BROOKINGS BIG IDEAS FOR AMERICA

BROOKINGS BIG IDEAS
FOR AMERICA

MICHAEL E. O'HANLON

EDITOR

BROOKINGS INSTITUTION PRESS
Washington, D.C.

Copyright © 2017
THE BROOKINGS INSTITUTION
1775 Massachusetts Avenue, N.W., Washington, D.C. 20036
www.brookings.edu

The Brookings Institution is a private nonprofit organization devoted to research, education, and publication on important issues of domestic and foreign policy. Its principal purpose is to bring the highest quality independent research and analysis to bear on current and emerging policy problems. Interpretations or conclusions in Brookings publications should be understood to be solely those of the authors.

Library of Congress Cataloging-in-Publication data are available.

ISBN 978-0-8157-3131-3 (cloth : alk. paper)
ISBN 978-0-8157-3132-0 (ebook)

9 8 7 6 5 4 3 2 1

Typeset in Minion Pro

Composition by Elliott Beard

Contents

Foreword

STROBE TALBOTT

President, Brookings Institution

The prospect of a new administration taking office has always inspired Brookings scholars to come up with ideas for the consideration of the nation's new president and his advisers, cabinet secretaries, and agency heads. We and our predecessors have focused on the challenges and opportunities facing an incoming chief executive 19 times, starting with Woodrow Wilson's handover to Warren Harding in 1921, five years after our founding. Like all Brookings products, these suggestions for policymakers have reflected our scholars' fact-based research, intellectual rigor, political independence, and the overall goal of improving governance.

We have also used our convening power, partnerships with other organizations, and publishing facilities to share our ideas with a wide audience. That includes, of course, outreach to the U.S. Congress and elected officials at the state and metropolitan levels, as well as the American people at large.

At the core of our mission is a commitment to engage the public in civil debate and adhere to Thomas Jefferson's injunction that a healthy democracy requires an informed citizenry.

Presidential campaigns are often a trial in that regard. These quadrennial contests between opposing parties for power frequently shed more heat than light. Because the stakes are so high and the rivalries so fierce, civility is often a casualty. So is respect for facts. In the midst of the race to the White House, the complex and urgent issues of policy waiting there for the winner are often eclipsed by the passion of the fray.

The campaign of 2016 was an extreme example of this aspect of America's democratic process. That did not stop our scholars from doing their professional and civic duty throughout the primaries and the general election. Now that Donald Trump is preparing to govern, my colleagues have been in contact with several of his transition teams.

The contents of this book, under the organizational and editorial guidance of Mike O'Hanlon, were delivered to the incoming administration. The Institution does not have a party line on any issue. As you will see in the pages that follow, our scholars have strong, diverse, and debatable views in the realms of their expertise. We hope these big ideas will contribute to elevating public discourse and illuminate areas where the American government can better serve its own constituents and reinforce its leadership in the world.

An Agenda for America

MICHAEL E. O'HANLON

Despite all the innuendo and intrigue, the 2016 presidential race actually delivered some serious policy debates. Donald Trump directly challenged the long-standing, bipartisan support for American internationalism, most of all trade and immigration policy. Hillary Clinton, borrowing in part from Bernie Sanders, questioned certain trade agreements herself while championing a higher minimum wage, free community college, gender equity in the workplace, more generous child care for the middle class and working poor, and needed repairs to the Affordable Care Act.

However, as in most campaigns, these issues and policy positions were arguably caricatured and sloganeered more than they were discussed, debated, and analyzed. At Brookings, we have sought to develop more detailed proposals for moving the nation forward that could be of use to the future President Trump and new Congress. There is no single Brookings view or institutional plan of action. Many of the ideas could plausibly be labeled either left or right, and might be of interest to both political parties going forward.

I have had the privilege of helping coordinate and edit some three dozen essays on big issues facing the country written by a range of colleagues in the immediate as well as what might be called the extended family at Brookings. I hope you will read many of them, for the background material they provide as well as for their prescriptions, which are often big and bold but are always smart and judicious.

In the rest of my brief introduction to this volume, I will focus only on a subset of the essays that could together help form an overall agenda that might be loosely entitled "Restoring the American Dream." Other essays focus on matters such as America's role in the broader world. On that subject, it is safe to say that most authors favor shoring up U.S. alliances and the global order to ensure the prosperity and security of Americans going forward, and to avoid the risk of throwing ourselves back to a more dangerous period of history.

This is not an institutional agenda, but if one were to attempt to construct a unified plan out of much of the wisdom that appears in the rest of this book, one could devise seven broad approaches that could be interwoven into an agenda for America and its middle class:

1. **Don't obsess too much about the deficit and the debt.** The United States has not been a great steward of fiscal policy in recent decades, allowing publicly held debt to rise to 75 percent of GDP. In one sense, this is not good, of course, and leaves us vulnerable to future fiscal shocks or higher interest rates. But as essays by Doug Elmendorf and others argue, given today's low interest rates, perhaps an even higher priority than driving down the debt is to invest in the future, while reorienting expenditures. We should spend more on infrastructure and education, while protecting benefits for the working poor and low-income children and elderly. We can pay for this by steps such as reducing or taxing the Social Security benefits of higher-income Americans, who have tended to benefit from the very trends in automation and globalization that have worsened the prospects of many other American citizens.

2. **Simplify tax policy.** Whether we use reforms to drive down tax rates, drive down the deficit, or both, some steps make good sense, as Bill Gale and others argue. For example, capping deductions at a certain percent of total income while also raising the earned-income tax credit would tend to help the poor and middle classes without unduly punishing the wealthy—and without attempting a wholesale revision of the tax code that would probably bog down in partisan gridlock.

3. **Fix (and possibly rename) Obamacare, largely through the states.** The Affordable Care Act, or Obamacare, has been a partial success, but

only partial, as Alice Rivlin and Bob Reischauer acknowledge. While it presents far too partisan an issue to expect easy resolution, or to allow much likelihood of a major fix like creation of a public option, there are natural paths forward for partial reform. Perhaps the central one is to encourage more states to opt out of Obamacare (or its successor), as existing law allows, provided that they devise health care reforms of their own that would achieve similar standards of coverage and (relative) affordability. Some other ideas such as facilitating the import of cheaper pharmaceuticals could help too.

4. **Increase annual infrastructure spending by $50 billion to $75 billion.** The nation is underinvesting in infrastructure, as Hillary Clinton and Donald Trump agree—not to mention Brookings scholars such as Bill Galston, Robert Puentes, Adie Tomer, and Joseph Kane. Some of this increase can be funded through public-private partnerships that require only modest federal, state, and/or local government contributions. Just as important as the amount of money, though, is the way projects are selected. Increases in spending should focus predominantly on urban areas, which need the help the most, have the worst infrastructure today, and can deliver the greatest economic bang for the buck with properly selected investments. An increase of this magnitude (or perhaps somewhat less) would be adequate to beef up the nation's defenses today too, as retired general David Petraeus and I argue in our own chapter. Together, these ideas suggest a way in which the 2011 Budget Control Act might be revised (lifting caps on domestic and defense spending by roughly the same amount).

5. **Address the crisis in black America.** As Belle Sawhill and Bill Galston, as well as Dayna Matthew, Richard Reeves, and Edward Rodrigue, argue in their respective essays, African Americans continue to suffer in this country. Unemployment and incarceration rates are very high, as are out-of-wedlock births; strong families and high school diplomas are too rare; black communities are still very segregated and lack the kind of net wealth needed to escape problem-plagued neighborhoods. Of course, this age-old set of problems will not be solved by the next president. But there are many "mid-size" reforms that could help substantially. They range from promoting greater involvement of parents with their kids' education (encouraged by a number of specific, relatively economical programs like home visitations); to a revision of prison

sentencing guidelines for nonviolent offenders in particular (since far too many young, black Americans are behind bars), and greater help for those prisoners in developing skills and finding jobs after jail; to withholding federal housing funds until states and localities develop plans to reduce segregation within their housing programs. Creation of more and smaller schools, as well as of "career academies" that focus on technical skills, can also help.

6. **Address the crisis in white America.** Carol Graham and Sergio Pinto's fascinating work on happiness tells us that working-class whites—the leading demographic of the Donald Trump voter, but also many of those who supported Bernie Sanders—are particularly frustrated and angry with their lot in life. Ben Bernanke provides very helpful perspective on this same question as well. It is not just a question of material well-being, but of hope, or lack thereof, and a sense that the American dream is vanishing. They often no longer expect to live as well as their parents and hold out less hope for their children as well. The causes of this dilemma are deep and result largely from the disappearance of many manufacturing jobs due to automation as well as globalization. Much of the solution must be through education, which also can address the decline in productivity growth that David Wessel discusses. That means not just making community college free or capping college-loan debt, but making community colleges and apprenticeships responsive to the shifting character of the modern economy—revising and improving the contents of their curricula. There are many more jobs in health care, information technologies, and other technical areas than American employers are able to fill; there is a basic mismatch between what the economy demands and what the educational system in America is generating. Some of the answer may also be simply to encourage people to move away from towns and locales where traditional manufacturing jobs have left, probably often for good.

7. **Repair trade.** Neither Hillary Clinton nor Donald Trump supported the Trans-Pacific Partnership, President Obama's top trade priority and a centerpiece of the so-called Asia-Pacific "rebalance" that Clinton herself championed when secretary of state. Both were savvy enough to recognize the country's growing angst on the subjects of trade and globalization. David Dollar suggests that the United States not allow

Chinese state-owned companies to buy American firms until certain reforms are made in areas such as the access of American firms to China's market. There is a huge undeveloped agenda on what to do about the American worker displaced, not only by trade but even more commonly by automation and technological advance. This is partly addressed in the current book—and will also surely constitute a major focus of our future work at Brookings as well.

The U.S. presidential race is over. But the debate over America's future is just beginning. The chapters here will help to inform that debate.

Most of these essays are updated versions of policy briefs posted on the brookings.edu/americasfuture website during the fall of 2016.

PART I

The Pulse of America

1

Are Americans Better Off than They Were a Decade or Two Ago?

BEN S. BERNANKE and PETER OLSON

SUMMARY: Traditional proxies of economic welfare, such as real median household income, provide an incomplete picture of economic well-being. This chapter describes an alternative, more comprehensive approach, developed by Charles Jones and Peter Klenow, that translates per capita consumption, leisure, life expectancy, and inequality into equivalent units of consumption, making it easy to compare economic well-being in the United States to that of the rest of the world. Jones and Klenow find with this method that many developed nations, such as those in Western Europe, have welfare levels much closer to that of the United States than traditional measures suggest, while developing or emerging nations fare more poorly relative to the traditional measures. Jones and Klenow also compare the United States to itself over time, an analysis that this chapter extends through 2015. Based on this analysis, Americans' well-being has improved considerably over the past few decades, but the rate of improvement has slowed in recent years.

Economically speaking, are we better off than we were ten years ago? Twenty years ago? When asked such questions, Americans seem undecided, almost schizophrenic, with large majorities saying that the country is heading "in the wrong direction," even as they tell pollsters that they are optimistic about their personal financial situations and the medium-term economic outlook.[1]

In their thirst for evidence on this issue, commentators seized on the recent report by the U.S. Census Bureau, which found that real median household income rose by 5.2 percent in 2015, as an indicator that "the middle class has finally gotten a raise."[2] Unfortunately, that conclusion puts too much weight on a useful but flawed and incomplete statistic.[3] Among the more significant problems with the Census's measure are that (1) it excludes taxes, transfers, and nonmonetary compensation like employer-provided health insurance; and (2) it is based on surveys rather than more complete tax and administrative data, with the result that it has been surprisingly inconsistent with the official national income numbers in recent years.[4] Even if income data are precisely measured, they exclude important determinants of economic well-being, such as the hours of work needed to earn that income.

On this question, a recently published article by Charles Jones and Peter Klenow proposes an interesting new measure of economic welfare.[5] It is by no means perfect, yet it is considerably more comprehensive than median income, taking into account not only growth in per capita consumption but also changes in working time, life expectancy, and inequality. Moreover, as the authors demonstrate, it can be used to assess economic performance both across countries and over time. This chapter reports some of their results and extends part of their analysis (which ends before the Great Recession) through 2015.[6]

The bottom line: According to this metric, Americans enjoy a high level of economic welfare relative to most other countries, and the level of Americans' well-being has continued to improve over the past few decades despite the severe disruptions of the financial crisis and its aftermath. However, the rate of improvement has slowed noticeably in recent years, consistent with the growing sense of dissatisfaction evident in polls and politics.

CROSS-COUNTRY WELFARE COMPARISONS

The Jones-Klenow method can be illustrated by a cross-country example. (Comparisons over time will be discussed in greater detail below.) Suppose that a researcher wanted to compare the economic welfare of citizens of the United States and France in a particular year—following the paper, 2005 will be the sample year.

In 2005, as the authors observe, real GDP per capita in France was only 67 percent that of the United States, and real consumption per capita (a more direct measure of living standards) was only 60 percent as high, making it appear that Americans were economically much better off than the French on average. However, that comparison omits other relevant factors of economic well-being. Jones and Klenow choose to focus on three such factors: leisure time, life expectancy, and economic inequality. The French take long vacations and retire earlier, and so they typically work fewer hours; they enjoy a higher life expectancy at birth (80 years in 2005, compared to 77 in the United States), which presumably reflects advantages with respect to health care, diet, lifestyle, and the like; and their income and consumption are somewhat more equally distributed than is the norm in the United States. Because of these mitigating differences, comparing France's per capita GDP or consumption with that of the United States overstates the gap in economic welfare.

How much do these other factors matter? To quantify their effect in a single measure, the authors formalize the following question: If someone had to choose between switching places with a random person living in the United States—with its consumption, inequality, life expectancy, and leisure—or a random person living in France, how much would U.S. consumption have to change before he or she would be equally happy with either outcome?[7] To answer this question, Jones and Klenow use detailed data for each country to convert the factors into "consumption equivalents," using a simple model of household preferences and some plausible assumptions about, for example, the relative value of leisure and consumption.[8] At the end of this exercise, they estimate that, in units of consumption equivalents, in 2005 a randomly chosen French citizen was actually about 92 percent as well off, on average, as a randomly picked U.S. citizen, despite the large gap between the two countries in consumption per capita.[9]

Similar calculations can be used to compare the United States and other countries. Table 1.1 shows the Jones-Klenow estimates of economic welfare, as well as income per capita, in a number of selected countries in the early to mid-2000s. (The exact years of comparison vary based on data availability.) U.S. values are set to 100, so the entries in table 1.1 should be interpreted as percentages of the U.S. level.

Table 1.1 confirms the conventional view that, broadly measured, American living standards are comparable to those of the richest Western

TABLE 1.1   WELFARE ACROSS COUNTRIES

COUNTRY	ECONOMIC WELFARE	INCOME PER CAPITA
United States	100.0	100.0
United Kingdom	96.6	75.2
France	91.8	67.2
Italy	80.2	66.1
Mexico	21.9	28.6
Russia	20.7	37.0
Brazil	11.1	17.2
China	6.3	10.1
India	3.2	5.6

Source: Charles I. Jones and Peter J. Klenow, "Beyond GDP? Welfare across Countries and Time," *American Economic Review* 106, no. 9 (2016): 2442 (table 2).

European nations but much higher than the living standards in emerging market economies. For example, this calculation puts economic welfare in the United Kingdom at 97 percent of U.S. levels, but estimates Mexican well-being at 22 percent. Interestingly, this comparison shows that Western European countries such as the United Kingdom, France, and Italy are considerably closer to the United States in terms of economic welfare than differences in per capita income or consumption would suggest, reflecting the fact that Western European countries do relatively well on the other evaluated criteria (namely, leisure, life expectancy, and inequality). For emerging and developing economies, however, differences in income or consumption per person generally understate the advantage of the United States, according to this measure, largely due to the greater levels of inequality and lower life expectancies in those countries.

IMPROVEMENTS IN ECONOMIC WELL-BEING OVER TIME

The Jones-Klenow measure can also assess an economy's performance over time. Since the Jones-Klenow published results cover only the period before the 2007–9 financial crisis and the Great Recession, publicly available data are needed to estimate U.S. results through 2015 based on the Jones-Klenow computer program available online.[10] Where the published and the estimated results overlap, they are comparable.[11] (Obviously, however, Jones and Klenow are not responsible for either the assumptions that the authors of the chapter made to determine their results or the accuracy of their calculations.)

Table 1.2 shows the results for the 1995–2015 period and for two subperiods. The first two columns report the annual growth rates of per capita GDP and of the data-based estimates of the Jones-Klenow measure of economic welfare. Also shown in the table below and displayed in figure 1.1 is the decomposition of the economic welfare growth estimates into four components: changes in life expectancy, consumption, leisure, and consumption inequality.[12]

Table 1.2 shows that economic welfare improved at quite a rapid pace over the two decades before the crisis (1995–2007), at more than 3 percent

TABLE 1.2   U.S. ECONOMIC WELFARE, AVERAGE ANNUAL GROWTH RATES, 1995–2015

YEARS	PER CAPITA GDP	ECONOMIC WELFARE	ECONOMIC WELFARE DECOMPOSITION			
			LIFE EXPENTANCY	CONSUMPTION	LEISURE	CONSUMPTION INEQUALITY
1995–2015	1.45	2.34	0.91	1.54	0.08	−0.19
1995–2007	2.13	3.32	1.17	2.30	0.01	−0.16
2007–15	0.42	0.88	0.54	0.40	0.18	−0.24

Source: Authors' calculations based on Jones and Klenow, "Beyond GDP? Welfare across Countries and Time"; BEA; CDC; Conference Board; U.S. Census; OECD.

FIGURE 1.1   SOURCES OF GROWTH IN U.S. ECONOMIC WELFARE

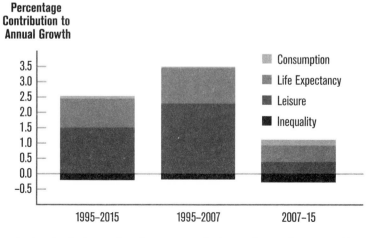

Source: Authors' calculations based on Jones and Klenow, "Beyond GDP? Welfare across Countries and Time"; BEA; CDC; Conference Board; U.S. Census; OECD.

per year, notably faster than the growth rate of per capita GDP, at about 2 percent.[13] As shown by the four rightmost columns of table 1.2 and graphically in figure 1.1, the gains in welfare were driven primarily by increases in per capita consumption and by improvements in life expectancy, which rose by 2.3 years over the period, from 75.8 to 78.1 years. Rising consumption inequality subtracted between 0.1 and 0.2 percentage points from the annualized growth rate in welfare during the precrisis period, and changes in leisure/work hours per person (which were stable) made only a very small contribution.

What about the more recent period (2007–15)? As can be seen in the table and the accompanying figure, economic well-being has continued to improve (growth in welfare is positive), but the pace of improvement has slowed considerably, to just about 0.9 percent per year. The biggest reason for the slowdown is the decline in the growth rate of per capita consumption to only about 0.4 percent per year since 2007—about the same as the growth rate of per capita GDP. In other words, disappointing economic growth, including the slow improvement in consumer spending power, is the dominant reason for the decline in the pace of welfare gains, even by this broader measure. Life expectancy has continued to improve since 2007, adding about a half percentage point to welfare growth; however, the contribution from this source is less than in the precrisis period, a difference that accounts for about 0.6 percentage points of the slowdown.[14] The longer-term trend toward inequality continued and intensified slightly after 2007, subtracting about a quarter percentage point from welfare growth.[15]

CONCLUSION

This analysis presents several conclusions:

1. Broad economic indicators like GDP, disposable income, and median household income are important measures of economic welfare, but inherently are incomplete. Jones and Klenow have provided a concrete example of how to construct a more comprehensive measure of economic well-being from existing data.

2. According to the Jones-Klenow measure, as of the early to mid-2000s, the United States had the highest economic welfare of any large country. However, several Western European countries, in-

cluding the United Kingdom and France, came close to the United States when differences in leisure, life expectancy, and inequality are taken into account. In terms of welfare, emerging market and developing economies were further behind the United States than per capita income or consumption figures indicate, largely because of greater inequality and shorter life expectancies in those countries.

3. Longer-term trends in economic welfare in the United States are mostly positive. According to our extension of the Jones-Klenow analysis, U.S. economic welfare has increased at about 2.3 percent per year since 1995, for a cumulative gain in two decades of 60 percent. Gains in income and consumption per capita and in life expectancy are the major reasons for improved welfare. Increased inequality of consumption has subtracted about 0.2 percentage points a year from the welfare measure since 1995.

4. Since 2007, economic welfare in the United States has continued to improve, according to our calculation. However, the pace of improvement has slowed markedly relative to the precrisis era, reflecting slower economic growth, some slowdown in the rate of improvement in life expectancy, and continuing increases in inequality.

5. This measure confirms that life in America is good, compared to other countries and to the country's own past, and is still improving. But there has been a significant slowdown in the pace of improvement that requires attention from policymakers.

Methodologically, the lesson from Jones and Klenow's research is that economic welfare is multidimensional. Their approach is flexible enough that in principle other important quality-of-life changes could be incorporated—for example, the 63 percent decrease in total emissions of six of the most common pollutants from 1980 to 2014 and the decline in crime rates.[16] We need better measures of how well Americans are being served by the economy, and frameworks such as this one are a promising direction.

Notes

1. Ben Bernanke, "How Do People Really Feel About the Economy?," Brookings, June 30, 2016, www.brookings.edu/blog/ben-bernanke/2016/06/30/how-do-people-really-feel-about-the-economy/.

2. Bernadette D. Proctor, Jessica L. Semega, and Melissa A. Kollar, *Income and*

Poverty in the United States: 2015, U.S. Census Bureau Report P60-356 (September 13, 2016), www.census.gov/library/publications/2016/demo/p60-256.html.

3. Matthew Yglesias, "5 Ways the Census Income Report Misleads Us about the Real State of the Economy," *Vox*, September 15, 2016, www.vox.com/2016/9/15/12915 038/census-income-report.

4. Gary Burtless, "Census Report of Big Jump in Income Is a Little Too Good to Be True," Brookings, September 16, 2016, www.brookings.edu/blog/up-front/2016/09/16/census-report-of-big-jump-in-income-is-a-little-too-good-to-be-true/.

5. Charles I. Jones and Peter J. Klenow, "Beyond GDP? Welfare across Countries and Time," *American Economic Review* 106, no. 9 (2016): 2426–57, http://dx.doi.org/10.1257/aer.20110236.

6. Jones and Klenow build on earlier work. See, for example, Marc Fleurbaey and Guillaume Gaulier, "International Comparisons of Living Standards by Equivalent Incomes," *Scandinavian Journal of Economics* 111, no. 3 (2009): 597–624, https://papers.ssrn.com/sol3/papers.cfm?abstract_id=1489058.

7. To state the obvious, this comparison is assumed to be made based only on the four factors considered. It ignores (among many other things) cultural preferences, like a taste for fresh baguettes or a consuming interest in the National Football League.

8. Jones and Klenow report that the results are not much changed by moderately varying their assumptions. Note that they are making the usual economist's assumption that leisure is a "good," which may underweight some positive psychological and social benefits of work. Note also that high levels of inequality are a negative in this framework only because, holding constant the average level of consumption, a person in a very unequal country has a high chance of living in poverty; this risk is assumed not to be compensated for by the fact that, in an unequal country, there is also a higher probability of having a very high living standard. "External" effects of inequality—the possibility that people prefer to live in a more equal society, whatever their own personal living standard—are not included here.

9. In other words, the Jones-Klenow calculation implies shifting from the United States to France is economically equivalent to losing 8 percent of average consumption.

10. For recession periods, the Jones-Klenow method has the problem that it does not differentiate "voluntary" leisure, such as vacations or earlier retirements, from cyclical unemployment. So, interpretation of their measure for a period of high cyclical unemployment, like 2008 or 2009, would be problematic. Our extension of their results below mitigates this problem by making comparisons between the precrisis period and 2015, a year in which cyclical unemployment was closer to normal levels.

11. Jones and Klenow use detailed microlevel surveys for some analyses, but for comparing broader sets of countries they instead use more easily available macro data. (They refer to these as their "micro" and "macro" approaches.) Where there is an overlap, they find that the two sets of results correspond closely. For data availability reasons, this chapter uses "macro" data for the United States in constructing table 1.2.

Differences with the Jones-Klenow results reflect data revisions, different sample periods, minor adjustments in assumptions, and (in two cases) a switch to U.S.-specific data sources: consumption data come from the National Income and Product Accounts instead of the Penn World Tables, and life expectancy data come from the Centers for Disease Control and Prevention (CDC) instead of the World Bank.

12. Since the CDC has not published life expectancy numbers for 2015, this calculation assumes that it stayed at its 2014 level of 78.8 (which was also its level in 2012 and 2013). Regarding inequality, the OECD estimate of the Gini coefficient for U.S. disposable income used here only goes through 2014, so the 2015 number has been imputed based on the 10-year average relationship between the OECD figure and the Gini coefficient for (pretax, pretransfer) income produced by the Census Bureau. Following Jones and Klenow, this chapter imputes the consumption Gini coefficient for the United States based on cross-country evidence on the relationship between Gini coefficients for disposable income and consumption.

13. For the period from 1980 to 2007, Jones and Klenow find that the growth rate of welfare was 3.11 percent per year (table 9, p. 2455). Using more detailed micro data, they calculate a growth rate of 3.09 percent for 1984–2006 (table 3, p. 2445).

14. The Jones-Klenow calculation does not include inequality in life expectancy, which in principle could be incorporated. In a 2016 article in the *Journal of the American Medical Association* (JAMA), Raj Chetty and colleagues showed that between 2001 and 2014 life expectancy rose considerably more for people in the upper portion of the income distribution than in the lower portion; in *PNAS*, Anne Case and Angus Deaton have pointed out the relative increases in mortality among U.S. white men with lower education. Another issue is how to treat the reduction in hours of work, which, as shown in table 1.2, contributes about 0.2 percentage points to welfare growth since 2007. Some of this reduction might reflect remaining cyclical influences or structural factors, particularly the absence of good job opportunities for less-educated, prime-age men. However, retirements and the aging workforce account for a substantial part of the decline in hours worked. Finally, the data on life expectancy go only through 2014 (see note 12 above), so that any more recent improvement on that dimension has been missed. See Raj Chetty and others, "The Association Between Income and Life Expectancy in the United States, 2001–2014," *JAMA* 315, no. 16 (2016): 1750–66, www.ncbi.nlm.nih.gov/pmc/articles/PMC4866586/; and Anne Case and Angus Deaton, "Rising Morbidity and Mortality in Midlife among White Non-Hispanic Americans in the 21st Century," *PNAS* 112, no. 49 (2015), www.pnas.org/content/112/49/15078.full.pdf.

15. Using detailed micro data, Jones and Klenow report (table 3, p. 2445) that increasing consumption inequality subtracted about 0.24 percentage points from welfare growth annually over the 1984–2006 period. In addition, increasing inequality in leisure subtracted another 0.08 percentage points.

16. "Air Quality—National Summary," U.S. Environmental Protection Agency, July 21, 2016, www.epa.gov/air-trends/air-quality-national-summary; and Andrew McGill, "Is Violence in America Going Up or Down?," *The Atlantic*, July 15, 2016.

2

Unhappiness in America

Desperation in White Towns, Resilience and Diversity in the Cities

CAROL GRAHAM and SERGIO PINTO

SUMMARY: The 2016 election highlighted deep social and political divisions in the United States, and related unhappiness. The starkest marker of desperation is the trend of increasing mortality rates—driven by preventable deaths—among middle-aged, uneducated whites. That stands in sharp contrast to gradual improvements in health and well-being of blacks and Hispanics over the past decades, and high levels of optimism about the future among these same groups. The trends among poor whites—and the frustrations that they are generating—have complex causes that we do not fully understand. Yet they constitute a social crisis that the next president will have to face. There are no magic bullets. We highlight the importance of documenting the extent of the crisis and exploring its causes as a first step toward finding solutions in the safety net, health, and well-being arenas.

According to most observers, the 2016 election is one of the most unusual in decades. In large part this is due to the anti-establishment and unpredictable nature of the Republican president-elect, which has wreaked havoc within the party. More fundamentally, though, the surprising level of political support for a populist platform rife with nativism, racism, and unrealistic proposals has exposed deep divisions in our society, as well as pockets of extreme desperation. Most notably, it is not minorities who have traditionally been discriminated against who are unhappy, but rather poor and uneducated whites who live primarily in suburban and rural areas in the heartland. This desperation is most starkly reflected in rising mortality rates among middle-aged uneducated whites, driven by preventable deaths such as suicides and opioid poisoning.

This is a social crisis with multiple and complex causes, not all of which we fully understand. We do know that it is dividing our society and polity in damaging ways. The next president must find ways to address it. There are no magic bullet solutions, which makes it more difficult to attract limited resources and craft policies to solve the problem. An important first step will be to document the extent of the crisis and to strive to better understand its causes. Our research—based on metrics of well-being, such as life satisfaction and hope for the future on the one hand, and stress, worry, and pain on the other—could be a useful starting point.

In November 2015 Anne Case and Angus Deaton published a study showing a marked increase in the all-cause mortality of high school (and below) educated white middle-aged non-Hispanic men and women between 1999 and 2013.[1] The change reversed decades of progress in mortality; it is unique to the United States and to non-Hispanic whites in particular. The change in the mortality rate trajectory was driven by drug and alcohol poisoning, suicide, chronic liver diseases, and cirrhosis. Those respondents with the least education saw the greatest increases in these diseases. Self-reported health, mental health, and ability to conduct activities of daily living in this group also saw a marked decrease and also suggest growing stress in this cohort.

At the same time that the mortality data were released, our research, based on extensive Gallup data for approximately 600,000 respondents in American metropolitan statistical areas (MSAs), exposed some stark trends and markers. We found marked differences in life satisfaction, hope for the future, and stress across poor blacks, Hispanics, and whites living in metropolitan areas.[2] Our econometric analysis included an array of widely used socioeconomic and demographic controls. These include age, gender, education, income, and employment status, as well as religion and place of residence, among other things. Among the poor, controlling for sociodemographic factors, blacks are by far the most optimistic cohort, and are close to three times more likely to be higher up on the optimism scale than poor whites (figure 2.1). Poor Hispanics also fared better than poor whites although the differences are less marked.

FIGURE 2.1   ODDS OF BEING IN A HIGHER LEVEL OF OPTIMISM DEPENDING
ON RACIAL GROUP (VERSUS WHITE), AMONG POOR INDIVIDUALS

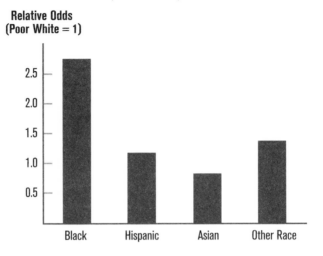

**Relative Odds
(Poor White = 1)**

Source: Author calculations: Gallup Healthways.

Large differences exist across races in stress, an important marker of
ill-being (figure 2.2). Poor whites are the most stressed group and are 9
percent more likely to experience stress in the previous day than middle-
class whites. Poor blacks are 47 percent less likely to experience stress than
poor whites (that is, their odds of experiencing stress are roughly half
those of poor whites), a difference between blacks and whites that remains
constant over the other income groups as well.

There are many explanations for these findings. One is gradual, hard-
fought progress by minorities, accepting that challenges remain. Meanwhile poor whites have fallen in status in relative terms, as competition
for low-skilled jobs has intensified. Blacks in general have improved their
status and well-being, and wage and education gaps have narrowed. Black
males earned 69 percent of the median wage for white males in 1970 and
75 percent by 2013.[3] And while the gaps in education achievement and
proficiency have widened across *income* groups, they have narrowed between blacks (and Hispanics) and whites at the same time. Fifty years ago,
the proficiency gap between black and white children was one and a half
to two times as large as the gap between a child from a family at the top
90th percentile of the income distribution and a child from a family at the
10th percentile. Today that has reversed, and the proficiency gap between

FIGURE 2.2   ODDS OF EXPERIENCING STRESS, DEPENDING ON
RACIAL GROUP (VERSUS WHITE), AMONG POOR INDIVIDUALS

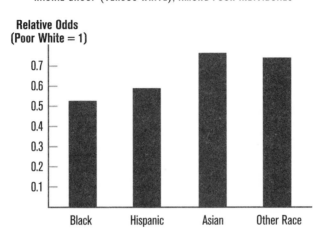

Source: Author calculations: Gallup Healthways.

poor and rich children is nearly twice as large as that between black and white children.[4]

Gaps in health status and life expectancy between blacks and whites, while still significant, have also narrowed. The gap in life expectancy between whites and blacks was seven years in 1990 (69.1 years for blacks versus 76.1 years for whites); by 2014 it had narrowed to three years (75.6 versus 79.0 years). Servin Assari and colleagues show that while black Americans have worse health indicators than white Americans *on average*, they (and minority groups in general) are better off in terms of mental health. Depression, anxiety, and suicide are all more common among whites than blacks.[5]

Assari and colleagues highlight higher levels of "resilience" among blacks and other minorities as an explanation. Resilience—defined as maintaining health in spite of a range of psychosocial risk factors—may be higher among blacks and minorities as they have had more experience with adversity. Community and religious factors may also be at play; a simple cross-tabulation of our data shows that blacks are the most likely of all racial groups to report that religion is important in their lives. This is corroborated by any number of accounts of the role of religion and community in African Americans' lives. While we control for religion in our analysis, so that it is not driving the optimism scores of our respondents, there are likely a number of indirect ways in which it still affects the lives—and optimism—of African Americans more generally.

These trends contrast sharply with the past experiences of whites in general. Paul Krugman notes that the economic setbacks of this group have been particularly bad because they expected better: "We're looking at people who were raised to believe in the American Dream, and are coping badly with its failure to come true." A recent study by Andrew Cherlin found that poor and middle-class blacks are more likely to compare themselves to parents who were worse off than they are when they are assessing their status. In contrast, poor and blue-collar whites, on average, have more precarious lives and employment stature than their parents did.[6]

Raj Chetty and colleagues, meanwhile, find that there are very strong geographic markers associated with these trends.[7] Mortality rates and the associated behaviors are particularly prevalent in rural areas in the Midwest and much less in cities. In part this is due to healthier behaviors associated with living in cities, such as more walking, and in part it is due to the combination of social isolation and economic stagnation that characterizes many of these rural locales. Krugman also notes the regional dimension to these trends: life expectancy is high and rising in the Northeast and California, where social benefits are highest and traditional values weakest, while low and stagnant life expectancy is concentrated in the Bible Belt (where economies are more stagnant as well).[8]

ONGOING RESEARCH

The mortality data and our well-being metrics highlight a paradox of rising well-being and improving health among minorities juxtaposed against the opposite trend among uneducated whites. We are exploring the extent to which our markers of well- and ill-being have a statistically robust association with the trends in mortality. We are doing this by matching our metrics with MSA data on mortality from the Centers for Disease Control and Prevention (CDC). Our preliminary results suggest that in addition to the differences across races, there are also important differences across *place*, which are reflected in differences in racial diversity and in health behaviors such as exercising and smoking.

We focus primarily on 103 MSAs for which sampling weights are available in all years of the Gallup data (2010–14) and which broadly correspond to the above 600,000 inhabitants. MSAs include relatively large urban and suburban areas; rural and micropolitan areas are comparatively sparser (there are approximately 800,000 observations for the MSAs, with over 600,000 corresponding to the 103 MSAs mentioned above, and just over 200,000 for rural and micropolitan areas).[9] We do not yet have the fully disaggregated CDC data, but were able to compute a composite measure that includes suicides, liver disease, accidental poisoning, and indeterminate deaths, and aggregate it up to the MSA level.[10] Our regressions include the usual controls for age, income, gender, education, employment, religion, and health status; we also include race and then race and income interaction terms, as above.

When we look at individual level well-being (and ill-being) markers and include MSA-level variables alongside the controls indicated above, we find that MSA-level mortality rates for those 45 to 54 years old are negatively correlated (for example, negatively associated) with optimism about the future. In addition, our regressions include a variable measuring reported pain, which Case and Deaton found to be correlated with suicide rates at the state and county level.[11] Pain is, not surprisingly, negatively correlated with life satisfaction and with optimism about the future, and positively correlated with stress. Our general results, though, hold whether or not we include pain. When comparing MSA with non-MSA areas, a simple cross-tabulation of our Gallup data for white low-income individuals is suggestive. We find that reported pain is higher in rural areas than in MSAs, and optimism about future life satisfaction is significantly lower (figure 2.3).

We also looked at average level MSA trends, with a focus on the role of place. When we looked at average levels of life satisfaction, future life satisfaction, and stress across MSAs, we find that all-cause mortality rates for 45–54-year-olds are negatively correlated with life satisfaction and positively correlated with stress. We find that percent of smokers per MSA is negatively correlated with life satisfaction and positively correlated with stress, while percentage of respondents who exercise is positively correlated with future life satisfaction and negatively correlated with stress. Our markers for overweight and obesity were insignificant, likely due to the inclusion of the exercise variable.

We also explored racial diversity as a characteristic of place, positing that there may be more social interactions in more diverse places. We find that the share of Hispanics per MSA is positively correlated with life satisfaction, while the share of blacks is positively correlated with future life satisfaction/optimism.[12]

FIGURE 2.3   PAIN INCIDENCE BY RURAL STATUS FOR
WHITE, LOW-INCOME INDIVIDUALS, 2010–14

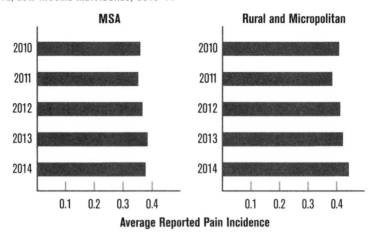

Source: Author calculations: Gallup Healthways.

Our research is still in progress, and we are hoping to have more fine-grained cohort and zip code level findings going forward. Yet even at this juncture, in addition to our strong findings on poor black and Hispanic optimism juxtaposed against poor white desperation, our data link robustly to patterns in mortality rates. It is not just a question of race and income, but also about place, with those places that are more racially diverse and where respondents engaged in healthier behaviors are also happier, more optimistic, and less stressed, all of which are markers of longevity and productivity in most places where well-being has been studied.[13]

POLICIES? SOLUTIONS?

What can be done in terms of policy? There is a clear need to restore hope and sense of purpose to places characterized by desperation and premature death, but it is not obvious how to do so. The solution will be multifaceted and should include a major effort to introduce healthier behaviors, focusing attention on premature mortality within those places. We also need to revisit the nature and reach of our safety nets. It is notable that when comparing the United States to other rich countries, those at the median and top of the U.S. distribution score higher in terms of absolute income, but the poor score worse than the poor in other rich countries.[14]

There has been some progress in recent years, and the new census data, released in September 2016, showed that median incomes rose by 5 percent on average across the country, and that poverty rates fell. Safety net programs such as the Earned Income Tax Credit (EITC) played an important role on the latter front.[15] While the EITC is very effective for working families, it is less so in isolated areas where employment opportunities have hollowed out—in other words, in the deepest pockets of desperation where mortality trends are most troubling. Anecdotal evidence suggests that these same places have low rates of Internet access, precisely at a time that the Internet is an increasingly important means to access safety net programs. This is an additional barrier for those who live in remote towns far from program administrative locales.

The reach of safety net programs across states is highly uneven. While the EITC has grown in importance in past decades, Temporary Assistance for Needy Families (TANF), the program that provides cash assistance to needy families, has been cut in many states, particularly Republican ones.[16] In the United States, continued reliance on food stamps as a means to assist the poor, while providing material assistance to the poor, is of questionable effectiveness on other fronts. Not only do food stamps stigmatize the poor, but obesity rates are higher among Supplemental Nutrition Assistance Program (SNAP) recipients than among non-SNAP recipients.[17] This stands in sharp contrast to the progress many countries—particularly in Latin America—have made in reducing poverty and improving health indicators with conditional cash transfer programs, which provide the poor with non-marginal cash transfers on condition that they send their children to school and to the health center.[18] Much of U.S. political dialogue stigmatizes recipients of welfare assistance, meanwhile, and the bureaucracies that administer it are particularly unfriendly and difficult to navigate, in sharp contrast to the efficient, semi-private bureaucracies that administer universal programs like Social Security and Medicare.

There are, no doubt, many other possible solutions, many of which are complex and long term in nature. Among these are improvements in education, vocational training, and possible incentives to relocate for some cohorts. The increasing number of 25–54-year-old men without work, which Nicholas Eberstadt projects will reach 25 percent of that cohort by mid-century, requires particular focus.[19] The men-without-work trend is in large part driven by the shrinking pool of low-skilled jobs and technology-driven growth and is likely to add to the growing unhappiness of uneducated, low-skilled citizens. There are also medical aspects to the solution. In addition to introducing healthier behaviors, we must address the manner in which opioids and other drugs are made easily available. And while the starkest trends in terms of lack of hope and mortality incidence are among poor whites, policies directed at improving opportunities and well-being of low-skilled workers should also benefit poor minorities whose challenges continue to merit sustained attention.

An immediate priority is to get a better handle on the causes of the problem. This will include listening to what desperate people themselves have to say, as well as learning from those who have shown more resilience when coping with crisis. Well-being metrics can play a role in this effort, for example by undertaking regular polling to gauge life satisfaction, optimism, pain, stress, and worry across people and places. Other countries such as the United Kingdom are already collecting these metrics annually. Reporting on the patterns and trends more regularly in public and policy discussions would be a simple and inexpensive way to monitor the well-being and ill-being of our society. It certainly seems a better path than waiting for mortality rates to sound the alarm bells.

Notes

1. A. Case A. and Deaton, "Rising Morbidity and Mortality in Midlife among White Non-Hispanic Americans in the 21st Century," *Proceedings of the National Academy of Sciences* 112, no. 49 (2015): 15078–83. Some recent work by Gelman and Auerbach suggests that these trends are driven in part by aggregation bias at the older ages of the 45–54 cohort, driven by the baby boomers, and that they are mainly driven by white women. See A. Gelman and J. Auerbach, "Age Aggregation Bias in Mortality Trends," *Proceedings of the National Academy of Sciences* 113, no. 7 (2016): E816–E817.

2. These initial findings are in Carol Graham, *Happiness for All? Unequal Hopes and Lives in Pursuit of the American Dream* (Princeton University Press, forthcoming). Graham is an academic adviser to Gallup and as such has access to the data. Our measure of optimism is a question that asks respondents where on a 0–10 scale they think their life satisfaction will be in five years.

3. A notable caveat is that most of the gains were made in the earlier decades. "Current Population Survey," 2014, U.S. Census Bureau (www.census.gov/people/households/currentpopulationsurvey).

4. E. Porter, "Education Gap Widens between Rich and Poor," *New York Times*, September 23, 2015: B1.

5. S. Assari and M. Lankarani, "Depressive Symptoms Are Associated with More Hopelessness among White than Black Older Adults," *Frontiers in Public Health 2016* (April 4): 82.

6. P. Krugman, "Despair, American Style," *New York Times*, November 9, 2015: A19; and A. Cherlin, "Why Are White Death Rates Rising?" *New York Times*, February 22, 2016.

7. R. Chetty, M. Stepner, S. Abraham, S. Lin, B. Scuderi, N. Turner, A. Bergeron, and D. Cutler, "The Association between Income and Life Expectancy in the United States, 2001–2014," *Journal of the American Medical Association* 315, no. 16 (2016): 1750–66.

8. Krugman, "Despair, American Style."

9. In practice, the smallest MSA has 12,000 people and the largest has just over 200,000. As such there is some overlap with the smaller MSAs (about 40 percent with less than 200,000 people). The number of observations for MSAs and rural and micropolitan areas indicated refer to those without missing observations for any of our variables of interest.

10. We used the publicly available CDC data, which impose significant limitations. For a substantial number of less populated counties, data are unavailable (due to privacy restrictions), which can introduce a bias into our composite measure. Similarly, we are unable to introduce the corrections suggested by Gelman and Auerbach, "Age Aggregation Bias in Mortality Trends."

11. A. Case and A. Deaton, "Suicide, Age, and Wellbeing: An Empirical Investigation," Center for Health and Wellbeing, Princeton University (June 2015).

12. Our population shares by race here are based on the percent of respondents in the Gallup survey; we will benchmark these against the population distribution in the American Community Survey (ACS) going forward.

13. C. Graham, "Happiness and Health: Lessons—and Questions—for Policy," *Health Affairs* 27, no. 2 (2008): 72–87; C. Graham, A. Eggers, and S. Sukhtankar, "Does Happiness Pay? An Initial Exploration Based on Panel Data from Russia, *Journal of Economic Behavior and Organization* 55 (2004): 319–42.

14. See www.demos.org/blog/1/5/15/when-it-better-not-be-america.

15. D. Trisi, "Safety Net Cut Poverty Nearly in Half Last Year," Center on Budget and Policy Priorities Blogs, September 14, 2016; and D. Trisi, "Three Essays on the State of the U.S. Safety Net," PhD dissertation, University of Maryland, College Park, 2016.

16. Ibid.

17. A. Carroll, "Limiting Food Stamps Choices May Help Fight Obesity," *New York Times* (*The Upshot*), September 27, 2016.

18. Nora Lustig, Carola Pessino, and John Scott, "The Impact of Taxes and Social Spending on Inequality and Poverty in Argentina, Bolivia, Brazil, Mexico, Peru and Uruguay: An Overview," CEQ Working Paper No. 13, Center for Inter-American Policy and Research and Department of Economics, Tulane University, and Inter-American Dialogue, August 2013.

19. N. Eberstadt, *Men without Work: America's Invisible Crisis* (West Conshohoken, Pa.: Templeton Press, 2016).

3

Time for Justice

Tackling Race Inequalities in Health and Housing

DAYNA BOWEN MATTHEW, RICHARD V. REEVES, and EDWARD RODRIGUE

SUMMARY: Despite undeniable progress since the civil rights era, the gulf that separates black and white Americans remains vast. This chapter reviews the reasons for this stubborn race gap, focusing in particular on data showing the extent, causes, and impact of housing segregation and health inequity. It proposes concrete recommendations for the new administration to shrink the racial divide, urging strong political leadership, improved housing market mobility, innovative focus on the social determinants of health, and tools to reduce unintentional biases in health care.

The first decades of the 21st century have been difficult for black America, despite the election and reelection of our first black president. There has been progress on some fronts, including narrower gaps in high school graduation rates, declining rates of teen pregnancy, and fewer suicides among black men. But the median black Americans will be just as far behind their white counterparts in 2017 as they were in 2000 in terms of income, wealth, unemployment, earnings, the risk of incarceration, and many measures of health. In the past few decades, progress toward broader equity for African Americans has been halting.

Compared to whites, black Americans face the same risk of unemployment today as in the 1960s.[1] Between 2007 and 2013, the net wealth of the median black household fell from 10 percent to 8 percent of median white household wealth, largely the result of the differential impact of the Great Recession. In other words, the median white household now has a net wealth 13 times greater than the median black households.[2] In 2000, the median black household had an income that was 60 percent of the median average white household income.[3] In 2015, that figure was 59 percent.[4]

In terms of housing and health, black Americans face a wide and stubborn race gap. It is perhaps no surprise that black and white Americans have starkly different views on progress toward racial justice. Nine in ten blacks say that African Americans have not achieved equality in this country. Four in ten are skeptical that they ever will. Yet 38 percent of white Americans think "our country has made the changes needed to give blacks equal rights with whites." Half of whites think there is more to do to achieve equality, but almost all of this group think that it will be achieved. Blacks and whites are, as the Pew Research Center puts it, "worlds apart."[5]

Many of the barriers blacks face are the result of an invisible, insidious force of unconscious bias. Whether it is water quality in Flint, Michigan; school quality in Ferguson, Missouri; environmental hazards in Dickson, Tennessee; or the inferior health care that the majority of black patients receive nationwide, the African American experience is *different*, and is allowed to be different, more than ever would be accepted within white communities. Racial injustice and inequality is a problem not just for poor and low-income blacks, but for moderate-income blacks as well, as we will show. Racism, even if unintentional, determines where, how, and how well black people live, relative to other groups in America. For most African Americans, in addition to the *tangible* inequalities captured in statistics, the *intangible experience* of being black in America is nothing like the experience of being a white person. Racial injustice lies not only in hard facts, but also in "the thick of everyday life."[6]

During his presidential campaign, Donald Trump appealed directly to whites, especially those who felt threatened by immigration, trade, and diversity. His choice of words and his choice of advisers have not suggested that the inequalities faced by black Americans are at the top of his agenda. He did point out, however clumsily, the difficulties that many blacks living in cities face in finding jobs or decent schools. If the new administration decides to treat the race gap seriously, there is much that can be done, right now.

RESIDENTIAL SEGREGATION: THE PROBLEM

More than half of black or white residents in 70 of the 100 largest U.S. metro areas would need to move to a different census tract in order to achieve integration despite the small reductions in racial segregation blacks have seen over the past two decaides.[7] Younger black city-dwellers (born between 1985 and 2000) are just as likely to live in a high-poverty neighborhood as the previous generation (born between 1955 and 1970). White Americans are also more segregated from black Americans than from either Asian or Hispanic Americans, according to analyses by William Frey from Brookings (see figure 3.1).

American neighborhoods have become more diverse in the past 20 years, but mostly because of the growth of the Asian and Hispanic American populations, rather than significant movement by either black or white Americans.[8] Native-born black Americans experience levels of urban neighborhood segregation nearly three times higher than native-born black British citizens.[9]

The causes of residential segregation are complex, enduring, and overlapping. It has been only a few decades since racial segregation was an explicit goal of public policy.[10] But even after the successes of the civil rights

FIGURE 3.1   **WHITE AMERICANS MORE SEGREGATED FROM BLACK AMERICANS THAN FROM OTHER GROUPS**

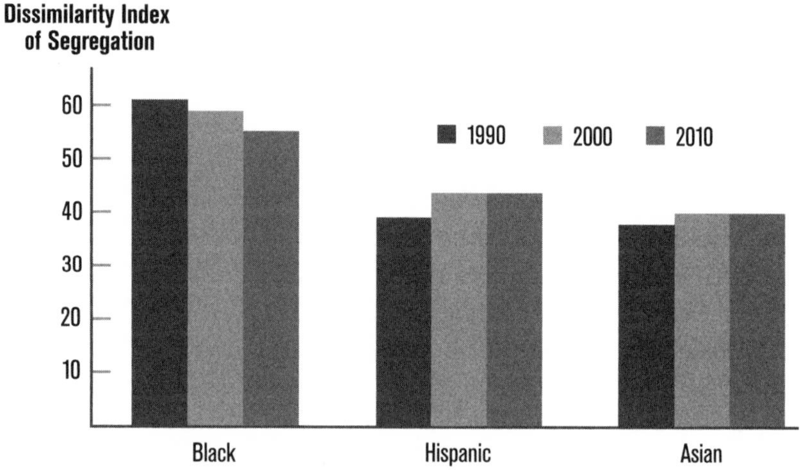

Source: William Frey, analysis of U.S. Census data.

movement, a number of factors continued to contribute to segregation—and, in many cases, still do so today. Five stand out:

1. **Zoning.** Even in the post–civil rights era, many forms of land use regulation have perpetuated segregation. Complex webs of covenants and zoning ordinances across U.S. cities—in particular for low-density development—superimposed on already highly segregated neighborhoods, have slowed integration.[11] When there are wide economic gaps by race, as we have in the United States, exclusionary land-use policies based on families' economic circumstances entrench racial segregation.[12]

2. **Transportation.** Highways and runways have often damaged or cut off black neighborhoods. "Highways cut the heart out of poor areas," as Transportation Secretary Anthony Foxx observed.[13] Meanwhile, public transit investments often fail to connect minority communities to opportunities for education and employment.

3. **"Steering."** Black and other minority homebuyers and renters receive different treatment from realtors and agents. In 2012, white and black "homebuyers" (in fact actors) were sent to 8,000 randomly selected realtors. Black home-seekers were shown 18 percent fewer homes.[14]

4. **Credit.** After being denied home loans before the civil rights era, black Americans have continued to be denied affordable credit, and have been pushed toward subprime loans.[15] SunTrust, Wells Fargo, and Bank of America have in recent years settled with the Justice Department (for $21 million, $175 million, and $355 million respectively) for pushing black homebuyers into subprime mortgage deals, overcharging them for home loans, and other breaches.[16]

5. **Attitudes.** Although such emotional aspects are harder to pinpoint, the attitudes and preferences of individuals and families likely play a role, too. Attitudes are shifting, but remain heavily influenced by race. Many white Americans strongly prefer to live with only a minority of black neighbors, up to roughly 20 percent of the neighborhood. Black Americans, meanwhile, prefer "50-50" neighborhoods and are averse to homogeneous neighborhoods.[17]

Physical segregation by race is costly to society simply in terms of race relations. It is harder to foster an equal, tolerant, multiracial society when people of different races live in their own enclaves. But there are more tangible costs, too, especially in terms of wealth disparities, educational opportunities, concentrated poverty, and neighborhood effects, with implications for well-being and health.

Wealth

The median black family has barely any wealth, in large part because blacks have not been able to participate in the wealth-generating momentum of the heavily subsidized housing market. Many blacks who did get a foothold before the Great Recession fell backwards once its full effects became known; black median household wealth almost halved from $19,200 in 2007 to $11,000 in 2013. The median wealth of white households is now 13 times greater than that for black households—the largest gap in a quarter-century (see figure 3.2).

Education

There are wide, well-documented race gaps in educational outcomes. School quality is a significant factor here, and since schools tend to serve specific areas, residential segregation leads to school segregation along racial and economic lines. The compounding effects of wealth, race, and place mean that even middle-income black students are more likely to attend high-poverty schools, as recent research by Sean Reardon, Demetra Kalogrides, and Kenneth Shore shows.[18] This may be one reason why black children born into middle-income families are twice as likely to be downwardly mobile as middle-income whites (see figure 3.3).[19]

FIGURE 3.2   **BLACK WEALTH BARELY EXISTS**

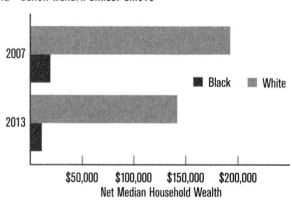

Source: Pew Research Center, analysis of Federal Reserve's Survey of Consumer Finances.

Neighborhood Effects

People living in areas with higher rates of poverty have worse outcomes across a range of social and economic measures. From sidewalks to social capital, differences in safety and neighborhood quality lead to differences in outcomes, as case studies jointly produced by the Community Affairs Offices of the Federal Reserve System and Brookings show.[20] Children in poor families who were able to use a voucher to move out of a poor neighborhood saw a 16 percent increase in college attendance, were much less likely to become single parents, and earned 31 percent more in their mid-twenties, compared to a control group.[21]

Residential segregation in terms of race is deep and damaging. What can be done?

RESIDENTIAL SEGREGATION: SOME SOLUTIONS

A complex and enduring problem like segregation will not be solved quickly or easily. It will require sustained political attention and policy

FIGURE 3.3   MOST BLACK MIDDLE-CLASS KIDS ARE DOWNWARDLY MOBILE

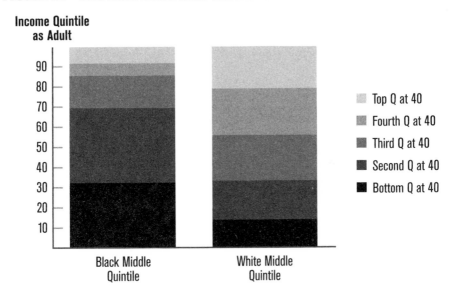

Source: Tabulations by Joanna Venator of Social Genome Model (Brookings and Urban Institute) results, based on data from the National Longitudinal Survey of Youth, 1979 and 1997 cohorts.

efforts from federal and local government. The president's role may seem limited at first. But there is plenty that can be done, even without new laws or funds. Many of the powers needed to make progress already exist; they simply need to be used. The following section sketches out a concrete policy reform, one element of a wider strategy to tackle segregation. But the most important ingredient is political leadership—not only from the new president, but also from the people that he appoints to critical roles in the administration.

Bring Back Romney (The Other One)

All of these proposals will require leadership from the new president, but they will also require bolder action from the Department of Housing and Urban Development (HUD). Leadership of HUD is critical. As we go to press, Donald Trump has announced Dr. Ben Carson as his pick for the position. Ideally, Carson will model himself after Romney: George Romney, that is, who was governor of Michigan during the tumultuous years of the mid-1960s.

"Some white people and public officials will advocate the return to state's rights as a way to legalize segregation," Romney said in the wake of the 1967 race riots. "As citizens of Michigan, as Americans, we must unhesitatingly reject all these divisive courses."[22] He then enacted a statewide fair housing law and told voters he wanted to end local zoning where it facilitated segregation and evenly distribute affordable housing around metro areas.[23]

Appointed secretary of HUD by President Richard Nixon, Romney did not hesitate to use the tools at his disposal—and which are still at HUD's disposal. As Nikole Hannah-Jones reported for *ProPublica*:

> Romney ordered HUD officials to reject applications for water, sewer and highway projects from cities and states where local policies fostered segregated housing. . . . [He saw his goal as using] his power as secretary of Housing and Urban Development to remake America's housing patterns, which he described as a "high-income white noose" around the black inner city.

Since the end of Romney's HUD tenure in 1972 there have been only a handful of occasions when the department cut funding to recipients for violating the Fair Housing Act of 1968. "HUD has sent grants to communities," wrote Hannah-Jones, "even after they've been found by courts to have promoted segregated housing or been sued by the U.S. Department of Justice."[24]

Scale Up "Small Area Fair Market Rents"

In many metro areas, HUD benchmarks the value of housing vouchers to costs in the entire metro. This means that voucher holders cannot afford to rent in more expensive, opportunity-rich neighborhoods and are effectively pushed into neighborhoods with cheaper housing.[25]

In some places, like Dallas, voucher amounts are indexed to ZIP codes rather than entire metro areas. This means the allowance falls slightly in lower-rent areas but rises in higher-rent areas. In a recent study of this "small area fair market rent" (SAFMR) approach in Dallas, Robert Collinson and Peter Ganong find that SAFMR led voucher families to enter neighborhoods with less poverty and violent crime.[26] Across five SAFMR demonstration sites, the total cost of the program actually fell by 5 percent between 2012 and 2014.[27] This finding does not mean that SAFMR will make sense everywhere, but HUD should permit and encourage more cities to adopt the approach, especially in those areas with concentrated poverty.

Expand Mobility Counseling

Opening up broader regional markets for voucher recipients will help to create more integrated cities; a powerful complement would be "mobility counseling" that helps voucher holders find a new residence. In Chicago, the Housing Opportunity Program offers a range of services, including housing search counseling and unit referrals, free credit reports, financial counseling, transport to potential new homes, expedited HUD Quality Standards inspections, legal workshops, and post-move support and house visits. The program helps families move to lower-poverty neighborhoods, according to longitudinal research, including a 2005 analysis by Mary Cunningham and Noah Sawyer.[28] Recent analysis of the Baltimore Mobility Program suggests that families who get this kind of extra support raise their neighborhood and school expectations and move to areas with higher-quality schools.[29]

HEALTH INEQUITY: THE PROBLEM

As the new administration and Congress design the ACA replacement,[30] it is important to remember that increased access is necessary but not sufficient to close morbidity and mortality gaps between blacks and whites. Health disparities resulting from racial inequity will persist as long as our nation continues to tolerate a separate and unequal health care system for black Americans.

The infant mortality rate for black babies is more than twice that for whites. This gap *persists* as the mother's education and income rise.[31] Babies born to well-educated, middle-class black mothers are more likely to die before their first birthday than babies born to poor white mothers with less than a high school education (see figure 3.4).[32]

These disparities continue into adulthood. Black men still have the shortest life expectancy of any other group in America. Racial inequities, compounded by education gaps, have a cumulative negative impact on health outcomes. White men and women with college degrees live an aver-

FIGURE 3.4 INFANT MORTALITY BY MATERNAL RACE AND EDUCATION, 2007–13

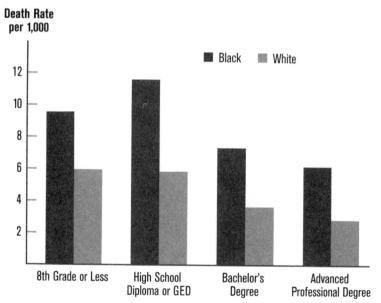

Source: Centers for Disease Control and Prevention (Wonder), Linked Birth/Infant Death Records, 2007–13

age of 14.2 years and 10.3 years longer than black men and women with less than a high school education.[33]

African Americans are disproportionately treated at health care facilities with the fewest technological resources, the most poorly trained professionals, and least experienced clinicians serve predominately black patient populations.[34] The most highly trained professionals serve predominately white populations.[35] When compared to whites, black patients are referred to see specialists less often, receive less appropriate preventive care such as mammography and flu vaccines, receive fewer kidney and bone marrow transplants, receive fewer antiretroviral drugs for HIV, receive fewer antidepressants for diagnosed depression, and are admitted less often than whites for similar complaints of chest pain.[36] No single cause explains these disparities, but five stand out.

1. **Unintended race discrimination.** The next president should take direct aim at the problem of unintended racial discrimination—also known as *implicit bias*—in medical care. Practices and policies that are race-neutral on their face actually result in inferior quality of and access to health care for blacks as compared to whites across geographic regions, diseases, facility types, and treatments.[37] Though different from intentional racism, the impacts of unintended discrimination are equally harmful. Because implicit bias is subtle and hidden, it allows discrimination in health care to persist although most Americans reject explicit racism.[38]

2. **Social determinants of health.** The next administration must also address racial disparities in the social determinants of health. These are the conditions in which Americans live, work, and play—including access to clean, safe, affordable house and health food choices. Health care alone accounts for only 10 percent of health outcomes. Social and environmental factors (20 percent), genetics (30 percent), and behavior (40 percent) all have a greater influence on health than health care. Closing the gap in health outcomes for blacks and whites means addressing inequity in upstream social and environmental factors that impact health.

3. **Housing disparities.** Housing inequity is an obvious place to start. Substandard housing conditions such as pest infestation, lead paint, faulty plumbing, and overcrowding disproportionately affect black families and lead to health problems such as asthma, lead poisoning,

heart disease, and neurological disorders. Blacks are 1.7 times more likely than the rest of the population to occupy homes with severe physical problems.[39] Concentrated housing inequity also disproportionately exposes black communities to environmental pollutants[40] and isolates black populations from essential health resources such as improved recreational spaces; quality pharmacies, clinics, and hospitals; and healthy food options (see figure 3.5).[41]

4. **Health behaviors.** Addressing housing disparities will encourage healthy behaviors. For example, reducing neighborhood violence and improving built environments will reduce sedentary behavior. Reducing the ratio of fast food and liquor outlets to healthy food options will reduce disparately unhealthy food consumption. [42]

5. **Criminal law enforcement.** The next administration can improve health equity by addressing instances of discriminatory law enforcement that disproportionately affect black communities. Black men and women are more likely to be arrested, charged, and convicted of crimes than whites who commit the same crimes (see figure 3.6);[43] disparate marijuana arrests are exemplary.[44] Once convicted, black men receive prison sentences that are nearly 20 percent longer than white men for similar crimes.

FIGURE 3.5   HOUSEHOLD FOOD INSECURITY, 2015

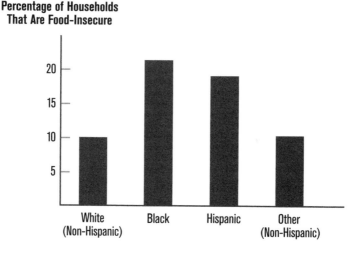

Percentage of Households That Are Food-Insecure

Source: Household Food Security in the United States in 2015, U.S. Department of Agriculture.

FIGURE 3.6A   ANNUAL MARIJUANA USE BY RACE, 2001-14

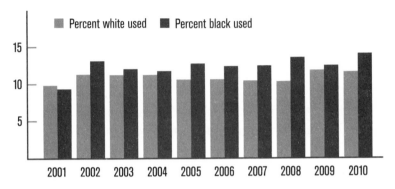

Source: National Household Survey on Drug Abuse and Health, 2001–10; FBI/Uniform Crime Reporting Program data and U.S. Census data.

FIGURE 3.6B   ARREST RATE FOR MARIJUANA POSSESSION BY RACE, 2001-14

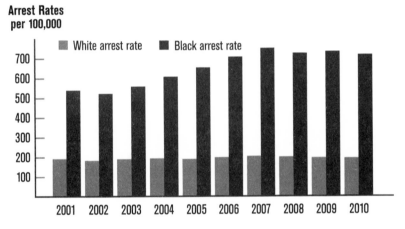

Source: Uniform Crime Reporting Program, U.S. Census Bureau. Data provided by Jon Gettman, Shenandoah University

The public health impact on black communities is staggering. Crowded living conditions in prisons increase transmission of infectious disease such as tuberculosis, viral hepatitis, and sexually transmitted diseases. The prevalence of mental illness and injection drug use among incarcerated populations is significantly higher than in the community at large. When prisoners are released, they bring a higher incidence of disease back to the detriment of the entire community's health.[45]

Incarceration affects the mental and physical health of communities left behind. Family members experience increased mental illness such as depression and anxiety disorders, and there is an increased risk of poverty and homelessness.[46] These health consequences are multigenerational. Incarceration, for example, is associated with a 30 percent increase in infant mortality.[47]

While there are some who express doubt that discrimination in the health care system is a cause of health disparities,[48] the costs of differences in black and white health outcomes are indisputable:

1. **Excess deaths.** In 2005, former surgeon general David Satcher estimated the cost in terms of lives lost due to racial discrimination in health care. He concluded that over 83,000 African American men and women needlessly lose their lives yearly due to unjust and avoidable differences in the quality and quantity of health care that they receive compared with the rest of the U.S. population.[49]

2. **Preventable hospitalizations.** A Centers for Disease Control and Prevention study estimated that if black Americans had the same adjusted rate of preventable hospitalizations as non-Hispanic whites from 2004 to 2007, the African American population would have had 430,000 fewer hospitalizations.[50]

3. **Dollars.** It is estimated that racial and ethnic disparities cost Americans $1.24 trillion between 2003 and 2006.[51]

HEALTH INEQUITY: SOME SOLUTIONS

The new president's most important step to achieve health equity will be to provide strong political leadership on this issue from day one. The president must publicly name the elimination of health inequity as a top priority of the new administration. We make three further recommendations:

Maintain Strong Agency Leadership Committed to Health Equity

The new president must ensure that political leaders are committed and empowered to fight health inequity to the full extent of the law. This must be true throughout the federal family, and especially so for Dr. Tom Price and Scott Pruitt, the people who will occupy the positions of secretary of health and human services (HHS) and administrator of the Environmental Protection Agency (EPA). Similarly, political leadership in both agencies' offices of general counsel and offices of civil rights must be individuals charged by the president and demonstrably committed to make the elimination of health disparities a top administration priority.

Make Efficient Use of Interagency Working Groups
Without any additional federal expenditures, the new president can strengthen the use of the Federal Interagency Health Equity Team to develop strategies, technical assistance tools, and accountability measures that will ensure that all federal agencies and departments, as well as all recipients of federal financial assistance, comply with health civil rights statute Section 1557.[52]

Section 1557 and its accompanying regulations provide powerful enforcement tools for the federal government to prohibit discrimination on the basis of race by health programs and activities. However, despite the strong final rule implementing the statute, Section 1557 is underutilized against racial health inequity. Currently, no sample or reported cases involving use of this statute to combat race discrimination in health care appear on the HHS website. The president can use existing interagency working groups to significantly enhance deployment of Section 1557 as a weapon against racial discrimination—whether conscious or unconscious—that produces health disparities.

Fully Implement Executive Order 12898
More than two decades have passed since President Bill Clinton signed the historic Executive Order 12898 on Environmental Justice, yet the order has not been fully implemented. The new president has an opportunity to live up to the promise that in America, "no matter who you are or where you come from, you can pursue your dreams in a safe and just environment."[53] Improving Title VI civil rights enforcement is the place to start. Currently, the EPA dismisses or rejects over 90 percent of Title VI complaints, takes an average of 350 days to complete jurisdictional reviews,[54] and has never in its history made a formal finding of discrimination. The EPA has never denied or withdrawn financial assistance from a recipient. And the agency's civil rights office has cases on its Title VI docket that were filed more than 10 years ago.[55] Making the promise of this executive order a reality will help reduce health disparities suffered by black Americans.

In sum, the new president can, by reducing the inequality that separates blacks, and whites, not only improve economic growth, social mobility, health, and opportunity for many, but also ensure justice for all Americans.

Notes

1. Drew Desilver, "Black Unemployment Rate Is Consistently Twice That of Whites," FactTank (blog), Pew Research Center, August 21, 2013, www.pewresearch. org/fact-tank/2013/08/21/through-good-times-and-bad-black-unemployment-is-consistently-double-that-of-whites/.

2. Richard V. Reeves and Edward Rodrigue, "Five Bleak Facts on Black Opportunity," Social Mobility Memos (blog), Brookings, January 15, 2015, www.brookings.edu/blog/social-mobility-memos/2015/01/15/five-bleak-facts-on-black-opportunity/.

3. Carmen DeNavas-Walt, Robert W. Cleveland, and Marc I. Roemer, "Money Income in the United States: 2000" (Washington, D.C.: U.S. Census Bureau, September 2001).

4. Bernadette D. Proctor, Jessica L. Semega, and Melissa A. Kollar, "Income and Poverty in the United States: 2015" (Washington, D.C.: U.S. Census Bureau, September 2016).

5. "On Views of Race and Inequality, Blacks and Whites Are Worlds Apart," Pew Research Center, June 27, 2016, www.pewsocialtrends.org/2016/06/27/on-views-of-race-and-inequality-blacks-and-whites-are-worlds-apart/.

6. This is a phrase used, in a different context, by Gerry Cohen in his book *If You're an Egalitarian, How Come You're So Rich?* (Harvard University Press, 2001).

7. William H. Frey, "New Racial Segregation Measures for Large Metropolitan Areas: Analysis of the 1990–2010 Decennial Censuses," Brookings Institution and University of Michigan Social Science Data Analysis Network, www.psc.isr.umich. edu/dis/census/segregation2010.html.

8. William H. Frey, "Census Shows Modest Declines in Black-White Segregation," *The Avenue* (blog), Brookings, December 8, 2015, www.brookings.edu/blog/the-avenue/2015/12/08/census-shows-modest-declines-in-black-white-segregation/.

9. John Iceland, Pablo Mateos, and Gregory Sharp, "Ethnic Residential Segregation by Nativity in Great Britain and the United States," *Journal of Urban Affairs* 33, no. 4 (2011): 409–29.

10. See, for example, racist lending practices within the Federal Housing Administration during the 20th century: Fair Housing Center of Greater Boston, "1934–1968: FHA Mortgage Insurance Requirements Utilize Redlining," www.bostonfair housing.org/timeline/1934-1968-FHA-Redlining.html.

11. White House, "Housing Development Toolkit," September 2016, www.whitehouse .gov/sites/whitehouse.gov/files/images/Housing_Development_Toolkit%20f.2.pdf.

12. Matthew Resseger, "The Impact of Land Use Regulation on Racial Segregation: Evidence from Massachusetts Zoning Borders" (Harvard University, November 26, 2013).

13. "Secretary Foxx Discusses a Transportation Plan for the 21st Century," You-

Tube video, 52:56, posted by "seeprogress," March 30, 2016, www.youtube.com/watch?v=QqtJgWaU0zM.

14. Margery Austin Turner and others, "Housing Discrimination Against Racial and Ethnic Minorities 2012" (Washington, D.C.: U.S. Department of Housing and Urban Development, June 2013), www.huduser.org/portal/Publications/pdf/HUD-514_HDS2012_execsumm.pdf

15. Redlining furthered segregation, and continues today. One example: Wisconsin's largest bank, Associated Bank, just settled with HUD over discriminatory lending and must now finance $200 million in home loans in minority census tracts, fork over $10 million in down-payment assistance, open four new offices in minority neighborhoods, and spend $1.4 million on marketing to these underserved communities. Emily Badger, "Redlining: Still a Thing," *Washington Post* Wonkblog, May 28, 2015; Alexis Madrigal, "The Racist Housing Policy That Made Your Neighborhood," *The Atlantic*, May 22, 2014; and Brentin Mock, "Redlining Is Alive and Well—and Evolving," *The Atlantic* Citylab, September 28, 2015.

16. Rick Rothacker and David Ingram, "Wells Fargo to Pay $175 Million in Race Discrimination Probe," Reuters, July 12, 2012; Ylan Mui, "For Black Americans, Financial Damage from Subprime Implosion Is Likely to Last," *Washington Post*, July 8, 2012; and Ta-Nehisi Coates, "The Case for Reparations," *The Atlantic,* June 2014.

17. Even fairly small differences in the kinds of communities people prefer to live in can have significant aggregate effects, as Thomas Schelling's work famously showed, especially in his book *Micromotives and Macrobehavior* (New York: W.W. Norton and Co., 2006). Maria Krysan and others, "Does Race Matter in Neighborhood Preferences? Results from a Video Experiment," *American Journal of Sociology* 115, no. 2 (2009): 527–59; and John Wihbey, "White Racial Attitudes over Time: Data from the General Social Survey," Journalist's Resource, August 14, 2014.

18. Mokoto Rich, "Nation's Wealthy Places Pour Private Money into Public Schools, Study Finds," *New York Times*, October 21, 2014; Mokoto Rich, "School Data Finds Pattern of Inequality Along Racial Lines," *New York Times*, March 21, 2014; and Mokoto Rich, Amanda Cox, and Matthew Bloch, "Money, Race and Success: How Your School District Compares," *New York Times*, April 29, 2016.

19. Reeves and Rodrigue, "Five Bleak Facts on Black Opportunity."

20. "The Enduring Challenge of Concentrated Poverty in America: Case Studies from Communities Across the U.S." (Washington, D.C.: Community Affairs Offices of the Federal Reserve System and Metropolitan Policy Program at the Brookings Institution, 2008).

21. Raj Chetty, Nathaniel Hendren, and Lawrence Katz, "The Effects of Exposure to Better Neighborhoods on Children: New Evidence from the Moving to Opportunity Project," *American Economic Review* 106, no. 4 (2016): 855–902.

22. Nikole Hannah-Jones, "Living Apart: How the Government Betrayed a Landmark Civil Rights Law," *ProPublica*, June 25, 2015.

23. Mark Santow and Richard Rothstein, "A Different Kind of Choice: Educational Inequality and the Continuing Significance of Racial Segregation" (Washing-

ton, D.C.: Economic Policy Institute, August 22, 2012), www.epi.org/publication/educational-inequality-racial-segregation-significance/.

24. One example Hannah-Jones provides: "New Orleans . . . has continued to receive grants after the Justice Department sued it for violating that Fair Housing Act by blocking a low-income housing project in a wealthy historic neighborhood." Hannah-Jones, "Living Apart."

25. Will Fischer, "Neighborhood-Based Subsidy Caps Can Make Housing Vouchers More Efficient and Effective" (Washington, D.C.: Center on Budget and Policy Priorities, June 10, 2015).

26. Robert Collinson and Peter Ganong, "The Incidence of Housing Voucher Generosity," SSRN, 2016, https://papers.ssrn.com/sol3/Papers.cfm?abstract_id=2255799.

27. Fischer, "Neighborhood-Based Subsidy Caps."

28. Greg Duncan, "New Lessons from the Gautreaux and Moving to Opportunity Residential Mobility Programs" (University of California–Irvine, 2007), http://merage.uci.edu/researchandcenters/cre/resources/documents/duncan.pdf; and Mary Cunningham and Noah Sawyer, "Moving to Better Neighborhoods with Mobility Counseling" (Washington, D.C.: Urban Institute, March 2005).

29. Marina L. Myhre and Nicole Elsasser Watson, "Housing Counseling Works" (Washington, D.C.: U.S. Department of Housing and Urban Development, May 2016).

30. The Department of Health and Human Services reports that the uninsured rate among black non-Hispanics dropped by more than 50 percent, from 14.3 percent to 7.0 percent, because of the Affordable Care Act. U.S. Department of Health and Human Services, "20 Million People Have Gained Health Insurance Coverage because of the Affordable Care Act, New Estimates Show" (March 3, 2016).

31. Lindy Washburn, "Medical Mystery Endures: Black Babies at Twice Risk of Whites for Death, Study Indicates," *Medical Press*, March 2, 2011, http://medicalxpress.com/news/2011-03-medical-mystery-black-babies-whites.html.

32. Laudan Y. Aron, "Despite Fifty Years of Improvements in Infant Mortality, Large Black-White Gap Remains Unchanged," Urban Wire (blog), Urban Institute, August 26, 2013, www.urban.org/urban-wire/despite-fifty-years-improvements-infant-mortality-large-black-white-gap-remains-unchanged.

33. S. Jay Olshansky and others, "Differences in Life Expectancy Due to Race and Educational Differences Are Widening, and Many May Not Catch Up," *Health Affairs* 31, no. 8 (2012): 1803–13.

34. Justin B. Dimick and others, "Black Patients Are More Likely to Undergo Surgery at Low Quality Hospitals in Segregated Regions," *Health Affairs (Millwood)* 32, no. 6 (2013): 1046–53; and Laurent G. Glance and others, "Trends in Racial Disparities for Injured Patients Admitted to Trauma Centers," *Health Services Research* 48, no. 5 (2013): 1684–1703.

35. Ioana Popescu, Peter Cram, and Mary S. Vaughan-Sarrazin, "Differences in Admitting Hospital Characteristics for Black and White Medicare Beneficiaries with Acute Myocardial Infarction," *Circulation* 123, no. 23 (2011): 2710–16. Differ-

ences in hospital quality, which may be due in part to ZIP code differences, may contribute to disparities.

36. Kevin Fiscella and others, "Inequality in Quality: Addressing Socioeconomic, Racial, and Ethnic Disparities in Health Care," *JAMA* 283, no. 19 (2000), 2579–84.

37. U.S. Department of Health and Human Services, "2015 National Healthcare Quality and Disparities Report and 5th Anniversary Update on the National Quality Strategy," AHRQ Publication no. 16-0015 (Rockville, Md.: Department of Health and Human Services, April 2016).

38. Bianca DiJulio and others, "Kaiser Family Foundation/CNN Survey of Americans on Race" (Washington, D.C.: Kaiser Family Foundation, November 2015).

39. James Krieger and Donna L. Higgins, "Housing and Health: Time Again for Public Health Action," in *Urban Health: Readings in the Social, Built, and Physical Environments of U.S. Cities*, edited by H. Patricia Hynes and Russ Lopez (Burlington, Mass.: Jones and Bartlett Publishers, 2009), 106.

40. Liam Downey and Brian Hawkins, "Race, Income, and Environmental Inequality in the United States," *Social Perspectives* 51, no. 4 (2008): 759–81.

41. D. R. Williams and C. Collins, "Racial Residential Segregation: A Fundamental Cause of Racial Disparities in Health," *Public Health Report* 116, no. 5 (2001): 404–16.

42. Angela Hilmers, David C. Hilmers, and Jayna Dave, "Neighborhood Disparities in Access to Healthy Foods and Their Effects on Environmental Justice," *American Journal of Public Health* 102, no. 9 (2012): 1644–54.

43. Dylan Matthews, "The Black/White Marijuana Arrest Gap, in Nine Charts," *Washington Post* Wonkblog, June 4, 2013.

44. Joe Palazzolo, "Racial Gap in Men's Sentencing," *Wall Street Journal*, February 14, 2013.

45. Sandro Galea, "Incarceration and the Health of Populations," Boston University School of Public Health, March 22, 2015, www.bu.edu/sph/2015/03/22/incarceration-and-the-health-of-populations/.

46. Editorial Board, "Mass Imprisonment and Public Health," *New York Times*, November 26, 2014.

47. Christopher Wildeman, "Imprisonment and (Inequality in) Population Health," *Social Science Research* 41 (2011): 74–91.

48. Jonathan Klick and Sally Satel, *The Health Disparities Myth: Diagnosing the Treatment Gap* (Washington, D.C.: American Enterprise Institute Press, 2006).

49. David Satcher and others, "What If We Were Equal? A Comparison of the Black-White Mortality Gap in 1960 and 2000," *Health Affairs* 24, no. 2 (2005): 459–64.

50. Carrie Hanlon and Larry Hinkle, "Assessing the Costs of Racial and Ethnic Health Disparities: State Experience" (Rockville, Md.: Health Care Cost and Utilization Project, June 24, 2011).

51. Thomas A. LaVeist, Darrell J. Gaskin, and Patrick Richard, "The Economic

Burden of Health Inequalities in the United States" (Washington, D.C.: Joint Center for Political and Economic Studies, 2009).

52. See, for example, Executive Order 11246, as amended by Executive Orders 113575 and 10286 and applicable regulations.

53. See, for example, Lisa Garcia, "President Obama's Proclamation on Environmental Justice," EPA blog, February 25, 2014, https://blog.epa.gov/blog/tag/executive-order-12898/.

54. Editorial Board, "The E.P.A.'s Civil Rights Problem," *New York Times*, July 7, 2016.

55. U.S. Commission on Civil Rights, "Environmental Justice: Examining the Environmental Protection Agency's Compliance and Enforcement of Title VI and Executive Order 12,898" (Washington, D.C.: September 23, 2016).

4

Health Policy Issues and the 2016 Presidential Election

ROBERT D. REISCHAUER and ALICE M. RIVLIN

SUMMARY: The new president and Congress will face the question of how to deal with the Affordable Care Act. Repealing and replacing it will not be simple. Politicians also will have to focus on the rising public and private costs of health care, driven by an aging population and the advent of new drugs and treatments, and will need to make decisions about how to preserve the highly popular Medicare program, whose current funding is unsustainable. This chapter explores the available options and some of the realities that constrain action.

H ealth policy has become a highly charged partisan issue in American politics. Each party claims that its policies will improve the quality, efficiency, and availability of American health care, while the other party's policies will destroy what is good about it. Realistically, however, any major sustainable changes in federal health policy will require broad public support and bipartisan agreement in Congress, even when one party controls both the White House and the legislative branch of government.

In a less polarized political atmosphere, the 2016 campaign could have allowed candidates to articulate realistic positions, help voters understand the options, and provide a basis for legislation when the new president and Congress take office in 2017. Unfortunately, the 2016 campaign has mainly featured slogans such as "Repeal Obamacare!" and "Save Medicare!" and mutual accusations of nefarious intentions that only deepen the partisan divide and raise barriers to constructive action in 2017 and beyond. The new president and Congress face at least three big health policy issues:

- Resolving the future of the Affordable Care Act (ACA);

- Slowing projected growth of national health spending on the federal, state, and private levels; and

- Reforming the Medicare program in a way that extends the life of the Medicare HI Trust Fund and moderates the growth of the Supplementary Medical Insurance trust fund to ensure the program's viability for ever more beneficiaries.

The American health care delivery and payment systems are extraordinarily complex. Proposed policy changes involve controversial tradeoffs and are hard to make clear to most voters. The three issues are also highly interrelated. For example, the ACA increased federal spending for health by creating subsidies for the purchase of health insurance and expanding Medicaid. At the same time, it reduced spending for Medicare and introduced reforms likely to make health care delivery more efficient. Hence, repealing the ACA in its entirety would make Medicare reform and spending concerns harder to resolve.

PARTISAN IDEOLOGY AND POLITICAL REALITY

Traditionally, the Republican and Democratic parties have had different approaches to health care, especially in campaigns, even though members of both parties have diverse views on health policy. Republicans emphasize market solutions, consumer choice, reduced waste and regulation, and more state-level flexibility in designing and executing health programs. They argue for tort reform to reduce malpractice premiums, health savings accounts to give consumers more control over health spending, and interstate health insurance markets to enhance competition. Democrats emphasize universal health insurance coverage, support enlarging the government's role in ensuring access to health care, and tend to favor health sector regulation to improve quality and moderate cost growth. They emphasize the millions of elderly and vulnerable people benefiting from Medicare and Medicaid and the ACA extension of health insurance coverage, and push for further expansions in coverage and benefits under federal programs.

As President-elect Trump and Congress begin to tackle these challenges, however, they will find their options severely limited. The American public generally is apprehensive about change in anything as vital and personal as health care. Reducing benefits for people who have federally supported coverage is politically hazardous. Medicare is popular, and modifications to it must be designed to assuage the fear of current beneficiaries and their families that they might end up worse off. Moreover, the health care establishment—providers, insurers, suppliers—forms a large, politically sophisticated economic sector (close to 18 percent of U.S. GDP) whose powerful lobbies protect the system's existing jobs and incomes. Newly elected policymakers proposing major health policy changes will face a daunting battle with entrenched stakeholders determined to defend and enhance their interests.

THE FUTURE OF THE AFFORDABLE CARE ACT

The clearest policy divide between the presidential candidates was over the future of the ACA. Although the ACA broadened health insurance coverage in market-oriented ways that might have held appeal for Republicans, such as subsidies for the individual purchase of competing private insurance plans chosen on electronic exchanges, the act was passed by Democrats without any Republican support. Republican congressional leadership, hoping to discredit President Obama, opposed it from the beginning. In the 2016 campaign, Republican candidates demonized "Obamacare" as the federal government forcing people to buy health insurance even if they did not want it, punishing small business with mandatory costs, and raising premiums for everyone.

In the 2016 primaries, all Republican candidates trashed Obamacare and promised to "repeal and replace" the ACA, thereby aiming to fulfill the unsuccessful four-year effort of congressional Republicans and deliver on a major plank in the party's platform. Several Republican primary candidates offered ideas for replacing the ACA, suggesting tax credits for the purchase of health insurance and either retaining the ACA insurance market reforms or replacing them with federally supported state-based high-risk pools or other devices. Donald Trump, however, said only that he would replace ACA with "something great." His campaign materials stated his belief that "every American deserves access to high-quality, affordable health care," but provided few relevant policy details about how that could be achieved. He said he favored enabling those without employer-sponsored insurance to deduct their premiums from taxable income, allowing health insurance to be sold across state lines, expanding importation of prescription drugs, having Medicare negotiate drug prices with pharmaceutical manufacturers, and transforming Medicaid into block grants for states. He has since said that he favors retaining two popular insurance market reforms: prohibiting denial of affordable coverage to those with preexisting conditions and allowing young people to stay on their parents' health insurance until age 26.

In the Democratic primary campaign, Bernie Sanders argued forcefully for a single-payer system (Medicare for All), a proposal long popular with the progressive wing of the Democratic Party, and acknowledged that paying for such a program would require substantially higher federal taxes. Hillary Clinton celebrated the accomplishments of the ACA in drastically cutting the proportion of Americans without health insurance, argued for enhancing the incentives to states to expand Medicaid, and proposed policies that would make ACA insurance more accessible and affordable. As Democratic nominee, Clinton moved in the Sanders campaign's direction by suggesting that people over age 55 be allowed to buy into Medicare before they reach the current eligibility age of 65, and that a public option be available on the ACA exchanges in all states to compete with private plans.

Having won the White House and retained control of both chambers of Congress, Republicans are in a position to repeal Obamacare early in 2017. They could use the reconciliation process in a budget resolution to repeal the spending and tax provisions of the ACA, thereby circumventing the 60-vote hurdle needed to close down a Senate-level Democratic filibuster. The consequences of defunding the ACA without enacting replacement legislation, however, would be chaotic even if the repeal were stipulated to be effective one or two years in the future. Some 20 million people who currently benefit from ACA coverage would not know how comprehensive or affordable their future coverage might be or even whether a replacement plan would even be enacted. Insurers, uncertain about possible changes in the risk pool and with only a short period of time to recoup any investments they may need to make, could decide to stop offering coverage through the exchanges. Providers could be less willing to participate in the dwindling number of exchange plans. Compliance with the individual mandate, particularly among the healthy, would probably crumble. And the impetus behind many of the efforts to curb cost growth, which the ACA has spawned, could dissipate.

Replacement legislation will require bipartisan backing to be permanently viable, and it will take time to craft. A full year might be required. None of the existing replacement plans have specified the detail required to address the tradeoffs and stakeholder concerns that an implementable plan requires. Without such detail, it is impossible to know with any certainty how many people will be covered, how affordable that coverage will be, what costs the government will face, and what will happen to the quality of care. Beyond the legislation, the associated regulations will have to be drafted, commented upon, and revised before any replacement structure can be implemented, which could require another year of work.

One optimistic scenario is that the Trump administration and congressional Republicans will realize the enormity of the replacement challenge and work with congressional Democrats and key health stakeholders to craft workable replacement legislation. The new law could keep the ACA's popular insurance market reforms, preserve the current rate of insurance coverage, and make buying health insurance more attractive to younger, healthier people and selling individual insurance more financially rewarding to insurance carriers—a tall order for such legislation.

The ACA transformed health insurance markets so the carriers could no longer compete primarily by attracting healthy, less expensive customers with lower premiums while excluding or charging higher rates to the less healthy. Only age (within narrow limits) and smoking behavior were subject to consideration. The hope was that the combination of income-related subsidies and penalties for not buying insurance (the individual mandate) or for not offering it to employees (the employer mandate) would result in rapid expansion of insurance coverage. Medicaid expansion was counted on to cover the poor and near-poor.

Roughly 20 million more people now have coverage (about half on the exchanges and half through Medicaid expansion) and the proportion of people without coverage has declined. But stresses in the insurance market revealed problems in the ACA's design. Not surprisingly, the sickest people signed up. The complex mechanisms the ACA established to compensate insurers that attracted particularly costly participants proved inadequate. Healthier people, particularly the young, often faced higher premiums for individual insurance options because their insurance did not meet the ACA's higher benefit standards. The subsidies and penalties were insufficient to induce many of the "young invincibles" to sign up. Insurance carriers found that the new population of previously uninsured customers was more expensive than they expected. Some underpriced their offerings, experienced losses, and began to raise premiums or withdraw from some markets, leaving beneficiaries with fewer choices. Some states also chose not to expand Medicaid, leaving a substantial group of people without affordable coverage.

An optimistic scenario assumes that Republicans are sufficiently dedicated to the goal of broadening access to affordable, good-quality care—with private insurance competition as the preferred model—that they will be willing to hammer out a replacement plan that fixes ACA shortcomings and transitions current beneficiaries to the new structure. It also assumes that some Democrats are willing to work with them and to accept more Republican-friendly attributes rather than opposing such proposals. Elements of such a structure might include allowing insurance companies more flexibility to offer cheaper plans with more limited benefits, bigger differences in premiums by age, greater reliance on health savings accounts, and some ways of combining insurance pools across state lines. Capping the tax exclusion of employer-paid health premiums (espoused by some Republicans, including 2012 presidential candidate John McCain) could be substituted for the yet-to-be-implemented "Cadillac tax" on high-cost employer-sponsored plans and some of the other revenue-increasing measures. Some of the Clinton proposals might also appeal to Republicans, including a refundable tax credit for those with high out-of-pocket expenses, limitations on out-of-network charges for care delivered in in-network hospitals, greater price transparency, and relaxation of restrictions on the importation of prescription drugs.

None of this would be easy. A Republican replacement plan would doubtless eliminate both the employer and the individual mandates. Some independent analysts have concluded that the employer mandate has only a marginal impact on coverage (but not on costs).[1] However, some substitute would have to be found for the individual mandate that gave younger, healthy people more incentive to buy coverage and thereby reduce average costs. One option would be to follow Medicare's example by imposing a premium surcharge that increased each month that an individual failed to obtain coverage.

Republicans will also want to give more flexibility to states, not only in Medicaid but also in using federal money to subsidize purchases of private health insurance. This state flexibility could appeal to some Democrats as well. Indeed, the ACA moved in this direction in its Section 1332 waivers: starting in 2017, states are able to substitute a state-designed structure for the ACA as long as the plan achieved the access, coverage, quality, and cost goals of the ACA. This idea could be expanded in the replacement. Much would depend on the attitude of Republican governors toward Medicaid expansion. Some took advantage of the ACA's federal inducements to expand coverage. However, 19 conservative states did not expand Medicaid eligibility to 138 percent of the federal poverty level (FPL), which cost their states tens of millions of dollars and opened up a glaring inequity that developed after the Supreme Court decision made the state Medicaid expansion optional. The Obama administration has used Medicaid's Section 1115 waiver authority to extend coverage in six states, but roughly 3 million are still uninsured because they fall into the coverage gap—those whose incomes are less than the 100 percent of poverty threshold for eligibility for subsidized coverage in the exchange, but above their state's Medicaid eligibility level. Since the replacement for the ACA would no longer be associated with a Democratic administration, some Republican governors might be more willing to accept federal funds to fill this gap and broaden coverage in their states. Another approach would be to provide all states with the option of scaling back the Medicaid expansion threshold from 138 percent to 100 percent of the FPL while providing federally funded premium tax credits and cost-sharing subsidies to those with incomes between 100 and 138 percent of the FPL who enroll in fully federally subsidized exchange plans. This would assuage concerns about future state responsibility for Medicaid costs and would reduce the numbers of families shifting back and forth between Medicaid and exchange coverage.[2]

Beyond these policies, there is a long list of lessons from the ACA experience that should be drawn on to inform any replacement effort. One is the necessary level of subsidies/tax credits to ensure participation in a system without individual mandates. Much as Republicans would like to reduce the costs of premium and cost-sharing subsidies, analysts have suggested that even the levels provided by the ACA were likely to prove inadequate, making exchange policies increasingly unaffordable for middle-income and elderly families.[3] Another is the importance of information technology, education, outreach, and regulation oversight and enforcement. Of even more importance is the need to take measures to expand and stabilize the insurance offerings whether offered through exchanges or some other marketplace. A number of large for-profit insurers have withdrawn from the exchange marketplaces altogether, while others have reduced the counties in which they are offering coverage. Only 6 of the original 23 Consumer Operated and Oriented (CO-OP) plans will be offering policies in 2017. In some areas, plan premiums have increased while deductibles and cost sharing in lower cost plans have soared. Among the explanations suggested for these trends are that marketplace enrollees are less healthy than expected, enrollment is much smaller overall than projected (especially in rural areas), enrollees purchase insurance only when they need expensive care and then stop paying their premiums after treatment, and the revenue redistribution mechanisms failed to operate as planned.

Health insurance carriers have found it difficult to make profits in sparsely populated rural areas with few customers and few providers. ACA exchanges frequently offered limited choices in such areas. Democrats have suggested creating a public option to ensure competition, but Republicans are unlikely to support such a plan and might prefer it if the federal government paid for, through competitive bids, a private plan that would offer insurance in counties with no or few exchange offerings. Until the marketplaces for subsidized insurance stabilize, insurers need to be more comfortable with the accuracy, predictability, and adequacy of the new risk adjustment system.

MODERATING THE GROWTH OF NATIONAL AND FEDERAL HEALTH CARE SPENDING

The United States devotes an extraordinary 18 percent of its GDP to health care—a substantially larger fraction than other advanced countries with modern health care systems. For several decades, health spending per capita grew faster than most other spending and seemed likely to push the fraction of economic resources devoted to health care ever higher—to 20 percent and beyond—squeezing competing needs in public and private budgets, including investments in young people. However, recently, health spending slowed markedly. Over the past five years (2010–15), National Health Expenditures (NHE) rose at an average of 3.5 percent a year on a per capita basis, compared with 6.0 percent in the previous decade (2000–10). From 2010 to 2015, Medicare spending rose by 1.4 percent per beneficiary; the comparable Medicaid figure was 1.7 percent.[4]

The causes of the recent spending slowdown are the subject of a lively debate. The Great Recession, low overall inflation, the ACA's cost-reduction measures and other federal initiatives, employer efforts to constrain spending by shifting costs onto workers through high-deductible and narrow network plans and other mechanisms, the shift to generic drugs, a slow-down in the introduction of expensive new interventions and blockbuster branded drugs, and provider efforts to improve efficiency have all played some role in slowing the growth in per capita costs.

Even without election-related disruption in the health sector, spending growth is expected to accelerate. Per capita NHE are projected to rise 4.9 percent per year over the next 10 years, Medicare spending at a rate of 4.3 percent per beneficiary, and Medicaid expenditures at a rate of 4.6 percent per enrollee. When looking at total, rather than per capita, health care spending, demographic trends will exacerbate the situation. Over the next decade, the baby boomers will expand Medicare's rolls by almost 3 percent a year. While the under-65 population will be growing by 0.4 percent a year, an increasing fraction will be concentrated in the 50–64 age group, where average medical expenditures for the nonelderly population tend to be high.

The lull in new expensive medical innovations seems to be coming to an end. Pharmaceutical manufacturers are introducing expensive new drugs for cancer and other chronic conditions—often costing well over $50,000 per year—along with pricey innovations based on genomic and nano-technology breakthroughs. In addition, provider consolidation (hospital, nursing home, and home health agency mergers), acquisitions of insurance companies by other insurers, and the purchase of physician groups by hospitals threaten to reduce what little effective competition exists in the health care sector.

Faced with the prospect of rapid health care spending growth, the new administration should lay out its view on the seriousness of the challenge and how it proposes to address it. It will have to make clear what the ACA substitute will do to replace the health spending reductions. The ACA contains initiatives such as the Cadillac tax, Medical Loss Ratio limits, and premium rate reviews that are intended to dampen expenditure growth by private plans. What measures would replace these?

The ACA also reduces the growth of Medicare's spending significantly. It cut payments to most institutional providers and to Medicare Advantage plans, initiated multiple demonstrations and pilot programs to test various cost-reduction approaches, and established the Innovation Center within the Centers for Medicare and Medicaid Services to explore new payment methods for government programs and a nonprofit Patient-Centered Outcomes Research Institute to sponsor research on cost reductions and improved care delivery. It also called for creation of the Independent Payment Advisory Board, a body charged with instituting cost-reducing measures if Medicare's spending exceeds specified target growth rates.[5] Many of these initiatives have yet to show significant impacts on the pace of cost growth; the Congressional Budget Office has estimated that Medicare's direct spending would increase $802 billion over the 2016–25 period if the ACA were repealed.[6] Advocates of repeal will have to decide which, if any, of the ACA's cost-saving measures they would retain and what alternative approaches they would propose.

REFORMING MEDICARE TO EXTEND THE LIFE OF THE TRUST FUND

Beyond the ACA, the Trump administration and Congress also face looming challenges in preserving Medicare solvency. The Trust Fund, out of which Medicare pays hospital claims, is projected to be depleted in 2028, even with all of the ACA's Medicare savings.[7] At that point, revenues dedicated to Medicare will cover only 87 percent of Medicare's Hospital Insurance's (HI) costs. Unlike other components of the federal budget except Social Security, Medicare has no legal authority to run a deficit in the Trust Fund and would have to cut spending. Repealing the ACA in its entirety would accelerate, possibly to the middle of the next decade, the date of Trust Fund depletion, as spending would increase when the productivity-related reductions in payment updates for institutional providers (such as hospitals and skilled nursing facilities) and other cost-reducing measures disappear, and when the increase in payroll taxes on those with high earnings required by the ACA is terminated, thereby reducing the Trust Fund's revenue.[8]

Moderating the growth of spending of the physician and drug components of Medicare (Part B and Part D) is also important. Under current law, general revenues automatically cover any difference between spending in parts B and D and premiums collected, which increases the federal deficit. With total Part B and Part D spending projected to rise by an average of 7.3 percent and 9.7 percent a year respectively over the next decade, these programs will burden both federal budget resources and beneficiaries (who will face rising premiums tied to increased program costs). Over the next two decades, parts B and D expenditures are projected to grow by 0.67 percent of GDP.

The new administration and Congress should address the future of Medicare and not wait until HI trust fund depletion forces hasty action. Doing so will permit a wider range of solutions to be considered, solutions that can distribute the burden across more stakeholders and generations. Furthermore, significant policy modifications to Medicare (and Social Security) must be phased in gradually to allow affected individuals, businesses, and institutions adequate time to adjust. However, Medicare, perhaps even more than Social Security, is the third rail of American politics. The millions of older and disabled people who depend on Medicare—and their children—are extremely fearful of proposals to limit Medicare's benefits or increase beneficiary costs, even if such proposals are phased in far in the future. Moreover, older people tend to show up at the polls.

The list of suggested policies for improving the sustainability of Medicare's finances is long, and controversial. Such policies include transforming Medicare into a system of premium supports in which beneficiaries receive a government subsidy (voucher) that enables them to purchase insurance through an exchange; raising the age at which Medicare is available from 65 to the age at which unreduced Social Security benefits are available (or even higher); increasing parts B and D premiums; increasing deductibles and cost sharing; moving to new payment mechanisms such as reference pricing, and episode-, bundled-, or value-based payments; limiting payments for expensive pharmaceuticals; and raising Medicare HI payroll taxes. Any candidate with a plan for moving Medicare to sustainable solvency risks scaring older people and being demonized by the other side. Hence, both 2016 presidential candidates promised to preserve Medicare, and one argued for popular but inadequate policies compared to the actual need, such as relaxing limitations on the importation of drugs and allowing the government to negotiate prices with drug manufacturers.

It seems unlikely that Medicare solvency will be an early priority for the Trump administration, although Speaker Ryan, who has controversial ideas about moving Medicare to a premium support model, has said that he wants to address the issue. Congress has some experience with bipartisan cooperation on health care issues—for example, in replacing the defunct Sustainable Growth Rate formula with the new MACRA payment system that focuses on value rather than volume of health services.[9]

Congress should push the administration to participate in a constructive bipartisan effort to ensure the fiscal sustainability of Medicare.

CONCLUSION

The next president and the new Congress will have to address other health policy issues as well, including unhealthful food, drug abuse, violence, and other nonmedical factors that impact health; health disparities between affluent and low-income populations; new epidemics and drug-resistant pathogens; and biomedical innovation. But the issues in this chapter—how to improve the ACA, how to control rising health spending, and how to preserve Medicare for the growing elderly population—should be the focus of policymakers in 2017.

Notes

1. Linda J. Blumberg, John Holahan, and Matthew Buettgens, "Why Not Just Eliminate the Employer Mandate?," Urban Institute, May 9, 2014, www.urban.org/research/publication/why-not-just-eliminate-employer-mandate.

2. As of April 2015, 21 states offered no Medicaid coverage to childless adults, 13 states offered parents of dependent children Medicaid only if their incomes fell below 50 percent of the FPL, and 4 offered such parents Medicaid coverage if their incomes fell between 50 and 100 percent of the FPL. In Alabama and Texas, eligibility was restricted to parents with incomes at or below 18 percent of the FPL. Under federal law, all children in families with incomes below the FPL and assets below constricted thresholds are eligible for coverage. Kaiser Family Foundation, "Where Are States Today? Medicaid and CHIP Eligibility Levels for Adults, Children, and Pregnant Women" (Menlo Park, Calif.: April 2015), http://kff.org/medicaid/factsheet/where-are-states-today-medicaid-and-chip/.

3. Employees of firms that offer insurance to workers can enroll in exchange plans with tax subsidies rather than their employer's plan if the premium costs for the worker-only policy exceed 7 percent of their income. However, if the premium for a worker-only policy is below this threshold but the premium for a family policy exceeds this level, the family is precluded from accessing subsidized coverage through the exchange, unlike the situation facing workers whose employer offers no insurance.

4. "Projected," Centers for Medicare and Medicaid Services, July 14, 2016, www.cms.gov/Research-Statistics-Data-and-Systems/Statistics-Trends-and-Reports/NationalHealthExpendData/NationalHealthAccountsProjected.html.

5. If it objects to these proposals, Congress can either approve an alternative package with comparable savings or vote to reject the package. In the latter case, Congress probably would have to override a presidential veto.

6. "Budgetary and Economic Effects of Repealing the Affordable Care Act," (Washington, D.C.: Congressional Budget Office, June 2015), 10–11.

7. The Boards of Trustees, Federal Hospital Insurance and Federal Supplementary Medical Insurance Trust Funds, "2015 Annual Report of the Boards of Trustees of the Federal Hospital Insurance and Federal Supplementary Medical Insurance Trust Funds," Centers for Medicare and Medicaid Services, www.cms.gov/Research-Statistics-Data-and-Systems/Statistics-Trends-and-Reports/ReportsTrustFunds/Downloads/TR2015.pdf.

8. Trump has said he will not repeal certain Medicare components, although the Republicans in Congress in their reconciliation bill included repeals of most of the Medicare-related tax increases—extra payroll tax for high income folks, tax on investment income, and so on. The big one that no one is suggesting to repeal is the ACA's reductions in provider updates.

9. MACRA stands for Medicare Access and CHIP Reauthorization Act. The Centers for Medicare and Medicaid Services (CMS) released a final rule on October 14, 2016, giving details on the final regulations for implementation of MACRA, the historic Medicare reform law that repealed the Sustainable Growth Rate (SGR) formula.

5

A Government-Wide Reform Agenda
for the Next Administration

ELAINE C. KAMARCK

SUMMARY: Government reform is long overdue to position the U.S. federal workforce to be more efficient and effective in facing the challenges of the 21st century. A comprehensive approach to government reform should focus on modernizing several key aspects of governance, including federal budget and spending decisions, the civil service and contract employee workforce, and regulatory and policy structure.

In the early 1990s the Clinton administration ran a large-scale government reform program that introduced websites, performance metrics, and other new ideas into government. The two presidents since then have been preoccupied with a terrorist attack on the homeland and the biggest recession since the Great Depression. The immediacy of those crises pushed major, widespread governmental reform to the back burner of the president's attention, although in each administration there were important management initiatives. After two decades of war and recession, it is time for the next administration to evaluate the government in the light of the new century.

There are three ways to approach reform.

- To focus on governmental systems that cut across all governmental departments and agencies, such as hiring, purchasing, revenue raising, and budgeting.

- To focus on individual operations of government, such as sending out Social Security checks, landing airplanes safely, tracking down fruit and vegetables that cause disease outbreaks, or investigating gun crimes.

- To ask some big questions about what the government should or should not be doing in the 21st century. For instance, should the federal government be involved in housing policy, or is this a question best left to states and localities?

All three of these things are important aspects of a comprehensive approach to government reform. The first two require significant management expertise and the third requires significant political will. This chapter will begin by examining the first set of questions.

A COMPREHENSIVE APPROACH TO GOVERNMENT REFORM

A government-wide reform agenda should begin with:

- **The budget process.** Our federal budget process has not been reformed since 1974. While it worked well for a while, in recent years it has broken down completely. In the meantime, a third type of budgeting has gone on through the tax system and stands completely outside of the budget process. Budget reform must include tax expenditures.

- **Federal contracting.** In the past two decades, more and more government functions have been done under contract by nongovernmental employees. Much of this has been driven by ideology, not by what is cost effective and right for citizens. It is time to ask what makes sense in federal contracting and to review the distortions that have resulted.

- **The civil service.** The civil service was built for a government of clerks, not for a government of professionals. It cannot compete for the talent it needs in today's marketplace. We have been penny wise and pound foolish when it comes to the civil service. It is time to "normalize" the federal civil service so that it more closely resembles the overall labor market.

- **Federal regulation.** The federal regulatory system is obsolete and cannot keep up with the pace of change going on in many sectors of the American economy. This is especially evident in the sectors of the economy that are undergoing rapid technological change.

- **Scoring issues.** The Office of Management and Budget (OMB) and the Congressional Budget Office (CBO), the mandarins of the federal system, have a consensus on a set of scoring rules that from time to time cause irrational spending decisions on the part of the federal government. It is time to revisit the scoring rules that dictate so much about federal regulation.

- **Policy design.** For too many years, we have passed bills and appropriated money for policies without paying any attention to whether or not they work. Every policy passed should have built into it a method of evaluation and a reasonable end date if the policy does not produce the results intended.

REFORM THE BUDGET PROCESS

According to the 1974 Budget Act, the formal definition of a tax expenditure is "revenue losses attributable to provisions of the Federal tax laws which allow a special exclusion, exemption, or deduction from gross income or which provide a special credit, a preferential rate of tax, or a deferral of tax liability."[1] In plain language, tax expenditures are "loopholes"—legal ways that people or corporations get to avoid taxes. Loopholes get a bad rap from the public; nonetheless, in recent years the total amount of revenue lost to the federal government through tax expenditures has increased substantially. As the following chart (figure 5.1) from the Government Accountability Office illustrates, over the past 30 years, revenue lost to the government through tax expenditures has increased nearly every year, with the exception of a few years following enactment of the historic 1986 tax reform bill. These days, tax expenditures are almost as large as the entire discretionary portion of the budget.

Who is advantaged? Most tax expenditures in 2014 went to individuals—87 percent—while 13 percent went to corporations. Hence the first part of the political problem here: Americans are all for getting rid of those bad corporate loopholes that keep big companies from paying taxes, but they are far less enthusiastic about getting rid of tax breaks that they be-

FIGURE 5.1   TAX EXPENDITURES ARE COMPARABLE IN
             SIZE TO DISCRETIONARY SPENDING LEVELS

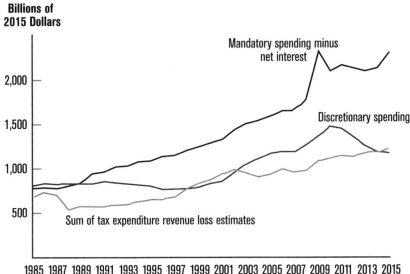

Billions of 2015 Dollars

Mandatory spending minus net interest

Discretionary spending

Sum of tax expenditure revenue loss estimates

2,000

1,500

1,000

500

1985 1987 1989 1991 1993 1995 1997 1999 2001 2003 2005 2007 2009 2011 2013 2015

Fiscal Year

Source: U.S. Government Accountability Office, "Tax Expenditures," www.gao.gov/key_issues/tax_expenditures/issue_summary.

lieve help them. Figure 5.2 shows who gets the tax expenditures. Figure 5.3 shows what the individual tax expenditures are for. Note that the two biggest ones are the exclusion for employer health insurance and for housing, notably the mortgage tax deduction.

Hence the second part of the political problem. Americans may hate loopholes, but they love their mortgage tax deduction and they would revolt if the employer contribution portion of their health care premiums were taxed. In fact, however, the advantages of individual tax expenditures are weighted extensively toward upper-income individuals—but the bottom quintiles do all right, too. The middle class is the least advantaged.[2]

Opinion about tax expenditures depends on which ones and who is looking. Liberals *and* conservatives value different expenditures. In budget terms, tax expenditures are like entitlement programs—they tend to live

FIGURE 5.2   **TAX EXPENDITURES IN BILLIONS, FISCAL YEAR 2014**

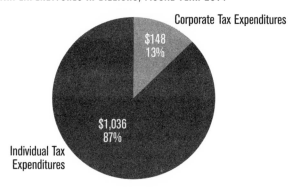

Source: Office of Management and Budget; http://taxfoundation.org/sites/taxfoundation.
org/files/docs/Chart1.png.

FIGURE 5.3   **INDIVIDUAL TAX EXPENDITURES IN MILLIONS, FISCAL YEAR 2014**

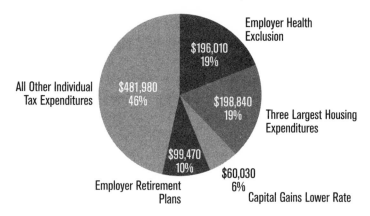

Source: Office of Management and Budget; http://taxfoundation.org/sites/taxfoundation.
org/files/docs/Chart2.png.

on with very little incentive or opportunity for examination. Three budget experts, Paul Posner, Steven Redburn, and Jonathan Breul, explain the tax expenditure situation as follows: "[Tax expenditures'] invisibility and institutional isolation makes them less subject to review and competition than other forms of spending. They arise in an entirely separate policy world centered in the revenue committees and the Treasury, considered apart from comparable spending programs that share common objectives and purposes and that are part of the budget process. Because they are separate they are not subject to the extensive reviews that regular spending programs come under."[3]

The time has come to integrate tax expenditures into the formal federal budget process. They should be presented alongside spending proposals in budget submissions and they should be subject to performance reviews. Finally, budget reconciliation should "provide savings targets to revenue committees requiring reduction of selected tax expenditures."[4] The creation of a tax expenditure budget does not mean the end of popular deductions such as the ones for mortgages and for health care. But it does expand the budget process in a significant way and provides another option for lawmakers *regardless* of their political objectives. The important point to this reform is to include in the budget process an important element in the overall budget picture.

RESTORE BALANCE TO THE FEDERAL CONTRACTING SYSTEM

The federal government buys lots of things and lots of different things— from pencils and staplers to laptop computers to laser-guided weapons systems, airplanes that can deflect radar, and spacesuits for astronauts. "Outsourcing" has always been a part of our federal operating system and often for the good. It can be argued that the U.S. government's decision to outsource weapons research and development during the Cold War— to universities like MIT and Cal Tech and to private companies such as Lockheed-Martin and Boeing—was a decision that helped us achieve the military superiority that ended the Cold War.[5]

Outsourcing or contracting out should not be an ideological decision. But in the first decade of the 21st century, that is exactly what it became, so that today the balance between official government work and contracted-out work is way out of balance. It is so out of balance that, in a provocative book called *Bring Back the Bureaucrats*, John DiIulio Jr. points out that while annual federal spending increased dramatically since 1960, the number of federal civilian workers has remained fairly constant. "In sum," he writes, "over the last half-century, the federal government increased its spending more than fivefold while the full-time federal civilian workforce remained largely flat."[6] There are no official statistics on the number of government contractors, but estimates suggest that there are as many as 7.6 million contract employees and as many as 2.8 million grant-based employees. This total—over 10 million—is more than twice the 4.3 million federal employees, including uniformed military.

The United States is ripe for a debate on the issue of federal contracting or, more broadly, on the issue of what is and what is not an "inherently governmental" function.[7] The next administration will need to work hard to restore the proper balance to the federal government between contractors and federal workers. First, it should create a "review board" to establish guidelines for what is inherently governmental on an agency-by-agency basis. This will make sure that we do not throw out the proverbial baby with the bathwater. There are many things that the federal government wants done—from building housing for soldiers to doing research on nanotechnology—that need not be done by federal workers. That said, we need to greatly enhance the capacity of the federal government to oversee these contracts, and the simplest way to do that is to pay them more. Every time the federal government embarks on a multibillion-dollar information technology acquisition, it should be able to hire the best from the private sector—no matter the price. Which brings us to the next section.

REFORM THE CIVIL SERVICE

The U.S. civil service has served the country well. But it was built for a government of clerks, not a government of professionals. In the mid-20th century, the federal government consisted of thousands of clerks who, working mostly with paper systems and primitive card readers, kept track of everything from veterans benefits to Social Security earnings records. But these clerks have been replaced by computers, and today's federal government has the most sophisticated and highly educated workforce in the world. According to a government report: "About 20 percent of Federal workers have a master's degree, professional degree, or doctorate versus only 13 percent in the private sector. A full 51 percent of Federal employees have at least a college degree compared to 35 percent in the private sector."[8] Today's civil service system is increasingly obsolete, with an approach to pay, recruitment, management, competition for talent, and dealing with poor performers that has been virtually unchanged since the 1978 Civil Service Reform Act. Although that act contains in it human capital flexibilities, these have tended to be underutilized, as have flexibilities granted to agencies as the result of legislation. Fear of change, inertia, and political pressure have left the federal government with a personnel system that is simply not up to the job.

The challenge for this century is to "normalize" the civil service. Federal hiring practices need to encompass recruiting flexibilities, and we need to expand the use of scholarships and ROTC-like programs to attract mission-critical talent. But the most important key to normalization is to allow, within the nonpolitical civil service, a compensation system that is more market-oriented and that would allow the federal government to hire competitively. In "A New Civil Service Framework," the Partnership for Public Service recommends that the government

> modernize the decades-old federal General Schedule (GS) job classification system to better reflect the work of today's federal professionals and administrators, and use it to match federal occupations and federal pay—to comparable jobs in the private and nonprofit sectors, as well as in state and local governments.[9]

In practice, this would mean that Congress would set an overall compensation budget for the federal government each year. Individual agencies would then have the freedom to determine, within ranges, the best mix of grades and occupations. They would create a process for determining pay that was based on market data, analyzing professions in comparison to pay that exists in the Fortune 500 companies, in large state and local governments, and in large nonprofit organizations since these entities compete for labor with the federal government. The Partnership's proposal would call for the retention of locality pay (something that might be reflected in a true market comparison in any event) and for salary caps on civil servant pay equivalent to the salary of the vice president. A more radical reform agenda would argue that salary caps should be abolished altogether.

The contracting problem and the civil service problem are part and parcel of the same story. By holding down civil service pay, by pretending that the 21st-century federal government is no different than the government in the 1950s, we have been spending a great deal more of the taxpayers' dollars than we need to.

REFORM THE FEDERAL REGULATORY SYSTEM

Just as the civil service system was built for another era, so was the federal regulatory system. It too is obsolete and cannot keep pace with the rapid technological changes going on in many sectors of the American economy. There are four commonly discussed reforms of the regulatory system that the next administration needs to follow up on. The first two are relatively straightforward and can be done quickly: mandate regulatory "look-backs" and expand cost-benefit analysis to independent government agencies.

The first "look-back" was conducted in the Clinton administration as part of the reinventing government effort, and another one took place in the Obama administration. In addition to making regulatory "look-backs" mandatory—perhaps every five years—there is an emerging consensus on the fact that the government should extend cost-benefit analysis to independent agencies such as the Federal Communications Commission and the Securities and Exchange Commission.

The bigger picture on regulatory reform, however, extends to those areas of the economy where the regulatory structure was built for another time. Take, for instance, online financial transactions such as those encountered in eBay or PayPal. The regulations currently governing transactions are based on a person-to-person banking system, even though PayPal is not a brick-and-mortar operation. Consequently, the rigid design standards that are in current law do not meet the reality, and so PayPal operates through a series of annual waivers to the regulations. Not a great way to do business.

A similar mismatch between a technologically advanced industry and its regulatory system occurs in the area of drug approval. Here, a widening chasm separates modern pharmacology and the emerging practice of molecular medicine. Currently, the Food and Drug Administration relies on testing protocols that use empirical studies and statistical correlations. However, as Peter Huber writes in *The Cure in the Code*, "modern pharmacology hinges on the scientific selection of the right drug-patient molecular combinations."[10] It is this area of regulatory reform that will pose the most profound challenges to the next administration.

REFORM SOME ELEMENTS OF SCORING

Everyone who has worked on policy in Washington understands that at some point a proposal can live or die based on how it is "scored." Scoring is a science and an art controlled by OMB in the executive branch and CBO in the legislative branch. Scoring rules often come under fire from both sides of the aisle. Republicans like to talk about "dynamic scoring" when it comes to tax provisions, since they like to argue that tax cuts actually spur growth and bring in revenue. Democrats like to talk about the importance of investments in the future such as those in education or health care that eventually will bring greater prosperity and greater tax revenue. Since both propositions can be true and false depending on the situation, it is no wonder that the establishment has held the line against such creative uses of scoring.

There are, however, some areas where the next administration should take a serious look at the current scoring rules. As Dorothy Robyn points out in a powerful op-ed, the current scoring rules of federal procurement of real property create real distortions and serious costs to the government. The major culprit in this is OMB Circular A-11, which since its inception has created unintended consequences. The most powerful is "the reliance on short-term operating leases to meet long-term federal facility requirements."[11] A second consequence has led agencies to postpone capital investments in their facilities. A-11 could be reformed to get rid of the costly incentives in federal property acquisition without changing all the scoring rules.

A second area that has long been ripe for reform is to change the way fraud control efforts are scored in entitlement programs. Half of the federal budget is now taken up by enormous entitlement programs—so called because they are not subject to annual appropriations. As any casual reader of the news knows, there is so much money in these programs that they invite fraud and abuse. Each program has a unit devoted to finding and investigating fraud and handing it over for prosecution. There is no doubt that these antifraud units more than pay for themselves. And yet, they are "scored" as part of the discretionary budget, meaning that when there are across-the-board budget cuts, these programs are cut even though they actually save money. An important reform would be to change the scorekeeping rules to ensure that mandatory cost savings derived from increased enforcement spending are scored as savings—as long as those savings exceed the increased enforcement funding.

SYSTEMATICALLY IMPROVE POLICY DESIGN

It is amazing that after all the time and money spent on government programs there are so many about which we know so little. The next administration should systematically build into any major spending program a method of evaluation and an end date to the program if the policy does not produce the intended results. For instance, in the 1990s the Department of Housing and Urban Development created a program known as "Moving to Opportunity," which had evaluation built in. The results were surprising: instead of showing increases in economic well-being, as predicted, the study showed increases in health and wellness. If more programs were designed to tell us something about whether a policy works and how, we would gain valuable knowledge about policy design.

CONCLUSION

These six areas are only an initial look at what has to happen in the federal government to bring it fully into the 21st century. But each of them has consequences for federal management in all areas of the government. As indicated initially, there are other pieces of a comprehensive reform package, which should look at duplication of efforts and consider what functions could be best given to the states or eliminated altogether. But starting with large, cross-cutting systemic reforms will yield advantages in both governmental cost and performance, and is therefore a good place to begin.

Notes

1. Joint Committee on Taxation, "Background Information on Tax Expenditure Analysis and Historical Survey of Tax Expenditure Estimates," JCX_15_11, February 28, 2011, www.jct.gov/publications.html?func=startdown&id=3740.

2. "The Distribution of Major Tax Expenditures in the Individual Income Tax System" (Congressional Budget Office, May 29, 2013), www.cbo.gov/publication/43768.

3. F. Stevens Redburn, Paul Posner, and Jonathan Breul, "Hidden in Plain Sight: The Mysterious Case of Tax Expenditures" (Brookings, February 6, 2014).

4. Ibid.

5. Waler LaFeber, *America, Russia, and the Cold War, 1945–2006* (Boston: McGraw-Hill, 2008), 340.

6. John DiIulio, *Bring Back the Bureaucrats: Why More Federal Workers Will Lead to Better (and Smaller!) Government* (West Conshohocken, Pa.: Templeton Press, 2014), 111.

7. The debate begins with an obscure OMB directive called OMB Circular A-76. It was created in 1966 to provide guidance to government agencies on whether they should "make or buy" certain goods and services and added to in 1998 with the FAIR Act. But contracting out was given new impetus during the George W. Bush administration. As a matter of pro-business ideology, the administration created

a "competitive sourcing initiative" that expanded the inventories in FAIR and set targets for expanding the A-76 competitions. This greatly expanded the possibility for outsourcing and modified, without much attention by Congress, the definition of what was "inherently governmental."

8. See chart 11-3 "Education Level Distribution in Federal vs. Private Workforce," at www.whitehouse.gov/sites/default/files/omb/performance/chapter11-2012.pdf.

9. "Building the Enterprise: A New Civil Service Framework" (Washington, D.C.: Partnership for Public Service, April 2014), 16.

10. Peter Huber, *The Cure in the Code: How 20th Century Law Is Undermining 21st Century Medicine* (New York: Basic Books, 2013).

11. Dorothy Robyn, "Reforming Federal Property Procurement: The Case for Sensible Scoring" (Brookings, April 24, 2014).

PART II

Growing the Economy

6

Recommendations for Federal Budget Policy

DOUGLAS W. ELMENDORF

SUMMARY: When the next president and Congress take office, decisions about the federal budget will be high on their "to do" list. Without changes in laws regarding federal spending or taxes, federal debt will rise indefinitely as a percentage of GDP. That is unsustainable. But the likely persistence of low Treasury borrowing rates means that the need to reduce debt is less urgent and that additional federal investment would be appropriate. Therefore, I recommend that we increase federal investment during the next decade and pay for that increase with lower benefits for better-off retirees and higher taxes, but allow debt to continue to rise. In the long run, though, we will need larger increases in taxes and reductions in benefits in order to put federal debt on a downward path relative to GDP, and we should enact those changes soon so that people have plenty of warning before they take effect. In addition, because the low level of interest rates reduces the Federal Reserve's ability to fight economic downturns, we should build stronger automatic stabilizers into the federal budget and prepare to use discretionary countercyclical fiscal policy.

Following are recommendations, as well as the economic analysis and value judgments that are the basis for those recommendations.

During the next decade, I think we should allow federal debt to rise as a percentage of GDP in line with what would happen under current law, but should shift the composition of the budget by increasing federal investment above what would occur under current law and paying for that increase with cuts in benefits for higher-income retirees and hikes in tax revenue. I also think we should enact larger cuts in benefits and increases in taxes to be phased in beyond the next decade so that debt declines gradually relative to GDP in the long term. Moreover, we should strengthen the automatic stabilizers in order to moderate the next economic downturn.

The *first* issue is the path of debt. Under current law, federal debt is projected by the Congressional Budget Office (CBO) to rise from 77 percent of GDP currently to 86 percent by the end of the decade and more than 100 percent 25 years from now. For comparison, debt averaged 39 percent of GDP over the past 50 years and was 35 percent in 2007 before the crisis.

Federal debt cannot increase indefinitely relative to the size of the economy, so current law regarding federal spending and revenues is not sustainable. Moreover, even if debt stops rising at some point, allowing debt to stay so high would have significant costs. Federal debt can crowd out private capital investment. Also, high debt reduces the "fiscal space" for responding to unexpected developments. If we hit another financial crisis or severe recession with debt at 77 percent or 86 percent of GDP rather than 35 percent, our options will be more constrained. Those points argue, all else equal, for reducing federal debt by a lot and for doing so quickly.

However, all else is not equal: interest rates on Treasury securities are very low by historical standards and will probably remain low for a prolonged period. The yield on 10-year Treasury notes was 8 percent at the end of 1990, 5 percent at the end of 2000, and 2 percent at the end of 2015—with CBO and a number of other analysts now predicting that the 10-year yield will rise only to about 3½ percent in the coming years, and many financial-market participants appearing to expect it to remain below that. That is a sea change in the economic backdrop for fiscal policy, and it has come into focus just in the past few years.

There are many possible explanations for why Treasury rates may remain much lower than historical norms, and different explanations have different implications for the optimal amount of federal debt. It is well understood that lower interest rates improve debt dynamics: For any given paths of revenues and noninterest spending, lower interest rates mean that debt will be lower. But it is not well understood how low rates should affect the amount of debt we should aim for. Together with Brookings senior fellow Louise Sheiner, I have analyzed alternative explanations for low

Treasury rates and the implications of each for budget policy.[1] We found that most explanations imply that the country should have a higher debt-to-GDP ratio than otherwise—and also that federal investment should be higher than otherwise. The intuition for these results is that interest rates show the direct cost to the Treasury of its borrowing and provide information about the indirect cost to the economy of Treasury borrowing—and if costs will be persistently much lower than we are accustomed to, then more borrowing, especially for investment, passes a cost-benefit test.

To be sure, interest-rate projections are very uncertain, and policy-making should be mindful of the risk that rates will rise above current expectations—especially because many large changes in fiscal policy are best made slowly. But we should not ignore a good deal of evidence that rates will probably be much lower than in the past.

In balancing those competing considerations, my judgment is that we should let debt rise gradually over the coming decade in line with what would happen under current law because the costs of doing so appear quite small and the benefits of maintaining or raising certain kinds of spending would be considerable. However, I think we should enact policy changes now that will reduce debt relative to GDP in the long run so that the changes can be phased in gradually and with a lot of advance notice.

How about the composition of the budget? The *second* part of my recommendations is to increase federal investment.

The traditional categories of federal investment are infrastructure, education and training, and R&D. Under the current caps on annual appropriations, federal non-defense investments of those sorts soon will be smaller relative to GDP than at any time in at least 50 years.

That is not forward-looking, growth-oriented budget policy. Cutting federal investments will reduce total output and income relative to what they would otherwise be. Moreover, cutting federal investment in education and training will reduce the incomes of lower- and middle-income people who are dependent on government help to have a real opportunity to advance. And with low Treasury interest rates, we should be doing more federal investment than otherwise. Therefore, in my view, we should raise the caps on non-defense appropriations substantially, in order to maintain federal investment as a share of GDP.

We should also work to increase the return on federal investments. Sometimes we build critical transportation links, and sometimes we build bridges to nowhere; sometimes education funding supports a breakthrough in a person's life, and sometimes it is dissipated. We can do better. For example, we should increase the role of careful cost-benefit analysis in deciding which specific investments to undertake.

It is also important to understand that some federal spending outside those traditional categories represents an investment in future income, especially for lower-income people. There is a small but growing body of evidence that certain benefits for lower-income families—such as health-care benefits and housing subsidies—raise future incomes of some young people. We should protect those investments as well.

The *third* piece of my recommendations is that we should reduce benefits for higher-income retirees but not for lower-income retirees or working-age people. I come to that view based on two sets of facts and one value judgment.

One set of facts is about the evolution of the federal budget under current law. If we look ahead 25 years, spending for Social Security and Medicare will continue to increase relative to GDP, mostly because of the aging of the population: by the time the last baby boomers become eligible for Social Security and Medicare, there will be more than 75 million beneficiaries of those programs, two-thirds more than the number just before the first boomers became eligible for early retirement benefits. Those beneficiaries will be more than one-fifth of the U.S. population. Meanwhile, defense spending is declining relative to GDP and, under current law, in a few years will be a smaller percentage of GDP than anyone can remember. All other non-interest spending taken together is about the same share of GDP now that it was 25 years ago, and in CBO's current-law projections, it is about the same share 25 years from now. Of course, there have been important shifts within this very broad category. But the key point is that the rise in federal spending does not stem from general growth in the federal government relative to the size of the economy but instead from a dramatic increase in spending for Social Security and Medicare, with a rising amount of interest payments as well.

The other set of facts is about the evolution of the income distribution. During the past few decades, the incomes of people across most of the distribution have risen quite slowly, while incomes at the high end of the distribution have risen very rapidly. According to estimates by CBO, between 1979 and 2013 market incomes—that is, incomes before taking account of taxes and transfers—rose 18 percent in the bottom quintile of the distribution, 12 percent in the middle quintile, and 85 percent in the top quintile. Those specific numbers substantially understate the true increases in people's incomes because the data do not fully capture quality improvements or the introduction of new goods and services, such as free digital products available through the Internet. Still, it is clear that most people in the country have gained very little directly from the growth of total output and national income in the past few decades.

The value judgment I make is that federal policies generally should be focused on raising incomes for people of modest means. Combining that value judgment with the facts about the evolution of the income distribution implies that it is especially important at this point in time to do so. And combining that conclusion with the fact that means-tested programs are not the principal obstacle to budget sustainability implies that we should not cut benefits focused on lower-income people. Moreover, I think we should avoid cutting benefits in programs like Social Security and Medicare in across-the-board ways, because such cuts would significantly reduce total retirement income for many lower-income people.

Therefore, I think that reductions in benefits should be focused on better-off beneficiaries of Social Security and Medicare. To be sure, that approach does not offer a free lunch. Making Social Security and Medicare more progressive would weaken the connection between an individual's taxes and benefits, which could undermine the earned-benefit character of the systems if taken too far. Also, because people with higher incomes would face lower benefits, their incentives to work and save would be reduced. But I think this approach is the best of the available alternatives for restraining federal debt without unduly burdening those Americans who have fared the worst in economic terms in recent years.

I want to comment here about the Affordable Care Act (ACA), which is the biggest expansion of federal means-tested programs in decades. The ACA is significantly increasing the share of Americans who have health insurance, and doing so at a cost of thousands of subsidy dollars per newly insured person and a collection of significant changes in insurance rules. That dollar cost is substantial, but not surprising given the high cost of health care. For context, the ACA subsidies will be only about 10 percent of total federal subsidies for health insurance over the next decade, with much larger subsidies provided through Medicare, Medicaid apart from the ACA, and tax subsidies for employer-provided health insurance. Of course, there are alternative policies regarding health insurance that we could adopt. But there are no policies that would achieve the substantial increase in insurance coverage occurring under the ACA without subsidies and rules similar to those of the ACA—or an even larger federal role. That is an analytic result. Then there is a value judgment about whether the increase in insurance coverage is worth those costs. My judgment is yes, largely because of my concern about the slow income growth at the lower end of the distribution.

The *fourth* part of my recommendations is to raise tax revenue above what will be collected under current law. There is no realistic way to reduce debt as a percentage of GDP that does not involve more revenue.

Over the next 25 years, spending for Social Security and Medicare is projected to increase by 3.5 percent of GDP, which would represent, for current GDP, more than $600 billion a year. That increase is driven primarily by the retirement of the baby boomers. Costs per beneficiary in Social Security are projected to rise roughly with real wages, as they have in the past few decades; costs per beneficiary in Medicare are projected to rise much more slowly than they have in the past few decades because of a combination of slow growth in payments per procedure under current law, ongoing changes in the health care system, and other factors. As a result, there are few ways to reduce spending that would not be felt directly by beneficiaries, and those beneficiaries generally like those programs a lot. As I mentioned earlier, my own recommendation is to reduce the benefits for better-off retirees, but that would not be nearly large enough to offset all of the increase in costs from the growing number of beneficiaries.

Meanwhile, the projections under current law show defense spending falling as a percentage of GDP. And, as I said, all other federal spending apart from interest is projected to be the same share of GDP in 25 years that it is today, which is about the same share as it was 25 years ago. At an abstract level, many people want government spending to be cut, but when one drills down to the level of individual programs within that broad category, cutting becomes much more difficult. People want highways repaired, medical research conducted, the borders secured, veterans cared for, food and drugs inspected, and so on. There is no evidence that most people want cuts in spending of the magnitude that would be needed to avoid any revenue increases. The Republicans have controlled the House of Representatives for nearly six years, and the number of bills they have approved that would cut spending substantially—apart from proposed repeal of the Affordable Care Act and the imposition of caps on annual appropriations enacted a few years ago—is zero.

To raise revenues, the natural places to start are to tax carbon emissions and to reduce the deductions and exemptions that narrow the tax base and thereby lower the revenue collected for any given tax rate.

Experts on the climate agree overwhelmingly that we should reduce carbon emissions substantially. Experts on the economy agree overwhelmingly that putting a price on carbon emissions is the most efficient way to reduce emissions. Putting a price on carbon can be achieved through a carbon tax or a cap-and-trade system, and we should establish one or the other.

Economists also agree overwhelmingly that reducing the deductions and exemptions that narrow the tax base would be the most efficient way to increase revenue from the personal income tax, the payroll tax, and the corporate profits tax. Those deductions, exemptions, and related features of the tax code are known as "tax expenditures" because they resemble federal spending in the sense of providing financial assistance for particular activities or to particular entities or groups of people. The revenue lost from all tax expenditures taken together is nearly as large as total revenue from the personal income tax, so considerable revenue could be raised by trimming them. And because those tax provisions can distort individuals' and businesses' decisionmaking, reducing the scope or scale of the provisions can improve efficiency.

The *fifth* part of my recommendations is to build stronger automatic stabilizers into the federal budget and prepare to use discretionary countercyclical fiscal policy.

When the economy falls into recession and unemployment rises, the economic and social costs of the lost output and lost jobs can be very large. Between 2008 and 2015, output was below the potential output of the economy—the amount we could produce if we had maintained nearly full employment—by trillions of dollars cumulatively, and millions of additional people were unemployed each year relative to what would have occurred without the recession.

To fight recessions, we rely on a combination of monetary policy and fiscal policy. In each of the past three recessions, the Federal Reserve has cut the federal funds rate by more than 5 percentage points. However, most current projections of the federal funds rate imply that the rate will stay below 5 percent in the years ahead. Therefore, when the next recession begins, the Federal Reserve will be unable to ease monetary policy nearly as much as it did in each of the three previous recessions.

Therefore, relative to what we have done in the past, we will need larger deficits during downturns and smaller deficits (or surpluses) during booms. Variability in the federal budget can itself be costly, and those costs should be considered in deciding what components of spending and taxes should vary most. For example, variation in tax rates and in the federal share of Medicaid spending probably have smaller costs than variation in infrastructure investment. But the general point is that we should build automatic fiscal stabilizers that are more powerful than existing stabilizers and respond very rapidly, and we should develop plans for discretionary fiscal policies that can be enacted when needed.

Note

1. Douglas W. Elmendorf and Louise Sheiner, "Federal Budget Policy with an Aging Population and Persistently Low Interest Rates," Hutchins Center Working Paper 18, Hutchins Center on Fiscal and Monetary Policy at Brookings, October 2016.

7

The Most Important Non-Issue
in the 2016 Campaign

RON HASKINS

SUMMARY: The Congressional Budget Office projects that the nation's debt will grow to equal 86 percent of its GDP by 2026. Other sources show the debt increasing even more rapidly. Under all projections, the debt will continue to increase and will become unsustainable unless Congress and the president enact a plan to reduce projected spending and increase revenues in the years ahead. The 2016 presidential campaigns paid little attention to this rising debt and neither candidate presented a plan to reduce it. Although no one knows at what level debt will interfere with economic growth and cause other negative consequences, few doubt that the current budget course can be sustained. The Trump administration appears poised to pass the buck as have others.

Presidential elections usually feature extended arguments by the respective candidates about the major issues facing the nation. If the candidates do not address the most important issues, the press and the presidential debate moderators are likely to raise them instead. Even so, skilled politicians have little trouble avoiding questions they do not want to answer, often by simply answering another question. In the election of 2016, neither candidate said much about the national debt, one of the top issues affecting the nation's long-term well-being.

The facts and projections that define the debt issue were not discussed in detail by either candidate. Nor did either candidate presented a plan to control the predicted increase in the nation's debt, let alone actually reduce the debt as a percentage of GDP. Given the stark and troubling nature of the debt figures, it is little wonder the candidates avoided them like the plague. According to the most recent report from the Congressional Budget Office (CBO), debt held by the public will equal 77 percent of GDP (about $14 trillion) by the end of 2016, the highest level since the end of World War II, and is predicted to rise to 86 percent of GDP ($23 trillion) within ten years.[1] Some economists believe that when a nation's debt reaches 90 percent of GDP, it begins to restrain economic growth.[2] Other economists believe that this dangerous figure is considerably above 90 percent, perhaps as high as 120 percent.[3] But whatever the level of dangerous debt accumulation might be, virtually every analyst recognizes that at some level the risks of deleterious consequences become likely.

According to CBO, the growth in the annual deficit and the amount each annual deficit adds to the nation's debt to reach 86 percent of GDP by 2026 is caused primarily by the growth of spending on Social Security, health care, and interest payments on the debt, combined with revenues that remain more or less fixed as a percentage of GDP (in CBO estimates, federal revenues over the next decade hold fairly steady at between 17.8 percent and 18.5 percent of GDP). Another factor that adds to the annual deficit is the congressional habit of financing "must pass" legislation by ignoring budget rules and simply increasing the debt.

CBO has supplemented its 10-year projections with 30-year projections to 2046.[4] These projections indicate that the debt is likely to continue increasing beyond the 10-year window and reach 141 percent of GDP by 2046. Even those who argue that the current level of debt is not a serious problem would be likely to agree that it would not be good policy to let the debt grow to more than 140 percent of the nation's economy. One of the reasons it is difficult to rouse politicians or the public about the rising debt is that there is no specific level of debt at which most economists, politicians, or the public would say, "This is it; we have to draw the line; we're about to go off the cliff."

As if these projections are not bad enough, there is good reason to believe that they could be underestimates of how much the nation's debt will grow. The biggest reason the estimates could be low is that the baseline that CBO uses to make its projections could be flawed. The budget baseline is itself an estimate, based primarily on projections of spending and revenues, projections of interest rates, and the likelihood of changes in current law. CBO projections are widely trusted because its analysts make projections according to a transparent set of rules, some of which CBO is mandated to follow. But many analysts believe the rules that CBO follows are too rigid.

A few organizations and individuals with the skills and experience to do their own projections create baselines that they argue are more reasonable than the baseline that CBO uses to produce its estimates. CBO assumes that current law will be implemented as written, but many analysts think it makes sense to form a baseline taking into account the way Congress is likely to behave in changing current law. Even CBO has often issued what its analysts call an "Alternative Fiscal Scenario" (AFS) that is based on what most analysts would agree are more realistic assumptions about what Congress is likely do with spending and taxation decisions than the assumptions in the official CBO estimates. These assumptions are based on what Congress has done in the past with regard to decisions like extending tax provisions that are about to expire and canceling spending cuts that are about to be imposed under previous laws. Congress tends to be bolder in raising taxes and cutting spending when these policies begin at some future date; it just changes them later to cancel tax increases and spending cuts that would impose burdens on politically important groups.

Because CBO did not perform a full AFS analysis in its 2016 update, the Committee for a Responsible Federal Budget created its own AFS following CBO procedures. Under the committee's version of an AFS, both the annual deficits and the impacts on the accumulated debt are greater than under the official CBO projections: the debt would increase from 75 percent of GDP this year to 109 percent by 2031 and 205 percent by 2046.

Both the official CBO debt estimates and the more alarming estimates based on the AFS show that the nation has a very serious long-term problem. CBO often uses the term "unsustainable" to label projections like those that result from its official scenario, let alone the picture revealed by projections based on the AFS.

The United States has maintained its credit since its founding and today enjoys an exalted position as one of the world's most reliable borrowers. Even so, threats from an increasing debt abound. One that is undeniable is the rising level of interest payments. This year, the nation will pay nearly a quarter of a trillion dollars in interest payments. By 2026, CBO estimates that interest payments will be well over $700 billion a year and rising. Whatever else might be said about the nation's debt, we are already paying a huge amount for previous failures to match spending with revenues. Without changes in the nation's fiscal policy, interest on our cumulative debt will continue to spiral upward.

A second consequence of the accumulation of debt and the federal government's growing spending on Social Security, health care, and interest is that other federal spending is being squeezed. A group of budget experts at the Urban Institute has been producing annual detailed reports of federal spending on children through programs such as food stamps, Medicaid, early childhood education, and the Earned Income Tax Credit. These projections show that spending on children has been declining as a percentage of GDP and has been flat as a percentage of federal spending (at about 10 percent). In fact, the budget group's projections show that spending on children will decline from the current 10 percent of the federal budget to 8 percent by 2026.[5] Meanwhile, spending on Social Security, Medicare, Medicaid, and net interest will continue to grow rapidly. To ensure that the young are not shortchanged, a more rational course than the one we are on would be to reduce Social Security payments and Medicare coverage for the elderly who are wealthy and spend the savings both on retiring debt and investing in the young. If we continue our current spending priorities, there will be ever increasing pressure on the rest of the budget, forcing the nation to forego opportunities for investments and emergencies.

Although neither of the 2016 candidates presented a plan for attacking the nation's debt, in the third debate, moderator Chris Wallace asked both candidates a tough question about the national debt. After reviewing the kinds of projections reviewed above and emphasizing how the debt is a threat to the nation's future, Wallace asked both candidates why they were ignoring the problem. Both claimed that they weren't ignoring the problem. Trump claimed that the projections are wrong because he would grow the economy at a rate as high as 6 percent a year and the debt problem would disappear. Clinton emphasized the point that she did not add "a penny" to the national debt because she proposes tax increases on the wealthy that would pay for her spending proposals. Although Trump claims that his "plan" would solve the debt by growing the economy at the highest rates since the end of World War II, virtually no one thinks a growth rate of this magnitude is possible. The result is that the debt would grow at a much higher rate than under current law because of the huge tax cuts contemplated by Trump. The Committee for a Responsible Federal

Budget estimates that under the Trump proposals, the debt would grow to 105 percent of GDP in 2026.[6] The committee agrees that Clinton would pay for her proposals by increasing taxes on the rich, but the debt would still rise in a fashion more or less identical to the current CBO projections because her plan did not use any of the money to reduce the annual deficit. In other words, Trump would make the debt problem worse and Clinton proposed nothing to address the debt problem.

If the debt problem is as threatening as claimed by CBO, the Committee for a Responsible Federal Budget, the National Academies of Science,[7] the National Academy of Public Administration, and many other organizations and analysts, why didn't the candidates discuss the issue and tell the American people how they would address the problem? Although there are many reasons for this failure, two seem especially important. Taken together, they lead to a most unfortunate conclusion.

First, Republicans and Democrats, whether in Congress or running for president, must go against the most basic political positions of their respective parties to balance the federal budget and reduce the national debt. Nothing of this magnitude can be accomplished in Washington without a grand compromise that involves both increased taxes and reduced spending as compared with projections. Arguably the single most important commitment of the Democratic Party is to protect federal social programs for the poor and insurance programs for the elderly, the latter of which are the main cause of the debt problem. Similarly, taxes will have to be increased as part of any debt control plan. Most Republicans have signed a pledge not to increase taxes under any circumstances, and many if not most congressional Republicans believe their next election would be jeopardized if they supported tax increases. It follows from these fundamental positions of the nation's two political parties that the prospects for compromise in the near future on a debt reduction package that involves spending cuts and tax increases is near zero—especially without leadership from the nation's president.

The second reason the candidates did not address the debt problem is that the debt does not loom as a clear and present danger to the nation. Not only are severe consequences unlikely to occur in the next few years, no one can predict when they will occur. Politicians are reluctant to tackle any problem of the magnitude of the national debt, let alone a problem that is unlikely to manifest its most serious consequences in the near future. Why should presidential candidates be any different?

After nearly a decade of failure by the nation's elected officials to come to terms with the debt, and at least three presidential elections in which candidates failed to produce serious proposals for reforming entitlements and increasing taxes to attack the nation's debt, it seems inevitable that nothing will be done until a debt-related crisis hits the nation. Let's give CBO the last word:

Large and growing federal debt over the coming decades would hurt the economy and constrain future budget policy. The amount of debt that is projected in the extended baseline would reduce national saving and income in the long term; increase the government's interest costs, putting more pressure on the rest of the budget; limit lawmakers' ability to respond to unforeseen events; and increase the likelihood of a fiscal crisis, an occurrence in which investors become unwilling to finance a government's borrowing needs unless they are compensated with very high interest rates.[8]

Notes

1. Congressional Budget Office, "An Update to the Budget and Economic Outlook: 2016 to 2026" (Washington, D.C.: CBO, August 2016).

2. Carmen M. Reinhart and Kenneth S. Rogoff, *This Time Is Different: Eight Centuries of Financial Folly* (Princeton University Press, 2011).

3. Thomas Herndon, Michael Ash, and Robert Pollin, "Does High Public Debt Consistently Stifle Economic Growth? A Critique of Reinhart and Rogoff" (Amherst, Mass.: University of Massachusetts, Political Economy Research Institute, April 2013).

4. Congressional Budget Office, "The 2016 Long-Term Budget Outlook" (Washington, D.C.: July 2016).

5. Sara Edelstein and others, "Kids' Share 2016: Federal Expenditures on Children through 2015 and Future Projections" (Washington, D.C.: Urban Institute, 2016).

6. Committee for a Responsible Federal Budget, "Promises and Price Tags: A Preliminary Update" (Washington, D.C.: Committee for a Responsible Federal Budget, September 22, 2016).

7. Committee on the Fiscal Future of the United States, National Research Council and National Academy of Public Administration, *Choosing the Nation's Fiscal Future* (Washington, D.C.: National Academies Press, 2010).

8. Congressional Budget Office, "The 2016 Long-Term Budget Outlook."

8

Infrastructure Issues and Options for the Trump Administration

WILLIAM A. GALSTON and ROBERT J. PUENTES

SUMMARY: Our nation's infrastructure facilities are aging, over-crowded, undermaintained, and in desperate need of modernization. The World Economic Forum ranks the United States 12th in the world for overall quality of infrastructure and assigns particularly low marks for the quality of our roads, ports, railroads, air transport infrastructure, and electricity supply. It is abundantly clear that to be economically competitive in today's world, adequate investment in infrastructure is critical. And yet, U.S. spending on infrastructure has declined over the past five decades.

Complacency is not an option for the next administration, should the president-elect hope to avoid a term marred by collapsed bridges, increasing traffic congestion, and overworked power grids. Rather, it is essential that the Trump administration develop coherent and targeted strategies for utilizing the federal government to address our basic infrastructure needs and shore up existing programs, especially in support of improving surface transportation, enhancing existing public financing mechanisms, and leveraging private capital to fund infrastructure projects that can yield an acceptable rate of return for investors.

By closing the infrastructure investment gap, the president will not only improve our nation's most critical assets but also help deliver on his promise of boosting job creation and enhancing economic growth. Doing so would also have the important benefit of connecting households across metropolitan areas to higher quality opportunities for employment, health care, and education and, finally, reducing greenhouse gas emissions and helping to protect the nation from an increasingly unpredictable natural environment.

INTRODUCTION: WHY INFRASTRUCTURE MATTERS

Since the beginning of our Republic, infrastructure—starting with transportation and water management—has played a central role in advancing the American economy. From the railroads that linked the heartland to industrial centers to the interstate highway system that forged regional connections, a sharp focus on prioritized, strategic, and rational infrastructure investments underscored periods of regional growth and national prosperity. But what the United States once understood, we seem to have forgotten. During the past three decades the United States has significantly underinvested in infrastructure. This shortfall has made it difficult to maintain existing infrastructure assets and impossible to create a globally competitive system. Our failure to meet long-term infrastructure requirements has impaired economic efficiency, impeded the creation of stable middle-class jobs, and slowed our response to the threat of climate change. It also is imposing direct costs on individuals and businesses. Several studies have documented sharply higher costs for vehicle maintenance and have attributed much of that increase to poor road conditions.[1]

Our nation's infrastructure is in desperate need of upgrades and modernization. From highly publicized bridge collapses and levee breaches to airport delays and traffic congestion, every American has experienced the frustration—and in some cases the dangers—of aging, overcrowded, undermaintained facilities.

Closing the infrastructure investment gap would have at least four beneficial consequences. First, it would boost the creation of jobs that often provide middle-class wages and opportunities to workers with modest levels of formal education. Second, it would enhance economic growth by decreasing overhead costs to businesses while efficiently moving people, goods, and ideas.[2] Third, it would better connect households across metropolitan areas to higher quality opportunities for employment, health care, and education.[3] Fourth, it could reduce greenhouse gas emissions while helping to protect the nation from an increasingly unpredictable natural environment.[4] For these reasons, among others, the president-elect would be well advised to address infrastructure issues.

THE PROBLEM

"In a growing economy," a Congressional Research Service paper notes, "infrastructure should hold its own, but other data show that that has not been the case. While total government spending on infrastructure adjusted for inflation increased from $92 billion in 1960 to $161 billion in 2007, it actually declined from $1.17 per capita in 1960 to $0.85 per capita in 2007."[5] According to one expert, "From 1950 to 1970 we devoted 3 percent of GDP to spending on infrastructure. . . . Since 1980 we have been spending well less than 2 percent, resulting in a huge accumulated shortfall of needed investment."[6] Just since 2002, the Congressional Budget Office (CBO) estimates, inflation-adjusted spending for highways at all levels of the federal system has fallen by 19 percent.[7]

The problem runs from top to bottom. Political wrangling and dysfunction mean that the federal government has ceased to be a reliable partner and an effective leader. Furthermore, the rise in federal interest payments, the increase in entitlement spending, and the decline in traditional sources of government revenue, such as the gasoline tax, mean that competition for limited resources is fierce.

By contrast, some cities and states now see budget surpluses due in part to increases in property tax revenues and state-level sales tax collections. However, it will take years for most localities to build back their reserves, repay debt incurred during the Great Recession of 2007–09, and pay for deferred maintenance on a range of infrastructure assets. Cities and states typically rely on the bond market to finance long-term projects, yet even though interest rates remain at historically low levels, the ability of many governments to borrow from the capital markets is hindered by debt caps and weak credit ratings. Plus, because virtually all state and local governments have balanced budget requirements, they must establish their ability to repay before borrowing. In addition to managing the lingering effects of the Great Recession, many states and localities must confront a limited fiscal capacity, as they are squeezed between soaring costs for health care and for criminal justice but slowly growing revenue sources.[8] Combined, these circumstances constrain their ability to self-finance projects, leading officials to scale back, delay, or cancel projects altogether.

This shortfall renders the United States less competitive in the global market. The World Economic Forum's 2014–15 Global Competitiveness Report ranks the overall quality of U.S. infrastructure 12th in the world, down from seventh place just eight years ago. We rank poorly in every category, with especially low marks for the quality of our roads, ports, railroads, and—most precipitously—air transport infrastructure and electricity supply.[9] As the Urban Land Institute succinctly put it: "To be competitive in today's world, it is imperative to invest in infrastructure."[10]

Possible Responses: Fix the Basics

First, the Trump administration needs to use the federal government to fix the basics and shore up existing programs, especially for surface transportation (roads, bridges, and transit).

The Highway Trust Fund   Funded primarily through the federal gas tax, the Highway Trust Fund distributes grants to the states to support the interstate system and other highway projects.[11] These grants, however, are not subject to scrutiny, competition, or even basic calculations to assess need. Instead, they are allocated based on formulas, yielding not only inefficiencies but also perverse incentives.[12] The U.S. Government Accountability Office found that the federal transportation program is functioning to some extent as a "cash transfer, general purpose grant program."[13] The federal government must lead in those areas where there are clear demands for national uniformity to match the scale or geographic reach of certain problems, such as global logistics and freight movement.[14]

The gas tax, which currently stands at 18.4 cents per gallon, has not been increased since 1993—despite the fact that project costs have gone up significantly.[15] As cars and trucks become more efficient and infrastructure ages, revenues cannot keep up with demand. But congressional resistance to a federal gas tax increase to support the current program is intense.[16] The result: an endless series of short-term funding patches that make planning and completing long-term projects much harder than it should be. If raising federal gas taxes is politically infeasible, lawmakers and candidates should propose viable alternatives.

Passenger Facility Charges   The federal government should allow greater flexibility for states and cities to innovate on projects that connect metropolitan areas. For example, passenger facility charges, which are used to fund airport modernization, are artificially capped at $4.50 and do not come close to covering many airports' operating and long-term investment costs. The busiest passenger airports need to be empowered to meet their larger-than-average congestion and investment costs without federal impositions or caps.[17]

Tolling and Pricing Mechanisms   The archaic restrictions on interstate tolls should also be lifted. Acting in conjunction with the states, metropolitan and local leaders are in the best position to determine which interstate roadway segments are the strongest candidates for tolling strategies.[18]

Innovation and Financing

Second, the Trump administration needs to quickly clarify how it would use the federal government to enhance existing innovative financing mechanisms.

Tax-Credit Bonds   Tax-credit bonds such as Build America Bonds (BABs) are a cost-effective means of subsidizing borrowing because every dollar of federal revenue forgone by the tax credit is transferred directly to the borrower (states or localities) rather than the investors (purchasers of the bonds). They also offer a more generous subsidy of interest costs and have the added benefit of broadening the pool of investors to include those that do not normally hold tax-exempt debt, such as pension funds (which are already exempt from taxes) and sovereign wealth funds (which also have no U.S. tax liability). By attracting new investors, BABs have eased the supply pressure in the municipal bond market and brought down borrowing costs. Tax-credit bonds could also be used to support a wide array of infrastructure investments, among them transportation, water and sewer projects, environmental and energy projects, public utilities, and the renovation of schools and hospitals.[19]

Transportation Infrastructure Finance and Innovation Act (TIFIA)   TIFIA bonds leverage federal funds with local and private investment by providing credit assistance through direct loans, loan guarantees, or lines of credit. While TIFIA assistance must be repaid through a dedicated revenue source (such as tolls, user fees, and other special assessments such as sales taxes), the terms are very favorable. Unfortunately, arguably the greatest strength of TIFIA—the competitive nature of the process and strong selection criteria—was eliminated in the 2012 transportation bill—a retrograde action that should be reversed.[20]

Other Financing Mechanisms   There are a handful of other federal programs that have expanded funding for transportation infrastructure and encouraged private sector participation in major projects. These programs include the Transportation Investment Generating Economic Recovery (TIGER) grants, Railroad Rehabilitation and Improvement Financing (RRIF) loans, and Private Activity Bonds (PABs). One benefit of these programs is that they can be combined with TIFIA loans as well as local and private investments to further leverage federal dollars. Additionally, each program takes an innovative approach to funding and does not rely on the classic formula-based grant distribution that defines the majority of federal investments in this area.[21]

Although these programs are helpful, they are not sufficient to meet the 21st-century infrastructure demands of the United States. The public funds available for appropriation fall far short of the needs, and as long as the ongoing squeeze in federal discretionary programs continues, significant increases will remain unlikely at best. In addition, all of the innovative funding strategies reviewed in this section (save for BABs, which have expired) deal primarily with surface transportation and are unable to address other areas that require investment—to our aviation system, electric grid, and so forth.

Technical Assistance for States and Localities   State and local governments often lack the technical capacity to ensure project quality and to protect the public interest. For that reason, the Trump administration should create a national-level public/private partnership unit. Housed within the Office of Management and Budget, the largest component of the Executive Office of the President, the unit would provide states, cities, and metropolitan entities with support and technical assistance, create an environment that encourages private infrastructure investment, and begin the process of forging an integrated national infrastructure agenda.[22] The new office should be modeled after the existing Build America Bureau at the U.S. Department of Transportation but expanded to include all sectors of infrastructure.

Selecting Projects

Third, the Trump administration needs to make good on its pledge for a new mechanism to select a set of projects that make economic sense and finance them with mostly private capital.

Numerous legislators and policy experts have suggested that the creation of a National Infrastructure Bank (NIB) would attract private investment for public purposes while ensuring that projects are funded on the basis of economic and social benefit, not political gain. Despite differences of detail, many proposals employ the same basic elements. The

NIB would be a financially self-sustaining government-owned corporation established to provide a market-oriented service. A modest amount of public seed capital would secure substantial private capital. An analytical staff would provide policy entrepreneurship identifying unique opportunities to leverage private capital for public needs. Once such possibilities are identified, bank executives could convene the necessary parties and work to broker agreements among them. This approach would encourage creativity in solving infrastructure needs. And by insulating the selection of projects from the political process, it would better align infrastructure investments with real social and economic needs.[23]

Donald Trump's victory on November 8 energized what was already an active bipartisan discussion about the best ways of boosting overall infrastructure investment. There is broad agreement that this objective must include private as well as public capital—and that it would be more likely to occur in the context of significant tax reform than as a free-standing policy.

As the failed efforts of recent years have shown, moving from consensus on the need for tax reform to agreement on a specific plan is no easy matter. Nonetheless, momentum seems to be building. Whether President-elect Trump's campaign proposal—an 82 percent tax credit for private sector equity investment in infrastructure—will pass muster as a cost-effective strategy remains to be seen.

In any event, we judge it unlikely that this measure by itself would suffice to meet Mr. Trump's overall objective of increasing infrastructure investment during the next decade by $1 trillion over current projections. This is why his administration should consider additional options, including the ones we have laid out.

CONCLUSION: STRUCTURAL DIFFICULTIES AND STRATEGIC DIRECTIONS

American infrastructure received considerable attention during the presidential campaign as the foundation of a healthy economy and society. And it is an issue that leaders at every level of our federal system, including the president-elect, recognize they have no choice but to address, hopefully sooner rather than later. The need is great and growing. If the expert estimates are correct, between now and 2020, we should be investing roughly $150 billion annually in transportation and port projects, water and sewage systems, the energy grid, and much else besides.[24]

President-elect Trump promised to spur $1 trillion in infrastructure investments over the next decade. Yet in the current political and fiscal environment, this will not be easy. There are four structural obstacles. First, citizens are being asked to pay now for investments that will yield a return over a lengthy period. But when household budgets are squeezed, patience to wait for future returns on spending is limited. Second, different regions have different needs: some rural and small-town voters often must drive long distances to work and shop and are highly resistant to gas tax increases. Third, it is hard to explain why tax dollars should travel to Washington, only to be returned to the states and localities. Why not just cut out the middleman? And finally, a basic difference between the federal government and other jurisdictions—Washington's ability to borrow readily for public purposes—is diluted in times when the people disapprove of budget deficits, whatever the purpose.

Two realities will continue to play out that directly impact the federal response in infrastructure. One is that on Election Day we clearly saw that voters in states and localities across the country are more than willing to tax themselves for projects if they can expect to reap the benefits directly, rather than shoring up broad national objectives. Nearly $300 billion in infrastructure ballot box measures went before voters, of which about three quarters were approved.[25] This reinforces the fact that governments closer to the people enjoy higher levels of trust than the federal government.

Second, it is clearly time for a new partnership between the public and private sectors. Individual investors and large investment pools are flush with cash seeking a reasonable return at a bearable level of risk. Mobilizing private dollars for public purposes should be an easier sell than is commandeering those dollars through our system of taxation.[26] At the same time, it is more important than ever to make sure these partnerships are delivering projects that meet clear public policy goals and benefit all segments of society, not just the private financiers.

The devil, as always, is in the details. But the bottom line is this: an efficient modern economy cannot be sustained without public goods that the market, left to its own devices, will undersupply. As always, governments face the challenge of mobilizing public support for these goods. The art of legislation is finding the path of least resistance to reach these essential public goals. And legislators will be more motivated to seek that path when they enjoy sustained leadership and support from the executive branch. Working with governors, mayors, and the private sector, the Trump administration must break the logjam and create a new model of infrastructure finance for the 21st century.

Notes

1. TRIP, *Bumpy Roads Ahead: America's Roughest Rides and Strategies to Make Our Roads Smoother*, July 2015 (www.tripnet.org/docs/Urban_Roads_TRIP_Report_July_2015.pdf).

2. Michael Greenstone and Adam Looney, *Investing in the Future: An Economic Strategy for State and Local Governments in a Period of Tight Budgets*, strategy paper (Hamilton Project, Brookings, February 2011).

3. Adie Tomer and others, *Missed Opportunity: Transit and Jobs in Metropolitan America* (Brookings, May 2011).

4. Robert Puentes, "Why Infrastructure Matters: Rotten Roads, Bum Economy," *Washington Examiner*, January 19, 2015 (www.washingtonexaminer.com/infrastructure-rotten-roads-bum-economy/article/2558743).

5. Claudia Copeland, Linda Levine, and William J. Mallett, *The Role of Public Works Infrastructure in Economic Recovery* (CRS Report No. R42018) (Congressional Research Service, 2011), 3.

6. Sherle R. Schwenninger, "A Capital Budget for Public Investment" (Washington: New America Foundation, 2007), 61.

7. *Public Spending on Transportation and Water Infrastructure, 1956 to 2014* (CBO 49910) (Congressional Budget Office, March 2015), 2.

8. Copeland, Levine, and Mallett, *The Role of Public Works Infrastructure*, 1–2.

9. Klaus Schwab and Xavier Sala-i-Martín, *The Global Competitiveness Report 2014-2015* (New York: World Economic Forum, 2014), 378–79.

10. Jonathan D. Miller, *Infrastructure 2009: Pivot Point* (Washington: Urban Land Institute and Ernst & Young, 2009), iv.

11. While most of the federal gas tax accumulates in the Highway Account of the trust fund, the remainder is distributed to the Mass Transit Account and supports public transit systems.

12. Robert Puentes, "The Problem with the Gas Tax in Three Charts," *The Avenue* (blog), Brookings, June 18, 2015 (www.brookings.edu/blog/the-avenue/2015/06/18/the-problem-with-the-gas-tax-in-three-charts/).

13. *Federal-Aid Highways* (GAO-04-802) (U.S. Government Accountability Office, August 2004), 5.

14. Joseph Kane, Adie Tomer, and Robert Puentes, "Metro Freight Series: Global Goods Trade and Metropolitan Economies," Brookings, June 16, 2015 (www.brookings.edu/research/metro-freight-series-global-goods-trade-and-metropolitan-economies-2/).

15. Puentes, "The Problem with the Gas Tax."

16. A recent poll found that a majority of voters would support a gasoline tax increase if it were targeted to roadway maintenance; see Keith Laing, "Poll: Voters

Would Support 10-cent Gas Tax Hike," *The Hill*, April 29, 2015 (http://thehill.com/policy/transportation/240527-poll-voters-would-support-10-cent-gas-tax-hike).

17. Robert Puentes, "A Federalist Agenda for Transportation," *The Avenue* (blog), Brookings, May 13, 2015 (www.brookings.edu/blog/the-avenue/2015/05/13/a-federalist-agenda-for-transportation/).

18. Ibid.

19. Robert Puentes and Patrick Sabol, "Building Better Infrastructure with Better Bonds," Brookings, April 22, 2015 (www.brookings.edu/research/building-better-infrastructure-with-better-bonds/).

20. William A. Galston and Korin Davis, *Setting Priorities, Meeting Needs: The Case for a National Infrastructure Bank* (Brookings, December 13, 2013), 7–8.

21. Ibid., 8–10.

22. Robert Puentes, "Strengthen Federalism: Establish a National PPP Unit to Support Bottom-Up Infrastructure Investment," Brookings, November 13, 2012 (www.brookings.edu/research/strengthen-federalism-establish-a-national-ppp-unit-to-support-bottom-up-infrastructure-investment/).

23. Galston and Davis, *Setting Priorities, Meeting Needs*, 18–19.

24. Susan Lund and others, *Game Changers: Five Opportunities for US Growth and Renewal*, McKinsey Global Institute, July 2013 (www.mckinsey.com/global-themes/americas/us-game-changers).

25. "Ballot Measures by State," Eno Center for Transportation (www.enotrans.org/publications-resources/ballot-measures-state/).

26. Patrick Sabol and Robert Puentes, *Private Capital, Public Good: Drivers of Successful Infrastructure Public-Private Partnerships* (Brookings, December 2014).

9

Short- and Long-Term Strategies to Renew American Infrastructure

ADIE TOMER and JOSEPH KANE

SUMMARY: Donald Trump has prioritized infrastructure investment as a way to accelerate economic growth, looking to modernize aging roads, rails, ports, and other facilities. The president-elect and the new Congress, though, will face daunting challenges around governance and finance. For example, federal leaders must separate what can be accomplished in short order—such as reinstating the Build America Bonds program, expanding competitive grant programs, and advancing other measures that have already gained traction in recent years—from what will require a more sustained conversation with political allies and adversaries. Before focusing on how much to invest, federal leaders must first recognize where to invest for the best results. This policy brief lays out a blueprint for a modern federal infrastructure strategy. It begins to detail a broad array of short-term strategies and long-term policy reforms necessary to build and maintain a strong system of infrastructure that supports sustained and broad-based economic growth.

Calls for increased infrastructure investment have been echoed for years now, and the 2016 election season was no different. As the U.S. economy continues to make strides following the Great Recession, infrastructure remains one of the more attractive areas to improve productivity and create jobs. Of course, finding reliable ways to pay for such improvements and investing more wisely remain central to delivering on those economy-enhancing objectives.[1]

Fortunately, now is a great time to boost public investment. With historically low interest rates and the potential for infrastructure projects to deliver long-run economic returns, economic writers such as Paul Krugman, Lawrence Summers, and Tyler Cowen all believe infrastructure investment could address the country's sluggish aggregate growth rates. Nevertheless, simply building more will not guarantee economic growth on its own, as infrastructure booms in Japan, China, and other countries reveal. This lesson is particularly important considering the falling returns from public investment in U.S. highways.[2]

There is demonstrated need across the country to justify higher investment rates. Many roads, bridges, and other systems are reaching the end of their useful lives. As the U.S. population grows, as climate pressures intensify, and as concerns rise over health and safety, pipes, sea walls, and treatment facilities are buckling under pressure. Yet total public spending on infrastructure—at $416 billion annually—is on the decline according to most measures.[3] As a share of gross domestic product (GDP), infrastructure spending now stands at around 2.5 percent—down from a high of 3 percent in 1959—and federal purchases have fallen by nearly 19 percent in real terms since 2003. Meanwhile, states and localities have picked up the slack, but they, too, can struggle to keep up with mounting maintenance and capital expenses.

While the need is clear, the politics still are not. Infrastructure claimed a central position on Donald Trump's campaign platform, proposing federal tax credits to incentivize up to $1 trillion over the next decade in private investment. Of course, this platform only represents a start; the real work will begin once the new president is in office and congressional leaders are in place—and congressional interest in infrastructure is unclear. At that point, reforming the federal infrastructure program will require recognizing the major challenges facing this critical policy area.

First, the country's greatest infrastructure needs are in metro areas, yet federal infrastructure investment too often runs through states. America's 100 largest metropolitan areas are the hubs of the U.S. economy. They house two-thirds of the country's population, generate three-quarters of its GDP, and do so on only about one-tenth of the country's land mass. The spatial design and industrial composition of each metro area vary considerably. The variety requires different solutions to maximize each place's economic potential. From Portland to Milwaukee to Miami, local leaders know this quite well as they customize new plans, develop new metrics, and spearhead new investments, including the use of ballot measures and public-private partnerships. Federal infrastructure policy must support a new federalism that recognizes metropolitan economies and supports metropolitan innovation.

Second, the federal government's approach to infrastructure planning and investment remains highly fragmented and has few formal requirements to test for economic returns, leading to inconsistent performance measures and a failure to account for costs and benefits efficiently.[4] For example, the U.S. Department of Transportation (DOT) does not always coordinate with the U.S. Department of Commerce when setting economic priorities for freight movement.[5] Multiple divisions within DOT operate in silos and use scarce budget resources ineffectively.[6] This haphazard organizational structure presents challenges to identifying reliable, stable sources of funding, particularly as the federal gas tax generates less revenue for future projects.

In the face of these challenges, the past eight years have proved that Washington can still advance infrastructure ideas, but many efforts have failed to move the dial enough. The period began with the American Recovery and Reinvestment Act of 2009 (ARRA), an enormous public works program that at times had questionable project selection criteria. In December 2015, Congress approved the first long-term transportation bill in nearly a decade, dubbed Fixing America's Surface Transportation (FAST) Act, which provides more certainty for local spending but also falls short in advancing multimodal planning efforts and developing durable sources of funding. Other federal efforts—including DOT's Ladders of Opportunity initiative, the Environmental Protection Agency's Clean Water rule, and the Federal Communications Commission's expanded Lifeline program—have helped improve economic opportunity, environmental sustainability, and digital connectivity, but more work remains.

POLICY RECOMMENDATIONS

The next administration and Congress should adopt a two-pronged infrastructure strategy to (1) advance immediate proposals that build on existing reform efforts and (2) begin to develop new platforms for long-term policy change. Federal leaders are at a crucial inflection point to advance reforms across a variety of infrastructure sectors and geographic scales, where they should continue to draw inspiration from regional innovations and best practices.

This chapter touches on four major infrastructure priorities in this respect: transportation, water, broadband, and infrastructure workforce development. Although they do not cover all infrastructure sectors, these four priority areas demonstrate the need for additional federal investment, financial flexibility, and programmatic direction. Again, rather than focusing on how much infrastructure investment should occur—in total or within each sector—this chapter aims to inform a more extensive conversation on funding and financing once the new administration and Congress take office.

Transportation

In the short term, federal legislators and the DOT should design competitive and financially innovative programs, and then Congress should appropriate enough funding to execute them.

- Congress should increase appropriations for the Transportation Investment Generating Economic Recovery (TIGER) grant program, which pumped billions of dollars into a range of multimodal projects nationally, but additional funding should require reformed accountability measures.

- Reinstating the Build America Bonds program and exempting private activity bonds from the alternative minimum tax could leverage low interest rates and tax advantages to promote investment in economically critical infrastructure projects.[7]

- Congress must recognize that the aviation network's hub-and-spoke system is here to stay. Whether within broader legislation or a stand-alone vehicle, policymakers should raise the current cap on passenger facility charges and adjust formulas under the Airport Improvement Program to facilitate movement of passengers within the U.S. aviation network.[8]

- Finally, intense interest for the Smart Cities Challenge should motivate Congress to consider developing a funding pool for similar future-looking competitive programs.

Likewise, executive branch agencies should continue to use the rule-making process where possible to modernize regulations under current authorizing legislation. Performance measures are a vital area in this regard, as evidenced by ongoing debates around whether congestion and greenhouse gas emissions are appropriate measures of highway performance or whether consolidating the country's dizzying number of metropolitan planning organizations would lead to a more efficient planning process. The next four years are also ripe with potential for automated vehicle (AV) guidance, creating an opportunity for DOT to better understand the kinds of flexible safety and urban planning standards that can allow the market to grow while preparing policy responses for potential market failures.

In the long term, the federal government must determine its 21st century priorities and develop dedicated revenue sources to pay for multimodal transportation needs.

Coming surface transportation and aviation reauthorizations are enormous opportunities to execute such reforms. Without greater financial certainty, the Highway Trust Fund—the primary vehicle for federal and state transportation investment—will continue to teeter on the edge of insolvency, and many regions will delay needed projects. Ongoing experimentation with new user fees, expanded loan programs, and federal formula adjustments—including a "fix it first approach," prioritized freight investments, and a reformed TIFIA program—should be part of the next multiyear surface transportation bill.

Yet hanging over the surface transportation program is a debate over priorities; the highway expansion era is over, but what is next? Since the FAST Act expires in four years, that debate should start now. In the case of the national aviation network, the public and private sectors are already settled on implementing a satellite and digital navigation system. At this point, Congress should determine whether a NextGen approach can work—and therefore fund it in full—or start planning for a superior alternative.[9]

The development of new metrics and investment standards should also be a hallmark of future federal efforts. The country needs to define a new approach to transportation, ideally centered on improving accessibility as opposed to reducing roadway congestion. Policymakers and practitioners must collaborate more extensively on connecting users to greater economic opportunity and a range of different services,[10] which will require new data, planning tools, and models of investment. These efforts must also better define the role of new technologies and services, including transportation network companies (TNCs), in supporting a more accessible built environment. The same goes for environmental quality. The federal government should continue to implement more stringent Corporate Average Fuel Economy (CAFE) standards and complement that effort with support for more widespread electric vehicle infrastructure.

Water

In the short term, federal leaders should investigate additional funding options for regional water infrastructure. Although the country's water needs are often highly fragmented and localized—and most federal agencies, including the EPA, tend to focus more on regulatory oversight—the growing number of local needs justifies a clearer, more active federal role. The scale of needed infrastructure investment—up to $1 trillion over the next two decades—combined with declining federal support is putting enormous pressure on states and localities to cover operational and capital improvements to drinking water, wastewater, and storm water systems, where the moment is ripe for federal action.

- Currently, the federal government primarily supports water investment by capitalizing state revolving funds (SRFs). The next administration and Congress should consider providing SRFs with an infusion of new support, while continuing to encourage the development of innovative infrastructure projects already eligible for SRF funding.

- Federal leaders should also explore new dedicated funding sources for local water projects, such as a Clean Water Trust Fund, including potential staffing, financial, and administrative needs to get it started.

Beyond increased federal funding, states and localities could also benefit in the immediate term from more certainty on a range of financing options. The new Water Resources Development Act (WRDA) in Congress shows some promise in this respect, but additional legislative vehicles and program changes could help build greater momentum.

- For example, providing long-term funding for the newly created Water Infrastructure Finance and Innovation Act (WIFIA) program could help localities gain easier credit assistance beyond the initial pilot phase, which began in 2014. However, federal leaders should closely monitor how WIFIA interacts with existing SRF funding, ensuring that localities are still able to support a variety of smaller projects.

- The next administration and Congress should maintain the tax-exempt status of municipal bonds for water projects and encourage the wider use of private activity bonds by eliminating state volume caps for water projects.

- Federal policymakers should also consider new resilience bonds and a "Disaster Deductible Program" to improve disaster relief and climate adaptation.[11]

In the long term, federal agencies, particularly the EPA, should provide greater programmatic direction and clearer technical guidance and maintain closer working relations with regions about regulatory compliance and other available financing tools for water infrastructure.

- Building on efforts of the EPA's Water Infrastructure and Resiliency Finance Center, for instance, the federal government should increase transparency regarding different financial tools available to individual communities, including expanding initiatives such as the WaterCARE program.

- The next administration should establish a more robust, cross-agency "Urban Water Center" to serve as a centralized destination for city-level water innovations and best practices to tackle these challenges. The current "Urban Waters Federal Partnership," for instance, has helped coordinate action among several federal agencies and a variety of regional stakeholders, an effort that should be further elevated with increased financial support and staffing resources.

Improving data collection efforts and implementing more comprehensive affordability standards should be a priority for federal leaders as well.

- To more accurately quantify water needs across different regions, the EPA and the U.S. Geological Survey should partner with state and local experts to create more granular data sets, particularly to inform investment gaps measures and to identify areas of regulatory concern, such as groundwater management.

• In addition, the EPA should work with individual states and regions to develop more consistent, comprehensive standards on water affordability—looking beyond the current 2.5 percent median household income standard, which tends to focus only on a narrow subset of all water users in a given market.[12] By doing so, regions can better weigh the effects of potential rate increases on lower-income households and improve customer assistance programs.

Broadband

In the short term, the next administration and the Federal Communications Commission (FCC) must work collaboratively to continue expanding programs related to broadband adoption and digital skills training to address the digital divide.

The Obama administration and the FCC deserve enormous credit for advancing significant programs related to both goals, including launching the ConnectHome Initiative for people living in rental-assisted housing; expansion of the Lifeline Program to reduce costs of broadband subscriptions for low-income households; and expanding the E-Rate Program and launching the ConnectEd Initiative to ensure schools and libraries can help students and individuals acquire the skills to succeed in the modern workforce. All of these programs are either new or significantly reformed, and their effects are only beginning to be felt. Moving forward, the next administration should continue to implement and rigorously measure the performance of these programs as it works with Congress around new strategies.

In the long term, the next administration must focus on how to use new digital telecommunications to unlock economic opportunity and accelerate e-government transitions.

Using sensors and digital telecommunications, the Internet of Things (IoT) promises to create efficiencies in nearly every aspect of daily life, from how the country manufactures goods to how those goods move between markets and how buildings consume energy. Designing federal support for civic IoT could help American communities achieve greater efficiency in their infrastructure operations and generate new data sources to understand how places function in real time. The launch of 5G networks—the next iteration in major wireless telecommunications technology expected to roll out during the next administration—is likely to undergird the civic

IoT, support new technologies such as driverless vehicles, and offer enormous potential to get more people online. The federal government's positions on 5G networks should be part of a modern "pipe policy" that, in collaboration with state and local governments, smartly manages spectrum, streamlines construction, and incentivizes sensible competition among Internet service providers.[13]

Infrastructure Workforce Development

In the short term, the next administration should build on efforts at DOT, the Department of Labor, and the Department of Education, among other agencies, to expand workforce development throughout the infrastructure sector.

More than 14.5 million infrastructure workers are employed across the country,[14] crucial to operating, constructing, designing, and governing all types of facilities, but nearly 3 million of these workers will retire in the next decade. Increasing the visibility of this infrastructure jobs gap and the enormous wage potential in these positions would help grab attention from local employers, workers, and job seekers. Federal agencies should highlight the specific training needs in this sector and support regional innovations already under way, including promoting additional grants within DOT's Ladders of Opportunity initiative and other environmental workforce grants.

Continued federal coordination and information sharing can easily and effectively drive more robust workforce development efforts. For example, federal agencies should look to convene public and private stakeholders in individual regions—from transit agencies and water utilities to ports and shipping companies—to explore new apprenticeships, technical education, and recruitment opportunities. The Department of Transportation, for instance, has led the creation of a National Network for the Transportation Workforce (NNTW), which partners with local educational institutions to drive engagement on these pressing workforce issues.

In the long term, a wide range of federal actors must develop more durable and sustainable pipelines of talent to fill infrastructure jobs over many decades.

More uniform training guidelines would help educators, employers, and workers alike better understand the evolving skill sets needed to fill these infrastructure positions. A consolidated federal approach—via the U.S. Department of Education, for instance—could help guide future action in this respect. Identifying existing education and training programs that have worked well in different regions could help further inform these efforts. Finally, reaching a wider group of prospective workers, particularly those in lower-income communities, would promote diversity and unlock greater economic opportunity.

CONCLUSION

While infrastructure is likely to generate interest and spur action as part of President-elect Trump's 100-day agenda, it is difficult to imagine sweeping legislation passed within such a short period—nor is there a major need to do so. The political and economic dynamics are quite different than during President Barack Obama's first days in office, when large-scale infrastructure investment aimed to provide an immediate jolt to the U.S. economy. Today, the country is experiencing more robust growth and construction unemployment sits near 5 percent. As such, Congress and the next administration should focus on the first 365 days in office to better define the country's most pressing infrastructure challenges and craft a truly comprehensive strategy, recognizing that the benefits should last for decades. Quickly passing an infrastructure bill based solely on federal tax credits would not do this and adds the greater danger of deep public financial losses while failing to invest around the public good.

Instead, a comprehensive approach should balance greater public investment with policy reforms. Economic, social, and environmental challenges vary considerably from place to place, meaning the country can no longer afford to deploy federal spending programs that aim for geographic equity. The approach laid out here attempts to address these core demands, using federal investments and regulations to empower metropolitan areas and states to invest in improved transportation access, cleaner water, modern data networks, and more well-paying jobs. These short- and long-term proposals will ensure the country does not miss the opportunity to build the assets that will deliver a stronger economy for future generations.

Notes

1. Aaron Klein, "Time to Fix Our Crumbling Infrastructure," Brookings, October 6, 2016, www.brookings.edu/research/time-to-fix-our-crumbling-infrastructure/.

2. Chad Shirley and Clifford Winston, "Firm Inventory Behavior and the Returns from Highway Infrastructure Investments," *Journal of Urban Economics* 55 (2004), 398–415.

3. *Public Spending on Transportation and Water Infrastructure, 1956 to 2014,* (49910 CBO) (Congressional Budget Office, March 2015).

4. *U.S. Infrastructure: Funding Trends and Opportunities to Improve Investment Decisions* (GAO/RCED/AIMD-00-35) (U.S. Government Accountability Office, February 2000).

5. Adie Tomer and Joseph Kane, "It's Time for a National Freight Investment Program," *The Avenue* (blog), Brookings, February 25, 2015 (www.brookings.edu/blog/the-avenue/2015/02/25/its-time-for-a-national-freight-investment-program/).

6. National Transportation Policy Project, *Performance Driven: Achieving Wiser Investment in Transportation* (Washington: Bipartisan Policy Center, June 2011).

7. Robert Puentes, Patrick Sabol, and Joseph Kane, "Cut to Invest: Revive Build America Bonds (BABs) to Support State and Local Investments," Brookings, August 28, 2013, www.brookings.edu/research/cut-to-invest-revive-build-america-bonds-babs-to-support-state-and-local-investments/.

8. Adie Tomer, Robert Puentes, and Zachary Neal, "Global Gateways: International Aviation in Metropolitan America," Brookings, October 25, 2012, www.brookings.edu/research/global-gateways-international-aviation-in-metropolitan-america/.

9. *Next Generation Air Transportation System: Improved Risk Analysis Could Strengthen FAA's Global Interoperability Efforts* (GAO-15-608) (U.S. Government Accountability Office, July 2015).

10. Adie Tomer and Jeffrey Gutman, "Shifting Gears to a New Transportation Model," *The Avenue* (blog), Brookings, May 31, 2016, www.brookings.edu/blog/the-avenue/2016/05/31/shifting-gears-to-a-new-transportation-model/.

11. Shalini Vajjhala, "Financing Infrastructure through Resilience Bonds," *The Avenue* (blog), Brookings, December 16, 2015, www.brookings.edu/blog/the-avenue/2015/12/16/financing-infrastructure-through-resilience-bonds/.

12. Joseph Kane and Lynn E. Broaddus, "Striking a Better Balance Between Water Investment and Affordability," *The Avenue* (blog), Brookings, September 12, 2016, www.brookings.edu/blog/the-avenue/2016/09/12/striking-a-better-balance-between-water-investment-and-affordability/.

13. Blair Levin, "Cities, Technology, the Next Generation of Urban Development, and the Next Administration, Part 3," *The Avenue* (blog), Brookings, July 20, 2016, www.brookings.edu/blog/the-avenue/2016/07/20/cities-technology-the-next-generation-of-urban-development-and-the-next-administration-part-3/.

14. Joseph Kane and Robert Puentes, *Beyond Shovel-Ready: The Extent and Impact of U.S. Infrastructure Jobs* (Brookings, May 2014).

10

Productivity and the Trump Administration

DAVID WESSEL

SUMMARY: Only half of all Americans tell public opinion pollsters that they expect today's young people to have a better life than that of their parents, a remarkably pessimistic view given the economic and technological progress that the United States has enjoyed over the past several generations.[1] Will those pessimists be proven correct? The answer depends on how fast we can increase productivity, the amount of goods and services produced for each hour of work.

Productivity growth—making more stuff with less effort—is the magic elixir of rising living standards. It's the reason why wages rise over time. It's the reason why we have more and better goods and services than our grandparents did, even though we work fewer hours on average.[2] Lately, productivity growth in the United States has been distressingly slow. If this persists, it's bad news for everyone.

Although economists find it hard to ascertain which policies will pay productivity dividends in the future, they do offer a menu of policies that stand a good chance of making a difference, including taking steps to increase competition across the U.S. economy, encouraging more private investment, increasing public investment, and aggressively improving the quality of education and training. President Donald J. Trump should put some of these policies toward the top of his economic to-do list and set a goal of doubling the American standard of living by 2050.[3]

First, a bit of economic history. From World War II to 1973, labor productivity—output per hour of work in the business sector—grew at a brisk 3.3 percent a year, and living standards (measured in GDP per capita) nearly doubled in a quarter of a century, or roughly a single generation. Around 1973 productivity growth slowed, a drought that lasted for about two decades and was accompanied by a lot of angst about the capacity of the U.S. economy to deliver for the American middle class. But then around 1995, productivity growth perked up, rising to almost post–World War II levels, a boom tied in part to the spectacular drop in the price of computing power, which also helped spread the benefits of the Internet throughout the economy. That spurt lasted for about a decade and then abated. Since 2004 labor productivity growth has been growing at only 1.3 percent a year on average, and even more slowly lately (see figure 10.1). At the pace that Federal Reserve policymakers expect the U.S. economy to grow over the next decade or so, it would take more than 70 years—close to three generations—for per capita GDP to double.[4]

The causes of the recent slowdown aren't clear. Some analysts blame much of it on flawed statistics, the failure of official government data to properly account for the explosion of free Internet services (like Google Maps) and such innovations as mobile phones that have evolved to replace still and video cameras, tape recorders, radios, compasses, and flashlights.

FIGURE 10.1   DECOMPOSING CHANGES IN PRODUCTIVITY GROWTH, 1948–2015

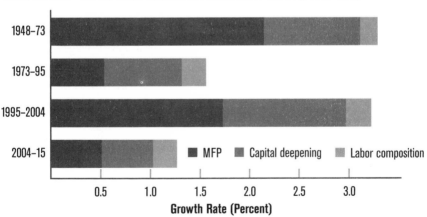

Source: Bureau of Labor Statistics Multifactor Productivity (MFP) Database for Private Business Sector. From Martin Neil Baily and Nicholas Montalbano, "Why Is U.S. Productivity Growth So Slow," Hutchins Center Working Paper 22, Brookings, September 2016 (www.brookings.edu/wp-content/uploads/2016/09/wp22_baily-montalbano_final4.pdf), figure 1.

Yet it is hard to believe that mismeasurement, although undoubtedly substantial, has increased so much in recent years that it explains the entirety of the recent productivity slowdown.

So if the problem is not mostly mismeasurement, then what is it? A couple of culprits emerge from a quick glance at the data. Economics textbooks teach that productivity of workers rises when they have more capital with which to work—more and better tools, machines, computers, software. Growth in business investment spending has been substantially slower than in the past. At the same time, there appears to have been less kick from technological progress across the economy. Whether that is likely to persist is a matter of spirited debate. Northwestern University's Robert Gordon argues that it will—that we should not expect a return to rapid, technology-driven productivity growth despite all the headlines about driverless cars and artificial intelligence. We cannot expect new technologies to match the power of electricity or even air conditioning to transform the economy, he argues. As the *Wall Street Journal*'s Tim Aeppel has reported, Gordon's down-the-hall Northwestern colleague Joel Mokyr disagrees—and he is not the only one.[5]

Other scholars find clues to the origins of the productivity slowdown from data on individual firms and industries. Economists at the Organization for Economic Cooperation and Development, for instance, find that firms at the technological frontier have been moving ahead but that other firms in the same industries are lagging behind.[6] They find a large and widening gap both in manufacturing and service industries between the most and least productive firms.

A team of economists from the University of Maryland, the Census Bureau, and the Federal Reserve observe that productivity growth depends on new successful and innovative firms pushing out older, less productive firms.[7] They point to a decay in the dynamism of the U.S. economy, particularly a decline in the number of new firms being born and old firms dying, as a potential cause of the productivity slowdown. A related line of work sees diminishing competition in the U.S. economy as a contributor to the slowdown in productivity growth. When shielded from competition, companies and industries tend to stagnate and simply count their profits, whereas competition forces old, established companies to change and helps spread productivity-enhancing innovations throughout the economy. There is evidence that there's less competition in the United States now than there was in the past, at least partly the result of explicit government policies (such as patent rules) or government inaction (such as on the antitrust front). Academic research suggests that more than three-quarters of U.S. industries have become more concentrated over the past two decades.[8]

It probably will take a decade or more for scholars to unravel the productivity riddle. But the new president and members of Congress need not—and should not—wait for a consensus diagnosis to take measures to treat the productivity slowdown. Suppose Mr. Trump declared that a national aspiration was to double the American standard of living over the next 35 years by pursuing policies that could nudge productivity growth up. What policies might plausibly improve the chances of reaching that goal?

Before we answer that question, there is one very important caveat to consider. Faster economic growth by itself will not solve all of America's economic problems. The forces of globalization and technology are widening the gap between economic winners and losers. Recent history demonstrates that faster growth hasn't always produced faster-growing incomes for working- and middle-class Americans. Recent research by Stanford's Raj Chetty and co-authors finds only half of the children born in 1980 were at age 30 in households with inflation-adjusted incomes greater than their parents'. In contrast, 90 percent of the children born in the 1940s were making more at age 30 than their parents earned.[9] If we are to achieve widely shared prosperity, we cannot rely exclusively on faster growth or the unfettered market. Progress will require public policies—on taxes, education, health care, labor market rules, and the like—that will counteract market forces driving wider inequality. We should pursue such policies, but that's a subject for another essay.

So if we were summoned to the Oval Office and asked what policies might help double American living standards by 2050, broadly speaking, where should we look?

PROMOTING COMPETITION

If absence of competition restrains productivity growth by allowing players with market power to make big profits without innovating, to squelch upstarts, and to restrict the adoption and spread of new ideas, then the obvious answer lies in government policies to foster more competition. Vigorous, thoughtful antitrust enforcement—making sure that companies do not collude and that mergers are not anticompetitive, while also avoiding counterproductive interventions in the market—is an obvious avenue. Picking the right people for key politically appointed positions at the Justice Department and Federal Trade Commission is crucial. But there are other, perhaps less immediately obvious, ways the government might stimulate competition.

A thorough rethinking of the patent system would be a good place to start. We should be sure that the United States is striking the right balance between, on the one hand, creating incentives for inventions and innovation—"to promote the progress of science and the useful arts," as the U.S. Constitution puts it—and, on the other hand, granting papers that create monopolies that last longer than necessary, raise prices, and block technologies from widespread adoption. Some learned observers say that it's simply too easy to get a patent. "Most of those who look closely at [the patent system] . . . think that the requirement for novelty is a little too low," says Bronwyn Hall of the University of California at Berkeley. Others question the length of time that patents protect inventors in some fast-moving industries, and wonder if the maze of patent laws and patent litigation is doing more for law firms' profit than for the overall economy.[10]

Curtailing and perhaps rolling back occupational licensing is another promising option. More than a quarter of U.S. workers now require a license to do their jobs, according to the White House Council of Economic Advisers. The share of workers licensed at the state level has risen fivefold since the 1950s, and about two-thirds of this increase stems from an increase in the number of occupations that require a license.[11] Licensing can and should protect consumers and maintain health and safety standards, but it can (and in many instances does) serve to protect professionals by limiting newcomers. As Brookings's Martin Baily puts it: "You need a license to be a florist [in some states]; you need a license to do all kinds of things. We certainly know in health care there are a lot of restrictive practices that make it difficult for nurses to do some of the things that they probably should be able to do, technical stuff. You can't have X-rays read in India. It's hard for the Mayo Clinic to enter the Texas medical market because the doctors don't want the competition. So there are a lot of these restrictive practices that are around that maybe we need to get rid of." Excessive occupational licensing can have several unwelcome consequences, one of which is hurting economy-wide productivity growth by making it difficult for workers to move to careers or places where they could be more productive.

Of course, it's also important to avoid policies that, though politically popular, can restrain productivity growth and end up hurting people they were intended to help. "If you think about the ongoing political campaign," says Robert Barro, a Harvard University economist, "the policies that have been given a lot of attention include things like restrictions on trade and immigration. . . . These are not the kinds of policies you want to think about if you're going to think about enhancing productivity." Free trade has acquired a bad reputation in the United States, at least in part because the rhetoric about aiding those whose livelihood has been hit hard by foreign competition hasn't been matched by effective effort. But there is ample evidence that trade—both the much-maligned competition from imports and investment by foreign companies in the United States—prods American companies to become more efficient and boosts U.S. productivity.

PROMOTING MORE PRIVATE INVESTMENT

Not all private investments pay off, of course, but the more businesses invest, the better the chances that the pace of productivity growth will quicken. Economists and governments have been trying to figure out what drives business executives to invest for decades. The great 20th-century economist John Maynard Keynes, writing in his *General Theory*, said that investment decisions involve something more than a straightforward cost-benefit calculation: "Most, probably, of our decisions to do something positive, the full consequences of which will be drawn out over many days to come, can only be taken as the result of animal spirits—a spontaneous urge to action rather than inaction, and not as the outcome of a weighted average of quantitative benefits multiplied by quantitative probabilities."[12]

The government does have a couple of levers. To some extent—economists and executives differ on exactly how much of an impact it has—uncertainty about public policies is the enemy of business investment. This argument can be overdone, but surely flirting with government shutdowns or debt default and perennially applying short-term fixes to long-term problems discourages business investment. Perhaps the most potent lever the government has is the U.S. business tax code, which is overly complicated, packed with perverse incentives, and incompatible with a world in which giant corporations spill over national borders.

Business tax reform is long overdue. Of course, any tax reform creates winners and losers, so there will be lots of political wrangling. Scrapping the entire U.S. tax code and starting from scratch, as appealing as that seems to some, is not likely to happen; the goal ought to be moving toward a business tax code that makes sense for the 21st century. This means a tax code that raises money to pay for government but also encourages investment without favoring politically connected industries, that makes the United States an attractive place to do business, and that reduces incentives to waste millions on tax avoidance while closing loopholes that companies have exploited to avoid paying taxes. No one said this was going to be easy.

SPENDING MORE ON PUBLIC INVESTMENT

With private investment so weak and interest rates extraordinarily low, there is room for spending more on public investment today without crowding out private investment, particularly investments that the private sector will never make because it cannot capture the returns. Federal non-defense investment spending—defined by the White House budget office as physical infrastructure, research and development (R&D), and education and training—soon will fall to its lowest level in at least half a century, measured as a share of GDP.[13] State and local spending on physical infrastructure has been muted despite very low municipal borrowing costs. Increased federal investment spending makes sense now.

Donald Trump has called for a substantial increase in federal spending on physical infrastructure. Politicians sometimes argue that this would create jobs immediately, recalling the "shovel ready" rhetoric of the 2009 Obama fiscal stimulus. But the stronger case for infrastructure and other federal investment spending is that it will pay off in the future, whether or not it creates a lot of jobs now. To be sure, it's much easier to make the case for more federal investment spending in general than to identify ways to direct added public investment to those projects that are most likely to pay off. Bridges to nowhere—shorthand for public investment projects that have no value—will not boost productivity growth. The political pressure to spread spending across all 50 states to win votes in the U.S. Senate is enormous. This is always true with federal programs, of course, but there are ways to direct money to projects likely to have the highest returns. For instance, more than 80 percent of the National Institutes of Health funding is awarded through competitive grants.[14] And the Obama administration's "Race to the Top" education approach was crafted to encourage states to pursue reforms of their K-12 systems to get additional federal money. Some federal transportation funding is awarded in a similar fashion,[15] but there's room for more of that.

Federal R&D spending—especially on basic science and projects too risky for the private sector to undertake—can be an important stimulant to productivity growth but has been declining for decades relative to the size of the economy. That is short-sighted, and it should be reversed. It would take a 50 percent increase in annual federal non-defense R&D spending—that is, about $30 billion more a year—to return spending to the levels of the early 1980s, as a share of the economy. This is a good goal, even if it takes some time to reach it.

IMPROVING THE QUALITY OF LABOR

Investing in human capital is as important as investing in physical capital and infrastructure, particularly in an era when machines and computers are handling more and more chores that once only humans could do. The more capable American workers are, the more productive they are likely to be. That argues for spending more where necessary and spending more wisely on everything from pre-K to college and worker training. One good measure of the economic value of education is wages: More educated workers, on average, earn more than less educated workers. It may be hard to prove that education is the cause—as opposed to a proxy for underlying ability—but there is a strong case that sound investments in education increase a person's productivity, the value of the goods and services he or she produces for each hour of work. This is about more than adding average years of schooling, though. Years of schooling is a familiar metric because its's easy to track, but what really matters is harder to measure: the skills, flexibility, understanding, and habits of workers. These aspects are what we need more of—and we should pay particular attention to continuing to improve the quality of high school and high school graduation rates, and to strengthening community college and other training programs to lift the job prospects and wages of Americans who otherwise likely will end up in very low-wage jobs, if they find work at all.

When I was at the *Wall Street Journal* in the early 1990s, Randy Kehl, an idealistic Air Force major assigned to Vice President Dan Quayle's Council on Competitiveness, came to see me and a colleague. The council had a well-deserved reputation as a toady for big business, as a vehicle for lobbyists to enlist vice presidential aides to derail proposed environmental or safety regulations. But Kehl wanted to "pick our brains" about a national crusade he had in mind. During the George H. W. Bush presidency, economic growth was so slow that it would have taken a century to double living standards. Why, he wondered, weren't people outraged? Why did it have to take that long? And how would a White House initiative to double living standards more rapidly be received by the press?

We told him that journalists report on what policymakers do, rather than give the White House advice, and that we didn't have much to give anyhow. But his questions stuck with us. He was asking the right questions, though the Bush administration never really sought to answer them. President Trump's administration should.

Notes

1. Some 54 percent of respondents to a June 2016 Gallup poll said that it is likely that today's youth will live better than their parents, a response up from a recent low of 44 percent (April 2011) but down from the levels of the late 1990s and early 2000s, when more than 70 percent said that it was likely. See Jeffrey M. Jones, "Views of Opportunity in U.S. Improve, but Lag the Past," Gallup, June 29, 2016, www.gallup.com/poll/193247/views-opportunity-improve-lag-past.aspx?g_source=better%20life%20than%20their%20parents&g_medium=search&g_campaign=tiles.

2. Robert Whaples, "Hours of Work in U.S. History," *EH.Net Encyclopedia*, August 14, 2001, http://eh.net/encyclopedia/hours-of-work-in-u-s-history/.

3. This policy brief draws from Martin Neil Baily and Nicholas Montalbano, "Why Is U.S. Productivity Growth So Slow? Possible Explanations and Policy Responses," Hutchins Center Working Paper 22, Hutchins Center on Fiscal and Monetary Policy at Brookings, September 2016, www.brookings.edu/wp-content/uploads/2016/09/wp22_baily-montalbano1.pdf; and "The Productivity Puzzle: How Can We Speed Up the Growth of the Economy?" (conference at the Brookings Institution, Washington, D.C., September 9, 2016).

4. In September 2016, Federal Reserve policymakers projected the long-term growth rate at 1.8 percent a year, and the U.S. Census Bureau projects that the U.S. population will grow at about 0.8 percent a year over the next decade. That works out to a 1 percent per year increase in GDP.

5. Timothy Aeppel, "Economists Debate: Has All the Important Stuff Already Been Invented?," *Wall Street Journal*, June 15, 2014.

6. Da Andrews, Chiara Criscuolo, and Peter N. Gal, "The Global Productivity Slowdown, Technology Divergence, and Public Policy: A Firm Level Perspective," Hutchins Center Working Paper 24, Hutchins Center on Fiscal and Monetary Policy at Brookings, September 23, 2016, www.brookings.edu/wp-content/uploads/2016/08/andrews-et-al.pdf.

7. Ryan A. Decker, John Haltiwanger, Ron S. Jarmin, and Javier Miranda,

"Declining Business Dynamism: Implications for Productivity?," Hutchins Center Working Paper 23, Hutchins Center on Fiscal and Monetary Policy at Brookings, September 19, 2016, www.brookings.edu/research/declining-business-dynamism-implications-for-productivity/.

8. Gustavo Grullon, Yelenda Larkin, and Roni Michiaely, "Are U.S. Industries Becoming More Concentrated?" (paper presented at the 2016 China International Conference in Finance, Xiamen, China, July 8, 2016), www.cicfconf.org/sites/default/files/paper_388.pdf.

9. Raj Chetty, David Grusky, Maximilian Hell, Nathaniel Hendren, Robert Manduca, and Jimmy Narang, "The Fading American Dream: Trends in Absolute Income Mobility Since 1940," Working Paper 22910 (Cambridge, Mass.: National Bureau of Economic Research, 2016), www.equality-of-opportunity.org/.

10. See "Time to Fix Patents," The Economist, August 8, 2015.

11. U.S. Department of the Treasury, Council of Economic Advisers, and U.S. Department of Labor, Occupational Licensing: A Framework for Policymakers, White House Report, July 2015, www.whitehouse.gov/sites/default/files/docs/licensing_report_final_nonembargo.pdf.

12. John Maynard Keynes, The General Theory of Employment, Interest and Money (London: Palgrave Macmillan, 1936).

13. See Douglas W. Elmendorf and Louise Sheiner, "Federal Budget Policy with an Aging Population and Persistently Low Interest Rates," Hutchins Center Working Paper 18, Hutchins Center on Fiscal and Monetary Policy at Brookings, February 5, 2016, www.brookings.edu/wp-content/uploads/2016/02/wp18_elmendorf-sheiner_final.pdf; and Douglas W. Elmendorf, "Federal Investment," Congressional Budget Office, December 2013, www.cbo.gov/sites/default/files/cbofiles/attachments/44974-FederalInvestment.pdf.

14. "What We Do: Budget," National Institutes of Health, April 4, 2016, www.nih.gov/about-nih/what-we-do/budget.

15. "Fixing America's Surface Transportation Act or 'FAST Act': Fostering Advancements in Shipping and Transportation for the Long-Term Achievement of National Efficiencies (FASTLANE) Grants," Federal Highway Administration, U.S. Department of Transportation, February 2016, www.fhwa.dot.gov/fastact/factsheets/fastlanegrantsfs.cfm.

11

Major Tax Issues in 2017

WILLIAM G. GALE and AARON KRUPKIN

SUMMARY: The federal tax system is beset with problems: It does not raise sufficient revenue to finance government spending, it is complex, it creates outcomes that are unfair, and it retards economic efficiency. This chapter discusses several ways to improve taxes, including creating a value-added tax, increasing environmental taxes, reforming the corporate tax, treating low- and middle-income earners equitably and efficiently, and ensuring appropriate taxation of high-income households.

A good tax system raises the revenues needed to finance government spending in a manner that is as simple, equitable, and growth-friendly as possible. The United States does not have a good tax system. This chapter highlights five areas where tax policy could be improved: raising long-term revenue; increasing environmental taxes; reforming the corporate tax; treating low- and middle-income earners equitably and efficiently; and ensuring appropriate taxation of high-income households.

RAISING LONG-TERM REVENUE

Under current law projections, public debt as a share of the economy will rise from 77 percent currently—the highest level ever except for a few years around World War II—to about 129 percent by 2046.[1] Revenues will rise slightly, but spending will rise much faster, due to increases in net interest, Social Security, and health programs. Under reasonable policy alternatives, the debt figures will rise even higher. High and growing levels of debt will crowd out future investment and stymie growth. They will also reduce fiscal flexibility, or the ability to respond to future recessions.

Alan Auerbach of the University of California at Berkeley and William Gale estimate that in order to return the debt level to its 1957–2007 average of 36 percent of GDP by 2046 immediate and permanent (through 2046) spending cuts and/or tax increases equal to 4.2 percent of GDP will need to be implemented. Just to maintain the 2046 debt at its current share of GDP would require adjustments, starting in 2017, of 2.7 percent of GDP.[2] It seems unlikely that changes of this magnitude could be managed on the spending side. Entitlements have proven difficult to reform, especially Social Security, as there is significant public and political backlash against cutting benefits. Moreover, any Social Security changes would likely be phased in slowly, and reasonable changes in the program would not affect the overall fiscal balance that much. In addition, discretionary spending has already been cut dramatically and is already slated to fall to historically low shares of GDP over the next 25 years. As a result, tax increases need to be part of a long-term fiscal solution.

One way to raise revenue is to broaden the tax base by reducing the number of specialized credits and deductions in the tax code.[3] For example, under current law, a dollar's worth of deduction reduces taxable income by a dollar and hence reduces the tax burden in proportion to the marginal tax rate. A high-income household saves 39.6 cents for a given dollar of deduction, whereas a low-income household saves only 10 cents or nothing at all. Setting the tax benefit of each dollar of itemized deductions to 15 cents would affect mostly high-income households and raise, on average, about 0.6 percent of GDP per year over a decade, or roughly a cumulative $1.4 trillion over the next 10 years. Current itemized deductions are expensive, regressive, and often ineffective in achieving their goals. The mortgage interest deduction, for example, does not seem to raise home ownership rates, yet it will cost the federal government around $70 billion in 2017. Limiting the benefits of the deductions for high-income households is a way of reducing the distortions created by the tax code, making taxes more progressive, and increasing revenue. Alternatively, the United States could cap the total amount of tax expenditures that an individual can claim.[4]

An alternative way to raise revenue is through the creation of a federal value-added tax (VAT), as a supplement to the current income tax system, rather than as a replacement.[5] A VAT is essentially a flat-rate consumption tax with administrative advantages over a national retail sales tax. Although it would be new to the U.S., the VAT is in place in about 160 countries worldwide and in every OECD country other than the United States. Experience in these countries suggests that the VAT can raise substantial revenue, is administrable, and is minimally harmful to economic growth. Additionally, a properly designed VAT might help the states deal with their own fiscal issues. Although the VAT is regressive relative to current income, the regressivity can be offset in several ways, and we should care about the distributional impact of the overall tax and transfer system, not just specific taxes. The VAT is not readily transparent in many countries, but it would be easy to make the VAT completely transparent to businesses and households by reporting VAT payments on receipts, just like state sales taxes are reported today. While the VAT has led to an increase in revenues and government spending in some countries, higher revenues are precisely why the VAT is needed in the United States, and efforts to limit government spending should be part of an effort to enact a VAT. A new 10 percent VAT, applied to all consumption except for spending on education, Medicaid and Medicare, charitable organizations, and state and local government, could be paired with a cash payment of about $900 per adult and about $400 per child to offset the cost to low-income families (the equivalent of annually refunding each two-parent, two-child household the VAT owed on the first $26,000 of consumption).[6] In all, this VAT could raise about a net 2 percent of GDP or about $390 billion in 2017, after allowing for the offsetting effect on other taxes.

INCREASING ENVIRONMENTAL TAXES

Economists have long recommended specific taxes on fossil-fuel energy sources as a way to address global warming. The basic rationale for a carbon tax is that it makes good economic sense: unlike most taxes, carbon taxation can correct a market failure—namely, that people and businesses do not pay the full cost of emitting carbon—and make the economy more efficient.[7] It could also serve to raise revenue as an alternative to the taxes described above.

Although a carbon tax would be a new policy for the federal government, the tax has been implemented in several other countries. On average, a reasonably designed U.S. carbon tax alone could raise gross revenue by about 0.7 percent of GDP each year from 2016 to 2025 (around $160 billion per year).[8] Carbon taxes are a good idea even if we did not need to increase revenues, because they can contribute to a cleaner, healthier environment by providing price signals to those who pollute. They have foreign policy benefits as well, as they plausibly reduce U.S. demand for oil and dependence on oil-producing nations. The permanent change in price signals from enacting a carbon tax would stimulate new private sector research and innovation to develop new ways of harnessing renewable energy and energy-saving technologies. The implementation of a carbon tax also offers opportunities to reform and simplify other climate-related policies that affect the transportation sector. The regressivity of a carbon tax could be offset in a number of ways, including refundable income or payroll tax credits.

REFORMING CORPORATE TAXATION

In the standard textbook setup, the earnings of equity holders are taxed twice: once under the corporate tax when they are earned, and then again under the individual income tax when they are paid to shareholders as dividends or capital gains. This summary both overstates and misstates the real problem. First, no corporate income is fully taxed under the individual income tax, since dividends and capital gains are taxed at preferential rates and capital gains are only taxed when the asset is sold. Second, a significant share of dividends and capital gains accrues to nontaxable entities—nonprofits or pensions—thus reducing the tax burden further. Third, a large share of corporate profits is never taxed at the corporate level in the first place. Aggressive corporate tax avoidance, including shifting funds out of the country through transfer pricing or other mechanisms, is an important factor in corporations reducing their tax burden.

The United States has the highest top corporate rate in the world at 35 percent. For many businesses, the tax distorts choices in favor of the non-corporate sector over the corporate sector. For other businesses, the corporate tax burden is offset by tax preferences. In the corporate sector, the tax favors debt over equity and retained earnings over dividends. As a result of numerous loopholes, aggressive corporate tax avoidance, and the large share of U.S. businesses that takes the form of non–C-corporation activity (which is in itself a form of corporate tax avoidance), U.S. corporate tax revenues as a share of GDP are only average compared to other countries, despite the high tax rate. In recent years, for example, corporate profits have equaled 12 percent of GDP, but corporate tax revenues have hovered around 2 percent of GDP.

Hence, the problem is not just that some forms of corporate income face two levels of tax; it is also that some forms face no tax. As a result, the main goal of corporate tax reform should be to tax all corporate income once and only once, at the full income tax rate. Given all of the flaws in the corporate tax, it should not be surprising that there are several approaches to reform that could help. None is without problems; each would address different aspects of the system.

One option would be to replace some or all of the corporate income tax with a tax on shareholder wealth accumulation, as proposed by Eric Toder and Alan Viard. Under this approach, there would be no corporate tax. Instead, "American shareholders of publically-traded companies would be taxed on both dividends and capital gains at ordinary income tax rates, and capital gains would be taxed upon accrual," rather than realization.[9]

Alternatively, the U.S. corporate income tax could be converted into a corporate cash-flow tax. This idea, proposed by both the House Republicans[10] and Alan Auerbach,[11] would essentially be a VAT with a wage deduction. It would encourage new investment by replacing deductions with immediate expensing for physical investment. The tax would be applied on a destination basis, which essentially limits the focus of the tax to transactions occurring exclusively on domestic soil and thus avoids all international transfer pricing issues.

A major change in the treatment of foreign source income should also be considered. In a pure worldwide system, all income from around the world is taxable, and all costs are deductible. In a pure territorial system, income earned outside the country is not taxable, and costs incurred outside the country are not deductible. A key issue, of course, is how income and expenses are allocated to each country because firms go to great lengths to move income to low-tax countries and deductions to high-tax countries. Most advanced countries lean toward a territorial system. The United States, by contrast, leans toward a worldwide system, but there is an important exception—taxes on actively earned foreign income are deferred until the income is repatriated to the United States. Currently, U.S. firms have more than $2 trillion in actively earned funds overseas that have not been repatriated and therefore go untaxed. This income is often described as being "trapped" outside the United States.[12] This characterization is only partially correct, though. The money may actually be in a bank in the United States and funding investment in the United States. However, the funds cannot be used to pay dividends to shareholders or to buy back firm shares until the funds are "repatriated" to the corporation, a legal procedure that generates a tax liability.

There are two general proposals to deal with the issue of funds sitting "abroad." One is to move to a worldwide system without deferral.[13] The other is to move toward a territorial system.[14] As noted, a big issue with territorial systems is that they increase the incentives that already exist to shift income into low-tax countries and deductions/costs into high-tax countries. The implementation of a territorial system would need to be accompanied by very stringent rules about income and cost-shifting. There has been a desire on the part of some lawmakers to have a one-time repatriation tax holiday, perhaps to finance infrastructure.[15] This would be a mistake, and would simply encourage firms to shift more funds overseas in an effort to gain a future tax advantage.[16]

REVISING TREATMENT OF LOW- AND MIDDLE-INCOME EARNERS

Under a progressive income tax, the highest statutory marginal tax rates are placed on the highest-income households. Under our current system, however, low- and middle-income earners often face very high effective marginal tax rates. These earners are in income ranges where increased earnings cause phaseouts of tax subsidies and benefit programs. The net effect of earning more—including higher wages, higher income tax payments, and lower program benefits—can impose quite significant effective tax rates on such households. This situation is unfair to those families, is inefficient, and discourages actions that would enhance social and economic mobility.

For example, Melissa Kearney and Lesley Turner note that a secondary earner in a married household typically pays a higher effective tax rate on the margin than the primary earner. This issue arises because the two incomes are combined to form one tax unit, even though the secondary earner often has a lower *individual* income than the primary earner (and would have a lower marginal tax rate if filing as a single person). This is particularly problematic for low- and middle-income households because it discourages additional work to support their family, which could result in extra income that may reduce their benefits or even render the family ineligible for programs such as food assistance or the Earned Income Tax Credit (EITC). On both fairness and economic grounds, Kearney and Turner propose a 20 percent secondary-earner tax deduction until a cap is reached. This deduction would improve the incentive to work, provide more economic security to working low- and middle-income families, and mitigate the secondary-earner penalty. On net, the authors estimate that their proposal would cost the federal government $8.2 billion per year.[17]

Of course, another option to mitigate the tax burden faced by low- and middle-income earners is to expand eligibility for the EITC or transform the Child and Dependent Care Credit (CDCC) to a refundable benefit.[18] Both of these programs are already executed through the tax code in an effort to aid low- and middle-income families, and changes to the programs could expand economic opportunity or increase the degree of fairness in the system. Specifically, EITC benefits could be raised for families with fewer than two children, especially for childless workers. This improves the incentives for work in these households, and it can lead to better economic outcomes for the associated families. By converting the CDCC to a refundable credit, low-income families would be able to reap greater benefits from the program and retain more disposable income. Additionally, it would incentivize the use of higher-quality child care. To make these options revenue neutral and prevent them from exacerbating the long-term revenue issues described above, the income eligibility caps for these programs could be lowered or other provisions could be removed.

TAXING THE RICH

There are three reasons to increase the tax burden on high-income households. First, their income has increased dramatically over the past several decades, yet their tax payments have not kept pace. Second, if the fiscal reforms described above are implemented, the main benefit will be economic growth, but such growth in the past several decades has accrued largely to high-income households, who should thus be expected to pay for it. Third, despite much rhetoric to the contrary, reasonable variations in taxes on high-income households do not appear to have any negative discernible impact on growth.[19]

There are many ways to boost revenue collected from high-income households. The most prominent examples would include higher taxes on capital gains and dividends, restrictions on tax expenditures, higher income tax rates, or a tighter estate tax. Taxing carried interest as ordinary income also makes sense in principle, but is difficult to implement without creating new forms of avoidance and, as a result, would raise very little revenue.

CONCLUSION

The U.S. tax system is far from ideal, and there are several areas for improvement. Reforming the system so that it pays for government spending, treats taxpayers fairly, and improves incentives for productive activity can alleviate many issues and only be a plus from an economic standpoint.

Notes

1. For current law projections, see Congressional Budget Office, "The 2016 Long-Term Budget Outlook" (Washington, D.C.: 2016). For current policy assumptions, see Alan J. Auerbach and William G. Gale, "Once More unto the Breach: The Deteriorating Fiscal Outlook" (Brookings, 2016).

2. Authors' calculation based on current policy assumptions and starting the adjustments in 2017.

3. William G. Gale, "Why Higher Taxes Will Have to be Part of the Medium- and Long-Term Fiscal Solution," *Tax Vox* (blog), Tax Policy Center, January 23, 2012, http://taxvox.taxpolicycenter.org/2012/01/23/why-higher-taxes-will-have-to-be-part-of-the-medium-and-long-term-fiscal-solution/.

4. For further analysis of tax expenditure reform options, see Daniel Baneman and others, "Options to Limit the Benefit of Tax Expenditures for High-Income Households" (Washington, D.C.: Tax Policy Center, 2011).

5. Yale University law professor Michael Graetz also has proposed a VAT, but he would use the revenues gained to cut the income tax substantially—raising the exemption to about $100,000 and taxing income above that level at a flat 25 percent—and to halve the corporate tax rate. See Michael J. Graetz, "100 Million Unnecessary Returns: A Fresh Start for the U.S. Tax System," *Yale Law Journal* 112 (2004): 263–313.

6. For more discussion, see William G. Gale and Benjamin H. Harris, "Proposal 10: Creating an American Value-Added Tax" (Hamilton Project, Brookings, 2013); Eric Toder and Joseph Rosenberg, "Effects of Imposing a Value-Added Tax to Replace Payroll Taxes or Corporate Taxes" (Washington, D.C.: Tax Policy Center, 2010).

7. William G. Gale, "The Tax Favored by Most Economists," Brookings, March 12, 2013, www.brookings.edu/research/opinions/2013/03/12-taxing-carbon-gale.

8. Donald Marron, Eric Toder, and Lydia Austin, "Taxing Carbon: What, Why,

and How," Tax Policy Center, June 24, 2015, www.taxpolicycenter.org/publications/taxing-carbon-what-why-and-how.

9. Eric Toder and Alan Viard, "A Proposal to Reform the Taxation of Corporate Income" (Washington, D.C.: Tax Policy Center, 2016).

10. "A Better Way: Our Vision for a Confident America," Tax Reform Task Force, Speaker of the U.S. House of Representatives, June 24, 2016, https://abetterway.speaker.gov/_assets/pdf/ABetterWay-Tax-PolicyPaper.pdf

11. Alan J. Auerbach, "A Modern Corporate Tax" (Hamilton Project, Brookings, 2010) www.americanprogress.org/wp-content/uploads/issues/2010/12/pdf/auerbachpaper.pdf.

12. "Companies Invest 'Trapped' Untaxed Foreign Profits in U.S.," *Bloomberg*, December 15, 2011, www.bloomberg.com/news/articles/2011-12-14/companies-hold-46-of-untaxed-foreign-profits-in-u-s-assets-1-.

13. Office of Management and Budget, *Fiscal Year 2016 Budget of the U.S. Government* (Washington, D.C.: U.S. Government Printing Office, 2015) www.whitehouse.gov/sites/default/files/omb/budget/fy2016/assets/budget.pdf

14. H.R. 1, *Tax Reform Act of 2014*, December 2014, www.congress.gov/bill/113th-congress/house-bill/1.

15. See the July 2015 "Bipartisan Framework for International Tax Reform" on Senator Robert Portman's website at www.portman.senate.gov/public/index.cfm/files/serve?File_id=146abc53-1763-4a0a-93ee-3d4eecf2a61c.

16. William G. Gale and Benjamin Harris, "Don't Fall for Corporate Repatriation," Brookings, June 27, 2011, www.brookings.edu/opinions/dont-fall-for-corporate-repatriation/.

17. Melissa S. Kearney and Lesley J. Turner, "Giving Secondary Earners a Tax Break: A Proposal to Help Low- and Middle-Income Families," Discussion Paper 2013-07 (Hamilton Project, Brookings, 2013) www.hamiltonproject.org/files/downloads_and_links/THP_Kearney_DiscPaper_Final.pdf.

18. Hilary Hoynes, "Building on the Success of the Earned Income Tax Credit" (Brookings, Brookings, June 19, 2014); and James P. Ziliak, "Supporting Low-Income Workers through Refundable Child-Care Credits" (Brookings, 2014).

19. William G. Gale and Andrew A. Samwick, "Effects of Income Tax Changes on Economic Growth" (Brookings, 2016).

12

The Future of U.S.-China Economic Relations

DAVID DOLLAR

SUMMARY: Protectionist rhetoric during the 2016 presidential campaign stressed the damage that trade with China has done to the U.S. economy and domestic employment rates over the past decade. Rather than simply retreat from competition and further demonize U.S.-Chinese economic relations, however, the incoming presidential administration should use a combination of incentives and restrictions to rebalance its approach to China and to encourage China itself to show greater openness in its trade and investment policies both at home and abroad.

China in the past few decades has emerged as the world's largest exporter and the United States' second-largest trading partner after Canada. Despite being a relatively poor developing country, China has built up the largest trade surpluses in human history, creating economic problems for the United States. Trade with China has led to the loss of American manufacturing jobs, reduced real wages for semiskilled workers, and devastated some communities dependent on low-end manufacturing jobs. These negative effects have naturally given rise to protectionist sentiments in the U.S. presidential campaign and given trade in general a bad name.

While protectionism is tempting, it is almost certain to backfire and cause more economic harm to the United States. Inducing China to become a more normal trading and investing nation will require a mix of carrots and sticks from the next administration, a policy that could be characterized as "responsible hardball." As a departure from current policy, the most promising option would be imposing new restrictions on Chinese state enterprises purchasing their competitors in the United States until China opens up reciprocally. The United States can also use leverage over China's desire to be granted market economy status in order to negotiate significant reductions in excess capacity in steel and other heavy industries.

BACKGROUND

Economists generally agree that trade between the United States and China has had negative effects on U.S. manufacturing employment, though estimates of the impact vary. What is not in dispute is that U.S. manufacturing employment declined sharply in the 2000s, dropping from 17 million in 2000 to 11 million in 2010. Some have estimated that China's reform and opening up explained 25 percent of the decline in American manufacturing jobs between 1991 and 2007, and 40 percent of the loss after 2000.[1] Others emphasize that the U.S. trade deficit was already large in 2000, and that trade accounted for little of the job loss in the 2000s. However, most agree that if the U.S. trade deficit were eliminated completely—a big "if"— then U.S. manufacturing employment would be 25 percent higher (3 million more jobs on the current base).[2]

The United States had problems earlier with large trade surpluses in Asian partners such as Japan, South Korea, and Taiwan. China was different from these three economies in at least three ways. First, China's trade surpluses emerged at an earlier stage of development than in the other Asian economies. China was still a relatively poor, capital-scarce economy when it started running trade surpluses. Second, China has a much bigger population than its East Asian neighbors, making it a greater challenge for the world to absorb Chinese surpluses. Third, the Chinese economy is a complex hybrid of private entrepreneurship on the one hand and a large state enterprise and government sector on the other. A trade surplus reflects an excess of savings over investment. China has had a lot of economic distortions that have tended to keep both savings and investment high, but savings in particular has been especially high. In recent years, China is a complete outlier among major economies, with a national savings rate near 50 percent of GDP.

One of the key distortions in the economy has been management of the exchange rate. In 1994, China pegged its currency, the yuan, to the U.S. dollar at a rate of 8.3:1. This was a reasonable and not unusual choice for a developing economy. At that rate, the trade balance was close to zero for the first few years, making it hard to argue against that level. The problem is that China had rapid productivity growth that required some appreciation over time. China was becoming competitive in more and more goods, but it resisted adjustment of the exchange rate. It was at this point that China developed a very large trade surplus that rose above 10 percent of GDP. Pegging the currency to the dollar in the face of a large trade surplus requires the central bank to accumulate reserves, and China's reserves over this period rose to a global high of $4 trillion.

Currency manipulation was one important distortion in the Chinese economy, but not the only one. China still has a large state-enterprise sector that earns profits but effectively pays no dividends to anyone. If firms were owned by households, then some of the profits would end up stimulating consumption; but in China those profits all end up as savings. For many years, Chinese state-owned enterprises (SOEs) largely deployed the savings in-country. But now, with problems of excess capacity emerging in many sectors, SOEs have turned outward and are on a global buying spree.

These economic factors create a new set of problems for the United States and other advanced economies. First is the issue of the trade surplus. China shifted off the peg to the dollar in 2005, and over the past decade it has allowed its currency to appreciate significantly—about 20 percent against the dollar since 2005. As a result of this new currency policy, China stopped intervening in the foreign exchange market to accumulate reserves. In fact, since 2015 China has been selling reserves to keep the value of its currency high, and its $4 trillion reserves stockpile has declined to $3.1 trillion. In the face of this new currency policy, China's trade surplus initially declined. But now it has started to rise again, and one factor is the shift of SOE investment outward. There are also net private outflows of capital, though it is hard to measure these exactly. The growing net capital outflow from China is threatening to take China's trade surplus back to levels that pose problems for the global economy.

A second and related problem is that China's policy toward foreign direct investment is highly asymmetric. China is now encouraging its firms to invest abroad in virtually all sectors. Meanwhile, according to an Organization for Economic Cooperation and Development measure of investment restrictiveness, China is the most closed of major economies. It is significantly less open than other emerging markets such as Brazil, India, Mexico, or South Africa.[3] China is partially open in manufacturing, though important sectors such as motor vehicles have to operate through awkward 50-50 joint ventures that force global auto companies to pair with local partners. Most of the modern services sectors such as finance, telecommunications, media, and logistics are almost completely closed to foreign investment. Even in sectors that are ostensibly open, U.S. firms are often reluctant to invest in China because their intellectual property rights, as well as property rights more generally, are poorly protected. This creates an unlevel playing field in which Chinese firms can earn profits in a protected market at home and then buy their competitors in the United States and Europe. The interagency Committee on Foreign Investment in the United States (CFIUS) can review mergers and acquisitions for their national security implications, but there are relatively few transactions that can be legitimately stopped on those grounds. In recent years, the review process has approved Chinese purchases of Smithfield Foods (a U.S. pork production enterprise) and Syngenta (a Swiss agricultural chemical company with large U.S. operations).

In addition to trade with China, America's trade with other partners also has been called into question during the current election season. In particular, the North American Free Trade Agreement (NAFTA) has been castigated for costing U.S. manufacturing jobs—however, there is little evidence that NAFTA had this particular effect. The nonpartisan Congressional Research Service, in its study "NAFTA at 20," concluded that "NAFTA did not cause the huge job losses feared by the critics or the large economic gains predicted by supporters. The net overall effect of NAFTA on the U.S. economy appears to have been relatively modest."[4] NAFTA, unfortunately, was largely being implemented at the same time that China was entering the global economy, and effects on the U.S. economy from China trade were misattributed to NAFTA.

One reason that it is hard to find any net negative job effects of NAFTA is that trade between the United States on the one hand and Canada and Mexico on the other has been relatively balanced. The same point holds for the group of economies that have negotiated the Trans-Pacific Partnership (TPP). This group includes Canada and Mexico, as well as Japan and a total of 12 Asia-Pacific economies. China is not included. In 2014, the United States imported $750 billion of goods from these partners and exported a similar amount, $726 billion. In the same year, the United States imported $467 billion in goods from China, but exported only $124 billion. On average, TPP partners are also more open to investment than China's economy. At the end of 2014, the United States had more than $1 trillion of foreign investment stock in the TPP partners, 15 times more than its paltry $67 billion of investment in China.

A final important piece of background is that the growth of the U.S. economy slowed significantly between the 1990s and the 2000s. It would be hard to attribute any significant part of the slowdown to China. The large trade gap with China may be annoying, but it is still small compared with the overall U.S. economy. For example, the $467 billion of imports in 2014 represented less than 3 percent of the U.S. economy. The slowdown in U.S. growth can be attributed to a multitude of factors, including the aging population, underinvestment in education and infrastructure, and the 2007–9 financial crisis. And although the share of manufacturing in employment has been on a slow but steady decline since the 1950s, the share of manufacturing in GDP has been stable.[5] This pattern reflects the relatively faster productivity growth in manufacturing compared to services. What distinguishes the 2000s from the 1990s is that overall employment growth has been so slow. In thinking about how to deal with China, there is a risk that that issue will distract from more important considerations about how to make U.S. output and employment grow more quickly.

POLICY OPTIONS FOR U.S.-CHINA TRADE AND INVESTMENT

The next president will want to shape a policy of "responsible hardball" with China. Hardball, because China needs incentives to open up to the standards of other large emerging markets, and responsible, because there are real risks that trade and investment restrictions will be either ineffective or counterproductive.

Restrictions on SOE Investments

The new imbalance in the relationship is that Chinese state enterprises are buying their competitors in the United States and Europe, especially in high-tech sectors. U.S. firms are not allowed to make similar purchases in China because of China's restrictions. The CFIUS review process, by statute, is focused narrowly on national security issues, not on broader issues of national interest or economic fairness. The United States and China have been negotiating a Bilateral Investment Treaty, and for this treaty to be in the U.S. interest—not to mention for it to have any chance of being passed in Congress—it should require China to open up virtually all of its economy to foreign investment. Interestingly, President Xi Jinping's administration has prioritized this negotiation, but there is a lot of resistance from state enterprises and different parts of the government bureaucracy.

The next administration should consider legislation that restricts the ability of foreign state enterprises to invest in the United States, especially through mergers and acquisitions. It would be reasonable to have some exceptions, such as investments from countries with which the United States has investment agreements. This could be crafted to provide incentives for China to reach an investment agreement with the United States. Given that investment negotiations could drag on for years, it would also provide sensible protections for U.S. firms in the meantime.

Trade War with China

As a presidential candidate, Donald Trump proposed a 45 percent tariff on imports from China. This idea is likely to backfire. Chinese leaders would definitely not buckle under such pressure. For one, exports to the United States are not that important to the Chinese economy anymore, and China's leaders have many avenues to keep its economy growing. For another, China's authoritarian leaders could not buckle to U.S. pressure without risking their hold on power. The population is nationalistic, and its attitude toward the United States is quite ambivalent. A direct trade attack on China would certainly whip up popular support for retaliation. The retaliation would not have much direct effect on the U.S. economy, since the United States exports so little to China, but it would create an uncertain environment for trade and investment globally that would slow U.S. growth.

Trade Remedies

While all-out trade war with China is not a good idea, the United States does have tools that it can deploy to address China's World Trade Organization (WTO) violations, as well as dumping or import surges that violate U.S. trade laws. The Obama administration has brought more WTO cases against China than its predecessors, and has used trade remedies more often as well. These actions are sensible, but in general China is following WTO rules, which do not set a very high standard. The distortions in

China noted above— such as restricting foreign investment or maintaining a large state-enterprise sector—are not covered by WTO disciplines at all.

Still, using trade remedies is an important part of U.S. trade policy. One practical issue at the moment concerns China's status as a nonmarket economy. When China joined the WTO in 2001, it agreed that it could be treated as a nonmarket economy for up to 15 years. The practical import is that in antidumping cases, the United States can look at costs in similar economies (such as Brazil) in determining whether Chinese exporters are selling below cost. The 15-year term ended in December, and China is expecting to receive market economy status at this time—in fact, it may bring a WTO case against the United States if it does not. U.S. law has a definition of a market economy; although this definition is somewhat subjective, a good case can be made that China does not meet the standard. In the current political environment, it is impossible to imagine that Congress would vote in favor of giving China market economy status.

Antidumping procedures are very relevant at the moment, because China has developed extremely large excess capacity in steel and other heavy sectors. The next administration should use market economy status as a bargaining chip to negotiate specific reductions in excess capacity, especially in steel. China would have a good case in the WTO if it chose that route, but a WTO case would take years and China is likely to prefer a negotiated settlement.

TPP as an Incentive

It is ironic that China has given trade a bad name and that the negativity has spilled over to feelings about the TPP. As detailed in "The Trans-Pacific Partnership: The Politics of Openness and Leadership in the Asia-Pacific," the TPP is a gold standard agreement among like-minded countries with which the United States has relatively balanced trade, including both advanced economies and developing ones such as Vietnam, Mexico, and Peru.[6] Because these are relatively open economies, the economic benefits of further opening are modest. By the same token, any adjustment costs in the United States are likely to be small. The main value of the agreement in fact is strategic. Asia-Pacific partners are looking for U.S. leadership in maintaining and extending an open trading system with fair rules. China is not one of the negotiating countries, and it would be hard for China to meet TPP standards because these standards would require China to open up its trade and investment and to adjust other regulations. We should hold out hope that China will one day aspire to meet these standards and join the TPP, but we should not hold our breath about China's system changing quickly. If the TPP is implemented, South Korea and ASEAN members could be attracted to join. It has the potential to spur new supply chains among a group of countries that have to some extent harmonized their regulations on investment, environmental protection, and labor standards. The TPP could be a positive incentive for China to reform, but if the United States turns its back on the agreement, Asian economies will naturally adjust to a world in which the United States retreats from Asia and China rises as the economic power in the region.

Naming China as a Currency Manipulator

This option is truly fighting the last war. In 2015, Congress wrote a formal definition of a currency manipulator: at its heart is the criterion that the country in question is intervening in the currency market accumulating foreign reserves. For much of the past decade, China would have met this particular criterion. But for at least a year now, China has been selling reserves to keep the value of its currency high, not low. It is hard to find economists or investors who think that that situation might turn around. To the contrary, there are plenty of investors betting that China will not be able to prevent the market from depreciating its currency. The underlying problem is the enormous savings rate in China. With diminishing investment opportunities, a vast amount of capital is trying to get out of the country. At this point, it is a mistake to focus any dialogue with China on the currency market; we should in fact be happy that China is intervening to keep its currency high, since a large Chinese depreciation would likely destabilize global financial markets. Just the hint of significant devaluation in August 2015 and again in December sent financial markets tumbling.

Focusing the Economic Dialogue with China on the Distortions That Keep the Savings Rate High

The United States has a range of government-to-government dialogues with China. The most prominent, the Strategic and Economic Dialogue, has become too big and formal to be of much use. But certainly the United States will continue various dialogues at different levels. It makes sense to separate the economic dialogue from the strategic issues and to focus the economic dialogue on the distortions in China that keep the savings rate high—this is the fundamental problem behind China's large and growing trade surplus.

Adjustment Assistance

If China were to open up and reform, there would be many more export opportunities for U.S. firms and workers and more balanced trade between the world's two biggest economies. Still, there will be winners and losers on each side. Expanded trade with China on a balanced basis would create a lot of jobs in the United States, but would lead to job losses in some sectors. The United States has done a poor job providing retraining and other support to workers and communities hurt by trade (or by technological change, which is actually more common). To get the maximum benefit from trade and to maintain popular support for it, we need more extensive and effective adjustment assistance in the United States.

Notes

1. David H. Autor, David Dorn, and Gordon H. Hanson, "The China Shock: Learning from Labor Market Adjustment to Large Changes in Trade," Working Paper 21906 (Cambridge, Mass.: National Bureau of Economic Research, January 2016), www.nber.org/papers/w21906.

2. Lawrence Edwards and Robert Z. Lawrence, *Rising Tide: Is Growth in Emerging Economies Good for the United States?* (Washington, D.C.: Peterson Institute for International Economics, 2013).

3. David Dollar, "China as a Global Investor" (Brookings, May 2016).

4. M. Angeles Villareal and Ian F. Fergusson, "NAFTA at 20: Overview and Trade Effects" (Congressional Research Service, April 2014), http://digitalcom mons.ilr.cornell.edu/key_workplace/1261/.

5. Martin Baily and Barry Bosworth, "U.S. Manufacturing: Understanding Its Past and Potential Future," *Journal of Economic Perspectives* 28, no. 1 (Winter 2014): 3–26.

6. Mireya Solís, "The Trans-Pacific Partnership: The Politics of Openness and Leadership in the Asia-Pacific" (Brookings, October 2016).

13

The Case for Trade and the Trans-Pacific Partnership

MIREYA SOLÍS

SUMMARY: The fate of the Trans-Pacific Partnership (TPP)—a 12-nation trade pact covering close to 40 percent of world GDP—will be an important marker in the United States' march toward or away from economic and political isolationism. This chapter will clarify the connection of trade policy, and the TPP in particular, to the U.S. national interest with regard to prosperity, security, and governance; and will suggest policy prescriptions to recreate a domestic consensus in favor of economic internationalism by investing in human capital and fostering labor mobility.

The United States is confronted with a defining issue: are we to turn inward by questioning the economic benefits of trade, reneging on a major diplomatic success in updating multilateral economic disciplines, and failing to renew a rules-based order at a time of a profound power shift in Asia? More important, is the abdication of international leadership good for the American worker? How does the Trans-Pacific Partnership (TPP) match up with U.S. visions of prosperity, security, and governance—and what will be needed to renew U.S. support for international economic engagement?

TRADE AND THE NATIONAL INTEREST

Prosperity

Trade's main contribution to national wealth comes from enhancing competitiveness. Building on the forces of specialization and innovation, open markets allow for the most efficient use of productive resources, foster competition to dismantle monopolies and inflated prices, and help disseminate new ideas and technologies that propel future growth. At the most fundamental level, an open trade regime allows nations to escape the boundaries of their internal markets to service global demand. The empirical record across centuries and regions is unequivocal: nations that purposively avail themselves of the international marketplace outperform those whose sights remain constrained by national boundaries.[1]

One of the major contributions of free trade is the reduction in the cost of living for consumers by making available goods and services at a lower cost. This price reduction in everyday necessities is particularly important for consumers with the fewest resources. Tariff elimination has a pro-poor bias in *every* country. For example, a modeling exercise shows that a move toward autarky in the world would erode the purchasing power of consumers across all income brackets, but it would bring an outsize loss (over 60 percent) for consumers at the bottom of the distribution ladder.[2]

International trade, like all forces of economic change, both creates and destroys jobs. Sectors that enjoy international competitiveness will thrive, creating job opportunities, but those that are unable to meet competition from abroad will contract and cut back on employment. Both sides of the coin matter in assessing trade's impact. The job benefits of international trade for the U.S. economy are substantial. In 2014, exports sustained 11.6 million jobs[3]—a conservative estimate that does not take into account the job creation effects of imports (for example, the sourcing of foreign components that make user industries more competitive), and of foreign direct investments in the United States that result from operating an open and competitive economy. But the figure suffices to show that export activity benefits working Americans, especially considering that wages in the export sector are 18 percent higher on average.

Trade liberalization also destroys jobs, and the costs for affected workers are steep. Trade competition with China (which is not a signatory to a trade agreement with the United States) is estimated by some to have cost 985,000 manufacturing jobs between 1999 and 2011, at a time when U.S.

manufacturing employment fell by 5.8 million jobs. And contrary to the notion of fluid labor markets, displaced American workers have not easily bounced back, as they have been saddled by prolonged spells of unemployment or left the workforce entirely, and when reemployed they frequently have settled for lower pay.[4]

No finding has framed more the current debate on the merits of trade for the American worker than the "China trade shock" thesis.[5] These findings point to the need to incentivize China to reform its trading and investment practices, and the TPP in fact can play an important role to this end.[6] Moreover, they have cast the spotlight on what is our biggest policy mistake: to leave unabated the distributional costs of economic change writ large as a result of both technological change and trade liberalization.

However, the wrong conclusion drawn by antitrade critics is that by trading with China we have surrendered our economic strength and self-imposed deindustrialization, and that protectionism will bring manual jobs back. The predominant cause for the loss of manufacturing employment has been technological change (85 percent), not international trade.[7] Automation has transformed the American factory, rendering millions of low-skilled jobs redundant. That technology is the primary driver is corroborated by the fact that despite the steep decline in factory jobs, manufacturing leads the U.S. economy in productivity rates and industrial output has been growing. Efforts to take stock of the contributions of trade with China to the American economy must certainly weigh in the job loss of rising import penetration, but must also factor in the jobs supported through American exports of goods and services to China, and the millions of consumers who have access to lower-priced goods. Protectionist measures could cost millions of Americans their means of livelihood.[8]

The TPP represents a different balance of benefits and costs with sizable economic gains from trading with a group of like-minded countries adopting cutting-edge rules and smaller adjustment costs (the largest market the TPP opens for the United States is a high-wage economy, Japan) and with important geopolitical ramifications. With novel rules on the digital economy, high tariff elimination targets, and disciplines to address behind-the-border protectionism, the TPP creates opportunities for American sectors that enjoy competitive strength—services, advanced manufacturing, and agriculture. The U.S. International Trade Commission estimates a *net* positive (albeit small) effect of TPP on job creation (128,000 jobs) and an increase in real wage rates (0.19 percent) by 2032. Annual increases in real income for Americans (that is, an expansion in their purchasing power) range from $57 billion to $131 billion by 2032.[9]

Security

As a region characterized by both its unparalleled economic dynamism and the rise of an emerging power with global aspirations, Asia is an area of vital security interests for the United States. The strategic goals of U.S. trade diplomacy in the region are in fact straightforward:

- To partake in the growth dividend of Asia-Pacific integration as a means of national strengthening, but also to reap the influence benefits that come from deepening links of shared prosperity with common view partners;

- To update and disseminate rules that shore up a liberal trading order that reflects not only our economic and security interests but also our values;

- To strengthen reforming elites who want to use international commitments to gain leverage in advancing economic reforms toward more open economies;

- To reassure allies and rivals that the United States is a multidimensional power, fully anchored to the region and capable of supplying novel institutions for regional cooperation; and

- To develop a smart strategy vis-à-vis China's regional and global leadership bid by using trade policy in proactive ways (covering governance gaps) and inclusive ways (contemplating a future Chinese accession).

The United States can meet these goals through the TPP, but if it scuttles the trade deal there is *no other* diplomatic instrument that can advance these vital security interests in one fell swoop. If clout is defined by the existence of alternatives, the United States will be at a disadvantage. Both our partners and competitors have a Plan B if the TPP never materializes. This plan is not a lofty blueprint for a distant future. It is ongoing trade negotiations to establish a 16-nation East Asian trade grouping: the Regional Comprehensive Economic Partnership (RCEP) led by China.

It should be recalled that the United States joined the TPP negotiations to avoid being marginalized from the process of Asian regionalism, as countries there drafted plans for trade integration that did not include us. Now, we seem poised to deliver that precise outcome ourselves. The security challenge is not that China is flexing its muscle to establish an alternative trading regime, it is that we are handing China the leadership baton. To look at it another way, think about the reach and meaning of RCEP in alternative scenarios where the TPP is enacted or not. In the former, RCEP is a conventional trade agreement that is thin on rules and shields only the most sensitive sectors; in the latter, RCEP becomes the regional standard of economic integration and elevates China as the focal point of economic diplomacy—with a novel institutional portfolio to cover a wide array of policy arenas from trade to infrastructure finance. The intervening variable is vanishing U.S. leadership.

Governance

One of the least understood aspects in the public debate on trade policy is why trade negotiations are no longer solely or even principally about tariff elimination, but about rules on policy arenas behind the border. The nature of trade negotiations has been transformed by the reorganization of international production activities and the consequent change in patterns of foreign trade. Traditionally, trade was driven by the exchange of finished goods, but the dissemination of global value chains (where production is fragmented and dispersed across national boundaries) means that the exchange of components, machinery, and services represents more than two-thirds of the value of international trade. Two main policy implications should be readily apparent. One, imports are ever more essential to sustain export activities, making protectionism costlier. And two, leveraging the growth potential of the global value chain calls for international trade disciplines that match the reality of international trade operations. But we have yet to codify them at the multilateral level, given the dysfunction of the World Trade Organization.

Trade negotiations have become infinitely more complex and challenging. To the traditional concern with market access (which remains a central objective), we need to add the new market presence agenda. In other words, deep integration disciplines provide commitments on the liberalization and protection of foreign direct investment, on the internationalization of services and free cross-border data movements, on the protection of intellectual property, and on competition policy and rule of law that facilitate the operation of the global factory.[10] The TPP aims to close this governance gap. It places a different kind of bet: that by shifting the locus of negotiation to a cluster of countries willing to undertake far-reaching liberalization and to codify novel trade and investment rules, the momentum for trade liberalization can be sustained. This bet could not be more timely, given the marked slowdown in international trade growth in the years after the global financial crisis.

Trade policy is vitally connected to core national interests of enhancing economic competitiveness, anchoring our leadership role in Asia, and renewing a liberal economic order. But our leadership on trade is predicated on a much-needed domestic transformation—one that puts front and center a better distribution of economic opportunity.

CULTIVATING THE POLITICS OF OPENNESS

With the above context in mind, what can be done to recreate a domestic consensus on the benefits of international trade that will pave the way for trade agreements, such as the TPP, that advance our national interests and have a positive influence on jobs and wages?

Make the Case for Trade Differently, and Act Accordingly
The case for trade has been made by focusing on the potential gains of more open competition while downplaying the concurrent fears, whether because the adjustment costs are deemed relatively small or because the United States will have assistance programs for trade-impacted workers. But these arguments do not resonate in a context of marked increases in income inequality or with still-fresh memories of significant job losses when the economy was battered by the global financial crisis. A more compelling case will build from the insight that people who have not benefitted from economic change will naturally oppose it. It will make the case for liberalization with a laser focus on the issue that the public cares most about: jobs. This means making a U-turn from the classic economists' position: that jobs are a side issue in assessing the merits of trade because the economy will return to full employment in the long run, and that the gains from trade are supple enough to compensate losers.

It is possible to focus on jobs and make a robust case for trade, to underscore that we have a more fundamental problem at hand with the growing skills deficit in the workforce that cannot be solved by blaming liberalization, and to grasp that a protectionist turn will not bring old-economy jobs back but will kill both today's and tomorrow's jobs. By looking at the jobs figures, we can:

- Put the impact of trade on jobs in perspective: the mammoth size of the U.S. labor market (121 million full-time jobs in 2015) and its active churning (5.2 million hires and 4.9 million separations in a *single* month—July 2016);[11]

- Understand the much larger impact that technological change has had on the loss of manufacturing jobs in the course of a decade compared to trade with China: 4.815 million vs. 985,000, respectively;

- Realize the value of export activity to working Americans: 11.6 million jobs in the export sector in 2014 (951,000 jobs in exports to China);

- Grasp the job casualties of protectionism: 4.8 million jobs in 2019 in a full trade war scenario;[12] and

- Realize the enormous wasted opportunities of a growing skill mismatch and labor market rigidities: 5.9 million unfilled job openings in July 2016.

Transform U.S. Labor Markets from Flexibility to Mobility

Just as rehashing our arguments on the gains from trade will accomplish little, so will doubling down on existing Trade Adjustment Assistance programs. Currently, these programs cover only a section of American workers, have not effectively tackled the problem of wage erosion, have come short in providing effective training, and cannot tend to the larger needs of skill acquisition for the American workforce. Instead, we need a comprehensive and proadjustment safety net that allows all displaced workers to navigate difficult economic transitions brought about by technological change, trade liberalization, and/or macroeconomic shocks. Job dislocation imposes a heavy toll on affected workers. The challenge for laid-off workers in finding new employment at a comparable wage is steep, and it may compromise their lifelong earnings potential. A skill mismatch may also prevent the redundant workers from transitioning to new economic sectors with growth potential. Furthermore, job competition among redundant workers will be particularly steep during recessions, triggering high unemployment rates, mass layoffs in a specific industry, and in situations where limited geographical mobility hinders relocation from depressed communities, dire employment prospects.

American labor markets are well known for their flexibility in firing and hiring workers, but this trait alone is not sufficient to generate smooth adjustment. Policies that target labor mobility are required to enable workers to relocate geographically and to enter new occupations and fields. The foundation of this mobility will be skill acquisition and upgrading. A relaunched safety net must embrace and invest in active labor market policies that increase the employability of workers through training, job-search assistance, direct job creation, and employment incentives. Concrete initiatives include:

- An expansion of the Earned Income Tax Credit for lower-income workers by loosening eligibility criteria;

- An extension of the wage insurance program to cover all workers (not just people over 50 enrolled in Trade Adjustment Assistance programs), since this income supplement tackles the pervasive problem of wage erosion;

- Dedicated community college funding to allow individuals to acquire or retool their skills to become more employable;

- An increase in the number of apprenticeships that provide company training and a potential path to future employment; and

- Job opportunities in rebuilding our deteriorating infrastructure, for workers who are unlikely to shift occupations through new skills.

A secure middle class and investments in human capital are essential to the renewal of U.S. internationalism and our leadership in trade. Succumbing to protectionism will leave workers' needs unattended and make us all worse off.

ACKNOWLEDGMENTS: I greatly benefited from comments on an earlier draft from my Brookings colleagues David Dollar, Kenneth Lieberthal, Joshua Meltzer, and Michael O'Hanlon. This policy brief also appeared in the Brookings Order from Chaos, Asia Working Group paper series.

Notes

1. World Economic Forum, "The Case for Trade and Competitiveness," September 2015, www3.weforum.org/docs/WEF_GAC_Competitiveness_2105.pdf.

2. Pablo D. Fajgelbaum and Amit K. Khandelwal, "Measuring the Unequal Gains from Trade," *Quarterly Journal of Economics* 131, no. 3 (2016): 1113–80, doi: 10.1093/qje/qjw013.

3. "Employment and Trade," International Trade Administration, Department of Commerce, last modified September 22, 2016, www.trade.gov/mas/ian/employment/.

4. David H. Autor, David Dorn, and Gordon H. Hanson, "The China Shock: Learning from Labor Market Adjustment to Large Changes in Trade," Working Paper 21906 (Cambridge, Mass.: National Bureau of Economic Research, January 2016), www.nber.org/papers/w21906.

5. Not every economist agrees that imports from China have had such ravaging effects on U.S. manufacturing jobs. Martin Baily and Barry Bosworth note that structural changes in the U.S. economy resulted in a contraction of the share of manufacturing employment over the span of decades. This long-term trend combined in the 2000s with sluggish job creation to produce an absolute decline in factory jobs. See Martin Baily and Barry Bosworth, "U.S. Manufacturing: Understanding its Past and Potential Future," *Journal of Economic Perspectives* 28, no. 1 (Winter 2014): 3–26.

6. See chapter 12 by David Dollar in this volume.

7. This figure comes from a study by the Center for Business and Economic Research at Ball State University, cited in Douglas A. Irwin, "The Truth about Trade: What Critics Get Wrong about the Global Economy," *Foreign Affairs* 95, no. 4 (2016): 84–95.

8. Marcus Noland and others, "Assessing Trade Agendas in the U.S. Presidential Campaign," PIIE Briefing 16-6 (Washington, D.C.: Peterson Institute for International Economics, 2016), https://piie.com/publications/piie-briefings/assessing-trade-agendas-us-presidential-campaign.

9. U.S. International Trade Commission, "Trans-Pacific Partnership Agreement: Likely Impact on the U.S. Economy and Specific Industry Sectors," Pub. No. 4607, May 2016, www.usitc.gov/publications/332/pub4607.pdf; and Peter Petri and Michael Plummer, "Economic Effects of the Trans-Pacific Partnership: Distributional Impact," Vox (Centre for Economic Policy Research's Policy Portal), April 30, 2016, http://voxeu.org/article/economics-tpp-winners-and-losers.

10. Richard Baldwin, "21st Century Regionalism: Filling the Gap between 21st Century Trade and 20th Century Trade," CEPR Policy Insight No. 56 (London: Centre for Economic Policy Research, 2011), http://cepr.org/active/publications/policy_insights/viewpi.php?pino=56.

11. Figures for the first and last bullet points come from the U.S. Bureau of Labor Statistics.

12. Noland and others, "Assessing Trade Agendas in the U.S. Presidential Campaign."

14

Maximizing the Local Economic Impact of Federal R&D

SCOTT ANDES

SUMMARY: Federally funded research and development (R&D) is a hallmark of the U.S. economy. Two-thirds of the most influential technologies of the past 50 years were supported by federal R&D at national laboratories and universities.[1] Smartphones, autonomous vehicles, personalized medicine, and other transformational innovations owe key technical components to public R&D. Moreover, this federal commitment does more than produce new products. By fostering innovation, it translates into productivity growth, the most important mechanism for ensuring economic growth and broadly shared prosperity. Most federal R&D does not happen in Washington, but these investments "come to ground" in communities across the country, and these regions should share in the economic benefits of research. To maximize and make apparent the economic returns from R&D, the Trump administration should seek to improve the local economic impact of federal R&D.

In the United States and around the world, scientific and R&D-intensive firms situate themselves in proximity to universities and national laboratories to enjoy myriad "ecosystem" benefits. Local economic clusters, often anchored by cities and urbanized research parks, emerge to concentrate knowledge flows, specialized workers, and supply chains in a way that encourages innovation and leads to higher productivity.[2]

The next administration should direct the largest federal R&D funding agencies—the Department of Defense (DOD), the Department of Health and Human Services (DHHS), and the Department of Energy (DOE)—to adopt policies to better support local economic development. Not only do these departments represent the majority of federal investments in R&D, but they also have unique investment vehicles that can be leveraged by cities at different points in the development process and through different mechanisms.

DOD, through its own efforts and those that flow from partnerships and procurement, consumes technology to meet its mission objectives. No other federal agency has such a quasifiduciary relationship with the commercial outcomes of its own R&D funding, and DOD can better solve battlefield challenges by taking greater advantage of regional clusters of knowledge flows, specialized workers, and dense supply chains. In contrast to DOD, DHHS invests almost all its R&D funds externally through competitive grants distributed around the country. Its geographically diverse portfolio is ideally suited for blending regional economic development with its primary mission of improving health. DOE invests heavily in its 17 national laboratories around the country. Few are located in dense regional technology clusters and cities, but these labs could bring the frontiers of science to market more quickly by strategically locating and linking parts of their core competencies in the vicinity of large and small firms, venture capitalists, and other research institutions. In sum, each of these three agencies has unique potential to improve the economic return on investment of federal R&D by capitalizing on relationships with local economic clusters.

FOR DOD—A NETWORK OF APPLIED R&D FACILITIES

At over $70 billion invested annually, DOD is by far the largest funder of federal R&D. And because it invests in research that it will deploy throughout its own operations, DOD maintains strong private-sector relationships. According to its own accounting, between 2000 and 2014 DOD paid private companies that had licensing arrangements with its labs $3.4 billion for military technology; during the same period, companies that licensed technology from DOD labs generated $20 billion in sales outside of DOD.[3] In other words, companies pay to use technology generated by DOD and then develop products and services around the technological discovery to meet defense as well as market needs. This continuous cycle of development well positions the department's R&D to impact the broader economy in general and regional clusters in particular.

Although DOD has long-standing partnerships with the private sector to meet its mission, it can do more to increase the economic impact of R&D and technology procurement. First, procurements that flow from DOD R&D revolve around a few large defense contractors, leaving many regions without big defense contractors out of the game. Of the military sales resulting from DOD licenses, 58 percent were from large corporations because, according to a DOD study, "large defense contractors are the primary holders of munitions technologies developed in DOD laboratories."[4] But DOD has demands beyond munitions that include new technical competencies in software, material science, automation, batteries, medical devices, and robotics. For these, the department could look beyond its traditional suppliers.

To increase the breadth of R&D-based procurement, the next administration should create a network of applied defense R&D facilities around regional technology clusters. The network would be similar to the National Network for Manufacturing Innovation but with a greater number of smaller centers that are highly focused around the virtuous cycle of firms working with DOD labs and creating products and services that meet military needs. Given that DOD already operates dozens of laboratories across 22 states, in many cases existing labs could shift their research and commercialization strategies to better align with adjacent technology clusters. In other cities, the department would need to develop new assets.

DOD is already moving in this direction. For example, the Defense Innovation Unit Experimental (DIUx) seeks to create bridges between the Pentagon and the commercial technology sector. Currently, DIUx has locations in Silicon Valley, Boston, and Austin, Texas; last year it awarded 12 contracts worth $36.3 million.[5] While DIUx is a good start, its budget is paltry compared to the changing demands for new technologies within the military. DOD should invest $500 million to develop 50 similar centers in technology platforms across the country.

The new regional network for applied research labs could also serve as a testbed for new partnerships in new platform technologies such as genomics, material science, and next-generation energy, which are increasingly important to meet DOD mission priorities. Here again, DOD has pilot projects that are moving in the right direction. For example, the Naval

Surface Warfare Center has partnered with Ball State University in Indiana in its Military to Market program, which allows undergraduates in the university's entrepreneurial program to use military technologies to create new companies.[6] In Rhode Island, the Naval Undersea Warfare Center Newport established the country's first Center of Excellence in undersea technology at the University of Rhode Island.[7] Similarly, in New York the Griffiss Institute, a nonprofit business accelerator and training center, serves as an intermediary between the Air Force Research Laboratory and private companies, helping to develop research contracts, review patents, and perform commercial test agreements.[8] Under a network of urban applied research labs, these pilots could be scaled across the country.

FOR DHHS—REGIONAL CONSORTIA AND "ENTREPRENEURS IN RESIDENCE"

DHHS invests over $32 billion every year in research, the vast majority of which is conducted by and through the National Institutes of Health (NIH). The primary vehicle for NIH R&D is competitive grants: currently, more than 80 percent of NIH funding is awarded through 50,000 grants to more than 300,000 researchers at universities, medical schools, and other research institutions. NIH research dollars touch every state and almost every city, and so the agency is ideally situated to play an important role in improving the return on investment of federal R&D at the local level. Also, because the lion's share of investment comes from NIH's grants to research universities and medical schools, as opposed to being spent at its own labs, NIH is in a unique position to create incentives for commercialization across the U.S. university system. However, a number of constraints limit the local impact of NIH funding.

First, few research grants incentivize partnerships that lead to commercialization. While program project/center grants promote collaboration, research grants such as R01s (the most common NIH grant used to support specific research projects) could be structured to meet their scientific discovery mission while also supporting regional economies. Unlike many technology areas, in the life sciences there is often no clear line between basic science and product development, especially in cutting-edge areas such as gene therapy where lab discoveries can be directly relevant to drug developers. Connecting the dots between research and commercialization early will improve the economic impact of R&D locally, since life science companies, academic medical centers, and research universities often cluster near one another.

To improve the commercial impact of research grants, the next administration should support regional precompetitive consortia to address national health concerns. When applying for NIH grants, research institutions should be incentivized to coordinate with regional peers to solve national issues. Making the consortia precompetitive—uninvolved in patent development—will help to avoid intellectual property disputes and allow their efforts to dovetail more closely with the academic missions of NIH research grants. One way to further incentivize partnerships would be to give grant proposals extra weight if multiple technology transfer offices, private-sector actors, and others within a city are designated as principal investigators.

NIH already supports similar programs at the national level. To promote new drug discovery, the Accelerating Medicines Partnership brings together the NIH and 10 biotechnology companies and nonprofit research institutions to identify issues around compound collections. NIH could leverage its grant-awarding power to incentivize such partnerships locally. A number of precompetitive arrangements exist at the regional level, but these efforts are not consistently encouraged or rewarded by federal funders.

The second constraint limiting the impact of NIH funding is the fact that grants do not necessarily promote medical entrepreneurship. Universities and academic medical centers that receive NIH funding often follow the narrow and traditional path to commercializing research that revolves around patenting and licensing. In the "classic" model of technology transfer, researchers at universities and medical centers apply for NIH and other federal funds to pursue basic science and then patent their discoveries. The technology transfer office at the university or medical center then takes these patents and licenses their use to biotechnology and pharmaceutical firms for the development of products. This classic model can be an appropriate vehicle for commercialization, but it often lacks strong connections between firms and research organizations. For that matter, successfully scaling a life science startup requires social and capital networks, mentorship, public-private partnerships, and access to both scientific and managerial talent. Developing, recruiting, and coordinating these disparate pieces of the medical entrepreneurial ecosystem is difficult, but once achieved it can spur new economic clusters, firms, and employment.

To increase medical entrepreneurship, the next administration should establish an NIH entrepreneurs-in-residence program that locates entrepreneurs in medical technologies within NIH-funded research institutions or among NIH Small Business Innovation Research recipients. DHHS currently has an entrepreneurs-in-residence program, but its focus is on improving efficiency in the non-research areas of the department rather than creating startups around NIH grants. Creating a revolving door between national medical entrepreneurs (many of whom were once recipients of NIH funding) and local life science clusters would help disseminate best practices. The program could be structured based on DOE's i-Corp program, which places mentors at universities and national laboratories to help researchers build their own companies. As the largest federal R&D funder of U.S. universities and medical schools, NIH has enormous sway over medical discovery. Coupling its research grants with an entrepreneurship-in-residence program would help the agency cover the full commercialization spectrum.

FOR DOE—MICROLABS AND VOUCHERS

The primary DOE vehicle for the deployment of R&D is its system of 17 national labs, representing over $12 billion in federally funded R&D. The lab network constitutes much of the country's core technical capabilities in clean energy, weapons development, nuclear cleanup, new materials, and atomic energy. Few federal assets have the ability to influence technology-based economic growth as the DOE lab system (see figure 14.1).

Despite the economic opportunity of the lab system, two major factors have historically constrained DOE's ability to maximize the system's impact in cities: isolation and regulation.

On the issue of isolation, many of the national DOE laboratories are located in isolated regions of the country, far from urban technology clusters. The national lab system grew out of the nuclear weapons research of the Manhattan Project in World War II, and so safety and security justified the seclusion of many of the labs in highly isolated regions. But the labs also specialize in technologies such as lightweight materials, energy storage, and additive manufacturing, which are highly relevant to the private sector.

To connect remote labs with cities, the next administration should en-

FIGURE 14.1 LOCATION AND STEWARDING AGENCIES OF THE 17 DOE LABS

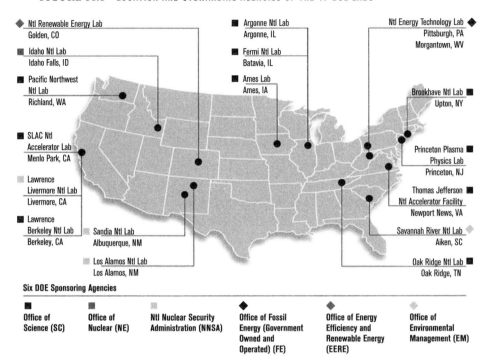

◆ Ntl Renewable Energy Lab
  Golden, CO

■ Idaho Ntl Lab
  Idaho Falls, ID

■ Pacific Northwest
  Ntl Lab
  Richland, WA

■ SLAC Ntl
  Accelerator Lab
  Menlo Park, CA

▒ Lawrence
  Livermore Ntl Lab
  Livermore, CA

■ Lawrence
  Berkeley Ntl Lab
  Berkeley, CA

▒ Sandia Ntl Lab
  Albuquerque, NM

▒ Los Alamos Ntl Lab
  Los Alamos, NM

■ Argonne Ntl Lab
  Argonne, IL

■ Fermi Ntl Lab
  Batavia, IL

■ Ames Lab
  Ames, IA

Ntl Energy Technology Lab ◆
  Pittsburgh, PA
  Morgantown, WV

Brookhave Ntl Lab ■
  Upton, NY

Princeton Plasma ■
  Physics Lab
  Princeton, NJ

Thomas Jefferson ■
  Ntl Accelerator Facility
  Newport News, VA

Savannah River Ntl Lab ◆
  Aiken, SC

Oak Ridge Ntl Lab ■
  Oak Ridge, TN

Six DOE Sponsoring Agencies

| ■ Office of Science (SC) | ■ Office of Nuclear (NE) | ▒ Ntl Nuclear Security Administration (NNSA) | ◆ Office of Fossil Energy (Government Owned and Operated) (FE) | ◆ Office of Energy Efficiency and Renewable Energy (EERE) | ◆ Office of Environmental Management (EM) |

Source: "Going Local: Connecting the National Labs to their Regions to Maximize Innovation and Growth" (Brookings, 2016).

courage labs to create off-campus "microlabs"—colocated within or near universities or private-sector clusters—that would cultivate key strategic alliances with regional innovation clusters.[9] Microlabs would help overcome the twin problems that most labs are located outside of major metropolitan areas and that most lab research occurs "behind the fence" of main campuses. Microlabs could take the form of additional joint research institutes or new facilities that allow access to lab expertise for untapped regional economic clusters. Accessible, off-campus lab space would also help labs engage with small and medium-size enterprises. Congress should legislate the creation of microlabs and require state buy-in, or state governments or regional consortia could create voucher programs in concert with DOE and particular labs.

Several national labs already operate external microlabs. Oak Ridge National Laboratory in Tennessee operates the Manufacturing Development Facility in Knoxville, away from its main campus. The facility has worked with over a hundred small and large companies to develop new manufacturing materials and new methods for 3D printing and energy storage. Oak Ridge is also in the early stages of opening an office in Chattanooga to work with local firms on smart grid technology.[10] In Chicago, Argonne National Laboratory and Fermilab are working with the University of Chicago to further the mission of the Polsky Center for Entrepreneurship and Innovation in its efforts to develop new research-based startups in the city.[11]

The second factor constraining national labs from having local impact is the rules that govern private-sector partnerships. It is extremely difficult for a small business that needs research or technical assistance to partner with a lab outside its geographic area. Just getting a contract with a lab to signature—a standard cooperative research and development agreement (CRADA)—takes on average 110 days, nearly half of which are spent negotiating terms and conditions (see figure 14.2). Small businesses grow based on attracting short- and moderate-term business contracts, and they generally do not have the cash reserves to wait five months to solve technical problems. Moreover, few small businesses have in-house legal departments to address the terms and conditions of signing a CRADA. Without greater access for these small companies, which generally operate in or near urban tech clusters, DOE labs will not be able to fully connect with cities.

To better connect small firms with DOE labs, the next administration should expand the Innovation Small Business Voucher Pilot to all DOE

FIGURE 14.2   NUMBER OF DAYS TO EXECUTE THE TYPICAL
NATIONAL LAB CONTRACT (CRADA)

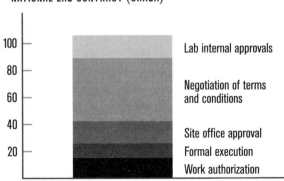

Source: U.S. Department of Energy, 2011.

labs. The pilot, created by DOE's Office of Energy Efficiency and Renewable Energy in 2015, has awarded $15 million to help small businesses access technical assistance at DOE labs.[12] Innovation vouchers are low-dollar grants that allow SMEs to purchase consulting services from labs. Because no financial exchange occurs, the time spent on terms and contracts is far less than for traditional user agreements and the benefits flow directly to the small business. Currently, five DOE labs participate in the pilot, but the voucher should receive significantly more funding and be expanded across the lab system.

In addition to expanding the Small Business Voucher Pilot, the next administration should support state government efforts to work with national labs to fund their own programs. Three national labs currently run innovation voucher programs with their state governments, including Oak Ridge's RevV! program with Tennessee and Los Alamos and Sandia National Lab's partnership with New Mexico on the New Mexico Small Business Assistance program.[13] By increasing programming and locations of the national labs through microlabs and by better connecting with small firms through innovation vouchers, DOE can go a long way toward linking its vast technological capabilities to regions' urban technology clusters.

CONCLUSION

The departments of Defense, Health and Human Services, and Energy have not only unique missions but also unique R&D portfolios, funding vehicles, and geographic footprints. For over 50 years, these strengths have propelled core American values around defense, health, and energy. Today, economic growth is lackluster, and federal R&D spending by these agencies could have a multiplier effect throughout local economies. The policies outlined in this brief and many others, if adopted by the Trump administration, will help bring federal R&D to ground and boost its impact on the entire U.S. economy.

Notes

1. Fred Block and Matthew Keller, "Where Do Innovations Come From? Transformations in U.S. National Innovation System, 1970–2006" (Washington, D.C.: Information Technology and Innovation Foundation, 2008).

2. See, for example, Mark Muro and Bruce Katz, "The New Cluster Moment: How Regional Innovation Clusters Can Foster the Next Economy" (Brookings, 2010). See also Stuart S. Rosenthal and William C. Strange, "Evidence on the Nature

and Sources of Agglomeration Economies," in *Handbook of Regional and Urban Economics*, vol. 4, edited by J. Vernon Henderson and Jacques-François Thisse (Amsterdam: North-Holland, 2004), 2119–71; Maryann P. Feldman and David B. Audretsch, "Innovation in Cities: Science-Based Diversity, Specialization, and Localized Competition," *European Economic Review* 43 (1999): 409–29; and Greg Tassey, "Competing in Advanced Manufacturing: The Need for Improving Growth Models and Policies," *Journal of Economic Perspectives* 28, no. 1 (2014): 27–48.

3. "National Economic Impacts from DOD License Agreements with U.S. Industry: 2000–2014" (Washington: Department of Defense, 2016).

4. Ibid.

5. Aaron Mehta, "DIUx Offers $36 million in FY2016 Contracts," *Defense News,* October 14, 2016.

6. Susannah Howieson and others, "Exemplar Practices for Department of Defense Technology Transfer" (Washington, D.C.: Institute for Defense Analyses, 2013).

7. "Naval Undersea Warfare Center Newport Establishes Center of Excellence in Undersea Technology with URI," University of Rhode Island, April 2007, https://today.uri.edu/news/naval-undersea-warfare-center-newport-establishes-center-of-excellence-in-undersea-technology-with-uri/.

8. Ibid.

9. For more information on microlabs, see Scott Andes, Mark Muro, and Matt Stepp, "Going Local: Connecting the National Labs to Their Regions to Maximize Innovation and Growth" (Brookings, 2014).

10. Mike Pare, "Oak Ridge National Laboratory Opening One-of-a-Kind Office in Chattanooga," *Times Free Press* (Chattanooga), October 20, 2016.

11. See "Polskey Center for Entrepreneurship and Innovation: Industry Partners & Investors," http://polsky.uchicago.edu/page/industry-partners-investors.

12. "The Small Business Voucher Pilot," U.S. Department of Energy, 2016, www.sbv.org/.

13. See "The New Mexico Small Business Assistance Program," www.nmsbaprogram.org/.

15

Why Cities and Metros Must Lead in Trump's America

BRUCE KATZ

SUMMARY: Donald Trump will assume the presidency at a time of enormous challenges for our country. But as all eyes focus on the president-elect, the actors most capable of confronting these challenges, and the ones best positioned to heal the divisions plaguing our country, are our cities and metropolitan areas. Cities and metropolitan areas are the engines of our economy and stand at the vanguard of our national progress. But they cannot do everything on their own. They need a reliable partner in Washington that upholds the core responsibilities of the federal government; empowers local communities to live up to their full potential; and helps leverage badly needed investments in innovation, infrastructure, and children and youth. Many of President-elect Trump's campaign positions stand in opposition to these principles and priorities. It remains to be seen whether he and the Republican Congress understand that for our nation to thrive, our metropolitan areas must succeed.

Over the past decade, American cities and metropolitan areas have firmly established themselves as the engines of the nation's economy and as the centers of technological innovation and global trade and investment.[1] Donald Trump's election and Republicans' continued control of the House and Senate put cities in uncharted territory.

Our country is facing a convergence of massive economic, demographic, and environmental challenges. The global economy becomes more competitive by the day while economic mobility at home remains stagnant. Our elderly population is growing while underserved minority groups represent a larger share of our nation. The effects of climate change disrupt the functioning of our society ever more frequently and dramatically.

These unprecedented challenges will not be overcome without an array of new investments. We must *spur innovation* through greater contributions to basic science and applied research, entrepreneurial startups, and business incubators and accelerators. We must *improve the standing of our middle- and lower-income populations*, not just through higher wages and more affordable housing but also through greater educational investments in specialized high schools, community colleges, and vocational training. We must *provide a strong platform for sustainable growth* through new transportation, energy, water, and other infrastructure. Yet even by conservative estimates, these investments will cost trillions of dollars over the next decade.[2] This "investment gap" should be at the forefront of policymakers' minds on both sides of the aisle.

Republicans' 2016 election victories at the federal and state level suggest that cities and metropolitan areas will be increasingly on their own in making these investments. In contrast to the partisan gridlock that characterized much of President Obama's time in office, Washington is now poised for a burst of conservative legislative and administrative activism not seen in decades. In a few areas, like infrastructure and defense spending, it is conceivable that greater federal investments will be forthcoming. But for the most part, the Trump era looks as if it will usher in a toxic mix of tax cuts, reductions in several types of entitlement spending, and policy shifts— like reducing our commitment to mitigating climate change—damaging to our long-term national interests. If this is the case, the responsibility for addressing major societal challenges will fall to local and metropolitan actors like never before.

THE NEW AMERICAN LOCALISM

As partisan gridlock paralyzed the federal government during President Obama's time in office, cities and metropolitan areas developed the capacity to take matters into their own hands. A New American Localism has emerged, filling the vacuum created by Washington's departure from normal functioning. Local cross-sector networks have joined together to become the vanguard of national problem solving and policy innovation. They are taking on issues as diverse and complex as economic competitiveness, social mobility, climate change mitigation, and immigrant integration.

Signs of this New Localism can be seen throughout the nation. Montgomery County, Maryland, and Sacramento and San Jose, California, are reducing income inequality by raising the minimum wage. Broward County in Florida, King County in Washington, and San Antonio, Texas, are generating hundreds of millions of dollars in local revenues to provide children with high-quality early education and other proven programs. In this election cycle, voters in Columbus, Ohio; Los Angeles; and Seattle approved $180 billion in additional taxes to spur ambitious transit expansions and more sustainable patterns of development. Private and civic investors in Indianapolis, Pittsburgh, and St. Louis are sharpening relationships between universities, companies, entrepreneurs, and business incubators, turning their cities into global centers of cutting-edge technology. These examples represent just a few of the places creating innovative solutions to our toughest problems. Every day brings new bottom-up approaches to improving the well-being of our communities.

The emergence of New Localism is particularly potent given the fact that our nation's 388 metropolitan areas house 84 percent of our population and generate 91 percent of our GDP. The top 100 metropolitan areas alone contain two-thirds of our population and generate three-quarters of our GDP.[3] The bottom line: as metropolitan areas succeed, so does the nation.

While the federal government must lead in many areas of national life—protecting the homeland, maintaining a strong military, providing a robust safety net for the elderly and disadvantaged, setting sensible immigration policies, ensuring civil rights, and investing in basic science—our federalist system is an exercise in shared power. In many of the matters most critical to our future prosperity and shared growth, Washington is a small player, providing, for example, only 12 and 25 cents of every public dollar spent on K-12 education and transportation infrastructure, respectively.[4] State and local actors play a much more important role in promoting the vitality of our businesses, the education of our children, the quality of our infrastructure, the vibrancy of our public spaces, and the skills of our workers.

By definition, localism manifests itself differently in every community across the nation. But the leading examples of the New American Localism share a number of common principles and characteristics. First, cities and metropolitan areas are addressing tough issues through the full collaborative power of their government, business, civic, philanthropic, university, and community networks. This contrasts with the old approach, which relied on public-sector solutions alone and focused on more traditional federalist relationships between levels of government (particularly the federal government and the states). Second, cities and metropolitan areas are forging their own responses to local problems that are holistic, multidisciplinary, and guided by community priorities. Spurring a local economy, improving outcomes for disconnected youth, or improving economic mobility requires comprehensive, tailored approaches to the specific circumstances at hand. This energetic response sharply contrasts with strategies employed in the past—taking on problems through siloed, narrowly defined, one-size-fits-all programs often administered by slow-moving, inflexible federal agencies.[5] Finally, cities and metropolitan areas are rethinking their approach to financing public activities by raising, pooling, and deploying capital from an array of local, national, and even global sources. They have recognized that rising mandatory spending at the federal level will inevitably push down spending on infrastructure, education, and other competitive levers, and that rising demand and population growth require greater investments and new forms of innovative finance.

Taken together, New Localism has demonstrated the power of metros to invest in solutions to our toughest problems, boost our economy, and generate quality jobs. It represents a striking contrast to the economic insecurity and fears about globalization that drove the 2016 election.

BRIDGING THE URBAN-RURAL DIVIDE

Economic dynamism aside, metropolitan areas are also the level at which our nation will bridge the chasm between cities and rural areas as well as racial and ethnic groups. The 2016 election showed that our country needs more than jobs and economic security. Overcoming the divides in our society cannot be achieved from our nation's capital.

Unlike politics at the national level, metropolitan areas unite geographies and disparate groups. They encompass central cities, suburbs, exurbs, and, due to sprawling development patterns, hundreds of rural communities. Fully half of the people living in rural areas are actually part of greater metropolitan regions.[6] All within a specific metro area are bound together by shared labor and housing markets. They are stuck in the same traffic jams, they root for the same sports teams, and they share an interest in improving their mutual quality of life.

Localism engages stakeholders across ideological and jurisdictional lines. In communities like Denver and Minneapolis/St. Paul, Democrats and Republicans have learned to do at the metropolitan level what they seem incapable of doing at the national level: namely, recognizing common interests and compromising to get things done. It is not always easy and there are often loud, impassioned detractors. But local community networks, unlike ideologically rigid national parties, ultimately reward action and punish obstruction.

Particularly in this time of raw division, metropolitan communities need to perfect a new style of collaborative governance, one that works across jurisdictions and alongside businesses and civic institutions. Coming together as a nation is not solely dependent on the federal government getting its act together—cities and metros have enormous potential here that has yet to be realized.

WHAT DO METROPOLITAN AREAS NEED FROM THE TRUMP ADMINISTRATION?

Historically, presidential administrations have taken too narrow a view of "urban policy." In reality, issues as diverse as health care, immigration, research and development, and climate change are all "urban" in their impact. Our cities must be vigilant in articulating the ways that changes to these policies will affect their communities. As the Trump administration begins to develop its policy platform, cities and metropolitan areas need to insist that the federal government *lead where it must*.

Many of the disruptive forces affecting communities across the nation—global trade, wage stagnation, technological change, environmental tumult, and international migration—transcend parochial borders and require thoughtful policymaking at the federal level. The Trump administration must see its core job as acting with vision, direction, and purpose on the things that cities and metropolitan areas cannot do on their own.

Many of the president-elect's campaign positions on platform issues like health care, immigration, and climate change are deeply troubling. Repealing the Affordable Care Act would take away health care from millions of Americans and shift responsibility for emergency care back to local governments, likely swamping local budgets that are already under enormous stress.[7] Reversals of climate policy could remove valuable incentives for investments in renewable energy. Shifts in immigration policy could divide communities, remove badly needed workers from local businesses, and distract local leaders from the many more pressing issues at hand. Cities and metropolitan areas need to describe—with evidence, granularity, and vigor—the implications of changes to these policies. Then they need to engage in the legislative debate with a unified voice, raising practical and widespread concerns that cross the artificial boundaries of cities, counties, suburban municipalities, and rural towns.

Second, cities and metropolitan areas need to demand that the federal government *empower where it should*. Given the extent to which cities have improved their performance over the past decade or so, President-elect Trump has a unique opportunity to reform Washington's relationship with metropolitan areas. He should consider providing them with greater flexibility to adapt federal discretionary investments in transportation, housing, workforce development, education, and other areas to their specific needs and local priorities. The resources the federal government provides to local areas are heavily prescriptive and compartmentalized, reaching their intended communities through stovepiped funding mechanisms that often roll out incoherently. This approach is fundamentally out of sync with the way problems are actually solved at the local level. Our metropolitan areas should call for greater flexibility in exchange for greater accountability. Any change in the provision of federal resources should be based on the principle of making federal investments more effective, not reducing their size. With the same total quantity of resources but more flexibility in how resources are spent, locally designed approaches have the potential to be more effective than federally administered ones.

President Trump and Congress should consider emulating the "City Deals" and devolution agreement process under way in the United Kingdom, which has created a vehicle for British cities to gain greater discretion in how central government funds are used locally.[8] To qualify for a City Deal, British cities propose distinct plans for how centrally provided resources might be better allocated around a specific purpose. If they are able to make the central government "an offer it cannot refuse," they are granted the flexibility to carry out their strategy. Congress could authorize a similar process, providing the opportunity for metropolitan areas to "apply" for the ability to allocate federal discretionary resources to a specific social, economic, or environmental outcome. This contrasts with the current system, where cities are forced to find ways to fit many small federal grants with rigid determinations into a coherent local strategy. City Deals—perhaps more appropriately labeled "Community Deals" in the United States—could better align federal resources with local priorities, fully unleash the problem-solving creativity of local actors, and correct the notion that the dizzying array of small federal grant programs provided to local governments can somehow match the drastically varying needs and conditions on the ground. Community Deals could also provide a vehicle for greater cross-party collaboration, as it would incentivize negotiation between local coalitions (often led by Democrats) and the Trump administration.

Finally, cities and metropolitan areas should demand that the federal government help *leverage private and civic capital to the maximum extent possible*. As described above, our nation needs dramatically greater investments in a range of policy areas, and these funds cannot be provided exclusively by the public sector. President-elect Trump has, to date, recognized this new reality inconsistently. His still-evolving infrastructure agenda seeks to provide incentives to private investors to engage. But his tax proposals follow a more traditional Republican penchant for general cuts rather than ones designed to achieve specific leverage.

From a city and metropolitan perspective on infrastructure, several things are clear.

- The infrastructure deficit is very deep and differs from place to place. Reliance on tax incentives might favor certain revenue-raising investments (such as toll roads) rather than others (such as mass transit). Congress should allocate resources in a way that enables cities and metropolitan areas to set their own priorities in accordance with market conditions and local preferences.

- Several tax expenditure programs, like the Earned Income Tax Credit and the Child and Dependent Care Tax Credit, have proven successful and should be expanded as part of any tax reform package.

- Several tax incentive programs, like the Low-Income Housing Tax Credit and the New Markets Tax Credit, work quite well and should be not only preserved but expanded.

Cities and metropolitan areas should also present their own proposals. Why not, for example, offer tax incentives for investments in qualified companies that seek either to grow jobs in distressed areas or craft market solutions to challenges in these communities?

WHAT CAN METROPOLITAN AREAS DO TO FILL THE INVESTMENT GAP AND STRENGTHEN NEW LOCALISM?

Regardless of the Trump administration's policy and investment platform, cities and metropolitan areas will still need to *raise substantial capital on their own* to make meaningful and durable contributions to innovation, infrastructure, human capital, children, and quality places in their communities—in other words, the investments needed to fuel productive, inclusive, and sustainable growth. The financing strategies used by cities and metros are becoming increasingly sophisticated. A new field of "metropolitan finance" is emerging that needs to be captured, codified, and leveraged across the nation.

First, *new financial instruments and practices have the potential to channel private and civic capital toward a number of nontraditional activities*, like inclusivity and environmental sustainability. Much attention has been paid to impact investing and Pay for Success bonds, recently used in Salt Lake County to expand prekindergarten to economically disadvantaged children. New instruments are also springing up in other areas of policy. Green Bonds, for example, have emerged as a way to fund clean energy and energy-efficiency projects. Consensus is also building around treating large regeneration projects as a single asset class, lowering the barriers to investing in massive, economy-shaping projects like London's Kings Cross.

Second, *new intermediaries are emerging to bring disparate sectors of society together*, a process essential in improving access to capital, creating opportunity, and spurring economic growth. Connectors like the Cambridge Innovation Center in Massachusetts have matched startups to experts and seed funding. Hubs like Chicago's 1871 have paired large companies like United Airlines and State Farm with entrepreneurial firms and talent. Social innovators like LaunchCode in St. Louis have linked newly minted coders to good jobs in mature companies.

Finally, *new breeds of special-purpose public, quasi-public, and civic institutions are forming to unlock the value of underutilized public assets and finance a wide range of transformative projects*. HafenCity Hamburg

GmbH, a company owned by the City of Hamburg, is overseeing the largest inner-city regeneration effort in Europe through the redevelopment of former port and industrial sites. In Copenhagen, CPH City and Port Development, a company jointly owned by the municipal and national governments, is developing areas along the waterfront. And CORTEX in St. Louis and 22@ in Barcelona have governed the build-out of innovation districts in those two cities.

REALITY CHECK

As Washington springs back to life under one-party rule, the notion that the president and Congress run the country will no doubt take hold. But the reality is more complicated. Washington is large, but it is not in charge.

America's resiliency is strengthened by a division of responsibilities that empowers communities to come together in improving the lives of their residents. Over the next several years, the hard business of investing in the future and uniting the nation most likely will not be conducted in Washington. Rather, it will occur in our metropolitan regions, where leaders and residents in our cities, suburbs, exurbs, and rural areas will work together to find common ground and purpose. It remains to be seen if Republicans, now in control of our national institutions, will choose to strengthen or stymie this dynamic.

Notes

1. See Bruce Katz and Jennifer Bradley, *The Metropolitan Revolution: How Cities and Metros Are Fixing Our Broken Politics and Fragile Economy* (Brookings Institution Press, 2013); Bruce Katz and Julie Wagner, "The Rise of Innovation Districts: A New Geography of Innovation in America" (Brookings, 2014); and Mark Muro, Jonathan Rothwell, Scott Andes, Kenan Fikri, and Siddharth Kulkarni, "America's Advanced Industries: What They Are, Where They Are, and Why They Matter" (Brookings, 2015).

2. See Laura D'Andrea Tyson, "The US Growth Opportunity in Infrastructure," McKinsey, 2013, www.mckinsey.com/industries/capital-projects-and-infrastructure/our-insights/the-us-growth-opportunity-in-infrastructure; and Justin Hicks and Robert D. Atkinson, "Eroding Our Foundation: Sequestration, R&D, Innovation and U.S. Growth" (Information Technology and Innovation Foundation, 2012), www2.itif.org/2012-eroding-foundation.pdf.

3. Alan Berube and others, "The State of Metropolitan America: On the Front Lines of Demographic Transformation" (Brookings, 2010).

4. For K-12 education, see "School Funding," New America Foundation, www.

newamerica.org/education-policy/policy-explainers/early-ed-prek-12/school-funding/; for transportation infrastructure, see "Funding Challenges in Highway and Transit: A Federal-State-Local Analysis," Pew Charitable Trusts, February 24, 2015, www.pewtrusts.org/en/research-and-analysis/analysis/2015/02/24/fund ing-challenges-in-highway-and-transit-a-federal-state-local-analysis.

5. Alaina J. Harkness, Bruce Katz, and Ross Tilchin, "A New Federalist Arrangement for Disconnected Youth" (Brookings, 2016).

6. See "Metro Nation: How U.S. Metropolitan Areas Fuel American Prosperity" (Brookings, 2007), 35.

7. Matthew Buettgens and Jay Dev, "The ACA and America's Cities: Fewer Uninsured and More Federal Dollars" (Robert Wood Johnson Foundation, 2014), www.rwjf.org/content/dam/farm/reports/issue_briefs/2014/rwjf413999.

8. Bruce Katz, "Unleashing Metro Growth—What the U.K.'s City Growth Commission Can Teach the U.S." (Brookings, 2014).

16

Climate Change and the Next Administration

NATE HULTMAN

SUMMARY: As the world's second-largest emitter of greenhouse gases, the United States has an essential role in ensuring the world can deliver on the promises of the 2015 Paris Agreement. American action can be a powerful incentive for the rest of the world to stay on the necessary path toward the deep emissions cuts needed to stabilize the climate at lower-risk levels. By the same token, inaction could dilute the interest and dampen the engagement of other countries, not only on climate but also on other issues of value to the United States.

The incoming administration has sent generally negative but confused signals on climate and energy, ranging from President-elect Donald Trump's early assertion that he would cancel the Paris Agreement to his postelection comment that he is keeping an open mind about it.[1] While it is still too early to predict how the next administration will engage the issue, a few options for Trump's administration are as follows. The first, and least likely, option would be to pursue a continuation of the Obama administration's regulatory strategy; second would be the "open mind" strategy of continuing international engagement to ensure American interests are represented alongside those of China and the EU; third would be working with Congress on supporting budgetary priorities and developing new legislative approaches to drive down emissions. Actions could include a tax reform and carbon pricing strategy, new investments in forests and other land-sector activities, and continued support for energy research and development, job training (or retraining), and finance and development aid for sustainable infrastructure for the poorest countries.

Regardless of how he chooses to proceed, engagement by President-elect Trump over the next four years is important for three overarching reasons.

TIMEFRAME CLOSING

First, the window for action to keep a lid on climate change is closing fast. Climate change is complex, with impacts felt at the local and regional levels that are often removed in time and space from their root causes. But ultimately, the science is clear regarding the basic cause-and-effect relationship that links emissions of greenhouse gases (GHGs) to a kind of "loading of the dice" that leads to increased temperatures, heat waves, droughts, floods, and other hazards. The globally agreed upon goal of keeping warming to no more than two degrees Celsius (2°C) above preindustrial levels will be difficult to secure. For reference, the world is now at about one degree of warming above preindustrial levels, and despite some recent slowing in the rate of change, our global economy is still producing large amounts of GHGs annually. Keeping warming under 2°C will require a rapid, near-term effort over approximately the next 10 to 15 years if we are to reach a peak in annual global GHG emissions and thereafter start a rapid decline. Without intensive reductions in the near term, by 2050 U.S. emissions would likely need to decrease by about 80 percent from 2005 levels.

THE INTERNATIONAL POLICY FRAMEWORK

Second, the appropriate international policy framework is now established but must be made real through national actions and continued international engagement. The Paris Agreement solves a difficult problem: harnessing what is useful in international agreements—goal setting, facilitating transparency, and organizing a process for increasing ambition over time—to encourage substantive action at the national level. The solution depends on a division of effort whereby countries provide national targets based on their own internal assessments, and the international process can in turn reassure countries that the other major players are doing their fair share. This global process reflects American interests, so for the United

States to walk away from it would leave an extraordinary amount of potentially helpful action on the part of other countries on the table.

AFFORDABLE—AND SUPERIOR—CLEAN TECHNOLOGY

Third, clean technology costs are rapidly dropping and many are nearing, but not at, tipping points relative to legacy technologies. Many technologies, particularly those that are mass manufactured, become cheaper over time as more units are produced (think of computers and cell phones). Historically, clean technologies were at a market disadvantage for three reasons: (1) they were immature and therefore, as expected, more expensive; (2) the clean benefits of the technologies were not reflected in their market prices relative to legacy technologies; and (3) for some technologies, their capital structure was weighted toward more up-front investment relative to legacy technologies, which would often be cheaper up front and have higher long-term operating costs. Nonetheless, the costs of many clean technologies have dropped to levels that are competitive with and even lower than their legacy competitors. Since 2009, costs for solar and for energy-efficient LED lighting have dropped 70 percent and 90 percent, respectively. Wind technology saw costs drop by 40 percent. Rooftop solar is now nearing and in some places is cheaper than grid-connected pricing. Still, because the costs of dirtier technologies are still not captured in their prices, the United States will likely continue to overinvest in these dirty technologies.

SECURING ACTION IN FIVE KEY AREAS

Continued engagement over the next four years is both in our own interests as well as right for the global climate. Recently, the United States has pursued a policy of integrating domestic actions with international leadership to encourage broad, global participation on climate change. We are currently the world's second-largest emitter of GHGs, emitting roughly 5,800 million net tons of carbon dioxide (CO_2) equivalent (MtCO2e) per year. China is the biggest emitter, having surpassed the United States about 10 years ago, and is now emitting roughly 10,500 MtCO2e per year. Other big emitters include the EU, India, Russia, Indonesia, Brazil, and Japan. Because the United States currently only emits about 13 percent of global GHGs, it cannot solve the problem alone. At the same time, though, others will be reluctant to act without full U.S. engagement. The United States is the top emitter among developed countries and is looked to for leadership in both policy and new clean energy technologies. For these reasons, the United States has pursued a policy of addressing domestic emissions and setting ambitious domestic targets, seeking to provide global leadership on what is fundamentally a collective action challenge. With this in mind, the Trump administration should pursue a set of initiatives that would collectively ensure action around five key areas.

1. Develop Great Infrastructure as Green Infrastructure

We all know that Donald Trump wants to Make America Great—he has talked about infrastructure and has made a career out of building things. As the next administration looks to enhance and expand American infrastructure, from transportation to power and more, it can note that the most impressive, forward-looking, modern, and job-creating infrastructure is often efficient and sustainable. Perhaps Trump could tour China and look at their high-speed rail (and even regular electric rail) network or go see the world's biggest solar facility in Morocco. Trump is right that our infrastructure lags, but looking backward to the dirty and inefficient technologies of the 19th century would just make the United States look antiquated and uncompetitive.

2. Lead in Energy Innovation and Jobs

While the level of interest in the rest of the climate agenda remains uncertain at best, the incoming administration may continue to support new technologies that will enable the clean energy transition at lower costs and with better outcomes. The United States has an excellent system of higher education, national laboratories, and funding for science and technology research and strong capital markets as well as a risk culture that supports new ventures. Stimulating investment in new technologies requires a broad effort aimed at both bolstering basic research and development but also fostering private-sector innovation and creating stable and predictable markets for new technologies. In addition, the U.S. government promised to double its budget for clean energy research and development. It will also be important to take steps to ensure that workers in old industries like coal are not cast aside. Restructuring causes disruption to real lives and efforts should be undertaken to partner with universities and the private sector to ensure that those workers from old industries can find new uses for their skills.

3. Promote Regulatory Approaches that Make Sense

The U.S. national climate target submitted in advance of the Paris negotiations sets a goal of reducing emissions by 26 to 28 percent below 2005 levels by 2025. The core element of the Obama administration's strategy was to implement existing U.S. law, such as the Clean Air Act or Energy Policy Act, in diverse sectors. This has led to a number of regulatory rulemakings over the past seven years that have focused on both CO_2 and non-CO_2 reductions. While Trump has made much of his interest in cutting regulations, many of the elements of the overall climate action plan are relatively mundane and end up both improving overall health and saving taxpayers and ratepayers money through energy efficiency. In addition, many of the regulations have long since been finalized and the new technologies are already being deployed. For example, once updated refrigerator or air conditioner efficiency standards are in place and new technologies are on the shelf, political benefits to rolling them back are virtually nonexistent. As such, a number of the programs included in the Obama climate action plan may well stay in place.

To lower carbon dioxide emissions from the U.S. energy system, which is the biggest source of our country's emissions, the Obama administration finalized a few major rules that would have a big impact but have also been criticized by Trump. The Clean Power Plan (CPP) would accelerate the decarbonization of the U.S. electricity grid through increased use of renewables and natural gas.[2] But recent indications show that market forces are at least as great, if not a greater, than forces accelerating the transition.

Another lower profile set of rules governs fuel efficiency in vehicles and accounts for close to the same volume of emissions reductions by 2030 as the CPP. Last but not least are energy efficiency standards promulgated by the Department of Energy (21 new standards were set since 2013 alone). These collectively should reduce about 3,000 MtCO2e by 2030—nearly half of what either the CPP or the transportation efficiency standards are likely to deliver individually. In addition to regulations aimed at energy CO_2, several other policies are designed to tackle non-CO_2 gases such as methane or hydrofluorocarbons (HFCs). At the federal level, these have included actions through tax policy to support deployment of solar and

wind energy and initiation of voluntary measures and public-private partnerships in areas such as land use, agriculture, and forestry. These federal
initiatives coexist with a patchwork of policies at the state and even local
level to encourage deployment of clean technologies and, in some cases,
pricing of emissions (such as California's emissions trading system).

These many policies provide a strong foundation for the United States
to reach its domestic 2020 and 2025 emissions goals. Ten years ago, projections for the United States estimated that emissions would be about 20
percent above 2005 levels by 2020. It now looks likely that the United States
will be in the range of 17 percent *below* 2005 levels by 2020, which means
we should be able to reach the 2020 target established in 2009. Such actions are part of a sound overall strategy to ensure global cooperation on
the issue. However, reaching goals for 2025 and creating the conditions
to continue lowering emissions at roughly the same rate through 2030
and beyond constitute a multipart challenge for the Trump administration. The United States can continue to support an approach of reasonable regulations in areas that support energy efficiency, renewables, and
reduction in short-lived climate pollutants. In other words, drawing on
existing law and using robust regulatory processes to establish reasonably
cost-effective pathways for reducing emissions will be a savvy way forward
and will preserve America's aspiration to be a leader on climate as well as
on clean energy and sustainable infrastructure.

To this end, the Trump administration should impartially consider the
regulatory actions that have not yet been finalized, such as for existing
oil and gas methane sources. Second, the next administration should continue to pursue options for reducing emissions through voluntary means,
including via partnerships with affected industries, and through support
of city- and state-level initiatives. Third, while the regulatory approach is a
solid way to deliver reductions through 2025 and beyond, there is a strong
case to be made for setting a price on emissions, which can be a more efficient way of raising revenue than corporate or income taxes. Pricing can
happen via a carbon tax or a cap-and-trade system, but the key element,
as mentioned above, is to improve the visibility of the costs of dirty technologies in investment decisions. States have the power to initiate pricing,
and regulatory actions can establish a pricing system in certain circumstances. A vital first step toward this will be for Congress to establish a
pricing policy that would encourage faster deployment of clean technologies, above and beyond regulatory actions.

4. Establish a Viable Pathway to Midcentury Deep Decarbonization
Given the structure of the energy economy, achieving major cuts on the order of 80 percent by 2050 will require a few broad measures. They include steps to decarbonize electricity, undertake massive energy efficiency reforms, switch as much demand as possible to electricity, and bolster carbon sinks as much as possible. Getting there requires connecting what we know about the future constraints to existing investment decisions—particularly those that have long lifespans. While a car may be replaced a couple of times before 2050, most industrial plants, buildings, and electricity generators will at most be replaced once. Moreover, the United States cannot easily reach its goals without healthy and growing forests and other carbon sinks; a major commitment to invest in and expand forests could help significantly in the post-2030 period. Even in the absence of a strong commitment to near-term action, the next administration can ensure that there is sufficient modeling and analytical capacity to understand all aspects of our emissions trajectory, including assessing potential land-sector sinks. We should in turn apply insights from this planning process to set medium-term policies and make the infrastructure investments needed to achieve deep decarbonization by midcentury.

5. Stay Engaged in the Paris Process
Because of the centrally important role of national targets and transparency embodied in the Paris Agreement, the United States should support countries in their efforts to reach their own ambitious targets. This can take the form of public-private partnerships for investment, facilitating improvement of national analytical capacity and techniques, and financing available through existing mechanisms (for example, bilateral partnerships, the World Bank, or the Green Climate Fund).

The United States should continue advocating for knowledge sharing, including by supporting and encouraging the international community to create a robust platform for transparency under the Paris Agreement. While not the only, or the most important, reason for continued engagement, China does remain committed to continuing climate action and could leverage nonparticipation by the United States to further its own agenda. On November 17, Liu Zhenmin, China's representative at the Marrakech climate conference, noted widespread concerns about a U.S. retreat on climate change. He signaled that, with or without the United States, China intends to be a frontrunner on climate action, partnering with other nations on adaptation to rising climate risks, public-private partnership investments in sustainable infrastructure, and more. China would certainly intend to use nonparticipation by the United States in contrast to the rest of the world to show who is the greater superpower—in China's argument, funding climate resilience in other countries and undertaking serious retooling of its energy economy demonstrates that China is moving ahead while the United States is returning to the 19th century.

Finally, the administration can continue to drive forward with other approaches to reducing short-lived climate pollutants that have other benefits, such as HFCs through the Montreal Protocol, methane through the Global Methane Initiative, and black carbon through the Arctic Black Carbon Initiative, collaborate on kerosene wick lamp dependence reduction, and participate in initiatives on climate-smart agriculture to reduce methane and nitrous oxide emissions.

While other countries have already decided to continue climate action for their own reasons, the Trump administration can nevertheless support a global approach to addressing climate change and keeping warming to lower-risk levels. Laid out above are five areas for particular focus as well as steps that need to be activated over the next four years. But to deliver the level of change needed, we must transform the politics of climate action. Environmental policy has not always been a one-party issue, nor should it be. The Environmental Protection Agency was initiated under former president Richard Nixon and the Clean Air Act amendments of 1990 were ushered in under former president George H.W. Bush. Climate change affects the health and well-being of all Americans. Resilience and preparedness for natural hazards and extreme weather are concepts that all Americans can support. Affordable clean energy is a positive choice.

A recent study by the University of Maryland's Program for Public Consultation found that 71 percent of respondents nationwide either strongly or somewhat strongly approve of a 2 percent annual emissions reduction goal.[3] That approval rating included more than half of Republican respondents (52 percent). Broken out by state, the researchers found support among 66 percent of respondents in Ohio, 69 percent in Oklahoma, 70 percent in Texas, and 71 percent in Florida. Seen in light of polarized attitudes, these results may seem surprising, but given the nature of the issue, the Trump administration may find value in some initiatives that garner broad support, such as job retraining for many coal industry jobs that are almost certainly not coming back. Undoubtedly, stronger bipartisan engagement will be helpful for the long-term robustness of a long-term U.S. strategy to address climate change.

At present, the unknowns regarding how President-elect Donald Trump will address energy and climate greatly outweigh the knowns. Undoubtedly there will continue to be action at the international level, with or without the United States, and at the level of individual states and municipalities. The market forces pushing the U.S. energy mix away from coal and toward renewables and gas are not something that Trump can control. But Trump may find that supporting aspects of the international approach to climate change could provide diplomatic as well as economic dividends that clearly serve American interests. Indeed, it may soon emerge that opportunities for sustainable infrastructure and clean energy fit well into Trump's still-evolving vision for the future.

Notes

1. "Framework Convention on Climate Change," United Nations, http://unfccc .int/paris_agreement/items/9485.php.

2. "Clean Power Plan for Existing Power Plants," U.S. Environmental Protection Agency, www.epa.gov/cleanpowerplan/clean-power-plan-existing-power-plants.

3. Steven Kull, Clay Ramsay, Evan Lewis, and Antje Williams, *Considering the Costs of Clean: Americans on Energy, Air Quality and Climate*, Voice of the People and University of Maryland's Program for Public Consultation, May 2016, www.cissm.umd.edu/sites/default/files/Considering%20the%20Cost%20of%20 Clean%20-%20050416.pdf.

17

Energy and Climate:
Moving beyond Symbolism

DAVID G. VICTOR

SUMMARY: Energy touches virtually every aspect of public policy. For all the importance of energy topics—from job creation and the economy to national security to the threats of climate change—it is very hard for federal policy to have large impacts on the structure of the energy system, which evolves slowly in ways often dominated by exogenous changes in technology and economic conditions. With a unified Congress, it might be possible to craft a major new energy bill, but there are many competing agenda items, and the areas of greatest consensus will have marginal effects. This chapter argues that the best strategy on energy is to chip away at the margins, such as through changes in the tax code that encourage investment and regulatory reforms that encourage greater use of markets. It also argues that the central energy challenges today are less with raw production of energy—oil, gas, coal—than they have been in the past but more with how energy is transformed and used, notably through electric power networks. The chapter also argues that while it will be tempting to focus on campaign promises that include rolling back regulation and abandoning efforts to address climate change, such policy initiatives would, in most cases, deliver symbolic benefits at potentially large costs to American business interests and also make it harder for the United States to advance important foreign policy goals.

IMPROVING ENERGY INFRASTRUCTURE

Physically, the energy system of the United States—which is typical of an advanced economy—is divided roughly into thirds. One portion of primary energy goes into transportation, which is dominated by oil—a prized fuel because it is a liquid at most relevant temperatures, has high power density, and is relatively cheap. Those attributes are crucial for mobile transportation that must carry its own energy supply. A second portion (about two-fifths) is transformed into electric power before being consumed in the economy; in power, there are many different sources of primary energy that compete effectively. The rest is utilized in a variety of stationary sources, such as for heating homes and providing process heat in factories—uses that are dominated by natural gas because in North America natural gas is quite cheap, thanks to huge new supplies from shale gas. Figure 17.1 summarizes the picture.

The overall picture in figure 17.1 changes slowly because the sheer size of energy infrastructures—such as oil and gas pipelines, roads, and electric power networks—impedes change. A costly, interconnected capital stock creates lock-in effects that slow down the rate at which evolution is possible. Nearly all the grand challenges in energy policy require fundamen-

FIGURE 17.1   BREAKING DOWN U.S. PRIMARY ENERGY CONSUMPTION, 2015

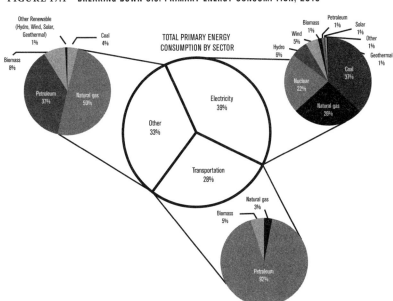

Source: Energy Information Administration, Monthly Energy Review, August 2015.

tal transformations in energy systems. Yet such transformations are slow and difficult to steer with policy. Historically, whole energy infrastructures need about 50 to 70 years for such transformations, although with active policies perhaps change could unfold faster in the future.[1]

Stopping climate change quickly—so that, for example, the United States and other nations can meet the bold goals they set in the Paris Agreement to stop warming at well below two degrees higher than preindustrial levels—would require transforming the energy system over about three decades, or twice the historical rate of turnover. Very few societies have ever done that, and pushing the energy system so quickly creates a high risk for economically and politically costly errors.

Over the last four decades—since the Arab oil embargo (1973–74)—the United States, like most other advanced economies, has made a huge shift toward the use of markets instead of direct regulation in governing the production and use of major fuels. Today there are global markets for oil; even though much oil still comes from dangerous and unreliable places in the world, global sourcing and efficient markets help make oil supplies more secure. A global market for gas is also emerging, and there is some global trade in coal. Within the country, all of these fuels trade in reasonably well-managed markets. The mission of creating efficient markets for primary fuels has been achieved.

Attention is now turning to how these fuels are transformed into useful services—in particular, electric power. Most studies suggest that the process of electrification of the economy—that is, the conversion of primary energy into electricity before it is used—will continue, especially if there are major efforts to cut pollution of all types. Even the area that has long been thought to be most difficult to electrify—transportation—is now seeing some inroads thanks to electric vehicles.

Because electricity is essentially impossible to move between continents, these markets are nearly always national and regional affairs. While the United States has three large grids, the interconnections within those grids are generally weak; thus, for practical purposes, the relevant size for U.S. power grids is even smaller and the role for state-level policy greater. This creates the central challenge for federal policy on electricity. The country overall stands to gain a lot from greater use of well-designed electric power systems, but the leverage available to the federal government is highly indirect. The Federal Energy Regulatory Commission (FERC) has jurisdiction over interstate power transmission and over markets broadly, but it cannot dictate many policies to the states.

INCORPORATING RENEWABLE ENERGY

A smart policy strategy around electricity must focus on places where the federal government has leverage. This administration should focus, in particular, on what is emerging as the central challenge for electric power: supporting growth in renewable energy while reconciling its inherent variability. There is a solid bipartisan consensus on the value of increasing use of renewable power—mainly solar and wind. That agreement across Republicans and Democrats is reflected, for example, in large, ongoing federal tax credits for renewable power as well as policies that actively require renewable power in 29 states.[2] Because new renewables get subsidies, advocates for other energy sources—such as hydropower, biomass, and, now, nuclear—are also seeking and obtaining subsidies. These many different subsidies are creating growing distortions in power markets—as evident, for example, in states such as Texas and Illinois where power markets with large amounts of subsidized supplies of wind power drive power prices negative at times. In such settings, base load power supplies—that is, gas, coal, and nuclear—cannot compete. This approach to power markets is unsustainable and is poised to have large, adverse, system-wide impacts such as the loss of large amounts of zero-emission nuclear power.

The new administration could usefully focus on three challenges for power grids laden with renewables. First is unwinding today's complicated and distortionary subsidy regime. There has been a compelling logic for subsidizing new energy sources—to promote innovation and commercialization—but for standard renewable power sources, those innovation goals have already been achieved. The opportunity to begin this unwinding will come with larger overhauls of tax and budget policies of the country. Subsidies for production of mature technologies should be scaled back while investment in fundamental pre-market innovation through research and development (R&D) should be scaled up. Compared with the size of the challenges the country faces in energy and the need for advanced technology to solve them, the United States massively underinvests—perhaps by a factor of two or three—in public sector R&D. While it is politically popular to bash examples of failures from past R&D

investments—failures that are intrinsic to any portfolio of investments in untested ideas and technologies—the reality is that the track record for energy-related R&D spending is generally excellent.

A second challenge—where R&D support as well as demonstration projects and market reforms could be pivotal—relates to integrating these renewable energy supplies into the grid. Parts of the United States are moving quickly to power grids that rely on large amounts of renewable power—California and New York have adopted laws to require 50 percent renewables by 2030, while Hawaii aims for 100 percent by 2045. A particularly high priority for the incoming president is to offer strategic guidance that can help states—starting with the states that are rapidly moving to renewables and soon other states as well—integrate renewables into the grid without undermining other goals, such as deep cuts in emissions and reliability. While this administration will disagree with these state governments on many topics, this is an area for useful common ground.

A third challenge relates to transmission infrastructure. Large integrated grids are usually better able to smooth out variations in pockets of supply and demand since those variations tend not to be correlated across large geographical areas. The incoming administration has signaled its interest in boosting investment in infrastructure. That effort, which seems to have focused mainly on roads and airports and other areas, should expand to include the power grid—and to building the elements of what could become a truly national grid system, such as exists in China. It should also engage with the need for massive investment in storage of power. So far, the federal government has played almost no role in the debate over storage, but the FERC should focus on potential needs for interstate storage projects that will need to integrate with bulk trade in renewable power. Grids that rely mainly on renewables will need multiday storage capabilities if electric power service is to be reliable.[3]

SECURING THE POWER GRID

In tandem with helping the nation make its power grids more capable of handling large amounts of renewable power, security of the grid will rise in importance. Much in modern society hinges on grid supply. After Superstorm Sandy hit the Northeast, for example, it proved extremely difficult to restore order and basic services in part because the failure of traffic lights had snarled the roadways.[4] Absent electric service, water and sewage services were shut down, public transport was largely unavailable, and electric gasoline pumps did not operate. The threats to the grid include nature and, perhaps increasingly, malicious attack. And the control systems on the grid may be vulnerable to cyberattack, as happened on parts of the Ukraine grid in late December 2015 through a skilled penetration that appeared to originate from Russian hackers.

The challenge for hardening the grid is not with small failures—such as those triggered by tornadoes or hurricanes or the errant foot of an unfortunate squirrel. Those happen regularly and the industry is extremely good at planning and responding to such knowable interruptions in service. Large-scale and long-duration outages are a different story because they are harder to predict and require a different form of preparedness. They require a more active program at the Department of Energy (DOE) to demonstrate technologies that can improve resilience to power loss. And they require the Department of Homeland Security (DHS) to lead a much more rigorous effort at regional planning for the impacts and recovery from long-duration grid failures.

These are the central, new challenges for the electricity supply and distribution system. The federal government must also stay abreast of many other issues related to energy supply and marketing. These include, for example, modernization of the management of the nation's strategic oil reserve—an anachronism left from an earlier era where government action had a larger impact on oil supply. Fuel economy standards for vehicles also need monitoring, but the Obama administration has already done extensive work in this area and the regime is in good shape for now. Some political forces will want to roll back those standards, but the automakers are already responding to existing rules, and little more of significance can be done in the next four years. Challenges include the economic impacts of energy production and utilization—including in sectors that are declining, notably coal. It is essentially impossible to rebuild the coal industry to its earlier status, but helping workers manage the transition to new jobs is important. The federal government will also be asked to help rethink the nuclear power industry, which is in the midst of a massive effort to make itself more competitive. Losing a large fraction of the existing U.S. nuclear fleet could be extremely harmful, not least to the nation's efforts to control emissions and provide diversity in power supply. In some areas, new legislation could help—such as efforts to adopt a rational long-term strategy for interim and then final storage of the spent nuclear fuel that is accumulating at the nation's reactor sites. Regulatory streamlining could also help. But most of the needed actions are within the industry, with the power markets, and at the state level—such as in Illinois and New York where state legislatures are being asked to help financially ailing local plants.

ENVIRONMENTAL REGULATION AND CLIMATE CHANGE

It will be tempting for Republicans, who have unified control of the presidency and Congress, to use this power to roll back many Obama-era and earlier environmental regulations, including national as well as international policies on climate change. That effort would be a mistake, but if it proves necessary politically, then it should be organized in a way that minimizes harm to U.S. foreign policy and business interests.

On environmental regulation generally, the period since the election has seen many plans for rolling back Obama-era rules. Caution is needed: many of those rules are already far along in implementation and rollbacks will create regulatory turmoil that is harmful to business investment. Rules on methane emissions from fracking, for example, are already being implemented in important producing states (indeed, those state rules were the model for the federal rules), and industry already knows it must manage these emissions. The Clean Power Plan offers a similar context where too much regulatory gyration would actually harm the interests the new administration says it wants to advance.

On climate, temptations to roll back the Paris Agreement are many. But it is important to take a sober look at how this agreement actually reflects and advances American interests. The United States played a central role in creating the Paris Agreement and making it much more flexible than the approach favored by the European Union and other important actors. Notably, the United States and China worked bilaterally to set the tone for the Paris talks and continue to cooperate on energy research and related topics.[5] Even as the United States and China face difficulties in their relationship elsewhere, this bilateral cooperation remains possibly the most effective example of what they can do together. The architecture of the Paris Agreement—which relies on countries to set their own commitments flexibly through a "bottom-up" process—largely mirrors U.S. and Chinese interests.[6] The United States has also developed a similar bilateral cooperation on climate and energy with India, although that process is less advanced. The United States has a strong interest in continuing to shape this process.

If the new administration aims to withdraw from United Nations co-operation on climate change, it should do it in a way that minimizes the inevitable harm to the U.S. reputation and foreign policy strategy. One model is that of the George W. Bush administration, which refused to ratify the Kyoto Protocol (and earned international scorn) but then slowly built up parallel efforts with a smaller number of countries, mainly in Asia. One area of immediate importance is to work with countries to review national policies to learn what is actually working (and at what cost). Such a review mechanism is envisioned under the Paris Agreement, and a constructive role for the new administration would be to participate with important countries—including China and India—in demonstrating how these systems work, just as the country has done bilaterally with China under the Group of Twenty (G-20), where countries self-volunteered for reviews of their national efforts to cut energy subsidies.[7] If the United States withdraws from the Paris process—either legally or de facto—then it should expect that other countries, notably China, will fill the vacuum in ways that could harm U.S. interests. Formal legal withdrawal from Paris would be the worst of many options—a softer withdrawal and shift in focus to other forums would be much more constructive.

CONCLUSIONS AND PREDICTIONS

The central challenges in energy policy have radically changed since the oil crises of the 1970s. As oil problems have waned, much more energy attention has shifted to electricity.

Making the federal government relevant to the process of electrification requires a strategy and a focus. Here, I've suggested three: making markets work, making infrastructure secure, and tackling climate change. Within each are some high-priority items—such as funding for R&D—and nearly all of the priority items will require that Congress and the administration work together to change laws and appropriate funds.

The most likely prediction for energy policy in the upcoming administration is that much of the real policy action will reside within the states. At the federal level, many of the most visible initiatives and disputes will likely be about symbolic policies—areas where policy action is relatively easy to organize and where decisions pretend to offer serious solutions to hard problems. There will be initiatives to promote renewables but persistent failures to build the grids and markets needed to integrate them reliably.

When the politics of serious energy policy become impossible to manage, then a torrent of symbolic actions fills the space. The biggest challenge for the next administration may be to manage the symbolic moves needed to placate organized interest groups while guiding the federal government toward a more rational and strategic approach.

ACKNOWLEDGMENTS: A special thanks to Tim Boersma, Charley Ebinger, Bruce Jones, Mark Muro, Michael O'Hanlon, Ric Redman, Janet Walker, and Philip Wallach for comments on a draft and to Jen Potvin for research assistance.

Notes

1. Bill Gates, "A Rational Look at Energy," *GatesNotes* (blog), October 13, 2010, www.gatesnotes.com/Books/A-Rational-Look-at-Energy-Energy-Myths-and-Realities; Kingsmill Bond, "The New Energy Transition: History Is Bunk," Trusted Sources, September 5, 2016, www.trustedsources.co.uk/new-energy/energy-demand/the-new-energy-transition-history-is-bun.

2. "State Renewable Portfolio Standards and Goals," National Conference of State Legislators, July 27, 2016, www.ncsl.org/research/energy/renewable-portfolio-standards.aspx.

3. Bryan Pivovar, "H2 at Scale: Deeply Decarbonizing Our Energy System," National Renewable Energy Laboratory, April 4, 2016, www.nrel.gov/docs/fy16o sti/66246.pdf; *Renewable Electricity Generation and Storage Technologies*, vol. 2, report NREL/TP-6A20-52409-2 (National Renewable Energy Laboratory, June 2012), www.nrel.gov/docs/fy12osti/52409-2.pdf.

4. Stephen Lacey, "Resiliency: How Superstorm Sandy Changed America's Grid," Green Tech Media, June 10, 2014, www.greentechmedia.com/articles/featured/resiliency-how-superstorm-sandy-changed-americas-grid.

5. David G. Victor, "The US-China Climate Deal Is a Model for World Diplomacy: Too Small to Fail," *The Guardian*, November 13, 2014, www.theguardian.com/commentisfree/2014/nov/13/us-china-climate-deal-diplomacy-paris.

6. David Victor, "Why Paris Worked: A Different Approach to Climate Diplomacy," *Yale Environment 360*, December 15, 2015, http://e360.yale.edu/feature/why_paris_worked_a_different_approach_to_climate_diplomacy/2940/.

7. *The United States' Efforts to Phase Out and Rationalise Its Inefficient Fossil-Fuel Subsidies*, G-20, September 5, 2016 (www.g20.org/English/Documents/Current/201609/P020160919418466525465.pdf); *China's Efforts to Phase Out and Rationalise Its Inefficient Fossil-Fuel Subsidies*, G-20, September 5, 2016, www.g20.org/English/Documents/Current/201609/P020160919413193754828.pdf.

18

Creating Opportunity for the Forgotten Americans

ISABEL SAWHILL

SUMMARY: The 2016 election revealed that there are a lot of "forgotten Americans" who have been hurt by trade, technology, and deindustrialization, and who voted for a change. With a unified government, we now have an opportunity to address this problem. We need to strengthen families, rethink education, and create more good jobs. This chapter contains a number of ideas for how these goals might be accomplished. One such idea is to empower young people to only have children when they want them. Another idea is to provide more career and technical education and to use charter schools as a source of innovation. A third idea is to lower taxes on repatriated corporate earnings and use the proceeds to fund a new infrastructure program that would simultaneously make America's public facilities great again and put people back to work. What we must not do is balloon the deficit or shred an already thin safety net in the process.

The 2016 election was a revolution. Americans voted for change, perhaps big changes, and the new president has promised to deliver, to make America great again. At issue is what kind of change we will have and whether it will satisfy the voters and remain consistent with our basic values of tolerance, inclusion, and respect for civil liberties.

One thing is certain. The era of gridlock is over. The ability to achieve big changes is now possible. It is no longer constrained by divided government. Republicans are firmly in charge in every branch and at every level of government. That could translate into an opportunity to achieve great things. It could also further fragment the country and make many people worse off. The path chosen matters—hugely.

This chapter provides a set of ideas that could turn this new era into one in which real progress is achieved for those who have been left behind—those who our new president calls the forgotten Americans. For too long, we have failed as a nation to expand opportunities for Americans of modest means. This chapter is focused on three key determinants of upward mobility: strong families; a better education and training system; and, most critically, jobs that provide an upward ramp into the middle class for low-income and working-class families.

How do we do that? There have long been three "norms" in American life: get an education, work to support your family, and be a good parent. In our research at Brookings, we have shown that if you graduate from high school, live in a family with at least one full-time worker, and wait to have children until you are married or at least are in a committed partnership with another adult, your chances of being poor drop to about 2 percent and your chance of joining the middle class climbs to over 70 percent.[1] (See figure 18.1.) We call this the *success sequence*.

What the country now needs is a new set of policies that give people a fair chance to succeed in their roles as parents, as students, and as workers in a 21st-century economy. These policies should be designed to reward, not punish, individual initiative and responsibility. But they must also recognize the web of disadvantages and changes in the economy that have made following the success sequence difficult for many Americans. There are no silver bullets. Government cannot do this alone. But government has a role to play along with civic and religious institutions dedicated to making the country whole again.

MARRIAGE OR A STABLE RELATIONSHIP BEFORE CHILDREN: IT IS ACHIEVABLE

The first prerequisite to forging an opportunity society is establishing stable families. Too many young adults are having children before they have formed enduring ties with another adult and too many are parenting children with more than one partner. Increasingly, it takes two paychecks to join the middle class; those who have children too soon and without a committed partner frequently end up not just with less education and job

FIGURE 18.1   PERCENT OF EACH NORM-GROUP IN POVERTY

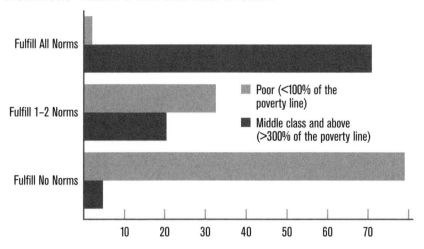

Source: Author's tabulations of March 2013 CPS.

Note: Statistics refer to calendar year 2012, since survey respondents are asked about income in the previous calendar year; data include only families with heads aged 25–64 who do not report receiving disability payments.

experience, but also without sufficient means to support a child on their own.[2] They end up experiencing less social mobility and more poverty as a result;[3] their children have poorer outcomes as well;[4] and they are often dependent on government assistance.

Most children now being born to unmarried women under the age of 30 are unplanned.[5] These women tell us that they either did not want a baby or did not want one (or another one) so soon.[6] If we could empower young adults to only have children when they themselves feel ready to become parents, we could reduce unplanned pregnancies and out-of-wedlock births. That alone would reduce poverty and lack of mobility. It would greatly improve the life chances of the children themselves.[7]

The solutions here are often nongovernmental and involve changing social norms around the importance of responsible, two-person parenthood. Nonprofit and faith-based organizations have a role to play. Some have called for a new generation of government-sponsored marriage programs and for reducing marriage penalties in tax and benefit programs. But these do not appear to be a cost-effective way to bring back the two-parent family. More promising are efforts to make the most effective forms of birth control (IUDs and implants) more widely available at no cost to women. IUDs and implants provide a virtually foolproof way for couples to delay parenthood until they are committed to each other for the long term and feel ready to be parents.[8] Efforts to provide women with good counseling and no-cost birth control in Colorado and a few other places have been highly successful and could be encouraged on a wider scale. A recent report from the consulting firm Bridgespan details the kinds of investments that are needed and recommends this approach not only as highly cost effective but also as one of the six "best bets" for improving opportunity in America.[9]

The Affordable Care Act addressed one of the barriers to responsible parenthood: the high cost of the most effective forms of contraception. If it is repealed and replaced, this cost issue needs to be addressed. Otherwise, we will have not just more poverty and less opportunity, but also higher government costs for Medicaid and other safety net programs and much higher rates of abortion.

EDUCATION: TIME FOR INNOVATION

High school graduation rates for the country as a whole have improved in recent years and are now over 80 percent.[10] In the urban districts of the nation's 50 largest metropolitan areas, however, only 59 percent of students who started high school in 2005 graduated four years later.[11] We can do better. For example, Mayor Bloomberg's Small High Schools of Choice in New York City[12] and a nationwide school model called Career Academies[13] have both proven remarkably successful.

In addition to scaling up successful programs, we need more innovation via charter schools or school choice. Not all charters have been successful, but the best ones have shown that it is possible to help all children achieve and to close racial and socioeconomic gaps.

Reform of K-12 schools is critical, but some postsecondary education is increasingly vital in today's economy. There are two pressing needs here. The first is more emphasis on career and technical education linked to good jobs that can enable more people to take pride in their specific skills and to launch—or relaunch—successful careers. The second is more emphasis on merit or student performance (along with need) as one basis for financial aid. American students have fallen behind students in other countries not because they spend too little time in school but because they do not learn enough in the process.[14] In most northern European countries (whose high school students routinely outscore U.S. students on international assessments), college attendance is more heavily subsidized than in the United States, but it is also more conditional on a student's academic performance and college readiness. In a similar vein, student financial assistance in the United States could be based not just on need, but also on performance in school, creating an incentive for middle and high schools and their students to better prepare for both college and career.[15]

WORK IS ESSENTIAL

Of the three pillars of opportunity (family, education, work), work is by far the most important. It has often been said that a job is the best antipoverty program. I would add that a full employment economy is the best jobs program.[16] But it is not just the poor who have suffered from lack of work. The recent election has revealed considerable voter anger or concern about the disappearance of jobs due to trade, technology, and the deindustrialization of the economy. Working-age men, especially those without much education, have been dropping out of the labor force for decades.[17] One reason is because they no longer have the skills that employers expect. A second is because mass incarceration has marked many of them as unemployable in the eyes of employers. A third is because the jobs available to them are largely in retail, in health care, or in other services where wages are lower than what they have come to expect.

While these problems are all too real, it would be easy for a new administration and Congress to misread the situation. First, it is not trade as much as technology that has destroyed manufacturing jobs; those jobs are not coming back, almost regardless of what we do. Second, there are no quick or easy solutions. Better education and training, especially career and technical education, have a critical role to play, but that approach will pay off only gradually over time. Third, there is much work to be done repairing our infrastructure and making bold investments in such things as highways for driverless cars and trucks, new technologies to combat climate change, or efforts to eradicate diseases such as cancer or Alzheimer's disease. But to make a discernible difference in the lives of struggling individuals and communities, these projects will require large amounts of both public and private funds, something akin to the Marshall Plan after World War II. Given our already debt-ridden fiscal future, such a plan would be possible only if there are new revenues, perhaps from a value-added tax (VAT) or carbon tax or from a modest tax on the repatriation of the $2 trillion in overseas profits held by American corporations. The challenge is huge; it is potentially transformational; but it is totally inconsistent with a major reduction in taxes that would balloon an already out-of-control national debt.

Many jobs, new or old, will realistically continue to pay low wages. So a new administration should also worry about making work pay. One way to do that is to raise the minimum wage and increase the Earned Income Tax Credit (EITC) as proposed by myself and Quentin Karpilow.[18] Our proposal would raise the EITC for families with very young children, eliminate the marriage penalty, and redirect some benefits from larger to smaller families and to single individuals. These provisions both incentivize work and encourage marriage and responsible child bearing. A reform with these elements—combined with an increase in the minimum wage to around $10.00 an hour—would reduce poverty by seven percentage points at virtually no cost to the government because a higher minimum wage reduces reliance on public programs. We could also provide an EITC bonus to those who work full time as a way to encourage more hours of work; the United Kingdom has done this with some success.[19]

A second possible option is a second-earner deduction. This proposal would also make work more rewarding by softening the blow of child care costs and other work-related expenses that affect two-earner households, while encouraging marriage.[20]

A third policy for getting more people working is to make it easier for Americans to combine work with raising families. That means more child care assistance and paid leave. Currently, our tax system tries to cover some child care expenses through the Child and Dependent Care Tax Credit (CDCTC). But because the credit is nonrefundable, much of the money goes toward families with incomes between $100,000 and $200,000.[21] Making the CDCTC refundable and capping it at $100,000 in income would make the program more equitable and facilitate low-income parents' labor force participation at little to no cost above the current spending on the CDCTC.

Meanwhile, the United States is the only advanced country that does not provide paid family leave as a matter of national policy. The four states that have shown the way here—California, New Jersey, New York, and Rhode Island—can serve as models for the rest of the country. Critics contend that paid leave will impose costs on employers and impede hiring. Yet 90 percent of employers surveyed after California's paid family leave law was implemented said it had either a positive or neutral effect on productivity, profit, morale, and costs.

Finally, there will always be some people who want to work but cannot find jobs, even when the economy is at full employment. They may have a prison record, have the wrong skills, or be new entrants to the job market. For people who are not able to find a job on their own, the administration and Congress should consider transitional job programs that provide subsidized low-wage work in either the public or the private sector. Evaluations of these programs have a mixed record of success, but some promising models exist.[22] These jobs also provide a way to identify which of the currently jobless are "truly unemployed" and how many are not interested in work. A transitional job offer could be tied to applications for safety net programs such as extended unemployment insurance to reveal who has the greatest need for such assistance, while simultaneously screening out those who refuse to work and reducing program costs.

CONCLUSION

The new administration and Congress have a historic opportunity to address some of the problems that have prevented both the poor and the working class from moving up the economic ladder and have undermined their self-respect, their health, and even their longevity.[23] Although the economy is now beginning to recover from a long and deep recession, structural problems remain. These include little or no gain in wages for these groups, difficulty accessing jobs, family fragmentation, alcohol and drug dependence, and deteriorating communities.[24] The ingredients of a new, new contract with America exist. They would include a new domestic Marshall Plan funded by a new source of revenue, such as a VAT or a carbon tax, and in the short run by a "re-entry tax" on corporate profits. They would also include a much more robust education and training system that prepared people for the jobs of the future. To this must be added an effort to produce more stable families. A brighter future for children begins with families and especially with responsible decisions about when and with whom to become a parent.

As important as what we should do is what we should *not* do. Protectionism will not help anyone in the longer run. It would raise prices, destroy jobs in export-oriented industries, and lead to retaliation that could usher in a worldwide recession. A new round of budget-busting tax cuts favoring the more affluent and corporate America is neither affordable nor likely to significantly increase long-run economic growth[25] (although the short-run effects could be very positive). Efforts to simplify the safety net and to provide more flexibility to the states have merit. But deep cuts in what is already a thin layer of protection for the most vulnerable must be avoided.

Notes

1. Isabel V. Sawhill and Edward Rodrigue, "The Three Norms Analysis: Technical Background" (Brookings, 2016).

2. Isabel V. Sawhill, *Generation Unbound: Drifting into Sex and Parenthood Without Marriage* (Brookings Institution Press, 2014).

3. I estimate that the growth of single-parent families since 1970 has increased the child poverty rate by 25 percent; Sawhill, *Generation Unbound*.

4. Isabel Sawhill and Joanna Venator, "Improving Children's Life Chances through Better Family Planning," CCF Brief No. 55 (Brookings Center on Children and Families, January 2015).

5. Sawhill, *Generation Unbound*.

6. Ibid.

7. Sawhill and Venator, "Improving Children's Life Chances."

8. Isabel Sawhill, "Reducing Poverty by Cutting Unplanned Births," Health Affairs Blog, http://healthaffairs.org/blog/2015/08/21/reducing-poverty-by-cutting-unplanned-births/

9. Ben Schiller, "Spending $1 Billion on Reducing Unintended Pregnancy Would Deliver $6 Billion to the Economy," *Fast Company*, September 21, 2016, www.fastcoexist.com/3063555/future-of-philanthropy/spending-1-billion-on-reducing-unintended-pregnancy-would-deliver-6-b; Michelle Boyd, Devin Murphy, and Debby Bielak, "'Billion Dollar Bets' to Reduce Unintended Pregnancies: Creating Economic Opportunity for Every American" (Boston: Bridgespan Group, August 2016).

10. See National Center for Educational Statistics, "Digest of Education Statistics, Table 219.10," 2013, http://nces.ed.gov/programs/digest/d13/tables/dt13_219.10.asp.

11. Christopher B. Swanson, "Closing the Graduation Gap: Educational and Economic Conditions in America's Largest Cities" (Bethesda, Md.: Editorial Projects in Education, April 2009).

12. Rebecca Unterman, "Headed to College: The Effects of New York City's Small High Schools of Choice on Postsecondary Enrollment" (New York: MDRC, October 2014).

13. James J. Kemple, "Career Academies: Long-Term Impacts on Labor Market Outcomes, Educational Attainment, and Transitions to Adulthood" (New York: MDRC, June 2008).

14. Isabel V. Sawhill, "Higher Education and the Opportunity Act," in *How College Shapes Lives: Understanding the Issues*, edited by Sandy Baum, Charles Kurose, and Jennifer Ma (New York: College Board, October 2013).

15. Isabel V. Sawhill, "Target Aid to Students Most Likely to Succeed," *Education Next* 14, no. 2 (Spring 2014): 58–64.

16. Dean Baker and Jared Bernstein, "Getting Back to Full Employment," CCF Brief No. 52 (Brookings Center on Children and Families, March 2014).

17. White House Council of Economic Advisers, "The Long-Term Decline in Prime-Age Male Labor Force Participation" (U.S. Executive Office of the President, June 2016); and Nicholas Eberstadt, *Men Without Work: America's Invisible Crisis* (West Conshohocken, Pa.: Templeton Press, 2016).

18. Isabel V. Sawhill and Quentin Karpilow, "A No-Cost Proposal to Reduce Poverty and Inequality," CCF Brief No. 51 (Brookings Center on Children and Families, January 2014); and Isabel V. Sawhill and Quentin Karpilow, "Raising the Minimum Wage and Redesigning the EITC" (Brookings Center on Children and Families, January 30, 2014).

19. The current version of the U.K. program, called the Working Tax Credit, provides individuals with £810/year (roughly US$1,250 in 2015) if they work at least 30 hours per week. See HM Revenue and Customs, "Tax Credits, Child Benefit and Guardian's Allowance," 2016, www.gov.uk/government/publications/rates-and-allow ances-tax-credits-child-benefit-and-guardians-allowance/tax-credits-child-benefit- and-guardians-allowance. See also Mike Brewer, Alan Duncan, Andrew Shephard and María José Suárez, "Did Working Families' Tax Credit Work? The Final Evalu- ation of the Impact of In-work Support on Parents' Labour Supply and Take-up Be- haviour in the UK" (London: HM Revenue and Customs, 2005) www.gov.uk/gov ernment/uploads/system/uploads/attachment_data/file/329203/ifs-laboursupply.pdf.

20. Melissa S. Kearney and Lesley J. Turner, "Giving Secondary Earners a Tax Break: A Proposal to Help Low- and Middle-Income Families," Discussion Paper 2013-07 (Hamilton Project, Brookings, December 2013).

21. James P. Ziliak, "Proposal 10: Supporting Low-Income Workers through Re- fundable Child-Care Credits," in *Policies to Address Poverty in America*, edited by Melissa S. Kearney and Benjamin H. Harris (Hamilton Project, Brookings, June 2014), 109–17.

22. Dan Bloom, "Transitional Jobs: Background, Program Models, and Evalu- ation Evidence" (New York: MDRC, February 2010), http://www.acf.hhs.gov/sites/ default/files/opre/tj_09_paper_embed.pdf.

23. Alan B. Krueger, "Where Have All the Workers Gone?" (paper prepared for the Federal Reserve Bank of Boston's 60th Economic Conference, October 2016); and Anne Case and Angus Deaton, "Rising Morbidity and Mortality in Midlife among White and Non-Hispanic Americans in the 21st Century," *PNAS* 112, no. 49 (December 2015): 15,078–83.

24. Charles Murray, *Coming Apart: The State of White America, 1960–2010* (New York: Crown Forum, 2012); Eberstadt, *Men Without Work*.

25. William G. Gale and Andrew A. Samwick, "Effects of Income Tax Changes on Economic Growth" (Brookings, February 1, 2016).

19

Making U.S. Development Fit
for the 21st Century

GEORGE INGRAM

SUMMARY: U.S. international interests rest on a triad of three Ds—
Defense, Diplomacy, and Development. They are co-equal in policy
statements, not in practice. Defense dominates in the budget arena.
Diplomacy dominates at the policy level. Development too often has
been the afterthought and not preeminent even in its own space. If
it is to fulfill its role in advancing U.S. international interests, the
American approach to development needs an upgrade in structure
and resources.

Foreign assistance and development are in the country's security, economic, and humanitarian interests. Countries that enjoy economic
progress and political and social stability are better able to create jobs,
educate their citizens, enjoy health systems that keep their populations
healthy and control potential pandemics, and invest in a stable international system; rarely are they breeding grounds for terrorism. Prosperous
countries are strong partners for U.S. trade and investment. Foreign aid to
the neediest fulfills our humanitarian values.

For those who grew up during the Cold War, the principal global challenges were few and clear—the threat of communism, inter-state and nuclear
war, and poverty in developing countries—with a few powerful countries
shaping the agenda. Today, the global agenda has exploded to, among other
challenges, ill-defined internal and regional strife, international trafficking

and terrorism, climate change, the impact of the technological revolution, terrorism, tax avoidance and illicit payments, and global pandemics. The players are no longer just a few powerful states but multiple countries with a wide range of capacities and interests as well as a host of non-state actors, the mix of which changes with each issue. The relevant responses sometimes involve the traditional tools of military power but more often require the deployment of smart tools of development and diplomacy that draw from an array of national economic, social, cultural, and political assets.

The most current example of the successful deployment of smart powers that joins development and security assistance toward a common objective is the decade-long investment in Colombia that has recently culminated in a peace accord between the government and the Revolutionary Armed Forces of Colombia (FARC).

THE DEVELOPMENT PILLAR

U.S. development capabilities, consolidated and strengthened with the passage of the Foreign Assistance Act of 1961 and the creation of the U.S. Agency for International Development (USAID) by President Kennedy, were eroded and dispersed during the 1990s and early 2000s. This led to under-appreciation of the critical role of development to U.S. interests around the world and to U.S. policies not being properly informed about how development cooperation could advance those interests. That course has been reset over the past decade with a rebuilding of USAID, restoring its policy and budget functions, hiring additional staff with specialized skills, and ensuring it is the lead agency on most development matters. An effort is well along to modernize the agency's operations through transparency, greater use of data for decisionmaking, more robust monitoring and evaluation, and a focus on results and local ownership priorities. As a result, a solid basis now exists from which the next U.S. administration can significantly advance U.S. development capacity so that it is a strong pillar of the three Ds.

BUDGET

A major disconnect in U.S. development programs is resources. The U.S. is either the most or least generous aid donor, depending on your perspective. Looking just at the amount of official development assistance (ODA), the U.S. provides more ODA than any other country.[1] As reported by the

FIGURE 19.1   TOTAL INTERNATIONAL AFFAIRS BUDGET FUNDING, FISCAL YEARS 2010-17

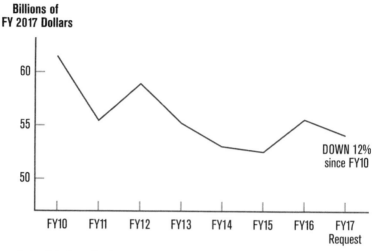

Source: U.S. Global Leadership Coalition, Washington, D.C.

Development Assistance Committee (DAC) of the Organization for Economic Cooperation and Development (OECD), U.S. ODA totaled $31.1 billion in FY 2015, with the United Kingdom next at $18.7 billion.[2] Additionally, in FY 2015 the United States provided over $12 billion in security and military assistance. Beyond the government, in 2013 private American voluntary international giving totaled $39 billion, almost 70 percent of an estimated global total.[3]

On the other hand, given the size of our economy, the U.S. government can be viewed as one of the least generous development donors. Six countries surpass the global target of donor nations providing ODA of 0.7 percent of GNI (gross national income), led in 2015 by Sweden at 1.4 percent and Norway at 1.05 percent. In contrast, the United States trailed near the bottom at 0.17 percent, in company with the least economically advanced members of the DAC. This is in sharp contrast to the role the U.S. played in the Marshall Plan in the immediate postwar period, when assistance was 3 percent of U.S. GDP.[4]

The American people think the United States is more generous than it actually is. Polls consistently show that Americans think that foreign assistance is 25 percent of the federal budget and believe it should be in the range of 10 percent. In fact, as shown in the accompanying chart, it does not reach 1 percent.

FIGURE 19.2   U.S. FOREIGN AID, 1948-2014

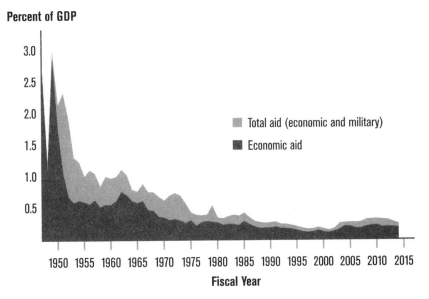

Source: Brookings Institution calculations based on U.S. Overseas Loans and Grants (Green-book) and OMB historical tables. Total aid includes economic and military obligations.

Why did the United States invest such large sums in the recovery of Europe after World War II? Americans are a generous people, but that is not the fundamental reason. The explanation is that the United States saw an existential threat to the world in which it wanted to live—yes, individual Americans opened up their wallets to help provide relief for the starving people of Europe, but American policymakers responded because they saw the potential of totalitarian government taking advantage of the devastation, poverty, and hunger rampant throughout the continent.

The recent decline in resources for foreign assistance has occurred at a time when the challenges confronting the United States internationally have surged—the pandemics of Ebola and Zika; the uncontrollable conflict in Syria; the humanitarian crisis of a historic level of 65 million refugees and displaced persons; child migration from Central America; earthquakes in Haiti and Nepal; Russian aggression in the Ukraine; the reach of ISIS and international terrorism; and civil strife in South Sudan and Yemen. U.S. development institutions and the diplomatic community are being asked to address these and many more issues with declining resources—an untenable situation if the United States is to fulfill its responsibility to protect the American people and preserve our country's preeminent role. We can address these problems using tools of diplomacy and development—and in a few instances by the threat or use of hard power—and curtail the potential explosion of these threats, or we can expend far greater effort and incur a terrible human cost when they spiral out of control. As our military leaders have said, fund development and diplomacy or give us more bullets!

RECOMMENDATIONS

There is a range of actions that can be taken to advance the development capabilities of the U.S. government. But first and foremost are actions in three areas that would further strengthen the principal development agency, USAID; ensure that the development voice is at the policy table; and provide the necessary resources.

1. Strengthen USAID

Several steps would consolidate the strengthening of USAID that has occurred over the past decade.

- **Cabinet rank:** Given the essential role of development in advancing the three Ds, the administrator of USAID should be conferred cabinet rank. Some presidents designated that status to the U.S. ambassador to the UN, the U.S. Trade Representative, and the head of the Small Business Administration. Just as other agencies operate in the international arena with the advice of the Secretary of State, so USAID would work in collaboration with the Department of State and under the overarching U.S. national security strategy. Cabinet status would provide the USAID administrator with the stature to be the voice for U.S. development policy, both within the administration and internationally, and bring coherence to U.S. development policy. Along with this status would come a permanent seat on the National Security Council and the position of chair or vice chair of other key development agencies— the Millennium Challenge Corporation and the Overseas Private Investment Corporation.[5]

- **Consolidation:** A key step in bringing coherence to U.S. development policy and programs is to bring into USAID other programs that are principally developmental in nature and fit USAID's mandate:

- *President's Emergency Plan for AIDS Relief (PEPFAR):* As suggested in the 2010 Quadrennial Diplomacy and Development Review (QDDR), the Global Health Initiative, the essence of which is PEPFAR, should be moved to USAID. PEPFAR is the largest single U.S. international health program. In recent years its scope has been broadened to include a focus on national health infrastructure, which makes it particularly important that it work in close harmony with USAID health programs. PEPFAR has taken impressive steps to embed data and transparency in its decisionmaking and to move in the direction of sustainability; bringing those capabilities into USAID would strengthen the agency. PEPFAR has become well respected internationally, and its brand and core operating modalities should be retained.

- *Middle East Partnership Initiative (MEPI):* Other programs of the Department of State that are principally developmental in nature, specifically MEPI, should be moved to USAID.

- **Budget Authority:** In 2010, the administration fully reinstituted USAID's policy function and partially restored the agency's management of its budget. To complete that process, as was recommended in the 2010 QDDR, USAID should be given full budget authority over the programs it administers. This action would require rethinking the role of the F Bureau (Office of U.S. Foreign Assistance Resources) and the several assistance coordinators at the Department of State, essentially limiting their purview to managing State's assistance programs and coordinating with USAID and other agencies and not attempting to exercise management authority over USAID programs. In addition, policy and budget should be joined in the same office to bring coherence to USAID's programs and budget and to have a single senior official responsible for ensuring that the two work in tandem.

2. Strategy

A U.S. global development strategy is an essential element to making this configuration work, as it would allow for policy coherence among the 26 U.S. government agencies involved in foreign assistance. The 2010 Presidential Policy Determination on Development (PPD No. 6) demonstrated the value of a government-wide policy statement that identifies the key development priorities of a new administration. Included in that policy statement was a recommendation for a global development strategy, which would be more comprehensive than a policy statement. Such a strategy should be developed through active involvement of Congress and civil society. It would bring all agencies under a common strategy, allow the United States to speak with one voice internationally, and bridge the chasm between the executive branch and Congress on key policy issues. It would also give the administrator of USAID a road map to direct and speak for U.S. development policy domestically and internationally.

3. Resources

Budgetary resources must be brought into line with expanding international challenges.

FY 2020: No one can calculate the exact level of funding that is required to meet U.S. global development responsibilities. But given the global challenges outlined above, and looking just at development assistance, a reasonable target would be by the end of the next administration to reach at least the average level of official development assistance by DAC members—0.30 percent of GNI—which for the United States would have been $54 billion for FY 2015. Reaching this target over four years would require an increase of about $5 billion a year to make U.S. programs fit to tackle the challenges of global development.

Notes

For a more in-depth discussion of ideas in this chapter, see George M. Ingram, "Aid Effectiveness: Reform in the New Administration and Congress," Brookings. November 2016.

1. ODA covers only development assistance, not security and military assistance. It is compiled by the Development Assistance Committee of the OECD.

2. Development Assistance Committee, OECD, "Development Aid in 2015 Continues to Grow Despite Costs for In-Donor Refugees" (Paris: April 13, 2016).

3. Hudson Institute, *The Index of Global Philanthropy and Remittances: 2013* (Washington, D.C.: 2013).

4. The table on U.S. Foreign Aid, 1948–2014, uses the category "economic aid" from the Greenbook (U.S. Overseas Loans and Grants) as a proxy for ODA as the only available data going back to 1948.

5. For more on this option, see Brian Atwood and Andrew Natsios, "Rethinking U.S. National Security," *Foreign Affairs*, December 1, 2016.

20

Securing the Future of Driverless Cars

DARRELL M. WEST

SUMMARY: The list of new technologies grows every day. Robots, augmented reality, machine-to-machine communications, and autonomous vehicles help people with a range of different tasks. These developments are broad in scope and have the ability to transform existing businesses and personal interactions. But people need to pay attention to the social and economic ramifications of emerging technologies. New devices carry a number of benefits but also disrupt existing patterns in significant ways.

Uber recently announced that it is offering automated car service in Pittsburgh, another sign of the coming transformation of U.S. transportation. Between now and 2021, according to the World Economic Forum, driverless vehicles are expected to generate $67 billion in economic value and $3.1 trillion in societal benefits.[1] By 2040 autonomous vehicles are expected to comprise around 25 percent of the global market.

The technology to power autonomous vehicles has advanced quickly and is poised for rapid deployment. But to realize possible benefits, the United States needs to address key policy, legal, and regulatory concerns. With forward-looking action, government and business can spur the marketplace and help the United States become a world leader in this area.

Currently, the major difficulty is overcoming the regulatory fragmentation caused by 50 states with differing preferences on licensing, car standards, regulation, and privacy protection. Right now, car manufacturers and software developers face conflicting rules and regulations in various states. This complicates innovation because makers want to build cars and trucks for a national or international market. Greater clarity in regard to legal liability and data protection is also needed. Addressing these issues would help manufacturers implement new technologies and help to spur economic growth in transportation.[2]

BACKGROUND

Autonomous vehicle technology involves the application of advanced technological capabilities to cars, trucks, and buses. This includes automated vehicle guidance and braking, lane-changing systems, use of cameras and sensors for collision avoidance, artificial intelligence to analyze information in real time, and high-performance computing and deep learning systems to adapt to new circumstances through 3D high-definition maps.

Light detection and ranging systems (known as LiDARs) and artificial intelligence are the keys to navigation capabilities and collision avoidance. LiDARs are a combination of light and radar instruments mounted on the tops of vehicles that use imaging from a radar and light beams to measure the speed and distance of surrounding objects in a 360-degree environment. Along with sensors placed along the fronts, sides, and backs of vehicles, these instruments provide information that keeps fast-moving cars and trucks in their own lanes, avoids other vehicles, applies brakes and steering when needed, and does so instantly so as to avoid accidents.

Because these cameras and sensors compile a huge amount of information that needs to be processed instantly in order to avoid the vehicle in the next lane, autonomous vehicles require high-performance computing, advanced algorithms, and deep learning systems to adapt to new scenarios. This means that software is the key, not the physical car or truck itself. Advanced software enables cars to learn from the experiences of other vehicles on the road and to adjust their guidance systems as weather, driving, or road conditions shift. Onboard systems can learn from other vehicles on the road through machine-to-machine communications.

Autonomous vehicles are likely to spread in niche markets before they become popular in the broader consumer market. The initial cost of automated cars will be high, due to the addition of cameras, sensors, lasers, and artificial intelligence systems, therefore precluding adoption by the typical consumer. Rather, businesses and niche areas are positioned to be the early adopters. The most likely adopters include those with an interest in ride-sharing cars, buses, taxis, trucks, delivery vehicles, transport vehicles for senior citizens and the disabled, and industrial applications.

Ride-sharing companies are very interested in autonomous vehicles. They see advantages in terms of customer service and labor productivity. All of the major ride-sharing companies are exploring driverless cars. The surge of car sharing and taxi services such as Uber and Lyft in the United States, Daimler's Mytaxi and Hailo services in Europe, and Didi Chuxing in China demonstrate the viability of this transportation option.

Delivery vehicles and "platoon" trucks traveling together represent another area likely to see quick adoption of autonomous vehicles. Purchases through online platforms and e-commerce sites are rising rapidly, and this has been a boon to home delivery firms. People want to order things electronically and get them delivered within hours.

BENEFITS OF AUTONOMOUS VEHICLES

Highway deaths are a major problem around the world. In the United States, an estimated 35,000 people die in auto accidents each year. Worldwide, according to the World Health Organization, 1.24 million people die annually due to highway accidents.[3] It is estimated that traffic fatalities cost $260 billion each year and that accident injuries account for another $365 billion. This represents a total cost of $625 billion annually from highway fatalities and injuries.[4]

According to a RAND Corporation study, "39 percent of the crash fatalities in 2011 involved alcohol use by one of the drivers."[5] This is an area where autonomous vehicles almost certainly will produce major gains in terms of lives saved and injuries avoided. Around 94 percent of U.S. vehicular accidents involve human error and therefore are potentially avoidable.[6]

Traffic congestion is a problem in virtually every large metropolitan area. In the United States, for example, drivers spend an average of 40 hours a year stuck in traffic, at an annual cost of $121 billion.[7] Research by Donald Shoup has found that up to 30 percent of the traffic in metropolitan areas is due to drivers circling business districts in order to find a parking space nearby.[8] That number represents a major source of traffic congestion, air pollution, and environmental degradation. Cars are thought to be responsible for "approximately 30% of the carbon dioxide ($CO2$) emissions behind climate change."[9] Autonomous vehicles can save on fuel and provide benefits for the environment as a whole.

Automobiles are major contributors to poor quality air. According to a RAND study, "AV [autonomous vehicle] technology can improve fuel economy, improving it by 4–10 percent by accelerating and decelerating more smoothly than a human driver."[10] Since smog in industrial areas is linked to the number of vehicles present, having more autonomous cars is likely to reduce air pollution. A 2016 research study estimated that "pollution levels inside cars at red lights or in traffic jams are up to 40 percent higher than when traffic is moving."[11]

NEEDED ACTIONS

The biggest U.S. challenge is overcoming the fragmentation of 50 state governments and implementing uniform guidelines across geographic boundaries. Public officials should address questions such as who will regulate autonomous vehicle technology and how will it be regulated and issues such as legal liability, privacy, and data collection.

Provide Guidelines for the States

Right now there are few agreed upon technical standards and a hodgepodge of regulation at the state government level.[12] Industry officials have to deal with 50 sets of state rules that can differ dramatically. According to Chris Urmson, formerly of Google, "In the past two years, 23 states have introduced 53 pieces of legislation that affect self-driving cars—all of which include different approaches and concepts. Five states have passed such legislation, and—although all were intended to assist the development of the technology in the state—none of those laws feature common definitions, licensing structures or sets of expectations for what manufacturers should be doing."[13] All of this complicates the task of car developers, who need a more unified approach. Companies cannot design cars for Texas that will not operate in Illinois, Florida, or New York.

California, in particular, has passed legislation that is overly restrictive. It sets back fully autonomous vehicles by requiring a driver in the front seat and prevents companies from removing human-operated steering wheels and brakes. That restriction potentially negates some of the benefits of driverless cars while also creating a barrier to innovation in the automotive industry.

In an effort to simplify the regulatory apparatus, the National Highway Traffic Safety Administration is expected to release new rules designed to promote innovation while protecting consumer safety. Among the likely features are the provision of guidelines for uniform regulations in the states, providing exemptions to outmoded safety regulations, operational guidance for new features, and new tools for encouraging autonomous vehicles.

But in a setback for manufacturers, the national government is insisting that fully autonomous vehicles retain a steering wheel and brakes and that a licensed driver be in the car. Some designers argue that having those override features opens the door to drunk drivers and creates a dangerous sense of complacency for drivers.

Address Legal Liability

Consumers cite lower insurance costs as one of the things they like about autonomous vehicles. Almost one-third of those polled gave that reason, followed by increased safety and the ability to switch to a self-driving model, as a reason they would buy a partially autonomous vehicle.[14]

It is not clear, though, how insurance companies will handle liability claims in the new world of transportation. Is the accident the fault of the driver, the writer of the software code that controls automated features, or the car manufacturer who made the hardware? It will take some lawsuits to resolve questions surrounding the attribution of responsibility. Insurance firms will take a while to develop actuarial tables based on accident records so that they will know what premiums to charge.

A RAND study recommends "no fault" insurance for autonomous vehicles. Its rationale is that driverless cars are less prone to human errors, and therefore they represent a fundamental change in legal liability.[15] Driverless cars essentially shift more of the responsibility from drivers to manufacturers and software designers.

For the latter, product liability law is a promising way to think about legal responsibility. Manufacturers are responsible for defective conditions, so their liability would hinge on whether there was a reasonable expectation that their products would operate as expected and not pose undue risks to passengers.

Improve Data Protection and Security

Data collected through vehicles enable new business models. For example, in the insurance industry "a connected vehicle allows an insurance company to really look at you individually in terms of your actual driving and your real risk and real time situational awareness, so they can innovate a lot of products and a lot of pricing strategies aimed at trying to keep you out of harm's way, and almost pivot from selling insurance to selling assurance."[16]

Several U.S. insurance companies such as State Farm and Progressive have safe driving policies that "collect the miles driven, acceleration, braking, right and left turns, speeds over 80 mph, and the time of day the vehicle is driven, and use the data to calculate insurance rates."[17] Consumer rights activists worry that this information will be sold to third-party vendors and used against drivers. It is clear that vehicles compile a wealth of information on people's locations, their text messaging, e-commerce purchases (including credit card numbers), and other activities in which they engage while in connected cars.

Given this situation, safeguards must be put into place to prevent hacking and to protect people's IP addresses, personal information, and GPS location data. According to Khaliah Barnes of the Electronic Privacy Information Center, the privacy policies of car manufacturers and service companies working on autonomous vehicles allow disclosure of driver information for "troubleshooting, evaluation of use, and research" and to unnamed third parties "for marketing purposes."

CONCLUSION

To summarize, the technology underlying semi- and fully autonomous vehicles is well developed and poised for commercial deployment. Major automotive companies and software developers have made considerable progress in navigation, collision avoidance, and street mapping.

Governments can accelerate or slow the movement toward self-driving vehicles by the manner in which they regulate. Addressing relevant issues and making sure regulatory rules are clear should be high priorities in all the countries considering autonomous vehicles.

There remain broader societal and ethical considerations, though, that must be considered as we move closer to commercialization. For example, if an automated car is facing the outcome between hitting one child or a group of 10 kids, how does it make that choice? One can imagine a wide variety of ethical issues that will come along, and software designers have to make choices regarding how to deal with them.

In addition, there are important ramifications for the workforce. Uber has around one million drivers on the road. Phasing in autonomous vehicles likely will mean that at least some of these individuals will lose their jobs and require retraining for other positions. Learning how to navigate these economic and social ramifications is a major challenge facing the world.

ACKNOWLEDGMENT: I want to thank Hillary Schaub for her valuable research assistance on this project.

Notes

1. Bruce Weinelt and others, *Digital Transformation of Industries: Automotive Industry*, report prepared for the World Economic Forum in collaboration with Accenture, January 2016.

2. For more details, see Darrell M. West, "Moving Forward: Self-Driving Vehicles in China, Europe, Japan, Korea, and the United States" (Brookings, September 2016).

3. World Health Organization, *Global Health Observatory Data: Number of Road Traffic Deaths*, 2010.

4. Morgan Stanley Research, *Nikola's Revenge: TSLA's New Path of Disruption*," February 25, 2014, 24–26.

5. James Anderson and others, *Autonomous Vehicle Technology: A Guide for Policymakers* (Santa Monica, Calif.: RAND Corporation, 2016), xiv.

6. Nathaniel Beuse, "Testimony before the House Committee on Oversight and Government Reform," November 18, 2015, p. 1. Also see Alyssa Abkowitz, "Baidu Plans to Mass Produce Autonomous Cars in Five Years," *Wall Street Journal*, June 2, 2016.

7. U.S. Department of Transportation, *Beyond Traffic, 2045: Trends and Choices*, 2015, 11.

8. Donald Shoup, "Cruising for Parking," *Access* 30 (2007): 16–22.

9. Weinelt and others, *Digital Transformation of Industries*, 4.

10. Anderson and others, *Autonomous Vehicle Technology*, xvi.

11. Tatiana Schlossberg, "Stuck in Traffic, Polluting the Inside of Our Cars," *New York Times*, August 29, 2016.

12. National Conference of State Legislatures, "Autonomous Self-Driving Vehicles Legislation," February 23, 2016.

13. Chris Urmson, "Testimony Before the Senate Committee on Commerce, Science and Technology," March 15, 2016, 4.

14. Xavier Mosquet, Thomas Dauner, Nikolaus Lang, Nichael Rubmann, Antonella Mei-Pochtler, Rakshita Agrawal, and Florian Schmieg, "Revolution in the Driver's Seat: The Road to Autonomous Vehicles," Boston Consulting Group, April, 2015, p. 11.

15. Anderson and others, *Autonomous Vehicle Technology*, 116.

16. Jeff McMahon, "Driverless Cars Could Drive Car Insurance Companies Out of Business," *Forbes,* February 19, 2016.

17. Khaliah Barnes, "Testimony Before the House Committee on Oversight and Government Reform," November 18, 2015, 13.

PART III

Security at Home and Abroad

21

America's Awesome Military

MICHAEL E. O'HANLON and DAVID H. PETRAEUS

SUMMARY: The United States has the best military in the world today, by far. U.S. forces have few, if any, weaknesses, and in many areas—from naval warfare to precision-strike capabilities, to airpower, to intelligence and reconnaissance, to special operations—they play in a totally different league from the militaries of other countries. Nor is this situation likely to change anytime soon, as U.S. defense spending is three times as large as that of the United States' closest competitor, China, and accounts for about one-third of all global military expenditures—with another third coming from U.S. allies and partners. Nevertheless, 15 years of war and five years of budget cuts and Washington dysfunction have taken their toll. The military is certainly neither broken nor unready for combat, but its size and resource levels are less than is advisable given the range of contemporary threats and the missions for which it has to prepare. No radical changes or major buildups are needed. But the trend of budget cuts should stop and indeed be modestly reversed, and defense appropriations should be handled more rationally and professionally than has been the case in recent years.

Most major elements of U.S. defense policy are on reasonably solid ground, despite innumerable squabbles among experts over many of the details. Throughout the post–Cold War era, some variant of a two-war planning framework (with caveats) has enjoyed bipartisan support and should continue to do so for many years to come. Forward presence and engagement in East Asia, Europe, and the Middle East remain compelling pillars of U.S. national security strategy. Robust research-and-development programs continue to be supported, as does an unparalleled intelligence community. The Defense Department's procurement budget—the first victim of budgetary austerity in the 1990s and in the early years of this century—is once again relatively healthy. Pentagon leaders are spurring innovation, and the men and women of today's armed forces display high standards of professionalism, expertise, and experience.

Yet there are also areas of concern. Excess base capacity remains a problem. The navy's fleet and the army are too small, and current budget trajectories imply further cuts rather than increases. And the scale of some hugely expensive weapons programs in the pipeline or on the drawing boards, such as the F-35 fighter jet and some new nuclear weapons, needs to be reassessed. The challenge for the next president will thus be how to build on the strengths, address the problems, and chart a course for continuing to maintain U.S. military dominance in a strategic environment that never stops evolving.

CHANGE VS. MORE OF THE SAME

The national interests that the U.S. military needs to advance remain constant: protecting the homeland; safeguarding U.S. citizens at home and abroad; and ensuring the security of U.S. allies, the global economy, and international order more generally. These days, threats to those interests come from five sources: great powers (such as China and Russia), extremist nonstate actors (such as al Qaeda; the Islamic State, or ISIS; and the Taliban), rogue states (such as Iran and North Korea), pandemics and environmental turbulence, and developments in advanced technology that could increase U.S. vulnerabilities (especially those related to cyberspace, space, and weapons of mass destruction).

Fortunately, the United States has many resources to draw on as it prepares for these threats, even beyond its military forces. The country's high-tech and innovative sectors are the best in the world. It has solid economic fundamentals, including a gradually growing population base, the world's best universities, and a large market at the center of global finance and commerce. And most important of all, the United States leads a globe-spanning system of alliances and partnerships that includes some

60 countries, collectively accounting for two-thirds of global economic output and military capacity.

A serious defense policy, however, needs to take into account the way war itself is changing. True military revolutions are relatively rare, as even major changes usually occur gradually, over decades. But there is clearly one such revolution now in process, perhaps halfway along: in airpower, particularly in the effects of precision ordnance combined with the vast increase of intelligence, surveillance, and reconnaissance (ISR) systems on the contemporary battlefield.

Harbingers of this revolution were apparent as far back as 1982, in the effectiveness of the French-made Exocet missiles used by the Argentinian military against British warships during the Falklands War. Around the same time, NATO put forward the concept of AirLand Battle, which envisioned using new types of advanced munitions to precisely strike critical targets behind the frontlines in the event of a conflict with the Warsaw Pact. (Hearkening back to the "first offset"—NATO's reliance on nuclear weapons to counter its foes' large land armies—some called this the "second offset," relying on the high-tech quality of its conventional forces to counter its foes' quantitative superiority.)

The public began to take notice of these developments during the Gulf War in 1990–91, as laser-guided bombing played as well on television as it did on the battlefield. GPS-guided bombs arrived a few years later, and they were eventually followed by armed drones. All these American weapons can now be employed in vastly greater quantities through "sensor-shooter loops" that take advantage of remarkable advances in reconnaissance systems, such as the "unblinking eye" of many dozens of drones and satellite-based communications that share targeting, video, and critical data across the military in real time.

Precision-guided bombs accounted for about 10 percent of the ordnance used in the Gulf War. In recent conflicts, they have accounted for about 90 percent, with a dramatic impact on the course of battle. As a result, Pentagon officials now talk of a "third offset"—the hope, championed by Secretary of Defense Ashton Carter and Deputy Secretary of Defense Robert Work, among others, that it will be possible to rely on modern-day ISR and precision assets to counter, say, larger Chinese missile, aircraft, ship, and submarine forces in the waters of the western Pacific.

For all this progress, however, there are limits to what standoff warfare and advanced technology can achieve by themselves. To make precision bombing effective, for example, targets need to be located accurately—something that can be difficult if those targets are in cities, forests, or jungles, or are concealed or underground. Moreover, advanced sensor and communications networks may prove fragile when fighting technologically sophisticated adversaries.

Land warfare also remains complex, particularly when fighting in cities or against an adversary trying to hide or disguise what is being done (such as Russia's seizure of Crimea in 2014 using "little green men"—mysterious soldiers in unmarked uniforms). Future war fighting could be complicated by the introduction of chemical, electromagnetic-pulse, or even nuclear weapons or take place in a war zone affected by pandemic infectious disease. And it is not hard to conjure up scenarios in which U.S. forces would be responsible for helping restore order in a chaotic environment marked by the breakdown of complex systems that usually provide essential services to millions of people.

Given all of this, how should the next administration handle defense policy? By building on existing policies and concentrating on preparing the army for multiple missions, continuing the navy's rebalance of attention to the Pacific, countering China and Russia, and maintaining adequate resources to support a robust force.

PREPARE THE ARMY FOR ANYTHING

After long, difficult wars in Afghanistan and Iraq, some critics have argued that the entire notion of attempting to prepare U.S. ground forces for complex missions beyond conventional combat is a fruitless or even counterproductive exercise. Reprising the army's attitude in the wake of the Vietnam War, when it eschewed counterinsurgency and focused instead on high-end maneuver warfare and the NATO–Warsaw Pact face-off, they favor developing a force with a more limited orientation. The Obama administration's 2012 Defense Strategic Guidance report, for example, stated that although U.S. forces would "retain and continue to refine the lessons learned, expertise, and specialized capabilities that have been developed over the past 10 years of counterinsurgency and stability operations in Iraq and Afghanistan," they would "no longer be sized to conduct large-scale, prolonged stability operations." Partly as a result of this logic, today's active-duty U.S. Army has been cut by almost 100,000 in recent years, to 470,000 soldiers. That is fewer than the number fielded in the mid- to late

1990s. Under current plans, moreover, the army would decline further, to 450,000 by 2018, and some key Pentagon officials have advocated cuts to 400,000 or below.

This reasoning—which was repeated in the 2014 Quadrennial Defense Review—is flawed. Washington might declare its lack of interest in large-scale land operations and stabilization missions, but history suggests that eventually it will find itself engaging in them nevertheless, driven by the pull of events and the logic of turbulent situations on the ground.

The 2014 Army Operating Concept, "Win in a Complex World," wisely recognizes that the current and future army must be ready to handle a wide range of possible challenges. It accords with the notion that the modern soldier must in effect be a pentathlete, with skills across a wide range of domains that apply to many possible types of operations. The document builds on earlier concepts, such as the belief of General Charles Krulak, former commandant of the Marine Corps, in preparing troops for a "three-block war," in which U.S. forces might be providing relief in one part of a city, keeping the peace in a second, and fighting intensively against a determined foe in a third. And it reflects awareness of what Raymond Odierno, former chief of staff of the army, has called the increasing "velocity of instability" in the world, with U.S. forces frequently participating simultaneously in a broad range of contingency operations in several different theaters—everything from combat to deterrence to the provision of humanitarian aid.

The George W. Bush administration took office averse to missions that smacked of nation building, but eventually it came to understand these realities. A Pentagon directive issued in 2005 stated, "Stability operations are a core U.S. military mission. . . . They shall be given priority comparable to combat operations." A decade on, that remains a sensible approach, while recognizing the imperative of having host-nation forces and coalition partners do as much as is absolutely possible to keep the United States' commitment in blood and treasure to a minimum—and thus sustainable over what are likely to be generational struggles.

CONTINUE THE NAVY'S REBALANCE

During its first term, the Obama administration put forward the notion of rebalancing U.S. power and attention toward the Asia-Pacific, reflecting the region's increasing significance to U.S. interests. This sensible proposal

met with broad bipartisan support and should be fleshed out and reinforced in coming years. To date, however, the Pentagon's moves in this direction have been relatively modest in scale, with a net shifting of assets to
the Asia-Pacific theater of no more than $10 billion to $15 billion worth out
of the approximately $600 billion annual defense budget, by our estimates.
If coupled with continued diplomatic efforts and economic measures such
as passage of the Trans-Pacific Partnership—not just a trade agreement
but also a crucial signal of U.S. commitment to the region in general—such
moves should suffice, at least for now. But it will take a healthy, predictable
defense budget to fund even moves of this scale, and anything less would
fall well short of what the strategic challenge requires.

No "pivot" to the Pacific is needed or even truly possible given the
United States' other interests and commitments. Nevertheless, the case for
reenergizing the nation's emphasis on the Asia-Pacific region is powerful.
North Korea remains a serious threat, with erratic and bellicose behavior
continuing under its current leader, Kim Jong Un. Pyongyang has now
detonated five nuclear weapons and apparently continues to expand its
arsenal and its missile-delivery capabilities. China, meanwhile, has established itself as a near peer of the United States by many economic and
manufacturing measures, has the second-largest military budget in the
world now, and could be spending half as much as the United States on its
armed forces within a few years, with much lower personnel costs and far
fewer regions on which to focus. Its stocks of advanced combat aircraft,
advanced submarines, other naval vessels, and ballistic and cruise missiles
have grown enormously, and the majority of its newer main platforms in
these categories are gradually approaching parity with the United States.
Factoring in everything from aircraft carriers to the latest planes and submarines, the U.S. military still has a major lead over the People's Liberation
Army, and the United States' total stock of modern military equipment is
worth perhaps 10 times that of China's. But the overwhelming superiority
once enjoyed by the United States is largely gone.

The bulk of the U.S. military's rebalance to the Pacific region involves
the navy. In a 2012 speech, then secretary of defense Leon Panetta stated
that by 2020 Washington would focus 60 percent of its naval assets on the
Pacific and only 40 percent on the Atlantic. But most of those ships will
be based in the United States, and many could still deploy to the Persian
Gulf from their new home ports on the Pacific coast. So the scale of the
rebalance is limited, and the changes in overseas basing arrangements as-

sociated with it are modest as well. Only four small littoral combat ships, for example, are currently planned to be based in Singapore, along with perhaps two to three more attack submarines based in Guam.

Other services are in on the act, too, but even more modestly. The army has created a four-star subordinate command at Pacific Command, in Hawaii, to strengthen its role in the region (although it may not get the funds to continue it). The Marine Corps will rotate up to 2,500 marines at a time to Darwin, Australia. New port and basing arrangements have been established with Vietnam and the Philippines. In 2013, then secretary of defense Chuck Hagel stated that 60 percent of many air force assets will also focus on the Asia-Pacific region, although their home airfields may not need to change much to make that possible. And regional missile defenses are being buttressed somewhat as well.

Yet the success of the rebalance will depend not just on how many U.S. forces are deployed to the region but also on how they are used. Wise recent actions in this regard include stepped-up freedom-of-navigation operations in the South China Sea, which challenge China's right to stake out new holdings near man-made islands and other land features there, and the Obama administration's public commitment to treat the group of islands known in China as the Diaoyu and in Japan as the Senkaku as being covered by the U.S.-Japanese security treaty. (Washington takes no position on the rightful owner of those islands, but since they are currently administered by Tokyo, it has agreed that they are covered by the treaty.)

As concerning as Beijing's actions have been, its recent assertiveness amounts more to moves in a long game of chess than preparations for some imminent war of aggression. Washington should thus respond, but do so calmly. The Obama administration's general policy of patient firmness is sound and should be continued by its successor, but the next administration should take care not to allow lags between rhetoric and action, as was the case when the United States promised to demonstrate its support for freedom of navigation in mid-2015 but then took months to deliver on it, sending mixed signals about its commitment. And if China continues to reclaim and militarize islands in the South China Sea, the logical response by Washington should be not a direct use of force but the development of closer security ties with various states in the region, possibly including new U.S. deployments or even bases.

COME LOADED FOR BEAR

The 2014 Quadrennial Defense Review was conducted before Russia's invasion and seizure of Crimea, and like all previous post–Cold War defense reviews, it did not consider a contingency involving the Russian Federation to be high on the list of priorities for force planning. That was then. Now, some members of the U.S. Joint Chiefs of Staff have described Russia as their top security concern. This makes sense, because the combination of Russia's sheer firepower and President Vladimir Putin's apparent ambitions make it a possible threat—indeed, a potentially existential one—that demands attention.

At the same time, however, perspective is needed. Putin is no friend of the West, nor of the smaller states near Russia that represent challenges to his drive for regional hegemony. But his moves to date have been select and calibrated. Crimea was historically Russian, is populated by a majority of Russian speakers, and is home to Russia's only Black Sea naval base. And when Putin moved into Syria last fall, he did so only after having determined that the Obama administration was keeping its own involvement limited. His intervention there allowed him to shore up an old ally, flex Russia's long-range power-projection muscles, retain Russia's only port on the Mediterranean, and demonstrate Russia's geopolitical importance. These actions may have been cynical and reprehensible, but they were not completely reckless or random, nor were they particularly brutal by the standards of warfare. And they do not likely portend a direct threat to more central NATO interests.

The Obama administration has been right to shore up its commitment to NATO, although it should go further and increase its assistance to Ukraine as well. Given Moscow's provocations of the Baltic states in recent years and its frequent buzzing of NATO military assets in the region, it makes sense to enhance deterrence of a Russian military threat to all NATO member states. The dramatic downsizing of U.S. capabilities in Europe over the last quarter century, to the point where the United States now has only 30,000 army troops and no heavy brigades on the entire continent, was never intended to signal a lack of U.S. resolve in maintaining its ironclad support for the transatlantic alliance, and so there is no reason not to reverse some of those withdrawals.

At least for now, it should not take much to reinforce U.S. commitments. Stationing a major NATO force in the Baltics, for example, not only is unnecessary but also could provoke Putin as easily as deter him, given his temperament and his desire to restore Russia's status. Firmness and prudence should be the watchwords, and for that, a reinforced tripwire is more appropriate than a robust forward defense posture. Current efforts, under the European Reassurance Initiative and Operation Atlantic Resolve, to maintain a nearly continuous U.S. presence through exercises, position four NATO battalions in the Baltic states and Poland, and sustain modest stocks of equipment in up to seven eastern NATO countries make sense. It also seems sensible to return a U.S. heavy brigade to Europe, perhaps to Germany, as is currently being considered. Greater participation by other NATO countries in the reassurance and deterrence mission, with a sustained military presence in the eastern states of a magnitude comparable to that of the U.S. level, would also be useful, demonstrating that alliance solidarity and security are truly collective efforts. It is heartening that NATO decisions now codify such initiatives.

Such moves in the military and diplomatic spheres will complement the ongoing impact of economic sanctions, which have played an important role both in making Russia pay a price for its actions and in demonstrating alliance cohesion. It is true that the drop in energy prices has hurt Russia's economy even more than the Western sanctions have, but the two pressures reinforce each other and have driven Russia into a recession for two straight years. Putin remains popular, having wrapped himself in the cloak of nationalism while suppressing domestic dissent, but he must worry that his popularity will not endure forever in the face of a protracted economic downturn. In fact, the success of sanctions in constraining Russia and in helping drive Iran to the negotiating table indicates that comprehensive strategies for dealing with regional threats these days should involve the Treasury Department and the Justice Department just as much as the Defense Department and the State Department.

STEADY AS SHE GOES

A national security strategy that maintains international order, checks China and Russia, and prepares properly for handling future threats and possible contingencies needs to be supported by a defense budget of appropriate size and composition. That means not only holding off on any further cuts but also adopting a thoughtful, measured increase. It is also time to end the perennial threats of sequestration and shutdown and place the Pentagon's budget on a gentle upward path in real terms.

Those who worry about an American military supposedly in decline should relax. The current U.S. defense budget of just over $600 billion a year exceeds the Cold War average of about $525 billion (in 2016 dollars) and greatly exceeds the pre-9/11 defense budget of some $400 billion. It is true that defense spending from 2011 through 2020 has been cut by a cumulative total of about $1 trillion (not counting reductions in war-related costs). But there were legitimate reasons for most of those reductions, and the cuts were made to a budget at a historically very high level.

We disagree with those who counsel further cuts, and we strongly resist a return to sequestration-level spending (as could still happen, since the chief villain and cause of sequestration, the 2011 Budget Control Act, remains the law of the land). There are good reasons why the United States needs to spend as much as it does on defense: because it has such a broad range of global responsibilities, because asymmetric foreign capabilities (such as Chinese precision-guided missiles and Russian advanced air defenses) can require large investments to counter convincingly, and, most important, because it should aim to deter conflicts rather than simply prevail in them. To be sure, many U.S. allies are wealthy enough to contribute substantially to their own defense and should certainly do more in that regard. But engaging in a game of chicken to try to persuade them to live up to their commitments would be a dangerous mistake.

Having reached nearly 5 percent of GDP in the later Bush and early Obama years, U.S. defense spending is now down to about 3 percent. That is not an undue burden on the U.S. economy and is in fact a bargain given the peace, security, and international stability that it underwrites. There is no need to return to significantly higher levels, such as the 4 percent of GDP that some have proposed. But nor would it be prudent to drop below 3 percent. That translates into perhaps $625 billion to $650 billion a year in constant dollars over the next few years for the overall national defense budget, including war costs (assuming they remain at roughly current amounts). That level is sensible and affordable, and what President Trump should work with Congress to provide. With that sort of support, there is every reason to believe that the country's fortunate military position can be sustained for many years to come.

22

Countering Violent Extremism in America

ROBERT L. MCKENZIE

SUMMARY: Since 9/11, the U.S. government has spent many billions and mobilized thousands of employees to thwart jihadi terrorist plots in America and abroad. Measured by American lives saved, the U.S. government has had extraordinary success using all elements of its national security toolbox to capture, arrest, and kill terrorists worldwide. Yet it is clear that kinetic operations alone will not solve the problem. The rise of the Islamic State has energized an estimated 27,000 jihadi foreign fighters from around the world to travel to Iraq and Syria, and recent attacks in Paris, Brussels, San Bernardino, Orlando, and Nice have demonstrated the organization's reach and ability to both inspire and guide homegrown violent extremists across the globe. To confront and address the threat of homegrown violent extremism, the next administration will need an innovative and refined agenda to counter domestic violence extremism—one that focuses on individualized interventions—rather than a faith-based approach that targets American Muslims writ large.[1]

To combat the enduring appeal of Salafi jihadism, the U.S. government and its allies have devoted an enormous amount of time, energy, and resources to counter violent extremism (CVE). At the UN General Assembly in September 2014, President Obama called on nations to do more to counter violent extremism, and in February 2015 he convened a White House summit on the topic.[2] There is a CVE Task Force hosted by the Department of Homeland Security and co-led with the Department of Justice.[3] Following bipartisan congressional support for the CVE Act of 2015,[4] a new CVE office was established at the Department of Homeland Security. At the Department of State, the Bureau of Counterterrorism was renamed the Bureau of Counterterrorism and Countering Violent Extremism. Additionally, there have been several important multilateral and international initiatives, such as the Global Counterterrorism Forum and the Hedayah Center in Abu Dhabi.[5]

Yet despite CVE's ascendancy as a policy paradigm, two significant and interrelated problems continue to confound practitioners and policymakers. The next president will need to address them.

The first concerns the lack of empirical knowledge about the root causes and drivers of violent extremism. This lacuna has led to conceptual confusion about CVE. It is difficult to design an effective policy when there is little consensus on what it means to counter violent extremism or what actions might be taken to do so. Consequently, CVE efforts are mostly designed and funded on the basis of anecdotal evidence, with unknown results.

Second, the Obama administration's domestic CVE policy has strained relations with an entire religious community, in large part because its policy perceives American Muslims through a security lens. The Department of Justice has led domestic CVE efforts, which primarily consist of outreach to Muslim leaders to keep the community involved and encourage information sharing about vulnerable youth. But the community rarely knows about youth who are radicalized in their midst. Moreover, the vast majority of Muslims do not embrace violent extremism, especially in America. Of the world's jihadi foreign fighter population, approximately 250 people[6] out of 3.3 million Muslims[7] in America (a mere .0075 percent) have been mobilized,[8] compared with 1,700 out of 4.7 million Muslims in France (.036 percent), and 6,000 out of 11 million in Tunisia (.054 percent).[9] What is more, the scale, scope, and complexity of the problem vary significantly by location. For example, two neighborhoods in Brussels have produced nearly two-and-a-half times as many foreign fighters as all of America, even though America has more than five times as many Muslims as Belgium does.[10]

This is not to suggest that there is no threat from Salafi violent extremism in the United States. Rather, it is neither the only nor by far the greatest threat to the country and its interests. It should go without saying that alienating an entire religious community undermines American principles and values. Worse yet, this alienation itself could very well spur radicalization, thereby undermining not only our principles and values but also our security. Therefore, it is not inconceivable that an alienating CVE agenda could in fact create the very problem it sets out to solve.

POLICY PROPOSALS

The policy proposals below follow from the abovementioned observations.

Learn from Past Failures

CVE efforts in the United States have struggled. There have been three recent CVE pilot programs in Boston, Los Angeles, and Minneapolis,[11] and each one has received widespread criticism from Muslim communities—the very communities that were intended as key partners. Many American Muslims feel that these programs securitized their relationship with the U.S. government. They point out that most Muslims who carry out or plot terrorist attacks are not active in their community, and almost none have been openly radicalized in social settings, such as at mosques or community centers. Most are radicalized online and in small cloistered groups, with limited contact with the wider community.

These points are not unfounded. Since 2014, 100 Americans have been charged in connection with the Islamic State and 43 have been convicted.[12] These 43 individuals were living in different parts of the country. To cite those states with the most cases: New York has 18 cases (14 pending and four convictions); Minnesota has 12 cases (four pending and eight convictions); and Virginia has 10 cases (seven pending and three convictions). In New Jersey and Michigan—two states with areas with dense Muslim populations—they have had only four cases (zero pending and four convictions) and three cases (three pending and zero convictions), respectively. In other words, there is no clear nexus between a particular city, neighborhood, mosque, or community center and violent extremism in America. Yet, the current CVE agenda suggests otherwise.

End FBI and Law Enforcement Outreach as a CVE Activity

In addition to the pilot projects listed above, the FBI and local law enforcement routinely have held meetings with Muslim community leaders across the country. Between 2012 and 2015, the FBI and local law enforcement convened more than 2,500 engagement events.[13] According to the Department of Justice, the aim is to "foster trust, improve awareness, and educate communities about violent risk factors in order to stop radicalization to violence before it starts." However, this type of outreach is sowing distrust in Muslim communities about government activities.

A recurrent complaint is that the government does no such outreach to white nationalist and far-right-wing Americans, despite the fact that before the Orlando terrorist attack there were roughly the same number of domestic deaths as the result of terrorism by far-right wing individuals compared to Muslims since 9/11 (48 deaths versus 45 deaths, respectively; since Orlando, the numbers now stand at 50 deaths and 94 deaths, respectively).[14] Muslims also point out that the number of jihadi terrorists pales in comparison to other criminal threats or leading causes of death in America. For example, there are 1.4 million gang members in America; in Chicago alone, there are 70 gangs, with 150,000 gang members.[15] In 2014, there were nearly 31,000 alcohol-induced deaths, and over 33,000 people died from firearm injuries, with homicides accounting for 32.6 percent (homicide was the 17th leading cause of death).[16]

Citing these kinds of examples, Muslims are concerned they are being singled out and that law-enforcement-led community outreach is merely a ploy to use the soft tools of public diplomacy to support the hard tools of law enforcement investigations. Well-meaning and creative ideas to include such things as liaison officers—Muslims working with or for the FBI and law enforcement—will only add to the growing belief that the government is deputizing Muslims to help provide surveillance on and build cases against other Muslims. Community members lament that if the government were truly interested in learning about their concerns, then outreach and engagement efforts would be led by the Department of Health and Human Services, municipal authorities, and civil society, not by federal and local law enforcement.

To be clear, the FBI and local law enforcement should continue to engage Muslim religious, business, civic, and community leaders to maintain a network of contacts across the country. This allows for open lines of communications, which is vital for when there are problems and also helps demystify the important work of federal and local law enforcement. However, this type of engagement should be decoupled from CVE efforts. Otherwise, it will continue to strain relations with Muslims and reinforce the impression—rightly or wrongly—that the government views them writ large as a potential security problem.

Reorient Domestic CVE Efforts away from Communities and toward Individual Interventions

The next president should refine and tighten the domestic CVE agenda so that, rather than a community-oriented approach targeting so-called "vulnerable communities," it focuses squarely on individuals who have demonstrated sympathy for propaganda produced by foreign designated terrorist organizations. Such a focus should favor intervening with or rehabilitating these individuals, depending on three primary interrelated factors: (1) whether indicators such as social media usage suggest high likelihood of committing a crime, (2) whether they have already committed a crime, and (3) what type of crime they have committed.

Introduce Nationwide Intervention Programs

The next president should introduce a nationwide intervention program that focuses on law-abiding citizens who have demonstrated a clear enthusiasm for violent extremism and/or terrorist organizations. Examples of such enthusiasm might include posting and/or promoting on social media "the virtues" of the Islamic State or al-Qaeda, or extolling the Islamic State, other terrorist groups, and/or related activities while in a public or social setting. The FBI has identified roughly 1,000 individuals as persons who have been radicalized online (and 80 percent by the Islamic State).[17] This is a manageable number for such intervention programs.

The interventions should be limited to minors who can be legally required by their parents to attend rehabilitation and similar programs. As for adults, interventions should be limited to those who have committed nonviolent crimes. Each intervention should be tailored to the specific needs of the individual, in a manner similar to community drug courts that deal with addiction. The Department of Health and Human Services should have federal oversight, but programs must be designed, implemented, and led at the local level with direct input and support from a range of professionals and local actors, including community and family members. A hotline should be incorporated to allow individuals or families to seek guidance on how best to support someone heading down the wrong path. In order to build and deepen trust, this hotline should not serve law enforcement and intelligence purposes. However, clear guidance should be provided as to when and how the FBI and law enforcement should be engaged if there are concerns about criminal activity or terrorist plots. Lastly, the next administration will need to ensure that those supporting intervention programs are not exposed to financial or criminal liabilities. At present, nongovernment officials who are involved in interventions can be exposed to a range of liabilities for having provided material support to a terrorist or related activities.

Include Local Actors and Listen to American Muslims at the Local Level

Intervention programs will require a significant amount of innovation and community buy-in at the local level. Therefore, the next president should ensure that these programs harness the voices and experiences of a range of local stakeholders: city officials, civic and business leaders, educators, and faith-based communities. These efforts would benefit from engagement with and lessons learned from two existing networks: 100 Resilient Cities, pioneered by the Rockefeller Foundation to address the physical, social, and economic challenges at the city level; and Strong Cities, a UN initiative to establish a global network of mayors and municipal policymakers to counter violent extremism in all its forms.[18] Drawing on these networks will allow for intervention programs to look to and benefit from the successes and lessons learned from interventions in places like Denmark and the Netherlands, where such programs have been in use.

Additionally, the next president should commission a series of 100 focus groups with Muslim youth, Muslim women, Muslim business and community leaders, and religious clerics. The purpose of these focus groups would be to better understand Muslims' views on a whole range of community-related and local issues. The focus groups should be conducted by a reputable research institution and take place in major metropolitan areas that would include Boston, Chicago, Cleveland, Detroit, Dallas, Houston, Los Angeles, Minneapolis, New York, northern Virginia, Orlando, Tampa Bay, San Francisco, and St. Louis. The FBI and law enforcement should play no role in the design, delivery, or analysis of the focus groups, and the findings should be made public. These focus groups may or may not offer deep insights about violent extremism, but they would go a long way to dispel myths and misinformation, possibly identify new mechanisms for addressing grievances, and engender the potential for richer and much-needed local dialogues with Muslim communities across the country.

Stress the Importance of Rehabilitation and Reintegration

In the United States, approximately 300 people have been convicted of terrorism-related charges since 9/11, with 88 people charged with ISIS-related offenses since 2014 (many for nonviolent offenses).[19] Given that many of those imprisoned on terrorism-related charges will be released at some point (roughly 40 people in the near future), the next president should establish a nationwide and comprehensive rehabilitation and reintegration program. The Bureau of Prisons should lead on the design and implementation of this program—but given the distinct nature and needs of this unique prison population, a full range of experts should be consulted: mental health professionals, psychosocial specialists and social workers, researchers and clinicians in the field of correctional psychology, education specialists, faith-based leaders, and family members when and where appropriate.

Rehabilitation and reintegration programs should also include a structured and systematic mechanism for input and participation from former terrorists. These individuals are important for at least two reasons: first, they can help provide a nuanced, empathetic understanding of the radicalization and deradicalization process, and second, their firsthand accounts provide powerful narratives in prison programs. Additionally, immediate family members of terrorists and former terrorists should be incorporated in these programs when and where appropriate. There is a wealth of literature on the measurement of recidivism and other indicators of effectiveness for rehabilitation and integration programs for incarcerated gang members, substance abuse offenders, and sex offenders. A comprehensive program should examine and build on the successes and lessons learned from these similar programs.

Stifle the Spread of Violent Extremism Online

Foreign terrorist organizations have long used the Internet to spread extremist ideology, inspire homegrown extremists around the world, and identify and mobilize foreign fighter aspirants.[20] In nearly 80 percent of the cases of foreign fighter aspirants in America, terrorist propaganda was transmitted or downloaded using social media. The next president should redouble efforts to get social media companies to identify and shut down accounts espousing violent extremism and terrorist propaganda. It is important to recognize that U.S. government-led efforts at messaging, countermessaging, and counternarratives have proven both difficult to conduct (because of U.S. laws) and ineffective (often because such government initiatives lack legitimacy).[21] The notion of empowering so-called credible voices online is undermined when these voices are identified, supported, or amplified by governments or government-funded entities. Recognizing these inherent and intractable difficulties, U.S. government efforts and resources would be better spent focusing on and working with Internet and social media companies to identify and shut down all accounts espousing any form of hate speech and violent extremism that violate these companies' terms of service.

Establish a Clearinghouse for Measurement and Evaluation

The next president should prioritize the establishment of a measurement clearinghouse that simplifies and aggregates data on CVE programs. Policymakers would use such a clearinghouse to replicate, adapt, or scale up successful programs, and avoid the mistakes of programs that have failed. The project should start in pilot form, focused on a set of countries, sectors, or a region, and scale up with proof of concept.

The State Department is piloting a technology platform called the International Counterterrorism and Countering Violent Extremism Capacity-Building Clearinghouse Mechanism (ICCM) to help governments coordinate their global counterterrorism and CVE efforts.[22] Yet the purpose of the ICCM is merely to map programs, identify gaps, and eliminate duplicative efforts in order to allocate resources more efficiently. It is not intended to measure the effectiveness of programs, and this is what is sorely needed. A CVE measurement clearinghouse, by contrast, would adopt a simplified ranking system of all global CVE efforts to make successful programs easy to fund. Although some may contest the scientific rigor of evaluating programs in such a way, the benefits far outweigh the costs of continuing to design programs in the dark.

CONCLUSION

In policy circles, the shortcomings of CVE efforts are often attributed to a lack of funding, inconsistent leadership, and poor coordination. To be sure, more resources, centralized leadership, and better coordination would be helpful. But these alone will not necessarily improve the efficacy of CVE efforts in America. What is needed is to clearly define the concept and practice—as well as tighten the scope of effort—while always adhering to American values and principles.

For these reasons, the U.S. government should jettison a faith-community-oriented approach. A better agenda would focus on individuals who have demonstrated a clear and sustained interest in jihadi propaganda. The more that the CVE agenda can identify and target specific individuals who have demonstrated sympathy for designated foreign terrorist organizations, the more the U.S. government will be able to measure and evaluate success, refine its programs and initiatives accordingly, and ultimately mitigate the threat of violent extremism in America.

Notes

1. See Drew DeSilver, "U.S. Spends over $16 Billion Annually on Counter-Terrorism," Fact Tank, Pew Research Center, September 11, 2013, www.pewresearch .org/fact-tank/2013/09/11/u-s-spends-over-16-billion-annually-on-counter-terror ism/. See Rosa Prince, "CIA Says Number of Islamic State Fighters in Iraq and Syria Has Swelled to between 20,000 and 31,500," *The Telegraph*, September 12, 2014, www.telegraph.co.uk/news/worldnews/northamerica/usa/11091190/CIA-says-number-of-Islamic-State-fighters-in-Iraq-and-Syria-has-swelled-to-between-20000-and-31500.html.

2. See U.S. Department of State and U.S. Agency for International Development, "Department of State & USAID Joint Strategy on Countering Violent Extremism," May 2016, www.state.gov/documents/organization/257913.pdf. Also see "The White House Summit on Countering Violent Extremism," White House Office of the Press Secretary, February 18, 2015, www.whitehouse.gov/the-press-office/2015/02/18/fact-sheet-white-house-summit-countering-violent-extremism.

3. "Countering Violent Extremism Task Force" (press release, Department of Homeland Security, January 8, 2016), www.dhs.gov/news/2016/01/08/countering-violent-extremism-task-force.

4. "Bipartisan Support in Congress to Counter Violent Extremism," Homeland Security Committee, U.S. House of Representatives, July 16, 2015, https://homeland. house.gov/press/bipartisan-support-congress-counter-violent-extremism/.

5. See the Global Counterrrorism Forum website at www.thegctf.org/ and the Hedayah Center website at www.hedayah.ae.

6. Ken Dilanian, "U.S. Says It's Slowing Flow, But Foreign Fighters Still Flock to ISIS," *NBC News*, January 16, 2016, www.nbcnews.com/storyline/isis-terror/u-s-says-it-s-slowing-flow-foreign-fighters-still-n494281.

7. Besheer Mohamed, "A New Estimate of the U.S. Muslim Population," Pew Research Center, January 6, 2016, www.pewresearch.org/fact-tank/2016/01/06/a-new-estimate-of-the-u-s-muslim-population/.

8. Out of the 250 Americans, 150 individuals were successful in traveling overseas as foreign fighters; 100 were arrested before they were able to leave the United States.

9. Conrad Hackett, "5 Facts about the Muslim Population in Europe," Pew Research Center, July 19, 2016, www.pewresearch.org/fact-tank/2016/07/19/5-facts-about-the-muslim-population-in-europe/; Richard Barrett and others, "An Updated Assessment of the Flow of Foreign Fighters into Syria and Iraq" (New York: The Soufan Group, December 2015), http://soufangroup.com/wp-content/uploads/2015/12/TSG_ForeignFightersUpdate3.pdf.

10. Aaron Williams, Kaeti Hinck, Laris Karklis, Kevin Schaul, and Stephanie Stamm, "How Two Brussels Neighborhoods Became 'a Breeding Ground' for Terror," *Washington Post*, April 1, 2016.

11. "Pilot Programs Are Key to Our Countering Violent Extremism Efforts," Department of Justice, February 18, 2015, www.justice.gov/opa/blog/pilot-programs-are-key-our-countering-violent-extremism-efforts.

12. Adam Goldman, Jia Lynn Yang, and John Muyskens, "The Islamic State's Suspected Inroads into America," *Washington Post*, November 15, 2016.

13. "Pilot Programs Are Key to Our Countering Violent Extremism Efforts."

14. Peter Bergen and others, "America's Layered Defenses," in "In Depth: Terrorism in America After 9/11," New America, n.d., www.newamerica.org/in-depth/terrorism-in-america/what-threat-united-states-today/#americas-layered-defenses.

15. Terry Frieden, "FBI Report: Gang Membership Spikes," CNN, October 21, 2011, www.cnn.com/2011/10/21/justice/gang-membership-increase/; "Chicago Most Gang-Infested City in U.S., Officials Say," *NBC Chicago*, January 26, 2012, www.nbc-chicago.com/news/local/chicago-crime-commision-gang-book-138174334.html.

16. Kenneth D. Kochanek, Sherry L. Murphy, Jiaquan Xu, and Betzaida Tejada-Vera, "Deaths: Final Data for 2014," *National Vital Statistics Reports* 65, no. 4 (2016), www.cdc.gov/nchs/data/nvsr/nvsr65/nvsr65_04.pdf.

17. Pierre Thomas, "FBI Tracking Nearly 800 ISIS-Related Cases Across US, FBI Director Says," *ABC News*, May 11, 2016, http://abcnews.go.com/US/fbi-tracking-800-isis-related-cases-us-fbi/story?id=39037540.

18. For 100 Resilient Cities programs, see www.100resilientcities.org/. For Strong Cities program, see http://strongcitiesnetwork.org/.

19. For those convicted of terrorism-related charges, see "Who Are America's 'Homegrown Terrorists'?," NPR, February 2, 2016, www.npr.org/2016/02/02/4652 57993/who-are-americas-homegrown-terrorists. On the ISIS-related offenses, see "Terrorism in the U.S.," Program on Extremism (Washington, D.C.: George Washington University, May 2016), https://cchs.gwu.edu/sites/cchs.gwu.edu/files/downloads/May%20Update.pdf.

20. "Final Report of the Task Force on Combating Terrorism and Foreign Fighter Travel," Homeland Security Committee, U.S. House of Representatives, September 2015, https://homeland.house.gov/wp-content/uploads/2015/09/TaskForceFinal Report.pdf.

21. Two initiatives were established to provide messaging and countermessaging: the Global Engagement Center, housed at the State Department, and the Sawab Center in Abu Dhabi, a joint collaboration between the United States and United Arab Emirates.

22. "Global Counterterrorism Forum Co-Chairs' Fact Sheet: The Deliverables" (press release, Department of State, September 27, 2015), www.state.gov/r/pa/prs/ps/2015/09/247368.htm.

23

Criminal Justice Reform

WILLIAM A. GALSTON

SUMMARY: Americans across partisan, ideological, and racial lines are rethinking the country's criminal justice system. This is entirely appropriate—and necessary. And yet, conversations, debates, and policy prescriptions around this issue often are not rooted in sound data. All too often, convoluted and even contradictory facts are cited, undermining efforts to improve a system that is in many ways broken. This chapter seeks to provide citizens and policymakers—including the next president—with a framework for assessing the opportunities and challenges of criminal justice reform by situating decades-long crime and punishment trends in appropriate historical and comparative contexts. The author has compiled the best substantiated data on five critical elements of the criminal justice system: nationwide crime rates; prison population and buildup; the costs of incarceration; and individuals killed by police. The evidence and facts presented here will allow interested parties to approach these complex issues from a common place of factual understanding. The author concludes by examining recent legislative efforts related to criminal justice reform and urging the next president and Congress to seize the opportunity afforded by contemporary bipartisan support and public demand for action around these issues.

I n recent years, the future course of the American criminal justice system has come under immense scrutiny. The White House indicated that substantial reform would be a leading priority for President Obama's last year in office, both chambers of Congress have seen legislation introduced and debated, Americans across the country have turned their passionate attention to the issue, and the subject was raised in all of the presidential and vice presidential debates in the 2016 campaign. At times, however, the passions of both citizens and lawmakers on this issue are fueled by incomplete, inaccurate, and insufficient data. For that reason, this chapter collects and compiles the best substantiated data on critical elements of the criminal justice system to provide an informed common framework for understanding the state of the system today, and the proposed reforms that will shape its future.

THE ISSUES AND FACTS

Five critical elements of the criminal justice system—nationwide crime rates; prison population and buildup; the costs of incarceration; and individuals killed by police—are worth assessing and evaluating in greater detail.

Crime

Despite recent speculation about a nationwide crime surge,[1] crime rates are near the lowest levels seen in decades. From 1980 to 2012, the most recent year for which comprehensive, nationwide data are available, there has been a 35 percent drop in the violent crime rate (from 597 to 387 crimes per 100,000 citizens) and a 47 percent decrease in the property crime rate (from 5,353 to 2,859 crimes per 100,000 citizens).[2] From 1980 to 2008, homicide rates declined for blacks as well as for whites, with a significant uptick and subsequent decline in the early 1990s. The homicide victimization rate for whites declined 49 percent (from 6.5 to 3.3 homicides per 100,000 citizens), and the offense rate dropped 47 percent (from 6.4 to 3.4 homicides per 100,000 citizens). Parallel to this trend, the black homicide victimization rate declined 48 percent (from 37.6 to 19.6 homicides per 100,000 citizens) and offense rate declined 50 percent (from 49.8 to 24.7 homicides per 100,000 citizens).[3]

While the nationwide arrest rate for all offenses decreased by 16 percent during this period, the arrest rate for drug crime increased by 93.4 percent.[4] Drug sale/manufacturing arrests increased by 55 percent and drug possession arrests increased 104.5 percent.[5] Arrest rates are not synonymous with rates of offenses, but rather reflect the frequency with which crimes are reported, police decisions regarding offenses on which they will concentrate their attention and resources, and the relative vulnerability of certain crimes to arrest.

The net decrease in nationwide crime coincides with the rapid buildup of the U.S. prison population. However, the relationship between decreased crime and increased incarceration is disputed. Historic decreases in crime and arrest rates stem from a number of complex social and political factors. Beyond increased incarceration, widely discussed hypotheses include:

- **Improved policing:** Over the past two decades, new technology has permitted police to use data to target and reduce crime.[6]

- **Waning demand for crack cocaine:** As the demand for crack has waned, so too has the associated violence and addiction.[7]

- **Shifting demographics: The average age of the U.S.** population has increased, and age is inversely related to propensity to commit a crime.[8]

- **The economy:** Favorable economic conditions in the 1990s and 2000s, including low unemployment rates and increased consumer confidence, reduced some of the impetus for crime.[9]

Prison Buildup

Over the past 30 years, the U.S. prison population has increased by 340 percent.[10] The incarcerated population is a function of the number of offenders admitted to and released from prison. For decades, the number of prisoners admitted greatly outpaced the number released, driving a surge in the local, state, and federal populations of incarcerated individuals.[11] As of 2013, the latest year for which comprehensive nationwide data are available, the United States incarcerated 2,220,300 individuals.[12]

There is vigorous scholarly debate on the causes and correlates of the burgeoning prison population.[13] Increased admissions can be attributed to various factors, including increased rates of investigation, prosecution, sentencing, and admission.[14] Decreased releases are due to factors such as increased sentence length and decreased eligibility for parole.[15] Many of these factors are the result of public policy choices, which vary with the nation's political mood. In the mid-1970s, for instance, reformers championed statutory sentencing standards, including mandatory minimums, to address "racial and other unwarranted disparities" in the criminal justice system.[16] A decade later, responding to surging crime rates and widespread concern about public safety, state and federal lawmakers enacted tough new measures—mandatory minimum laws, three strikes laws, and life in prison without the possibility of parole, for instance—to target violent and drug offenders.[17]

Prison Composition

In 2014, the state prison population was 6.4 times that of the federal prison population.[18] In state prisons, violent offenders comprise the majority (53 percent) of sentenced prisoners, while drug offenders make up just 16 percent of the population.[19] In federal prisons, drug offenders make up the majority (50 percent) of the population, while violent offenders constitute just 7 percent of the population.[20]

Of federal drug offenders, 95.1 percent can be classified as traffickers, while just 0.8 percent are imprisoned for unlawful possession. However, the drug offender category is quite broad and includes offenses ranging in culpability from drug mule to high-level supplier or importer. Fewer than half of federal drug offenders (41.4 percent) are involved with the organization and/or management of the drug trade. Indeed, the majority (56.7 percent) of offenders played a lesser and more replaceable role in drug distribution.[21]

Characteristics of the Prison Population

Although men comprise the majority (93.4 percent) of the U.S. incarcerated population, the proportion of incarcerated women has grown at almost twice the rate of men since the 1990s.[22] The underlying circumstances contributing to the dramatic increase in women's incarceration for drug offenses have yet to be thoroughly examined and addressed by researchers or policymakers.[23]

The United States incarcerates a disproportionate number of black and Latino individuals relative to their composition in the U.S. population.[24] The causes and correlates of this racial discrepancy in the criminal justice system are manifold. Studies suggest that a variety of factors contribute to racial disparities in criminal justice involvement, including law enforcement practices, neighborhood crime rates, offenders' socioeconomic status, and state and federal-level sentencing policy.[25]

Most (76.6 percent) offenders recidivate within five years of being released from prison, a striking trend observable across demographic categories.[26] Cyclical incarceration imposes tremendous costs on individuals, families, and communities; even after being released from prison, individuals face legal barriers to employment, housing, and voting.[27] Families with incarcerated loved ones suffer financial losses due to lost income. Studies show that children with incarcerated parents exhibit more negative behavioral, academic, and emotional outcomes.[28] These so-called collateral consequences compound and destabilize community support systems.

Cost of Incarceration

In 2010, total corrections expenditures totaled $80 billion—a 350 percent increase from 1980 (in real terms). Consistent with the distribution of the prison population, the majority of the expenditure occurs at the local and state, rather than federal, levels.[29]

Individuals Killed by Police

In 2015, 987 individuals were shot and killed by police officers. The vast majority (78 percent) of victims were armed with a deadly weapon: only 10 percent were killed while unarmed. Fifty percent of the individuals killed by police were white, but police killed a disproportionate number of minority individuals relative to the racial composition of the U.S. population. Although the data are not inconsistent with racial bias in police shootings, the best available evidence is too limited to allow us to substantiate claims of racial bias.[30]

The majority of police killings do not take place in major metropolitan areas. For example, only 2 out of the 15 fatal shootings in Maryland occurred in Baltimore. Chicago is a notable exception to this pattern; 9 out of the 21 (43 percent) of police shootings in Illinois occurred in Chicago.[31]

REFORM EFFORTS AND OPTIONS

In our hyperpolarized system, signs of emerging agreement across party lines are hard to come by, but criminal justice reform may be one of the few exceptions. During much of 2016, House and Senate Democrats and Republicans have engaged in serious discussions about legislation that could command broad support.

This effort rests on two widely held premises. First, although the tough steps taken in response to the crime surge of the 1980s and 1990s were justified in principle, some went too far, generating unanticipated consequences that need correction. Second, a revolving-door system in which three-quarters of all felons commit new crimes within five years of their release guarantees excessive rates of incarceration and criminal justice expenditures.

The House and Senate bills, which emerged from their respective judiciary committees before stalling mid-year, would attack both problems. With regard to what Senator Chuck Grassley (R-Iowa), Senate Judiciary Committee chair, has called "legitimate over-incarceration concerns," the reform proposals would reduce sentences for low-level drug offenders, the largest single category of federal felons, as well as for weapons offenders, the second-largest category. Some lawmakers see this reform as the leading edge of a broader reconsideration of "mandatory minimum sentences," a strategy adopted in the 1990s to prevent lenient judges from allowing convicted criminals to return to the streets too quickly. Regarding recidivism, the bipartisan Charles Colson Task Force on Federal Correction urged Congress to give the Federal Bureau of Prisons the authority and the resources to deliver evidence-based educational and job-related training to inmates, especially those at the greatest risk of reoffending. Here again, legislation moved forward in both the House and the Senate before hitting roadblocks. President Trump will have the opportunity to build on the progress made in 2016 and score an early bipartisan win.

Although this would be a good start, it would not be enough. To reverse the revolving door in and out of prisons, for example, localities backed by the federal government would have to set up comprehensive reintegration regimes for recently released inmates, including much better linkages between these individuals and potential employers. The current system of parole supervision is not up to this task or, more accurately, does not really try to do it. Some reformers have endorsed a proposal called "ban the box," which would prohibit employers from inquiring into a job applicant's criminal justice history. Skeptics point to evidence that programs along these lines have led to increased discrimination along lines of race and ethnicity: If employers cannot get information about individuals' criminal records, they go with the demographic odds. It will take patient experimentation and honest commitment to evidence-based policymaking to resolve such issues.

This leaves the thorniest issue of all—relations between local police forces and communities of color. In recent years, high-profile shootings of young minority males have led to protests and social unrest in numerous communities and even to lethal retaliation against police officers. These events have divided public opinion along racial and ethnic lines as well, with whites far less likely than African Americans to see unwarranted and discriminatory police conduct.

But even here, there are signs of hope. Earlier this year, the chair and ranking member of the House Judiciary Committee came together to call for "urgent congressional attention" to address the crisis of confidence between the police and the communities they have pledged to protect. At the same time, they recognized that quantitatively as well as politically, the bulk of the action must take place at the state and local level. While federal legislation may be helpful in some instances, individual communities have different histories and needs. Police-community relations may be similarly vexed in Chicago, Baltimore, and Baton Rouge, for example, but steps that work in one of these communities might not necessarily be equally effective in the others. Nevertheless, there are opportunities for bipartisan leadership that did not exist even a few years ago, and the new occupant of the Oval Office would be well advised to seize them.

Notes

1. Mariano Castillo, "Is a New Crime Wave on the Horizon?," CNN, June 4 2015; Aamer Madhani, "Several Big U.S. Cities See Murder Rates Surge," *USA Today*, July 10, 2015; Martin Kaste, "Nationwide Crime Spike Has Law Enforcement Retooling Its Approach," NPR, October 10, 2015; and Monica Davey, "Murder Rates Rising Sharply in Many U.S. Cities," *New York Times*, August 31, 2015.

2. Brookings analysis of "Estimated Crime in United States—Total," generated using the Uniform Crime Reporting Data Tool, Federal Bureau of Investigation, www.ucrdatatool.gov/Search/Crime/State/RunCrimeStatebyState.cfm.

3. Brookings analysis of Alexia Cooper and Erica L. Smith, "Homicide Trends in the United States, 1980–2008," Bureau of Justice Statistics, November 2011, 11–13, www.bjs.gov/content/pub/pdf/htus8008.pdf.

4. Brookings analysis of "Arrests in the United States, 1980–2012," dataset generated from the Arrest Data Analysis Tool, Bureau of Justice Statistics, www.bjs.gov/index.cfm?ty=datool&surl=/arrests/index.cfm#.

5. Brookings analysis of "Estimated Crime in United States—Total."

6. Jeremy Travis and Michelle Waul, "Reflections on the Crime Decline: Lessons for the Future?" (Washington, D.C.: Urban Institute, August 2002), www.urban.org/uploadedpdf/410546_crimedecline.pdf.

7. Alfred Blumstein and Joel Wallman, *The Crime Drop in America* (Cambridge University Press, 2005).

8. Alfred Blumstein and Richard Rosenfeld, "Factors Contributing to U.S. Crime Trends," in *Understanding Crime Trends: Workshop Report*, edited by Arthur

S. Goldberger and Richard Rosenfeld (Washington, D.C.: National Academies Press, 2008), 13, www.nap.edu/openbook.php?record_id=12472&page=13.

9. Franklin E. Zimring, *The Great American Crime Decline* (Oxford University Press, 2006).

10. "Table: Estimated number of persons under correctional supervision in the United States, 1980–2013," Key Statistics: Total Correctional Population, Bureau of Justice Statistics, www.bjs.gov/index.cfm?ty=kfdetail&iid=487.

11. John Pfaff, "The Myths and Realities of Correctional Severity: Evidence from the National Corrections Reporting Program on Sentencing Practices," *American Law and Economics Review* 13, no. 2 (2011): 491–531.

12. Brookings analysis of "Table: Estimated number of persons under correctional supervision in the United States, 1980–2013."

13. See "Prison Time Surges for Federal Inmates," Pew Charitable Trusts, November 2015, www.pewtrusts.org/en/research-and-analysis/issue-briefs/2015/11/prison-time-surges-for-federal-inmates; Kamala Mallik-Kane, Barbara Parthasarathy, and William Adams, "Examining Growth in the Federal Prison Population, 1998 to 2010" (Washington, D.C.: Urban Institute, 2012), www.urban.org/sites/default/files/alfresco/publication-pdfs/412720-Examining-Growth-in-the-Federal-Prison-Population--to--.PDF; Heather M. Washington and Shawn D. Bushway, "Review: *Why Are So Many Americans in Prison?* By Steven Raphael and Michael Stoll," *Social Forces* 94, no. 3 (2016): e82, http://dx.doi.org/10.1093/sf/sou052; Pfaff "The Myths and Realities of Correctional Severity"; and John Pfaff, "The Causes of Growth in Prison Admission and Population," Social Science Research Network, July 12, 2011, http://dx.doi.org/10.2139/ssrn.1884674.

14. See Mallik-Kane, Parthasarathy, and Adams, "Examining Growth in the Federal Prison Population, 1998 to 2010"; Pfaff, "The Causes of Growth in Prison Admission and Population"; John F. Pfaff, "Escaping from the Standard Story: Why the Conventional Wisdom on Prison Growth is Wrong, and Where We Can Go from Here," Fordham Law Legal Studies Research Paper No. 2414596, *Federal Sentencing Report* 26, no. 265 (2014), http://ssrn.com/abstract=2414596; and "Drivers of Growth in the Federal Prison Population," Charles Colson Task Force on Federal Corrections and the Urban Institute, March 2015, www.urban.org/sites/default/files/alfresco/publication-pdfs/2000141-Drivers-of-Growth-in-the-Federal-Prison-Population.pdf.

15. Mallik-Kane, Parthasarathy, and Adams, "Examining Growth in the Federal Prison Population, 1998 to 2010"; Pfaff, "The Causes of Growth in Prison Admission and Population."

16. Jeremy Travis, Bruce Western, and Steve Redburn, *The Growth of Incarceration in the United States: Exploring Causes and Consequences* (Washington, D.C.: National Academies Press, 2014), 71–74.

17. Ibid.

18. Brookings analysis of Ann Carson, "Prisoners in 2014," Bureau of Justice Statistics, September 2015, 3, www.bjs.gov/content/pub/pdf/p14.pdf; and Todd Minton

and Zhen Zeng, "Jail Inmates at Midyear 2014," Bureau of Justice Statistics, June 2015, 3, www.bjs.gov/content/pub/pdf/jim14.pdf.

19. Carson, "Prisoners in 2014," 16, table 11.

20. Ibid., 17, table 12.

21. William Galston and Elizabeth McElvein, "Criminal Justice Reform: The Facts about Federal Drug Offenders" (Brookings, February 13, 2016).

22. Nicholas Freudenberg, "Adverse Effects of US Jail and Prison Policies on the Health and Well-Being of Women of Color," *American Journal of Public Health* 92, no. 12 (2012): 1895.

23. "Caught in the Net: The Impact of Drug Policies on Women and Families," American Civil Liberties Union, Break the Chains, and Brennan Center for Justice at NYU, 2005, www.aclu.org/caught-net-impact-drug-policies-women-and-families.

24. Brookings analysis of Paul Guerino, Paige Harrison, and William Sabol, "Prisoners in 2010," Bureau of Justice Statistics, December 2011, appendix table 12, 26, www.bjs.gov/content/pub/pdf/p10.pdf

25. "Reducing Racial Disparity in the Criminal Justice System: A Manual for Practitioners and Policymakers" (Washington, D.C.: The Sentencing Project, 2008), 5, www.sentencingproject.org/wp-content/uploads/2016/01/Reducing-Racial-Dispar ity-in-the-Criminal-Justice-System-A-Manual-for-Practitioners-and-Policymakers .pdf.

26. Matthew R. Durose, Alexia D. Cooper, and Howard D. Snyder, "Recidivism of Prisoners Released in 30 States in 2005: Patterns from 2005 to 2010," Bureau of Justice Statistics, April 2014, www.bjs.gov/content/pub/pdf/rprts05p0510.pdf.

27. "Transforming Prisons, Restoring Lives: Final Recommendations of the Charles Colson Task Force on Federal Corrections" (Charles Colson Task Force on Federal Corrections, January 2015), 15, http://colsontaskforce.org/final-recommen dations/Colson-Task-Force-Final-Recommendations-January-2016.pdf.

28. Joseph Murray, David P. Farrington, and Ivana Sekol, "Children's Antisocial Behavior, Mental Health, Drug Use, and Educational Performance after Parental Incarceration: A Systematic Review and Meta-analysis," *Psychological Bulletin* 138, no. 2 (2012): 175–210; and Ross D. Parke and K. Alison Clarke-Stewart, "The Effects of Parental Incarceration on Children: Perspectives, Promises and Policies," in *Prisoners Once Removed: The Impact of Incarceration and Reentry on Children, Families, and Communities*, edited by Jeremy Travis and Michelle Waul (Washington, D.C.: Urban Institute Press, 2003), 189–232.

29. Melissa S. Kearney, Benjamin H. Harris, Elisa Jácome, and Lucie Parker, "Ten Economic Facts about Crime and Incarceration in the United States" (Hamilton Project, Brookings, May 2014), 13.

30. Brookings analysis of Julie Tate and others, "Investigation: People Shot and Killed by Police This Year," *Washington Post*, January 11, 2016.

31. Ibid. According to the 2015 *Law Enforcement Officer Fatalities Report*, 124 officers died "in the line of duty" in 2015. Of those, a majority were victims of either traffic accidents or job-related illnesses. Forty-two officers were fatally shot.

24

Lawful Hacking and the Case for a Strategic Approach to Going Dark

SUSAN HENNESSEY

SUMMARY: Technological advances in encryption and other forms of data security have created problems for government and law enforcement agencies. They may have an investigative need and legal right to access particular communications, but often lack the technical ability to do so. The federal government needs to take a more pragmatic approach to "lawful hacking" that will protect individual privacy and secure information but still allow law enforcement agencies to conduct criminal investigations that may be needed to protect its citizens.

Following two years of intense discussion and a series of mutually bruising legal stand-offs, the U.S. government and Silicon Valley are no closer to resolving the "going dark" debate. Going dark refers to the phenomenon by which government agencies have a legal right to access particular communications but lack the technical ability to do so, often because technology companies have deployed strong encryption to shield the information. Not only are the various participants unable to find a resolution to the problem, they are unable to agree on the proper analogy for it—or even whether there actually is a problem.

Legislative efforts have failed. Legal battles ended without producing additional clarity. Attempts at voluntary cooperation have gone nowhere. Finding a more productive path is critical to the future public-private cooperation that will be necessary for many unrelated cybersecurity efforts. A new approach is needed.

The federal government in a new administration should adopt and articulate a pragmatic approach that fully embraces lawful hacking as a possible alternative to legislative mandates. A coordinated interagency position should clearly communicate the tradeoffs, stakes, and strategic aims of lawful hacking. Moreover, recognizing that future legislative efforts may be required, the government should seek to develop empirical data to inform long-term decisionmaking on cybersecurity policy in law enforcement investigations.

BACKGROUND

In 2011, then–FBI general counsel Valerie Caproni used the term "going dark" to describe "a potentially widening gap between our legal authority to intercept electronic communications pursuant to court order and our practical ability to actually intercept those communications."[1] That prediction has proved largely accurate. Although some technological developments and trends have assisted law enforcement collection, a variety of pressures place ever more communications content beyond the reach of a warrant. The underlying factors include broader adoption of end-to-end encryption, full disk encryption, and stronger security defaults, but also extend to widely available anonymization tools, trends toward data localization, and the availability of large-storage removable media devices. In short, the factors underlying the phenomenon are varied and not limited to technological developments alone.

Although going dark also impacts intelligence collection, the most pressing concerns arise in the context of law enforcement. In ordinary criminal investigations, end-to-end encrypted messaging, stronger device encryption, and IP anonymization tools present acute challenges. The problem's scale has increased dramatically over the past few years, as a number of major communications providers have taken steps toward offering end-to-end encrypted messaging and sophisticated device encryption broadly and by default.[2] Anyone who does not hold the required keys, including the providers themselves, is unable to access communications sent using those platforms or stored on those devices. Unquestionably, these features offer substantial security benefits to consumers. But the effect, whether intentional or unintended, is that even when law enforcement obtains a warrant, the content is inaccessible unless investigators can obtain the keys directly from individuals.

What had been a simmering tension between the government and technology companies boiled over into a heated public debate in February 2016. That month, the Department of Justice sought a court order to compel Apple to assist the government in unlocking an iPhone belonging to San Bernardino terrorist Sayed Farook. The precise legal questions centered on whether a court could require Apple to provide a particular form of technical assistance, where it unquestionably retained the capacity to do so. The case resolved itself out of court when a third party demonstrated the ability to unlock the phone at issue and the government withdrew its motion. While the San Bernardino case was actually about what technical assistance a company must provide to the government where it is able, the public debate centered on a distinct and important question: should companies be required to ensure that the government has access to communications content when required for an investigation?

Broadly speaking, at issue are the relative risks and merits of requiring "exceptional access" for law enforcement, which is often characterized by opponents as a "backdoor." Most notably, Senators Dianne Feinstein and Richard Burr advanced draft legislation to require companies to retain the technical capacity to comply with court orders to produce plaintext communications.[3] This legislation would, in effect, prohibit companies from deploying security features that place communications content beyond their own reach. Critics decried the draft as technologically illiterate and dangerous, arguing that it compromised user security overall.

Unsurprisingly, the heated rhetoric allowed little room for facts and common sense. Most of the public engagements consisted of each side assuming and then dismissing the other side's concerns, either by insisting that exceptional access does not necessarily compromise information security or by alleging that law enforcement overstates its need to see communications content. One strain of criticism to "backdoors," however, recognized law enforcement's concerns and offered a potential solution: so-called "lawful hacking."[4] Instead of creating additional vulnerabilities to an already-fragile security ecosystem in the form of exceptional access, these commentators argued that law enforcement should exploit existing software and hardware vulnerabilities. In theory, the position offers a workable middle ground by which law enforcement is able to access a sufficient amount of communications and companies are unimpeded in

designing secure systems. But in order for lawful hacking to be a meaningful alternative—as opposed to a diversionary tactic to delay government
action—a number of questions must be addressed.

The government has employed hacking techniques since long before
the Apple v. FBI controversy, and it faces opposition to those actions from
many of the same groups that oppose exceptional access. Despite some express suggestions that pose lawful hacking as an alternative to backdoors,
the specific debates over the procedural rules, operational policies, and
legal standards central to the feasibility of lawful hacking have proceeded
largely in parallel to the conversation regarding going dark. In reality, the
two conversations are deeply related. Congress and the executive branch
are accountable to a public that expects the government to discharge law
enforcement functions. And despite critics who declare periodic victories
or insist that access to communications content is unnecessary for law
enforcement, the going dark problem is not going away. Therefore, if the
executive branch is unable to successfully develop lawful hacking tools to
address a sufficient amount of the need for government access to communications to meet the expectations of the general public, it becomes
dramatically more likely that it will feel compelled to seek comprehensive
legislative solutions mandating exceptional access.

A STRATEGIC APPROACH TO MOVING FORWARD

Thus far, the FBI has been the public face of the government's engagement.
This has created ambiguity as to whether FBI director Jim Comey speaks
on behalf of the federal government, on behalf of law enforcement, or only
for himself. The federal government is not monolithic, after all, and technological developments have uneven effects on the equities of different
agencies. Therefore, it is not surprising that there is no consensus view
even within government on the best way to address the problem. But the
lack of any clear government position gives the impression of internecine
battles and masks shared principles.

Stronger leadership is needed in order to clarify the government's interests and goals. A coordinated interagency position does not require reaching agreement on the ultimate solution. Instead, the White House should
coordinate a position that articulates the government's view regarding the
general scope and severity of the impact of going dark on law enforcement
specifically.

Some forms of communication will always remain inaccessible, and the proper balance of information security and law enforcement needs will require tradeoffs. But the government must be clear that the American people expect law enforcement to prevent, investigate, and prosecute crimes. It would be unacceptable and intolerable for the executive branch to simply accept that police function be significantly impaired, especially in the context of serious offenses. However, where experts agree that the most direct and comprehensive solution—a legislative decryption mandate—would have significant security downsides and potentially wide-ranging unintended consequences, prudence requires investigating potential alternatives.

The executive branch should deliberately set itself to solving as much of the going dark problem as is possible before resorting to costly and controversial legislation, especially since it is clear that a legislative solution is unlikely to become politically feasible any time soon. Under the best outcome, a genuine investment in varied alternative strategies, possibly coupled with technological developments favoring law enforcement equities, would create a stable situation moving forward. But even if it does not, it is useful to exhaust alternatives in demonstrating the necessity of comprehensive mandates.

Adopting a strategic position of pursuing alternatives also has the benefit of clarifying the opposition. Many companies and advocacy organizations state that they support law enforcement action and believe that crimes should be fully investigated; their objection is only to making imprudent security sacrifices to that end. This strategy would present a good faith attempt to reconcile those views by pursuing "least bad" alternatives. But those who oppose not only performance standard legislation but also all feasible alternatives in effect endorse a view that it is tolerable for law enforcement to be unable to detect, prevent, investigate, or prosecute certain offenses.

A NATIONAL STRATEGY ON LAWFUL HACKING

Lawful hacking is a necessary, though possibly not sufficient, element of a workable solution without mandated exceptional access. Therefore, lawful hacking should be viewed as the central element of a comprehensive alternative strategy, which includes investments in using metadata and the emerging Internet of Things to offset the losses to communication content that make up the going dark problem.[5]

The ultimate utility of lawful hacking will depend as much on legal developments as technological ones. This series of complex, interrelated legal questions is central to the future of law enforcement and U.S. national security. Those questions should not be answered haphazardly or based on the expedient incentives of individual criminal cases, and instead must be given adequate thought. To achieve this, the administration should direct the Department of Justice to develop a National Strategy on Lawful Hacking. Below are recommendations for elements of an effective national strategy.

Coordinate Lawful Hacking Investigations and Prosecutions

The Department of Justice should coordinate categories of cases related to lawful hacking, including those involving the use of sensitive government tools or novel network investigative techniques, or those where a single warrant is expected to result in prosecutions in numerous but unidentified jurisdictions. Coordination ensures consistent representation of the government's position on the legal questions central to the success of this alternative strategy.

The department's litigation strategy also should focus on obtaining the clearest possible answers, and not fear establishing unfavorable precedents. Here, the resolution of legal questions may be more important than the answers themselves. For example, one controversy currently being litigated is whether a defendant is entitled to review sensitive computer code related to law enforcement techniques. Hacking tools are necessarily perishable, but an obligation to disclose them in court would dramatically reduce their useful lifespan. While some proponents advocate for law enforcement to temporarily exploit and then quickly disclose a vulnerability for patching, this is infeasible in practice and would significantly limit the efficacy of lawful hacking as a broader solution. The sooner the executive branch knows whether such code must be disclosed, the sooner it can strategically invest resources in further pursing the strategy or instead seeking congressional legislation for it.

Support a Technologically Informed Judiciary

The executive branch should call on the Federal Judicial Center to develop a Reference Manual on Computer Science aimed at empowering the federal judiciary to independently evaluate the relevance and materiality of evidence involving computer code and information technology systems. The executive branch has a significant interest in ensuring correct, technologically informed judicial decisions related to lawful hacking, and it should provide technical support and expertise to aid the development of such a guide.

The executive branch also should, to the extent possible, support the designation of independent court-appointed experts. Pursuant to federal evidence rules, a court is entitled to appoint experts of its choosing.[6] In the context of lawful hacking investigations, designating experts would be valuable to assist judges in determining the relative credibility of defense and prosecution expert testimony. And where tools related to lawful hacking contain classified or highly sensitive information, the government should seek to designate specially cleared, impartial experts. This is a limited solution, but similar strategies have been successful mechanisms for independent assessment of highly sensitive materials in the context of the Foreign Intelligence Surveillance Court.[7]

Develop Ethical Use Guidelines for Federal Investigatory Agencies

Policy guidelines should specify the circumstances in which the use of lawful hacking is permitted. Broadly, policies should ensure that hacking techniques are deployed only after less intrusive means have been exhausted, as is required when wiretapping.

Government policy should also set guidelines, similar to those for undercover operations, governing lawful hacking that temporarily facilitates criminal activity. Standards should be set to balance probable harms and benefits and to ensure that criminal activity is facilitated only where strictly necessary to prevent ongoing harm.

Invest Resources in Investigating the Most Serious Offenses

Lawful hacking is resource intensive, both to develop or purchase the necessary tools and to properly coordinate investigations. Consequently, executive policy should invest these limited resources in investigations of the most serious offenses—violent crime, sexual offenses against children, large-scale narcotics trafficking, and terrorism. Limiting lawful hacking to serious cases ensures appropriate allocation of research and development resources, better protects tools, and facilitates coordinated prosecution strategies.

Embrace Mass Hacking

Lawful hacking often, though not always, constitutes a search under the Fourth Amendment and thus requires law enforcement to obtain a search warrant. Opponents of lawful hacking warn of the government's ability to target thousands of computers pursuant to a single warrant, calling it "mass hacking."[8] But the government should embrace mass hacking as a paradigm shift necessary for investigations to respond to going dark, and the Justice Department should clearly articulate how warrants for such operations can satisfy all constitutional requirements. Individuals who use computers to facilitate the most serious offenses, particularly those related to child sexual exploitation, avail themselves of the most sophisticated available technologies to hide their identities and crimes. Because of better tools and stronger defaults, those offenders make fewer mistakes, which limits available opportunities for law enforcement intervention. In investigations with opportunities to uncover serious crimes and rescue victims—and where warrants can be obtained—law enforcement should be encouraged to unmask as many offenders as possible.

Demand Security in Exchange for Disclosure

The government should clearly articulate the vulnerabilities equities process applicable to law enforcement hacking tools that rely on undisclosed flaws in commercial software. The public should have a clear understanding as to the considerations and safeguards in developing such tools and be confident that the balance between disclosure and use maximizes overall security benefits.[9]

The government also should mandate that technology companies that are notified of a vulnerability pursuant to the equities process either patch the flaw within a reasonable time period or provide periodic updates detailing the reason for their failure to protect consumers. This policy maximizes security benefits. The reason to disclose a vulnerability is so that it can be patched to eliminate the threat that bad actors will discover and exploit it; nonetheless, disclosure represents some degree of loss to the security interests served by government use. Typically, that loss is more than offset by the ubiquitous information security gains of patching, but both the government and the technology company affected should act to avoid the net harm that results when a vulnerability is disclosed and no patch is deployed.

Develop Empirical Data to Inform Long-Term Decisionmaking

The government should seek to develop data regarding the precise scope of going dark and the impact on law enforcement. This includes tracking instances in which law enforcement was unable to effectuate a court order to view communications content and the disposition of cases where such content could not be obtained.

The government should also support empirical research regarding the probable consequences of legislative options and lawful hacking methods. For example, while software updates might provide an existing mechanism to push malicious updates to the target of a warrant, experts fear that this type of action could result in fewer individuals updating software and could create widespread insecurity. Where probable behavioral responses are measurable propositions, the government should seek evidence to inform policy that promotes cybersecurity benefits by avoiding more drastic and potentially harmful solutions, and also minimizes harm. Similarly, research is needed into the genuine consequences of law enforcement retaining vulnerabilities, which is the most controversial element of lawful hacking.

CONCLUSION

Going dark presents fundamental tradeoffs. Maximally secure information technology systems exist at the real cost of how effective law enforcement can be. Conversely, maximally efficient law enforcement may require some genuine compromise to our information system security. Ultimately, that choice will have to be made either all at once through comprehensive legislation, or continually over time by refining the balance through "good enough" alternatives. Standing still, however, is not an option. The continued evolution of technologies alters the available options over time—solutions that are available today may not be in the near future. The choices here are neither easy nor obvious, but it is not yet necessary to determine the ultimate conclusion.

A strategic, solution-minded policy facilitates law enforcement function and allows for the development of much-needed evidence to inform law and policy choices. What is required now is pragmatic and clear leadership. The stakes are too high to wait.

Notes

1. Valerie Caproni, statement before the House Judiciary Committee, February 17, 2011.

2. "Report of the Manhattan District Attorney's Office on Smartphone Encryption and Public Safety," November 2015, 2–6.

3. Compliance with Court Orders Act, 114th Congress (2016).

4. Steven M. Bellovin, Matt Blaze, Sandy Clark, and Susan Landau, "Lawful Hacking: Using Existing Vulnerabilities for Wiretapping on the Internet," *Northwestern Journal of Technology and Intellectual Property* 12, no. 1 (2014).

5. Matthew Olsen and others, "Don't Panic: Making Progress on the 'Going Dark' Debate" (Berkman Center for Internet & Society at Harvard University, 2016), https://cyber.harvard.edu/pubrelease/dont-panic/Dont_Panic_Making_Progress_on_Going_Dark_Debate.pdf.

6. Federal Rule of Evidence 706(a).

7. 50 U.S.C. §1803(i)(1), "Designation of judges."

8. Ron Wyden, "Wyden Calls for a Vote on SMH Act to Stop Massive Expansion of Government Hacking into Americans' Personal Devices" (press release, September 8, 2016).

9. Ari Schwartz and Rob Knake, "Government's Role in Vulnerability Disclosure: Creating a Permanent and Accountable Vulnerability Equities Process" (Belfer Center for Science and International Affairs, Harvard Kennedy School, June 2016), 12–14.

25

To Preserve an Important U.S. Intelligence Tool, Trump Needs to Set a Different Tone

BENJAMIN WITTES

SUMMARY: At the end of 2017, a major U.S. intelligence collection authority is set to expire unless Congress acts to renew it. Reauthorization should have been a no-brainer. Under a Trump administration, it may not be.

W hether President-elect Donald Trump and his advisers know it or not, a complex challenge in the field of intelligence law will confront the new president almost immediately when he takes office: The legal authorization for one of the intelligence community's most important collection programs is set to expire on December 31, 2017.

The failure to reauthorize the law at issue—Section 702 of the FISA Amendments Act—would deal a body blow to the intelligence community. Yet the conduct of Mr. Trump as a candidate and immediately following his election will greatly complicate his task as president of bringing about its reauthorization. In the current environment, it will require care and prudence on the part of the new administration to put itself in a position to ask for and receive reauthorization of 702, since many people, based on the candidate's own words and actions, will reasonably fear abuses by intelligence agencies under his control.

But for Mr. Trump's election, the debate over 702 reauthorization was poised to be a relatively easy one. The law—which clarifies that the normal warrant requirements of the Foreign Intelligence Surveillance Act do not apply when the National Security Agency or the FBI is conducting surveillance of non-U.S. persons reasonably believed to be outside the United States—is a critically important tool.

Broadly speaking, it permits the intelligence community to target certified categories of foreign communications for collection as they pass through U.S. servers and tech companies. Information derived from the 702 program, sometimes known as PRISM, comprises a large part of the President's Daily Brief. Intelligence community insiders unanimously view 702 as one of the most important available instruments for foreign intelligence signal collection in the United States. The reason is that the FISA warrant requirement was never meant to apply to non-American targets overseas, and its cumbersome procedure—designed to protect civil liberties domestically—is simply incompatible with the volume of foreign intelligence information the United States collects abroad and the aggressiveness with which it does so. Yet much of this information, because of the dominance of U.S. technology companies in the global information architecture, now passes through servers in the United States. Without 702 to relieve the intelligence community of the strict terms of FISA, a lot of collection would grind to a halt.

What's more, despite the anxieties expressed over 702, particularly in the wake of the Edward Snowden leaks, there have been no serious allegations that the 702 program has been the subject of abuse, and there is a lot of evidence that it has been used responsibly. There is strong bipartisan support for the program among members of both the House and Senate intelligence committees. As of November 7, in other words, the only serious question about 702 reauthorization was whether it would be a "clean reauthorization"—one without significant changes—or whether Congress would seek to build in some limited number of additional protections.

Mr. Trump's election, however, substantially complicates the reauthorization picture. This is a man, after all, who campaigned promising abuses of power involving the intelligence community: spying on people because of their religion, torture, and retaliation against political opponents. This is also a man who, after the election, has left open the possibility of removing FBI director James Comey because the director concluded a criminal investigation without bringing charges against Mr. Trump's opponent, Hillary Clinton. We often think about 702 as an NSA authority, but it is also to a significant degree an FBI authority. Thus, the person and the integrity of the FBI director is critically important to the integrity of the program. When a president openly contemplates violating the strong customary norm against firing the FBI director, based on the president's predetermination that a citizen is guilty of a crime absent evidence, and replacing that person with someone acceptable to himself, it inevitably casts 702 in a very different light.

Unless and until Mr. Trump changes the environment with respect to the pervasive and justified anxieties about his intentions, 702 reauthorization may be extremely difficult, if not impossible. Even the Obama administration, which was not accused of significant abuses of intelligence authorities and which always struck a measured tone on those authorities, increasingly struggled to pass FISA-related laws. The USA Freedom Act, the last set of major changes to FISA, passed only after a divided Congress actually let an intelligence program lapse for a period of time. If Mr. Trump continues to send erratic and dangerous signals, it is not hard to imagine a bipartisan coalition in the House of Representatives preventing 702 reauthorization. It is even easier to imagine a group of 41 senators blocking consideration of a reauthorization bill in the Senate, either as an end itself or as a way of forcing Mr. Trump to stop some other activity or give in on some other matter.

Remember that inaction here produces repeal. The sunset provision requires positive congressional action for 702 to persist.

We might chalk all this up to the ordinary rough and tumble of politics, except for the fact that we need 702 and our security cannot afford even a temporary lapse. The Privacy and Civil Liberties Oversight Board concluded that 702 "has enabled the U.S. government to monitor . . . terrorist networks in order to learn how they operate and to understand how their priorities, strategies, and tactics continue to evolve" and notes that 25 percent of the NSA's reports involving international terrorism rely on data from the program. President Obama's review group following the Snowden revelations concluded that 702 "has clearly served an important function in helping the United States to uncover and prevent terrorist attacks both in the United States and around the world." This is one of the bread-and-butter programs of U.S. signals intelligence, and the incoming president must not let fears about his intentions or personality cause it to evaporate.

The burden is entirely on the new administration, and on Mr. Trump personally, to instill in Congress and in the public the kind of confidence that will make reauthorization possible. To this end, the new administration should take the following five steps:

First, the president-elect should immediately cease the speculation about replacing Director Comey. Comey is not a popular man these days in either political party, but his removal for refusing to indict Hillary Clinton would constitute the most dramatic politicization of the intelligence community since the Watergate era. Though the president undoubtedly has the raw constitutional authority to fire Comey, it would be a grave breach of the presidential obligation to take care that the laws be faithfully executed to fire an investigator for concluding that a U.S. citizen had committed no crime. If President-elect Trump wishes for Congress to continue reposing in him the awesome collection powers associated with 702, he immediately must cease contemplating such abusive behavior.

Second, the president-elect needs to choose Justice Department leadership of genuine stature and bipartisan regard. The first line of oversight of all FISA programs, outside the intelligence agencies themselves, is the men and women of the U.S. Department of Justice, who both restrain and represent the intelligence agencies in court. The persons of the attorney general, the deputy attorney general, and the assistant attorney general for national security thus matter a great deal. Are these people whose word—when they make factual representations to the court, Congress, and to the public—matters? Mr. Trump ran a remarkably fact-free campaign. The relationship between the intelligence community and the law, however, must be based on facts and trustworthy personnel. If Congress does not trust the Justice Department's senior leadership in its intelligence oversight role, and its representation role of the agency in the FISA court system, 702 will die. The selection of Senator Jeff Sessions represents, in this regard, an inauspicious start. The merits of the appointment are beyond the scope of this chapter, but suffice it for the present to say that we can expect a highly partisan fight over his confirmation. And we can expect as well Justice Department comments on 702 matters in the first year of the administration to be received, particularly by Democrats, in light of the fallout from that fight. All of this puts an enormous premium on whom Mr. Trump names for key positions beneath the attorney general.

Third, the president-elect needs also to choose a CIA director of genuine stature and bipartisan regard. The Central Intelligence Agency is not the epicenter of the FISA process. But it is the epicenter of a lot of intelligence controversies. And Mr. Trump's promises, particularly with respect to waterboarding and torture and targeting terrorists' families, make vivid the possibility of major confrontations over CIA activities. It is hard to imagine that Congress will easily renew authority for major NSA activities in the presence of real doubt as to whether the CIA plans to follow the law. Putting in charge of the agency serious leadership committed to legal compliance is critical to maintaining public and legislative confidence that the intelligence community more broadly, the NSA included, can be trusted with the 702 powers. The selection of Mike Pompeo as CIA director is more promising here than is the Sessions nomination. Pompeo has the regard of a bipartisan collection of former intelligence officials and colleagues on the House Permanent Select Committee on Intelligence. On the other hand, his views of the early Bush administration CIA interrogation program can be expected to spark serious controversy in the context of his confirmation.

Fourth, the president-elect needs to work with the bipartisan leadership of the two intelligence committees to verify publicly that he has not altered the NSA's operating authorities or guidance—or, alternatively, that any changes he does make are lawful and prudent. People need confidence, if they are to reauthorize 702, that the NSA they are empowering is the same entity with the same policies and practices that has not abused it in the past. They need to have confidence that the order they are reauthorizing is the regular order. The oversight committees have a critical job in this respect. But the incoming administration does, too. The more changes it makes, and the more it obscures its changes, the less confident people will be.

Fifth, and almost too obvious to mention, the incoming administration needs to assiduously avoid any actions involving the intelligence community that represent any appearance of departure from reasonable public expectations of intelligence community conduct. The early Bush administration took highly aggressive actions that raised serious legal questions. The later Bush administration and the Obama administration moderated those actions notably, with the result that there is now a high degree of consensus among a wide array of analysts about the proper scope of intelligence community activity. While disagreement remains on the precise contours of transparency and oversight, today there is a strong shared sense of where the lines of normalcy are. Actions that push those lines will gravely undermine the confidence on which stands the legislative coalition for 702.

Section 702, in short, is a palatable tool only because we have high confidence in the fidelity both to law and to a certain set of relatively settled expectations about intelligence community behavior. That is, we have high confidence that it is being used responsibly, by responsible people, and for genuine foreign intelligence, not political, purposes. Our president-elect must come to understand that it will survive only as a long as that continues to be the case, and he needs to behave accordingly, or his first year will see the loss of a critically important national security tool.

PART IV

Foreign Challenges
and Opportunities

26

America's Role in a Turbulent World

BRUCE JONES

SUMMARY: We live in a moment of global uncertainty and American confusion. Confidence in the Western order and its American backing has waned, and hope for a benign multipolar order has been shown to be hollow. We face a choice. We could stay home in splendid isolation, in the belief that our economy will thrive and terror will avoid us and great power tensions in Asia and Europe won't disrupt the global economy, pull us in, or threaten our way of life. This approach would be willing walls of sand around both the economy and our security. If you think hope isn't a strategy, try denial. Unfortunately, engagement with the world is the only option. The next president will have to orient the American public and its national institutions to a rapidly evolving set of security challenges that lack the clarifying virtue of a single, simple menace. But in making the case for internationalism, we have to go beyond the simple case for American exceptionalism, and we have to make a richer argument than for American military action alone. What America needs, what the world needs, in this time of testing is a new concept and a new architecture for action. Between the unsatisfying notion of American exceptionalism and the false lure of isolationism, we need a vision for how to act to keep the peace in a world defined by a weakened West and an ill-formed rest. We need a new model of burden sharing for a multipolar world.

We live in a moment of global change and American self-doubt. In the space thus created, a variety of adventurers and evil-doers have carved out new opportunity, and conflict and tensions are rising. The current debate about America's role in this uncertain world is dominated by two options, especially as relates to the unfolding and unyielding crises in the Middle East. The first, drawing on the tradition of American exceptionalism, focuses on U.S. military intervention. The second, based on a sense of fatigue and of poor outcomes from recent interventions, is a form of neo-isolationism.

These are unsatisfying options. Isolationism in the face of mounting chaos in the Middle East and growing strategic uncertainty is proving to be an inept, possibly disastrous course. Inaction in the face of strategic crisis in Syria is as likely to protect American security as tariffs on Chinese goods are likely to restore American manufacturing; these are walls of sand. But there is little domestic support for a strategy based on American exceptionalism, and the concept has been damaged by a long period of failed policy in the Middle East—a region where our posture was premised on relations with autocratic allies and served to defend an increasingly antidemocratic and unstable order. We need a third way.

AMERICA'S CHOICE

The Office of the President of the United States is unlike any other in the contemporary world. The man or woman who sits in it not only controls the most powerful military on earth—by many reasonable measures, the most powerful army in history—he or she inherits a specific and special responsibility, a responsibility that the United States chose for itself at the end of the Second World War—that is, to use its economic, political, and military might to deter and prevent another of the great wars between major powers that so consumed the early part of the 20th century. Subsequent presidents of the United States have discharged that responsibility with varying degrees of humility and arrogance, skill and ineptitude, but all of them have spent at least a portion of their presidencies managing the deployment of American power for the purpose of avoiding a great power war. No other leader has a responsibility on the same scale. International critics have legitimately questioned how American misadventures contributed to the cold peace with the Soviets, or more recently, how the Iraq War contributed to maintaining the peace in the Middle East. Domestic critics of the left argue that by maintaining a global military presence the United States is acting imperially, and no doubt at times it has been. But in the main, the large bulk of American military power, deployed in forward bases in Asia and in Europe, helped to check aggression in those two theaters, preserve the security of these regions' democracies, and avoid the outbreak of active hostility—with the attendant risk of nuclear escalation—among competing powers. These functions of American power are all crucial to the degree of peace we have had in key regions since the end of the Second World War, to say nothing of economic growth.

Critics of the right question why the United States should extend itself when friends and allies carry less than their share of the burden. And there is some logic in the critique. But what successive American presidents have come to understand is that the only real alternative to the United States playing these roles is not the United Nations, it is not a benign compact of the powers; it is a ruthless competition for power and security by the world's least peaceful and least democratic forces. And in the modern era, not only will ruthless state leaders seek power in the space left unoccupied by American power but so too will the most virulent and most violent non-state groups and networks. Logic and history tell us that the result of the United States' spending less effort to keep the peace means that these dangers will mount and become less and less manageable—ultimately posing greater direct risks to the United States—and be much harder to tackle when they eventually become too large to ignore. But this is a lesson easy to argue against and unpopular among the public, to say the least. And so, in 2017, the president of the United States will occupy the Oval Office and inherit this responsibility at a moment of flux. He will have to orient the American public and its national institutions to a rapidly evolving set of security challenges that lack the clarifying virtue of a single, simple menace. He will have to find the right balance between reassuring an uncertain world about America's willingness to continue to exercise its responsible role while avoiding commitments that too far exceed the tolerance of the American people. And he will have to do so after the first election in three generations that threw into doubt the basic tenets of America's postwar role.

A TIME OF MONSTERS

Part of the answer to the question of America's role depends on the nature of the international situation and the threats we confront. Here, the next president will encounter a debate—indeed, some of the least edifying debates in contemporary American foreign policy. Is the whole world on fire? (No.) Is the challenge to American security posed by great powers or non-state actors? (The answer, quite obviously, is both.) Are we in a new Cold War? (No.) If not, are we in the world of author Steven Pinker's "better angels," moving steadily toward great peace? (Ask the Syrians.)

Despite the attacks of 9/11 and the reality of two American wars in the Muslim world, we have lived for almost a quarter century through a period of steadily declining violence and steadily rising wealth, all occasioned by the absence of a great power conflict. Now, though, violence is rising again, albeit mostly in the Middle East, and geopolitical tensions are on the rise. We have not entered a new Cold War, nor are we beset by threat on all fronts—exaggeration does us no good in this debate. But nor are we at a moment when the United States can afford to ignore international security or the world can afford for the United States to retreat into an isolationist stance.

This is a moment of testing, a time when a range of actors—from revisionist powers to regional upstarts to powerful non-state actors—are testing the existing international arrangements, seeking to weaken them or simply to find a more advantageous position within them. Vladimir Putin is not a new Stalin, but he is an ambitious and determined leader of a country that, while far from the power it once was, has concentrated its still-substantial assets in a small number of industries and state tools, including its military, and he has his hand directly on those tools and can wield them efficiently to a disruptive effect. Xi Jinping is not Chairman Mao, and China's ambitions on the world stage, at this point in history, are less threatening than they are often made out to be. But his ambitions in the East Asian region are more assertive, and he is testing America's presence (and patience) there and risks disrupting an East Asian peace that has held for 50 years and helped bring that region to the position it holds now as one of the main economic engines of the world. In the Middle East, everyone from the Iranians to the Qataris to al-Baghdadi of ISIS to Mohammed bin Salman of the House of Saud is testing the established order, and the result is a sharp rise in violence. More benignly, countries like Brazil and India and Indonesia are testing the boundaries of the established order on issues like the governance of the Internet, the rules that govern nuclear energy, and the financing of global development. Some of this testing is legitimate and warranted, even overdue. But some of it is violent and dangerous. Few of the challengers actually seek a collapse of the international peace. But they could cause it.

This coincides with a period of doubt in the West, occasioned in large part by two things: the loss of faith in free trade and globalization to generate benefits, which is triggering antiglobal politics writ large, and a sense of futility of action, generated by a series of losses from military action in the Middle East. Both are overstated in the current debate, but both play into a dangerous stasis and paralysis, not to mention demagogy.

Taken together, all this is generating a kind of senescence of the established order, an aging and withering from within. The risk is that this gradual erosion of established roles—for all their lapses, all their inadequacies—will snowball into something far more dangerous. Rarely has Antonio Gramsci's famous quote seemed quite so apt: "The old is dying and the new cannot be born; in this interregnum a great variety of morbid symptoms appear."[1] A more pithy translation of the last part of this quote expresses perfectly the anxiety of our time: "Now is the time of monsters."

ON WHOSE STRENGTH CAN WE RELY?

When American presidents have seen such dangers on the world stage, they have often been tempted to turn to great powers to ask them, too, to share the burden of keeping the peace. Time and again, these coalitions run aground on fundamental political differences and basic mistrust between the powers.

When great power cooperation (and the United Nations) fails, the alternative is the West. Throughout the Cold War, we relied on the West and the alliance system in which it is embedded to support American action and to help maintain the stability of Europe and Asia—to keep the peace, in short. Right now the West is weakened, to be sure, and looking inwards; and as a mobilizing concept, the West is not the powerful mobilizing idea that it once was, either in American domestic terms or internationally. So the next American president will have to remind us and the world that between the United States and its core European and Asian allies, the western democracies still account for more than 70 percent of global GDP and an even larger share of military spending—we can still act in the world if we summon the will to do so.

What's more, American foreign policy has never stumbled on a justification for its extensive role in the Middle East that squares with the notion of American exceptionalism, responsibility, or the basic concept of keeping the peace. In Asia and in Europe, at least, American power and occasionally American force secures and protects a democratic order while preserving a stable or semi-stable peace. The American public is justifiably confused by our strategy in the region, such as it is, and understandably skeptical that throwing more American military resources into the mix will help.

And so, when American foreign policy elites call for American leadership, what the American public hears is "let's engage in more unilateral, ill-considered military adventurism in the Middle East." That's an easy call to rebuff. Lost in the debate are the vital questions of securing stability and democracy in Asia and Europe.

And yet, faced with the horrors of Syria, who other than the United States should act to seek an end to the violence and the disorder it is occasioning?

Here's the problem. We've built two international architectures to support our international engagement. First is a global one, anchored in the United Nations. Despite recurrent American cynicism about the UN, it does many useful things in the resolution of small wars. But the UN is ill equipped, politically or operationally, to tackle strategic crisis management in Europe or Asia or regional tensions in the Middle East, let alone to tackle the hell that is contemporary Syria. Then, second, we have a Western system grounded in NATO and the broader alliance arrangements. Despite critiques of the left, this is an absolutely vital pillar of international stability. But it is not a sufficient one. Putin has conceded that NATO can maintain the territorial defense of Europe; he's not challenging it. Nor is China in any serious way challenging the territorial stability of Asia—though its temptation to do so might grow if America's 7th Fleet withdrew from the Pacific. Rather, both are practicing what I call "insidious geopolitics"—using economic and political pressure to reshape the domestic politics of neighbors, or trying to. A military alliance is a necessary but not a sufficient response.

BURDEN SHARING FOR A MULTIPOLAR WORLD

What America needs, what the world needs, in this time of testing, is a new concept and a new architecture for action. It needs a new model of burden sharing for a multipolar world. Between the unsatisfying notion of American exceptionalism and the false lure of isolationism, we need a vision for how to act to keep the peace in a world defined by a weakened West and an ill-formed rest. Notwithstanding a routine reference to American decline or the rise of new powers, the United States remains the only power that can articulate this vision or that has a reasonable chance to build a sustained international coalition to support it.

Not every aspect of that vision can be spelled out here, but the broad principles on which America should *lead* seem clear. These are:

- **To keep the peace.** The rhetoric, signals, and actions of the use of American power should hew closely to the responsibility we've taken on since the end of the Second World War to maintain the global peace. When we deviate from that basic function and cast our role in terms of more assertive precepts, we lend credence to domestic and international critics about the misuse of our power and make it harder to maintain domestic and international support for our actions.

- **Diplomacy backed by power.** Diplomacy should always have pride of place in American strategy. But diplomacy will not always succeed: no amount of negotiation was going to stop Col. Qaddafi from brutal suppression of dissent and rebellion in Libya; no amount of negotiation is going to convince President Assad to sue for peace. The oldest lesson of American foreign policy is still the most germane: when America is in a position of strength—economically and militarily—it adds potency and effect to its diplomatic strategy.

- **Act in concert, and create new "standing coalitions."** When we act in the world to maintain the peace, we should do so with as many friends and allies as possible. Easily said, hard to do. But we have to have the honesty to acknowledge to ourselves and to our friends that as vital as NATO is, it is not a sufficient response to today's challenges and nor is the UN. If NATO and the UN are not sufficient tools, we need to create new ones. These should be built around those actors committed to keeping the global peace and willing to shoulder substantial responsibilities to do so. That will include a core of the West, but not all members of NATO, and should be open to participation by countries like India with a huge stake in global stability.

Rebuilding internationalism is the central challenge that confronts the next president of the United States. It has to be rebuilt from the ground up—that is to say, it has to be rebuilt on a wide basis of American domestic support. This election has mobilized every corner of the American body politic that has been disadvantaged or dislocated by globalization, as well as some darker corners of American politics that cast themselves against "globalism" to paint a veneer over an underlying racism. The next president should address what is real and concerning in the dislocation caused by globalization; and he will have to act both to try to correct real dislocation (from technology as much as from globalization, but they go hand in hand) as well as push the new American racism back under the rock from whence it was liberated. And he has to recover an older argument about America's security role in the world: not an argument based on American exceptionalism but an argument about keeping the global peace and underpinning an open international economy—a role that America need not and should not do alone but a role that cannot be done without the United States.

Note

1. Antonio Gramsci, "Wave of Materialism" and "Crisis of Authority," *Selections from the Prison Notebooks* (New York: International Publishers, 1971), pp. 275–76.

27

The Twilight of the Liberal World Order

ROBERT KAGAN

SUMMARY: In recent years, the liberal world order that has held sway over international affairs for the past seven decades has been fragmenting under the pressure of systemic economic stresses, growing tribalism and nationalism, and a general loss of confidence in established international and national institutions. The incoming U.S. administration faces a grave challenge in determining whether it wishes to continue to uphold this liberal order, which has helped to maintain a stable international system in the face of challenges from regional powers and other potential threats, or whether it is willing to accept the consequences that may result if it chooses to abandon America's key role as a guarantor of the system it helped to found and sustain.

The liberal world order established in the aftermath of World War II may be coming to an end, challenged by forces both without and within. The external challenges come from the ambition of dissatisfied large and medium-size powers to overturn the existing strategic order dominated by the United States and its allies and partners. Their aim is to gain hegemony in their respective regions. China and Russia pose the greatest challenges to the world order because of their relative military, economic, and political power and their evident willingness to use it, which makes them significant players in world politics and, just as important, because the regions where they seek strategic hegemony—Asia and Europe—historically have been critical to global peace and stability. At a lesser but still significant level, Iran seeks regional hegemony in the Middle East and Persian Gulf, which if accomplished would have a strategic, economic, and political impact on the international system. North Korea seeks control of the Korean peninsula, which if accomplished would affect the stability and security of northeast Asia. Finally, at a much lower level of concern, there is the effort by ISIS and other radical Islamist groups to establish a new Islamic caliphate in the Middle East. If accomplished, that, too, would have effects on the global order.

However, it is the two great powers, China and Russia, that pose the greatest challenge to the relatively peaceful and prosperous international order created and sustained by the United States. If they were to accomplish their aims of establishing hegemony in their desired spheres of influence, the world would return to the condition it was in at the end of the 19th century, with competing great powers clashing over inevitably intersecting and overlapping spheres of interest. These were the unsettled, disordered conditions that produced the fertile ground for the two destructive world wars of the first half of the 20th century. The collapse of the British-dominated world order on the oceans, the disruption of the uneasy balance of power on the European continent due to the rise of a powerful unified Germany, combined with the rise of Japanese power in East Asia all contributed to a highly competitive international environment in which dissatisfied great powers took the opportunity to pursue their ambitions in the absence of any power or group of powers to unite in checking them. The result was an unprecedented global calamity. It has been the great accomplishment of the U.S.-led world order in the 70 years since the end of the Second World War that this kind of competition has been held in check and great power conflicts have been avoided.

The role of the United States, however, has been critical. Until recently, the dissatisfied great and medium-size powers have faced considerable and indeed almost insuperable obstacles in achieving their objectives. The chief obstacle has been the power and coherence of the order itself and of its principal promoter and defender. The American-led system of political and military alliances, especially in the two critical regions of Europe and East Asia, has presented China and Russia with what Dean Acheson once referred to as "situations of strength" in their regions that have required them to pursue their ambitions cautiously and in most respects to defer serious efforts to disrupt the international system. The system has served as a check on their ambitions in both positive and negative ways. They have been participants in and for the most part beneficiaries of the open international economic system the United States created and helped sustain and, so long as that system was functioning, have had more to gain by playing in it than by challenging and overturning it. The same cannot be said of the political and strategic aspects of the order, both of which have worked to their detriment. The growth and vibrancy of democratic government in the two decades following the collapse of Soviet communism has posed a continual threat to the ability of rulers in Beijing and Moscow to maintain control, and since the end of the Cold War they have regarded every advance of democratic institutions, including especially the geographical advance close to their borders, as an existential threat—and with reason. The continual threat to the basis of their rule posed by the U.S.-supported order has made them hostile both to the order and to the United States. However, it has also been a source of weakness and vulnerability. Chinese rulers in particular have had to worry about what an unsuccessful confrontation with the United States might do to their sources of legitimacy at home. And although Vladimir Putin has to some extent used a calculated foreign adventurism to maintain his hold on domestic power, he has taken a more cautious approach when met with determined U.S. and European opposition, as in the case of Ukraine, and pushed forward, as in Syria, only when invited to do so by U.S. and Western passivity. Autocratic rulers in a liberal democratic world have had to be careful.

The greatest check on Chinese and Russian ambitions, however, has come from the combined military power of the United States and its allies in Europe and Asia. China, although increasingly powerful itself, has had to contemplate facing the combined military strength of the world's superpower and some very formidable regional powers linked by alliance or common strategic interest, including Japan, India, and South Korea, as well as smaller but still potent nations like Vietnam and Australia. Russia has had to face the United States and its NATO allies. When united, these military powers present a daunting challenge to a revisionist power that can call on no allies of its own for assistance. Even were the Chinese to score an early victory in a conflict, they would have to contend over time with the combined industrial productive capacities of some of the world's richest and most technologically advanced nations. A weaker Russia would face an even greater challenge.

Faced with these obstacles, the two great powers, as well as the lesser dissatisfied powers, have had to hope for or if possible engineer a weakening of the U.S.-supported world order from within. This could come about either by separating the United States from its allies, raising doubts about the U.S. commitment to defend its allies militarily in the event of a conflict, or by various means wooing American allies out from within the liberal world order's strategic structure. For most of the past decade, the reaction of American allies to greater aggressiveness on the part of China and Russia in their respective regions, and to Iran in the Middle East, has been to seek more reassurance from the United States. Russian actions in Georgia, Ukraine, and Syria; Chinese actions in the East and South China seas; Iranian actions in Syria, Iraq, and along the littoral of the Persian Gulf—all have led to calls by American allies and partners for a greater commitment. In this respect, the system has worked as it was supposed to. What the political scientist William Wohlforth once described as the inherent stability of the unipolar order reflected this dynamic—as dissatisfied regional powers sought to challenge the status quo, their alarmed neighbors turned to the distant American superpower to contain their ambitions.

The system has depended, however, on will, capacity, and coherence at the heart of the liberal world order. The United States had to be willing and able to play its part as the principal guarantor of the order, especially in the military and strategic realm. The order's ideological and economic core order—the democracies of Europe and East Asia and the Pacific—had to remain relatively healthy and relatively confident. In such circumstances, the combined political, economic, and military power of the liberal world would be too great to be seriously challenged by the great powers, much less by the smaller dissatisfied powers.

In recent years, however, the liberal order has begun to weaken and fracture at the core. As a result of many related factors—difficult economic conditions, the recrudescence of nationalism and tribalism, weak and uncertain political leadership and unresponsive mainstream political parties, a new era of communications that seems to strengthen rather than weaken tribalism—there has emerged a crisis of confidence in what might be called the liberal enlightenment project. That project tended to elevate universal principles of individual rights and common humanity over ethnic, racial, religious, national, or tribal differences. It looked to a growing economic interdependence to create common interests across boundaries and the establishment of international institutions to smooth differences and facilitate cooperation among nations. Instead, the past decade has seen the rise of tribalism and nationalism; an increasing focus on the "other" in all societies; and a loss of confidence in government, in the capitalist system, and in democracy. We have been witnessing something like the opposite of the "end of history" but have returned to history with a vengeance, rediscovering all the darker aspects of the human soul. That includes, for many, the perennial human yearning for a strong leader to provide firm guidance in a time of seeming breakdown and incoherence.

This crisis of the enlightenment project may have been inevitable. It may indeed have been cyclical, due to inherent flaws in both capitalism and democracy, which periodically have been exposed and have raised doubts about both—as happened, for instance, throughout the West in the 1930s. Now, as then, moreover, this crisis of confidence in liberalism coincides with a breakdown of the strategic order. In this case, however, the key variable has not been the United States as the outside power and its willingness, or not, to step in and save or remake an order lost by other powers. Rather it is the United States' own willingness to continue upholding the order that it created and which depends entirely on American power.

That willingness has been in doubt for some time. Increasingly in the quarter-century after the end of the Cold War, Americans have been wondering why they bear such an unusual and outsized responsibility for preserving global order when their own interests are not always apparently served and when, indeed, the United States seems to be making sacrifices while others benefit. The reasons why the United States took on this abnormal role after the calamitous two world wars of the 20th century have been largely forgotten. As a consequence, the American public's patience with the difficulties and costs inherent in playing such a role has worn thin. Thus, whereas previous unsuccessful wars, in Korea in 1950 and Vietnam in the 1960s and 1970s, and previous economic downturns, such as in the mid- to late 1970s, did not have the effect of turning Americans against global involvement, the unsuccessful wars in Iraq and Afghanistan and the financial crisis of 2007–09 have had that effect. President Obama pursued an ambivalent approach to global involvement, but the main thrust of his approach was retrenchment. His actions and statements were a critique of previous American strategy and reinforced a national mood favoring a much less active role in the world and much narrower definition of American interests.

With the election of Donald Trump, a majority of Americans have signaled their unwillingness to continue upholding the world order. Trump was not the only candidate in 2016 to run on a platform suggesting a much narrower definition of American interests and a lessening of the burdens of American global leadership. "America First" is not just an empty phrase but a fairly coherent philosophy with a long lineage and many adherents in the American academy. It calls for viewing American interests through a narrow lens. It suggests no longer supporting an international alliance structure, no longer seeking to deny great powers their spheres of influence and regional hegemony, no longer attempting to uphold liberal norms in the international system, and no longer sacrificing short-term interests—in trade for instance—in the longer-term interest of preserving an open economic order.

Coming as it does at a time of growing great power competition, this new approach in American foreign policy is likely to hasten a return to the instability and clashes of previous eras. These external challenges to the liberal world order and the continuing weakness and fracturing of the liberal world from within are likely to feed on each other. The weakness of the liberal core and the abdication by the United States of its global responsibilities will encourage more aggressive revisionism by the dissatisfied powers, which may in turn exacerbate the sense of weakness and helplessness and the loss of confidence of the liberal world, which will in turn increase the sense on the part of the great power autocracies that this is their opportunity to reorder the world to conform to their interests.

History suggests that this is a downward spiral from which it will be difficult to recover absent a major conflict. It was in the 1920s, not the 1930s, that the most important and ultimately fatal decisions were made by the liberal powers. Above all, it was the American decision to remove itself from a position of global responsibility, to reject strategic involvement to preserve the peace in Europe, and neglect its naval strength in the Pacific to check the rise of Japan. The "return to normalcy" of the 1920 U.S. election seemed safe and innocent at the time, but the essentially selfish policies pursued by the world's strongest power in the following decade helped set the stage for the calamities of the 1930s. By the time the crises began to erupt in that decade, it was already too late to avoid paying the high price of global conflict.

One thing for the new administration to keep in mind: History tells us that revisionist great powers are not easy to satisfy short of complete capitulation. Their sphere of influence is never quite large enough to satisfy their pride or their expanding need for security. The "satiated" power that Bismarck spoke of is rare—even his Germany, in the end, could not be satiated. And of course, rising great powers always express some historical grievance. Every people, except perhaps for the fortunate Americans, have reason for resentment at ancient injustices, nurse grudges against old adversaries, seek to return to a glorious past that was stolen from them by military or political defeat. The world's supply of grievances is inexhaustible.

These grievances, however, are rarely solved by minor border changes. Japan, the aggrieved "have-not" nation of the 1930s, did not satisfy itself by swallowing Manchuria in 1931. Germany, the aggrieved victim of Versailles, did not satisfy itself by bringing the Germans of the Sudetenland back into the fold. And, of course, Russia's historical sphere of influence does not end in Ukraine. It begins in Ukraine. It extends to the Baltics, to the Balkans, and to heart of Central Europe. The tragic irony is that, in the process of carving out these spheres of influence, the ambitious rising powers invariably create the very threats they use to justify their actions. The cycle only ends if and when the great powers that make up the existing power structure, in today's case, the United States, decide they have had enough. We know those moments as major power wars.

The new administration seems to be fixated almost entirely on the threat of radical Islam and may not believe its main problem is going to be great power confrontation. In fact, it is going to have to confront both sets of challenges. The first, addressing the threat of terrorism, is comparatively manageable. It is the second, managing great power competition and confrontation, that has historically proved the most difficult and also the most costly when handled badly.

The best way to avoid great power clashes is to make the U.S. position clear from the outset. That position should be that the United States welcomes competition of a certain kind. Great powers compete across multiple planes—economic, ideological, and political, as well as military. Competition in most spheres is necessary and even healthy. Within the liberal order, China can compete economically and successfully with the United States; Russia can thrive in the international economic order upheld by the liberal powers, even if it is not itself liberal.

But security competition is different. The security situation undergirds everything else. It remains true today as it has since the Second World War that only the United States has the capacity and the unique geographical advantages to provide global security. There is no stable balance of power in Europe or Asia without the United States. And while we can talk about soft power and smart power, they have been and always will be of limited value when confronting raw military power. Despite all of the loose talk of American decline, it is in the military realm where U.S. advantages remain clearest. Even in other great powers' backyards, the United States retains the capacity, along with its powerful allies, to deter challenges to the security order. But without a U.S. willingness to use military power to establish balance in far-flung regions of the world, the system will buckle under the unrestrained military competition of regional powers.

If history is any guide, the next four years are the critical inflection point. The rest of the world will take its cue from the early actions of the new administration. If the next president governs as he ran, which is to say if he pursues a course designed to secure only America's narrow interests; focuses chiefly on international terrorism—the least of the challenges to the present world order; accommodates the ambitions of the great powers; ceases to regard international economic policy in terms of global order but only in terms of America's bottom line narrowly construed; and generally ceases to place a high priority on reassuring allies and partners in the world's principal strategic theaters—then the collapse of the world order, with all that entails, may not be far off.

28

You've Got a Friend in Me

Why U.S. Alliances Make America Safer

RICHARD BUSH

SUMMARY: The United States' alliances with East Asian countries are not a fight-for-cash proposition, as Donald Trump continues to suggest. They are an important instrument of U.S. national security strategy, whereby we have chosen to defend the homeland by forward deployment of our armed forces in the Asia-Pacific. Moreover, our allies pay a significant cost of our presence (around 50 percent in the case of Japan and Korea) and bear the primary responsibility for defending themselves. To suggest that the United States would help their defense only if "the price is right" only fosters doubt in the minds of our friends regarding the credibility of our commitment.

President-elect Donald Trump argued during the 2016 campaign that U.S. alliances around the world are a bad deal for America, because our allies do not pay enough for the security we provide. Trump's approach displays a basic misunderstanding of the alliances' value *for the United States*. Regarding East Asia, he is seemingly unconcerned with the deep anxieties his ideas have provoked among our security partners in the region about the very credibility of our commitment. Yet Trump's proposal does serve something of a useful purpose. It provides an occasion to review why these arrangements benefit the United States.

BACKGROUND

The United States has had a naval presence in the Pacific and East Asia since the mid-nineteenth century, but it was not until after World War II that it decided to conclude alliances with friendly regional countries with a commitment to defend them in case of aggression. In the early 1950s, to facilitate the containment of communism, Washington struck bargains with countries on China's periphery—Japan, South Korea, Taiwan, the Philippines, Thailand, Australia, and New Zealand—committing itself to their defense in return for permission to base significant U.S. forces on their soil.

A fundamental judgment drove U.S. policymakers to pursue alliance building in East Asia and Europe: prewar isolationism had only rendered America more vulnerable, not less. The United States could best protect itself by establishing an active forward presence on both ends of the Eurasian landmass. Alliances and the overseas deployment of U.S. armed forces were therefore instruments in a larger strategy. Forward deployment of military forces not only pre-positioned the capabilities needed for war-fighting if war should ever come, but also enhanced deterrence by sharpening the risk calculus of friends and adversaries alike: reassuring allies and warning enemies. Like cops on the beat, moreover, the constant presence of American forces in East Asia fostered a long period of relative regional stability, with the Vietnam War as the exception that proved the rule. There were, of course, important economic, political, and cultural elements to U.S. policy, but forward deployment was the key. Asian alliances were never seen as favors to the countries concerned; American leaders believed that helping to keep our friends safe would better secure our homeland.

The United States thus became what Robert Gates, secretary of defense in the Bush and Obama administrations, would call a "resident power in East Asia." But the U.S.-led security order was not completely static. In a dramatic shift, presidents Richard Nixon and Jimmy Carter induced China's leaders to align their country with the West against the Soviets. America and its friends in the region worked to incorporate China into the international capitalist economy and to try to bind it to the institutions, regimes, norms, and laws that helped regulate international society. Even as the Cold War continued, its character in Asia had changed. The post-1978 emergence of China from its past isolation actually reinforced America's basic strategy, and the U.S. alliances and the forward deployment they enabled fostered a stable environment in which the countries of the region—including China itself—saw accelerated economic growth and, in some cases, made the transition to democracy. Although these alliances served the specific purpose of deterring the adversaries of the United States' allies, the broader presence that the alliances symbolized brought a strategic stability for allies and nonallies alike.

The collapse of the Soviet Union in 1991 naturally raised questions about whether East Asian alliances were necessary. The threat from Moscow no longer existed. China might be powerful in the long term, but not in the near and medium term. Meanwhile, trade and investment were drawing the countries of the region together, and fear of interstate conflict declined substantially. Thailand, New Zealand, and the Philippines even chose to let their alliances with America atrophy.

ALLIANCES TODAY

Even though the global Cold War had ended by the early 1990s, a Cold War–like phenomenon had emerged in northeast Asia. The source was Stalinist North Korea, which had maintained a conventional threat against the South since the end of the Korean War in 1953. By the 1980s, Pyongyang had systematic programs to develop nuclear weapons and the means to deliver them over long distances. Its economy was autarkic, and its political system was severely repressive. American and South Korean attempts to divert North Korea diplomatically from its hostile path were to no avail, for the simple reason that North Korea did not wish to be diverted. Pyongyang's nuclear and missile programs created an existential threat to both South Korea and Japan, which in turn have deepened their security cooperation with the United States.

Most significant for the long term, since the late 1970s China has gradually but systematically rebuilt its national power and ended almost two centuries of relative weakness. Beijing began by strengthening its economy and diplomacy, but it is now developing maritime, air, and missile capabilities to project military power within East Asia and beyond. The growth of China's power and the more assertive exercise of its political influence have increased anxieties through most of the region and sometimes worked to the diplomatic disadvantage of the United States. Still, China is not the old Soviet Union. It is more integrated economically with the world than the Soviet Union ever was. Its demand for natural resources and advanced components for assembly into high-tech electronic devices, plus the thirst of developed countries for low-cost consumer goods, has made China the engine of global economic growth. In different ways, the countries of East Asia depend on China for their prosperity, and declines in Chinese growth hurt their own economic prospects.

Still, as much as we might hope that East Asia might be a domain of peaceful coexistence, it is not. Dangers exist, and the friends and adversaries of the United States cannot help but prepare for the worst, even if they hope for the best. The conceivable circumstances in which war could occur are clear:

- North Korea initiates a low-level conventional attack against South Korea. South Korea carries out its threat to retaliate, the conflict escalates, and China and the United States get drawn in, with Beijing on Pyongyang's side and Washington in support of Seoul.

- In the East China Sea, a physical clash between Japanese and Chinese coast guard vessels destroys the current yet fragile standoff surrounding the Senkaku/Diaoyu islands. The navies of the two countries get drawn in and the conflict escalates, and the United States intervenes to assist Japan.

- Either China continues to expand its physical and military presence in the South China Sea, to the point of effectively seizing land forms held by Vietnam, the Philippines, and others, or there is a serious clash between U.S. and Chinese naval ships; and the conflict escalates.

- Taiwan's leaders take political steps that China interprets (rightly or wrongly) as moves toward *de jure* independence, which Beijing opposes. China then undertakes political, diplomatic, and military intimidation of Taiwan; the United States supports Taiwan; and the conflict escalates into a U.S.-China war.

The chance that any of these scenarios might occur is probably low, but it is not zero. Misperception, miscalculation, and domestic nationalisms would likely be at play. Leaders of all the countries concerned understand the economic stakes of military conflict, and they could use diplomacy and conflict-reduction measures to reduce the danger of war. They have done so successfully in the past.

The risks of conflict thus can be reduced, but they cannot be elimi-

FIGURE 28.1   OVERLAPPING CLAIMS IN THE SOUTH CHINA SEA

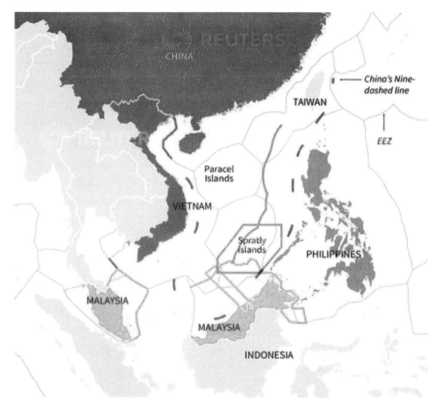

Six nations contest all or parts of the South China Sea, which has led to a series of confrontations between China and some of its neighbors over the potentially oil-and-gas-rich area. Here is a look at how each claim compares with the official exclusive economic zones (EEZ), the waters extending 200 nautical miles from the coast.

Source: U.S. State Department; U.N. Division for Ocean Affairs and the Law of the Sea; U.S. Energy Information Administration; Reuters.

nated. Nor can the possibility be dismissed that the United States might choose to intervene to defend its allies and protect its own interests. Yet the idea that the intervening American forces are latter-day Hessians—the equivalent of mercenaries subcontracted to foreign governments—is simplistic and wrong.

First of all, our alliances do not exist solely to defend our allies in the case of war. They have successfully deterred adversaries from initiating war in the first place. So far, our capabilities and those of our allies, plus the credibility of our willingness to use them, have convinced our adversaries that the risks and costs of conflict are not worth the benefits to be gained. But to raise doubts about U.S. resolve by suggesting, for example, that U.S. armed forces would defend our allies only if the price is right would only invite the adventurism that we wish to prevent. Smart deterrence is a good deal for the United States.

Second, it is wrong to assume that the United States would bear the combat burden. The Korean and Japanese armed forces are some of the most capable in the world. They plan on the assumption that if (God forbid) war occurs, they would have the primary responsibility to fight and die to defend their homelands. The United States would play a supporting role, with capabilities that only we possess. Despite our supporting role and the robust mechanisms that integrate our respective defense forces, our allies' knowledge that we have their backs gives them far greater confidence to fight and maybe die.

Third, the idea that the U.S. taxpayer is paying all the expenses for U.S. forces in East Asia has no factual basis. Objective data show that Korea and Japan each cover around half of the direct costs of the presence of U.S. forces in their countries. To take the forces we currently deploy in Japan and Korea and base them back in the United States probably would not save any money and certainly would make war-fighting harder.

The most graphic demonstration of the generosity of our friends has to do with the U.S. Marines that have been deployed on Okinawa. The U.S. and Japanese governments decided that 5,000 of these troops should be relocated to the American territory of Guam. Not only will Japan pay for the actual relocation costs, but it will also construct new facilities on Guam.

Deterrence and burden sharing aside, the United States and its leading allies—Japan and Korea—recently have used their alliances as vessels for much broader policy cooperation. In both cases, there is growing attention to issues of security outside East Asia, such as Iran's nuclear program, and an array of nonsecurity objectives including global economic growth, sustainable development and poverty reduction, global health, climate change and environmental protection, cybersecurity, and science and technology cooperation.[1]

To be sure, America's alliances do not come without liabilities:

- Each of our Asian partners has strong antennae to pick up any signal that Washington is about to abandon it. Each sometimes fears that alignment with the United States will lead to its entrapment in a conflict it does not desire.

- The United States is not always satisfied with how much our allies spend on defense and on what capabilities they acquire. This becomes very important if a U.S. ally is the victim of attack, for it must be able to hang on until U.S. forces intervene in strength, and the clear ability to hang on strengthens deterrence.

- Washington is periodically afraid that the actions of a U.S. ally or security partner will entangle it in an unnecessary dispute or conflict (that the "tail will wag the dog").

- America's friends in the region may disagree with Washington on the appropriate way to respond to the security challenge of the moment (for example, China's incremental campaign to expand its presence and capabilities in the South China Sea).

- Nationalistic public opinion in some countries of East Asia sometimes has been hostile toward the United States because of its security and political role.

Yet none of these problems is new, and Washington has a wealth of experience on managing each. There is no reason why it cannot apply past experience to new situations. That the countries of East Asia plus the United States with its forward presence have been able to keep the peace in East Asia should lend confidence that they can continue to do so. From this historical perspective, therefore, the Obama administration's "rebalance" or "pivot" is not a new policy at all, but more an adjustment of a decades-old strategy to new circumstances.

ALLIANCES IN A CHANGING ASIA (CHINA)

What *is* new in East Asia is how China's growing power—and the way it has been used—presents new challenges for America's friends in the regions and for our security relationships with them. East Asia is where China's revival as a great power will first take place, and the region already has its share of medium to strong powers. From China's perspective, creating strategic depth into the East and South China seas makes sense in terms of its defense strategy, and it has steadily built the military capabilities to create that depth. Yet it is encroaching into areas where other powers' armed forces are already present—first and foremost the United States, and secondarily Japan.

To make matters worse for Beijing, its neighbors keep a constant watch on the activities of its military and paramilitary capabilities. The way China has used its assets to establish a new presence in the East and South China seas and to assertively advance its territorial and maritime claims has made most of its East Asian neighbors nervous about its long-term intentions. Their default response is to align more closely with the United States, at least when it comes to security. On trade and investment, however, they reap the benefits that stem from a large and modernizing Chinese economy. The last thing that China's neighbors want is to have to make a choice between China and the United States.

Chinese officials and scholars have sought to turn the rhetorical tables on the United States by complaining more and more about the security architecture that Washington built and has sustained in its neighborhood. They start with the assumption that alliances exist by definition to counter an enemy, and then infer that China must be America's new adversary. This logic betrays a serious problem in China's decisionmaking system: reflexively viewing the actions of the United States as part of a plot to contain China, even though those actions usually have an alternative and benign purpose (or, sometimes, are a response to Chinese actions). This logic ignores the significant, long-term stabilizing impact that U.S. security policy has had in Asia, through alliances and other means. Moreover, Washington has played an important role in trying to resolve or mitigate disputes within the region so that they do not spin out of control, and has sometimes discouraged its friends from taking steps that would unnecessarily increase tensions. Both of these actions benefit China's interests.

Still, there is a security dilemma at play between the United States and China, one that can affect the region as a whole. Even if rivalry is not inevitable, neither is it impossible. Washington's actions may and do foster perceptions in Beijing that U.S. intentions constitute a hostile containment policy and require a robust response. China's actions create fears in the United States that Chinese leaders wish to drive it from the region, fears that are shared doubly by our regional allies and friends. The danger of a vicious circle is real. If the United States overreacts to Chinese moves, it may only invite more extreme steps by China. (As Harvard's Joseph Nye famously warned: "If you treat China as an enemy, you are certain to have an enemy.") But if Washington sits idly by in the face of Chinese provocations, our allies will be alarmed.

A serious and more practical challenge is the effect of China's military modernization capabilities. Sooner or later, it will have the ability to project significant air and naval power out to at least the first island chain (formed by Japan, Taiwan, and the Philippines). Simply acquiring the ability to project power in that way does not necessarily mean that Beijing will use that power. Nor does it mean that China will refuse to coexist with its littoral neighbors and the United States. But if China has this power-projection capability, it could change the way that the United States would have to fight China if there should ever be a major war, which in turn might require changes in alliance arrangements at political and operational levels.

Generally, the direction of U.S.-China policy might be summarized as "cooperate where we can but contend when we must." Washington's hope is that China will pursue a similar approach and the two states together can manage areas of contention well enough to avoid exacerbating mutual suspicions. For the United States, moreover, its alliances and security partnerships in East Asia remain a force for regional stability and an asset for setting benign parameters to channel China's rise. There will be frictions and contention between China and the United States and between China and its Asian neighbors. The task will be to mitigate and contain those problems through a variety of mechanisms, including diplomacy and military confidence-building measures. If China is prepared to exercise restraint as it projects power outward, that is the best outcome. If, through its own actions, it stimulates deterrence responses from the United States and its friends, alliance relationships are more likely to succeed than individual effort.

Note

1. For a more detailed discussion of U.S. alliances and security partnerships in Asia, see the "Alliances & Partnerships: U.S. Commitments in the Asia-Pacific" series of papers produced at Brookings in July 2016, available at www.brookings. edu/research/alliances-partnerships-u-s-commitments-in-the-asia-pacific.

29

U.S. Leadership in Global Education: The Time Is Now

REBECCA WINTHROP

SUMMARY: "Education is one of America's most important global investments, not just because it's the right thing to do—it's also the smartest," states the U.S. Global Leadership Coalition.[1] So far, however, U.S. government investment in global education is one-tenth of what is spent on global health. No U.S. president has made global education one of his signature initiatives. The next U.S. administration should make education a centerpiece of America's foreign assistance strategy. A presidential initiative on global education should put girls and women at the center and work toward ensuring that the millions of young people at risk of disenfranchisement can develop the breadth of skills needed to succeed in a rapidly changing world. To do this, the United States should leverage bilateral and multilateral mechanisms in support of quality early childhood development, better schooling, and youth workforce development programs.

Helping lift up those around us demonstrates our commitment to human dignity and human rights; it is also in our national interest. Investing in education globally, especially for girls and women, is one of the best investments we can make and has a high return, with benefits across a range of areas—from global security to poverty reduction and economic stability to women's empowerment and improved global health.

THE PRICE OF IGNORANCE

This past September, a report, *The Learning Generation: Investing in Education for a Changing World*, revealed that if we do not do something radically different, by 2030 half of the world's youth—over 800 million—will not have the basic high school–level skills needed to succeed in the world of work.[2] The bulk of these girls and boys will live in low- and middle-income countries. In fact, by 2030, in the poorest countries—from Afghanistan to Sudan—only 1 in 10 young people will have the basic skills he or she needs for a successful future. This is due to both limited access to schooling for the most marginalized and to the often poor quality of such education when it is available. Millions of children and youth are attending schools but are not mastering the competency they need, a problem that has serious implications for economic stability, peace and security, and women's empowerment.

Unlike in previous generations, technological innovations now and in the future will lead to more job destruction than creation. The recently released *Learning Generation* report argues that over two billion jobs are at risk of automation in the coming decades. In this context, the demand for skills will be transformed, with more advanced skills at a premium and limited employer interest in low-order skills. Because of this, education systems must pivot and focus on preparing young people by cultivating the breadth of skills needed for the 21st century.[3] Academic fundamentals will continue to be important, but so will competencies such as teamwork, problem solving, empathy, creativity, adaptability, and resilience. Fortunately, we know that cultivating a broader range of skills does not take away from academic achievement, but rather reinforces and improves it. Recent research in the learning sciences illustrates how young people who from an early age develop a range of competencies, from communication to critical thinking, are better at content mastery and academic success.[4]

THE RATIONALE FOR U.S. LEADERSHIP

To date, no U.S. president has made global education one of his major signature initiatives, although the Obama administration made inroads in that direction. Moral imperative aside, investing in education globally brings the United States benefits across a range of areas, from global security to poverty reduction and economic stability to women's empowerment and improvements in global health.

The timing is auspicious. Compared to eight years ago, the global education field has put in place key building blocks for success. There are now new measures for tracking the outcomes of global education efforts, along with new global coordination and investment mechanisms such as the reformed Global Partnership for Education (GPE), which kicks off a new strategy and replenishment cycle in 2017. The Obama White House, through its interagency Let Girls Learn initiative, laid the groundwork for a whole-of-government approach to education, and the U.S. Agency for International Development's (USAID) current education strategy is undergoing a refresh. Global education is a topic that rises above partisan politics and appeals strongly to both sides of the aisle. By the end of 2016 the Education for All Act had unanimously passed the U.S. House of Representatives, and the Senate Foreign Relations Committee, showing global education to be one of the few issues in America to garner strong bipartisan support.

Returns on Investment

Improving education levels around the world, particularly for girls and women, plays an important role in helping address many of top global concerns facing the United States.

Peace and security. Studies have long demonstrated the effect that increased levels of education have on reducing a country's risk of armed conflict. Indeed, higher levels of schooling within a population can significantly cut conflict risk. For example, an increase in secondary school enrollment from 30 percent to 81 percent is estimated to reduce the probability of civil war by almost two-thirds.[5] It can even significantly reduce the length of existing armed conflicts, something borne out in a meta-analysis by coauthor Corrine Graff and I in the Brookings research report "Beyond Madrasas: Assessing the Links Between Education and Militancy in Pakistan."[6]

Poverty reduction and economic stability. Investing in global education helps break intergenerational poverty and supports economic stability. UNESCO estimates that 171 million people could be lifted out of poverty if all students in low-income countries left school with basic reading skills—the equivalent of a 12 percent drop in world poverty.[7]

Improving education, particularly for girls and women, is also one important way to boost GDP. For example, a study of education levels from 1950 to 2010 found that an additional year of schooling for the average population could account for a 5 to 12 percent increase in economic growth; other studies have shown that GDP grows even faster when more women complete secondary schooling.[8] The benefits of lifting people out of poverty in the developing world are felt globally. Indeed, high education levels outside the United States not only help bolster economic growth in other countries, they also bring direct economic benefits back to the United States itself. Harvard professor and Brookings non-resident fellow Martin West argues that improvements to the quality of education abroad would boost global productivity and lower the costs of imports, increase technological innovation to the benefit of American industry, and improve global stability.[9] Studies have found that an overall increase in the skills of young people today would increase global GDP, growing both the global pie and America's slice therein.

Global health. Improving education levels, especially for girls, is one of the most impactful interventions for addressing global health concerns. Dubbed the "social vaccine for HIV/AIDS," girls' education reduces the risk of HIV transmission, as better-educated women have more knowledge about how HIV is transmitted, helping them avoid infection and prevent their spreading it to their babies. Educating women and girls also helps reduce malaria, as women who are educated are more likely to use preventative measures such as bed nets. Improvements in girls' education also have led to healthier families, and half the decrease in child mortality from 1970 to 2009 can be attributed to increased levels of girls' education.[10]

Women's rights and empowerment. It is the basic human right of all girls to be able to get a quality education. Currently, over 130 million girls are denied an education and an opportunity for a better life due to such things as early marriage, sexual slavery, crushing poverty, or simply living in out-of-reach areas. Quality education gives girls the skills they need to succeed in the changing world of work; it also has the power to help women better navigate the world around them and makes them better equipped to exercise their voice.

THE TIME IS NOW

A move by the United States to invest big in education would send a strong signal about America's commitment to human dignity globally. This visible investment, combined with the building blocks put in place over the past eight years and the ready-made global platform provided by the GPE replenishment, means that U.S. leadership would be catalytic for the sector. High-level leadership from the United States would be able to leverage and bring together new and stronger constituencies outside of the United States and allow for improved donor collaboration on education in the neediest and risky areas of the world.

Below is a selection of developments in the global education field over the past eight years that make it an opportune moment for fuller U.S. engagement.

Engaged Constituencies Ready to Partner

Education Commission. Global thought leaders from diverse walks of life—technology, academia, teaching, business, and politics—have mobilized through the international, high-level Education Commission.

United Nations. For the first time ever, the UN secretary-general has appointed a special envoy for global education, a position occupied for the past three years by former British prime minister Gordon Brown.

Civil society. Increasing numbers of internationally based civil society networks have been focusing on global education, which join the long-standing Basic Education Coalition, a group of almost 25 U.S.-based global education implementers and the Global Campaign for Education–U.S., a coalition of more than 80 U.S. organizations dedicated to ensuring universal access to quality education.

Teachers. Teachers and their organizations are more engaged at the policy level within the global education community. Through Education International, the global federation of teacher unions and organizations, teachers have a seat at the table at the major global policy dialogue forums and are actively engaged in codeveloping solutions together with government leaders.

Foundations and business. New coalitions of philanthropic and business actors have come together to support global education to find better opportunities for collaboration and partnership. Some of these include the International Education Funders Group, the Global Business Coalition for Education, and the Global Compact on Learning Donor Network.

Education Outcomes—Data and Measurement

Sustainable Development Goal (SDG) 4. The SDGs, and the accompanying implementation roadmap, the Education 2030 Framework for Action, have clearly placed improving learning outcomes and skills squarely on the global agenda.[11] With 193 countries signing on to this ambitious goal, there is more support than ever before for improving the skills and competencies of *all* children and youth.

New measurement tools. A broad-based global initiative to develop better shared measures for learning progress has spurred progress on a shared commitment to tracking learning and developing new tools to do so. For example, there is a new shared tool—Measuring Early Learning Quality and Outcomes—to assess the quality of early childhood development.[12] There are also new measures for understanding inequities in education access and outcomes from UNESCO's World Inequality Database on Education to FHI-360 and Save the Children's Education Equity Research Initiative.

Global tracking of student learning. For the first time ever, the international body that tracks global education data, UNESCO's Institute for Statistics, is monitoring data on learning outcomes and on who is enrolling in early childhood programs and school.

Multilateral Mechanisms

GPE. Newly relaunched in 2011, the Education for All Fast Track Initiative became the GPE, with a new governance mechanism and global role in coordinating global education efforts to strengthen education systems. GPE today is a multistakeholder partnership and funding platform operating in 65 low-income countries.

Education cannot wait. Launched this year at the World Humanitarian Summit in Istanbul, the Education Cannot Wait fund aims to provide education to over 13 million children and youth living in emergencies and protracted crises by 2030. To date, a range of countries have committed to supporting crisis-affected children through this mechanism, including the United States, the United Kingdom, Norway, the Netherlands, the European Union, Denmark, and Canada.

U.S. Initiatives to Build On

Let girls learn. As mentioned previously, through the efforts of First Lady Michelle Obama the White House has recently sought to elevate the issue of education for adolescent girls through its Let Girls Learn initiative. The initiative works across agencies and as such lays important groundwork for the incoming Trump administration to build and strengthen a high-level global education initiative.

Reading. Primarily through USAID, the United States has moved the agenda forward on improving reading levels for children in developing countries by working on a range of issues from measurement to teacher training to availability of books.

Refugees. The State Department and USAID have ongoing programs supporting education for refugee children and children who are internally displaced and otherwise affected by crisis, from armed conflict to natural disasters.

Education for All Act. Enjoying broad bipartisan support, the Education for All Act puts forward a strong commitment to global education goals and key principles.[13] The act was passed unanimously by the House of Representatives and the Senate Foreign Relations Committee by the close of 2016.

International Basic Education Caucus. One of the newest caucuses, the International Basic Education Caucus, enjoys bipartisan sponsorship and support and provides a useful mechanism for advancing global education issues in the U.S. Congress.[14]

A GLOBAL EDUCATION INITIATIVE WITH GIRLS AND WOMEN AT THE CENTER

A significant global education initiative cannot only help our global health investments to be more effective, but also can catalyze change for communities around the world and pay back dividends to the United States in multiple ways. The Trump administration should lead globally by establishing a presidential initiative on global education that uses an interagency approach to position education as a centerpiece in U.S. foreign assistance.

WHO: Women and Girls at the Center

This initiative should place girls and women at its center for two main reasons. First, it needs to ensure that global education programming reaches and fosters relevant learning outcomes for girls and is a way of recognizing that girls have a long-standing legacy of discrimination and underinvestment to overcome. Second, it must recognize that educating girls and women is one of the best investments the world can make because it yields high returns. Strong evidence shows that improving girls' and women's education levels leads to better lives for children, families, communities, and countries. In *What Works in Girls' Education: Evidence for the World's Best Investment*, my coauthor Gene Sperling and I find that girls' education increases economic growth, improves jobs and wages, saves mothers' and children's lives, leads to smaller and more sustainable families, results in healthier and better-educated children, reduces rates of HIV/AIDS and malaria, reduces rates of child marriage, empowers women, increases women's political leadership, and reduces harm to families from natural disasters and climate change.[15]

WHAT: Developing Breadth of Skills across the Lifecycle

The initiative must focus on giving young people the skills they need to thrive in a changing world. This requires not only building schools and increasing enrollments but also helping children and youth develop the breadth of skills needed for work and life, inclusive of academic competency and other essential 21st-century skills.[16] While the scaling-up of education in developing country contexts has mostly focused on increasing access to school, effective models for scaling up improvements in quality learning do exist.[17] With the right programmatic and policy design, learning outcomes across the breadth of skills can be improved. To achieve this goal, however, a lifecycle starting from early childhood to formal schooling to youth workforce development is required. The foundations for children's 21st-century skills and academic success are laid early, before children ever enter school. Recent estimates find that there are 250 million children under age 5 who are at risk of not meeting their developmental potential.[18] These recent studies find that the effects of such developmental delays impact brain development that can be seen in the first year, but worsen throughout childhood and persist throughout life. In fact, an earlier study estimated that developmental delays result in a 19.8 percent deficit in adult income.[19]

As children grow, these education deficits persist. There continue to be a large number of children and youth who are not in primary and secondary school, and millions more who despite attending school are not gaining even basic reading and math skills. Two hundred and sixty-three million children and youth of school age are currently out of school, and even more strikingly, 479 million are enrolled in school but are not achieving basic learning outcomes.[20] For the 142 million youth who today are not in school and likely never to return, alternative pathways such as skills training and workforce development are crucial.

WHERE: Communities with Greatest Need, Including Fragile States

Today we are in the midst of the greatest refugee crisis since World War II: over 60 million people have been forced to leave their homes and flee to another country. Any global education initiative must take seriously how to support the communities most in need. This includes those affected by armed conflict and disaster as well as those who may live in more stable contexts but are chronically marginalized.

HOW: Mutually Reinforcing Bilateral and Multilateral Approaches
The initiative should leverage both bilateral and multilateral channels of support. Bilateral mechanisms can allow for greater flexibility for advancing U.S. policy in the world and should continue to be an important mechanism for supporting children's education globally. However, the initiative should add to this existing bilateral work by ramping up its support of currently underfunded multilateral mechanisms like GPE and the Education Cannot Wait fund. Often in places where U.S. support is needed most, there is weak local governance, and support through bilateral mechanisms can be effectively complemented by multilateral mechanisms.

CONCLUSION

We should never underestimate the importance of investing in children and youth. Quality early childhood development and education are pivotal for putting young people on a path to success that contributes to vibrant societies. Far too many children are excluded from these opportunities and ultimately from a positive future. The next U.S. administration has an opportunity to capitalize on the groundwork that has been laid over the past eight years and make a significant difference for the education of young people around the globe, particularly for girls and women. This would be a historic contribution to the future of our children and an important contribution to our collective global prosperity.

Notes

1. Elizabeth Holtan, *Why Global Education Is One of America's Biggest Returns on Investment* (Washington, D.C.: U.S. Global Leadership Coalition, October 5, 2016).

2. See the report of the International Commission on Financing Global Education Opportunity at http://report.educationcommission.org/report/.

3. Rebecca Winthrop and Eileen McGivney, "Skills for a Changing World" (Brookings, May 19, 2016).

4. See Robert Michnick Golinkoff and Kathy Hirsh-Pasek, *Becoming Brilliant: What Science Tells Us about Raising Successful Children* (American Psychological Association, 2016).

5. Clayton L. Thyne, "ABC's, 123's, and the Golden Rule: The Pacifying Effect of Education on Civil War, 1980–1999," *International Studies Quarterly* 50 (2006): 733–54, www.uky.edu/~clthyn2/thyne-ISQ-06.pdf.

6. Rebecca Winthrop and Corinne Graff, "Beyond Madrasas: Assessing the Links between Education and Militancy in Pakistan" (Brookings, June 23, 2010).

7. *Teaching and Learning: Achieving Quality for All* (UNESCO, 2014), http://unesdoc.unesco.org/images/0022/002256/225660e.pdf.

8. Gene B. Sperling and Rebecca Winthrop, *What Works in Girls' Education: Evidence for the World's Best Investment* (Brookings Institution Press, 2015).

9. M. R. West, "Education and Global Competitiveness," in *Rethinking Competitiveness*, edited by K. Hassett (Washington, D.C.: American Enterprise Institute Press). An excerpt of this paper also appears in Martin R. West, "Global Lessons for Improving U.S. Education," *Issues in Science & Technology* 28, no. 3 (2012): 37–44.

10. Emmanuela Gakidou, Krycia Cowling, Rafael Lozano, and Christopher J. L. Murray, "Increased Educational Attainment and Its Effect on Child Mortality in 175 Countries between 1970 and 2009: A Systematic Analysis," *The Lancet* 376, no. 9745 (2010): 959–74, http://dx.doi.org/10.1016/S0140-6736(10)61257-3.

11. "High-level Meeting on the Education 2030 Framework for Action" (UNESCO, 2016), www.unesco.org/new/en/education/themes/leading-the-international-agenda /education-for-all/education-2030-framework-for-action/.

12. See information on the Measuring Early Learning Quality and Outcomes project on the "Readiness to Learn" website of the Learning Metrics Task Force, Brookings Center for Universal Education, www.brookings.edu/learning-metrics-task-force-2-0/readiness-to-learn/.

13. H.R. 4481, *Education for All Act of 2016*, September 7, 2016, www.govtrack. us/congress/bills/114/hr4481.

14. "The Path to Quality Education for All" (International Basic Education Caucus, Results, 2015), www.results.org/uploads/files/IC_2015_Education_Caucus.pdf.

15. Sperling and Winthrop, *What Works in Girls' Education*.

16. Christina Kwauk and Amanda Braga, "Are We Offering a Breadth of Skills in Girls' Education Programming?" (Brookings, October 11, 2016).

17. Jenny Perlman Robinson, Rebecca Winthrop, and Eileen McGivney, "Millions Learning: Scaling up Quality Education in Developing Countries" (Brookings, April 13, 2016).

18. Maureen M. Black and others, "Early Childhood Development Coming of Age: Science through the Life Course," *The Lancet* (online first), October 4, 2016, http://dx.doi.org/10.1016/S0140-6736(16)31389-7.

19. Sally Grantham-McGregor and others, "Developmental Potential in the First 5 Years for Children in Developing Countries," *The Lancet* 369, no. 9555 (2007): 60–70, http://dx.doi.org/10.1016/S0140-6736(07)60032-4.

20. "Target 4.1: Primary and Secondary Education," *Global Education Monitoring Report* (UNESCO, 2016), http://gem-report-2016.unesco.org/en/chapter/target-4-primary-and-secondary-education/.

30

U.S.-Mexican Relations

*After the Election's Vitriol, Ways to Strengthen
a Multifaceted Partnership*

VANDA FELBAB-BROWN

SUMMARY: Among the hallmarks of President-elect Donald Trump's "America first" approach, which would put the United States in a defensive crouch against others and deeply divide it internally, has been his antagonistic perspective on Mexico as a source of violent crime and illegal immigration, as well as a prime reason for job loss in the United States. As 2017 unfolds, the Trump administration should move beyond the campaign slogans and divisive rhetoric and work with Mexico in a cooperative spirit. Below are ways to advance the economic, security, and public safety issues that are of deep interest to both countries.

As a presidential candidate, Donald Trump called for the creation of a border wall between the United States and Mexico. That wall and the broader politics of division it represents would not only separate the United States and Mexico but would also further tear apart U.S. communities. He promised to get tough on crime and tough on immigration, making it difficult for Mexicans and Latinos to enter the United States, increasing deportations, and instituting very tough vetting procedures for Muslims seeking to obtain visas for entering the United States or refugee status and asylum. Trump also labeled the North American Free Trade Agreement

(NAFTA), the cornerstone of U.S.-Mexican-Canadian economic integration, "the worst trade deal ever" signed.[1]

Immigration, NAFTA, and criminality are interrelated. Not only is U.S. security enhanced by good cooperation with Mexico, but weakening U.S.-Mexico economic integration can exacerbate both criminality in Mexico and outmigration pressures to the United States. Weakening NAFTA and the economic progress it has brought to Mexico would reduce job opportunities and social development in Mexico, and thus would be likely to result in more impoverished Mexicans seeking to enter the United States illegally to make basic ends meet or face pressures to work in illegal economies and join criminal groups.

In fact, both basic facts and overwhelming evidence from economic studies show that it is in fact in the interests of the United States and Mexico (and Canada) to continue deepening their economic cooperation and integration. Equally in the realm of national security, including against terrorism and criminality, the three North American countries must continue and enlarge their cooperation—at their borders and beyond—assisting each other in advancing rule of law, justice, and public safety.

DEEPENING ECONOMIC PARTNERSHIP

Despite Trump's campaign rhetoric, the United States and Mexico will benefit from deepening and broadening their economic partnership. Mexico is the third-largest U.S. trade partner after China and Canada, and the third-largest supplier of U.S. imports. Some 79 percent of Mexico's total exports in 2013 went to the United States.[2] After Canada, the United States *exports* more to Mexico than to any other country. In merchandise, for example, the United States is by far Mexico's leading trade partner. It is also the top destination for exports from three U.S. states—Texas, Arizona, and California—and the second most important market for another 20 U.S. states.[3] But after twenty years of NAFTA, the U.S.-Mexico relationship has moved beyond trade. Investment between the two countries has grown enormously, and production is increasingly integrated and joint.

For the United States to attempt to renegotiate the basic text of NAFTA could spell the treaty's end. That would put U.S. workers (as well as Mexican ones) at a significant comparative disadvantage with regard to China, the very opposite of what President-elect Trump seeks to accomplish. Protectionist measures would undermine U.S. (and Mexican) competitiveness in a global market. Instead, tightening labor, environmental, anticorruption, and anti-money-laundering regulations is appropriate. Such deepening and tightening of the joint framework not only would be in the U.S. interest, but also would help promote rule of law and desirable standards in Mexico. The government of Mexico is willing to modernize NAFTA this way. But such revisions should be accomplished through negotiating binding side agreements, not opening the basic NAFTA text. Involving U.S., Mexican, and Canadian business, environmental, and labor communities in any such new discussions and negotiations will be crucial for making NAFTA a stronger and more effective deal. Moreover, many U.S. states and communities will want to continue their robust economic relations with Mexico, even if the new federal government gets in the way, because it benefits their economic growth and job opportunities.

A wise U.S. trade policy with Mexico must recognize that although economic integration with Mexico boosts the U.S. economy, not all U.S. workers have been able to share in the benefits. The appeal of Donald Trump's anti-NAFTA messages has been strongest among working-class white families who have struggled to make ends meet. Many do not have the capacity to provide for the kind of education their children need in order to successfully compete in the 21st-century economy. Many face an economic situation much tougher than white U.S. working-class families faced in the 1950s and 1960s. Their real wages have often declined and their living standards may have fallen as well, even when they work full time. The next U.S. administration must assist them with measures that will not only help them vent their frustration but will actually improve their well-being. Among those are safety nets, but also technical training programs and educational opportunities to develop new skills for competing in the information-age economy. Such effective and practical responses to their plight will allow the otherwise resentful and angry American workers to perceive that they are the beneficiaries of international commerce, and not its victims.

Trade, investment, joint production, and travel across the U.S.-Mexico border are a way of life for border communities, including U.S. cities and citizens. Disrupting them will not only create substantial economic costs for both countries, it will also create enormous social costs. The family ties and economic networks and connections of Mexicans increasingly reach deep into the United States. According to a 2015 fact sheet issued by the Mexican government, the 33 million people of Mexican origin in the

United States account for 8 percent of U.S. GDP; there are more than 2 million Hispanic entrepreneurs in the United States; and the trade between Mexico and the United States amounts to $530 billion per year.[4] The U.S. Hispanic consumer market was valued at $1.3 trillion in 2015, a number larger than Mexico's GDP, and is expected to grow to $1.7 trillion by 2020.[5] In 2012, the total consumer market in the United States was $12.2 trillion, and the spending power of Hispanics in the United States was larger than the entire economies of all but 13 countries in the word.[6] That year, Mexican immigrants to the United States contributed 4 percent to the U.S. GDP,[7] a proportion that has likely grown since.

The remittances from the United States are a significant lifeline for many poor Mexicans. They have tended to fluctuate between $20 billion and $25 billion annually during the George W. Bush and Barack Obama years. Remittances allow families to remain in their home country and provide better health care and education for their children, thus enabling human and economic development within their country and reducing further outmigration pressures. Over the past decade, remittances from the United States have amounted to about 3 percent of Mexico's GDP, representing the third-largest source of foreign revenue after oil and tourism. For many poor Mexican families, remittances can represent 80 percent of income, still barely enough for basic items such as food, clothes, and heath care. With a poverty rate set at $158 per month, 46.2 percent of Mexicans lived in poverty last year, an increase from the 45.5 percent in 2012.[8]

If U.S. anti-immigration policy and efforts to undo NAFTA worsen economic conditions in Mexico and undermine the country's efforts to reduce poverty, many more Mexicans will again seek to work in the United States, despite the risks and dangers from criminal organizations and U.S. law enforcement they will face in trying to get into the United States.

BUILDING 21ST-CENTURY BORDER SECURITY AND IMPROVING RULE OF LAW IN MEXICO

Thus, for economic as well as security reasons, the border needs to remain not a line of separation but a membrane of connection. The Bush and Obama administrations embarked on strengthening the U.S.-Mexico border by adding detection technologies and significantly increasing human resources devoted to patrolling the border. The U.S.-Mexico border is already tight and many fewer people manage to cross it than did a decade ago. In many areas where a wall is not already constructed, physical conditions do not easily allow it, and the costs of building such walls—whether in terms of financial outlays, environmental factors, or the effects on cross-border Native American communities—are enormous.

Donald Trump claimed that the wall would cost only $12 billion. Other estimates put the cost at $285 billion, with each U.S. taxpayer having to pay some $900 in new taxes.[9] He proposed that "remittances derived from illegal wages" would pay for the financial costs of erecting the fence. They will not. Even if there were a way to distinguish and trace legally and illegally derived remittances, the total level of remittances that Mexicans sent home in 2014, including from the very many living in the United States legally, was $23.6 billion.[10] This would be a tiny fraction of the likely cost of the wall.

Nor can every tunnel or wall breached be detected in time. Traffickers are adapting to the detection technologies and greater numbers of border personnel by deploying drones themselves to smuggle contraband across the border. And as in Europe, people can be smuggled in by boat. Instead of devoting a large amount of taxpayer money to erecting physical barriers, the Trump administration should explore ways to further deploy cheaper, smarter technologies along the border as a way of delivering on his key electoral promise.

The United States has also engaged with Mexico to tighten its southern border with Central America and limit the flow of migrants from Central America to the United States through Mexico. If President Trump adopts very confrontational policies toward Mexico, Mexico can retaliate by ending border security cooperation with the United States on both its northern and southern border, a dangerous and counterproductive outcome for both countries. Hopefully, President Trump will learn soon that good intelligence sharing, cooperation in policing, and trust among the neighbors are also crucial for achieving effective security at the border.

The new U.S. administration should also reinforce efforts to improve the efficiency of merchandise movement across the border by expanding goods inspection away from the border, deeper into Mexico and the United States, and close to loading points. Establishing such secure container monitoring away from the border and modernizing the flow of commerce were crucial elements of the Beyond Merida cooperation initiative, which the United States and Mexico signed during the early part of the Obama administration. In some parts of Mexico, this modernization has been a great success, significantly reducing wait times at the border and improving trade efficiency and border security. In other parts of Mexico, where insecurity and corruption persist—such as Michoacán, an important source of Mexico's agricultural exports but a place of poor rule of law, intense contestation among criminal groups, and inadequate state presence—there is a need and many opportunities to improve such infrastructure through mutual cooperation.

The new U.S. administration should continue to cooperate with Mexico on improving rule of law and reducing corruption. This is good for security and public safety in both countries, and will also facilitate trade. The Trump administration should build on Beyond Merida and encourage the following improvements in Mexico's law enforcement efforts:

- Making interdiction of criminal networks more strategic;

- Moving away from targeting the leaders of criminal groups piecemeal to targeting as many as possible of the middle operational layers of criminal groups at once;

- Resurrecting momentum on police reform and finally undertaking a deep reform of municipal police forces;

- Strengthening the deterrence capacity of law enforcement and prosecutorial capacities;

- Deepening Mexico's justice reform;

- Strictly and diligently protecting human rights and strengthening accountability, and

- Improving and deepening socioeconomic anticrime interventions.

IMPROVING POLICING IN THE UNITED STATES

It is remarkable that despite extraordinary and once-again escalating criminal violence in Mexico since 2006, the U.S. criminal market has remained by and large peaceful, with violent crime rates falling for two decades in most of the United States. Violence from Mexico has not spilled into the United States, even though Mexican drug trafficking groups are the dominant suppliers of illegal drugs in the United States. There are exceptions. Chicago is one example of a city where criminal violence remains distressingly high for multiple reasons, including fighting between local Latin and African American gangs over Chicago's drug distribution markets supplied by the Mexican criminal groups. Reducing homicides and improving policing in Chicago and in other U.S. cities where violent crime has been persistent or rising, such as Baltimore and New Orleans, is an urgent priority. Among the tools available are focused deterrence approaches pioneered in Boston in the early 1990s and successfully adopted in other U.S. cities. These approaches prioritize law enforcement targeting of and social intervention with the groups and actors most likely to initiate violence.[11]

An antagonistic U.S.-Mexico relationship will not help reduce persistent crime problems in both countries. Indeed, for a decade, the two countries have embraced the principle of joint responsibility, with the United States recognizing its responsibility for its drug consumption and illegal weapons flows into Mexico. Cooperation between the countries is necessary for effectively tackling organized and disorganized crime. But so is cooperation among police forces and local residents.

Pushing local police forces to check immigration papers and obligating them to hunt for undocumented residents ultimately will have detrimental effects on law enforcement. The Bush administration tried that policy: It did not help reduce crime, and local police departments resented it and found it counterproductive, diverting them from other anticrime priorities and alienating local communities. Communities will shut up and refuse to interact with police forces; alienation, refusal to cooperate with law enforcement units, and actual protests against police presence can escalate; and vital information on serious organized crime can be lost. In order to get to know and stop criminals, the police need to know and be accepted by their communities.

The opposite of a policy that divides communities and alienates minorities is needed: Public safety requires close cooperation with local communities, not racial or ethnic profiling. Protests by African Americans against excessive and heavy-handed policing and inappropriate killings by police should have driven that home to President-elect Trump. To reduce violent crime, a real solution requires reaching out to communities, establishing citizen-police liaison committees, and finding out what crimes actually most threaten local communities—not ostracizing minorities. In fact, increasing police recruitment from among minority groups, including Hispanic but also Muslim communities, is a far more useful tool. Such officers will be able to better understand local communities and develop their trust. This is particularly important for dealing with lone-wolf terrorist attacks where the most important "responder"—and often the only source of intelligence—can be the family, friends, and neighbors of a potential attacker. Beyond specialized counterterrorism units, such as fusion centers and task forces, it is local communities that can know about and prevent a lone-wolf attack by providing ground-up intelligence. Such good community-police cooperation is all the more necessary in smaller cities that will not be able to marshal counterterrorism resources on the scale of large cities, such as New York. Thus, neither Muslim nor Hispanic or African American communities should be ostracized and mistreated.

There are many other aspects of improving policing, corrections systems, and criminal justice broadly in the United States. Reducing—*not increasing*—the U.S. prison population is one of them. Crucially, reducing shootings and killings by U.S. law enforcement forces, as well as violence against them, must be a top priority. Effective policing is about communities that feel protected by and allied with the police, not ones that shy away from them.

The issues of trade, border security, and public safety hardly exhaust the agenda of U.S.-Mexico cooperation. Although they were featured in the 2016 U.S. presidential election and will be crucial components of the new administration's Mexico policy, the United States and Mexico will need to cooperate on a host of other matters. These include energy cooperation to build clean energy sources for both countries and mitigate climate change. Even though President-elect Trump has been skeptical of the reality of climate change and had promised to revive and increase U.S. fossil fuel consumption, clean energy sources—not fossil fuels—are the right way to go. Other large areas of the bilateral relationship comprise a broad range of environmental issues, from improving water sustainability and reviving joint watersheds to combatting cross-border and global illegal trade in wildlife, in which both countries are crucial actors. Cooperation, not a one-sided or antagonistic relationship, will help both countries to improve our peoples' well-being.

Notes

1. Maggie Severn, "Trump Pins NAFTA, 'Worst Trade Deal Ever,' on Clinton," *Politico*, September 26, 2016, www.politico.com/story/2016/09/trump-clinton-come-out-swinging-over-nafta-228712.

2. Data in this paragraph are from M. Angeles Villareal, "U.S.-Mexico Economic Relations: Trends, Issues, and Implications," Congressional Research Service Report No. 7-5700 (April 20, 2015), 2–3.

3. U.S. State Department, U.S. Embassy—Mexico City, "Bilateral Trade Factsheet," August 2013, http://photos.state.gov/libraries/mexico/310329/sept13/Bilateral-Trade-0913.pdf.

4. Cited in Joshua Partlow, "For Mexicans, the Donald Trump Candidacy Is Getting Scarier," *Washington Post*, August 18, 2015.

5. Nicole Akoukou Thompson, "Hispanic Consumers to Spend $1.3 Trillion in 2015, Prompting National Economic Growth," *The Latin Post*, September 28, 2015, www.latinpost.com/articles/82555/20150928/hispanic-consumers-will-spend-1-3-trillion-in-2015-prompting-overall-economic-growth.htm.

6. Jeffrey Humphreys, "The 2015 Multicultural Economy," Selig Center, Terry College of Business, September 2015, https://estore.uga.edu/C27063_ustores/web/product_detail.jsp?PRODUCTID=4606.

7. Mamta Badkar, "Here's the Real Economic Impact of Mexican Immigrants on the U.S.," *Business Insider*, July 29, 2012, www.businessinsider.com/mexican-immigration-us-economy-2012-7.

8. Data from a 2015 biannual Mexican government agency Coneval's report to the Mexican Congress, reported in Joshua Paltrow and Gabriela Martinez, "Mexico's Economy Was Supposed to Soar. It's Starting to Flop," *Washington Post,* August 8, 2015.

9. "Trump's America," *The Economist*, September 5, 2015.

10. "Mexican Remittances Jump 7.8% in 2014," Associated Press, February 3, 2014.

11. See, for example, David Kennedy, *Don't Shoot: One Man, A Street Fellowship, and the End of Violence in Inner-City America* (New York: Bloomsbury, 2011); David Kennedy, Daniel Tompkins, and Gayle Garmise, "Pulling Levers: Getting Deterrence Right," *National Institute of Justice Journal* 236 (1998): 2–8; Mark Kleiman, *When Brute Force Fails: How to Have Less Crime and Less Punishment* (Princeton University Press, 2009); and Vanda Felbab-Brown, "Targeted Deterrence, Selective Targeting, Drug Trafficking and Organized Crime: Concepts and Practicalities," IDPC-IISS-Chatham House, Modernizing Drug Law Enforcement, Report No. 2 (February 2013), www.brookings.edu/wp-content/uploads/2016/06/drug-law-enforcement-felbabbrown.pdf.

31

Dealing with a Nuclear-Armed North Korea

Rising Danger, Narrowing Options, Hard Choices

EVANS J. R. REVERE

SUMMARY: A nuclear-armed and belligerent North Korea presents the Trump administration with an urgent and dangerous challenge. North Korea believes that its nuclear weapons now deter the United States, thus setting the stage for the realization of Pyongyang's long-time goals: the end of the U.S.–South Korea alliance and national reunification on its terms. Meanwhile, the message of Pyongyang's nuclear threats to the United States is disturbingly clear: "We are willing to risk nuclear war to achieve our goals, are you?"

The rising threat posed by North Korea (Democratic People's Republic of Korea; DPRK) requires a new approach that will force the regime to choose between nuclear weapons and survival. President Trump should make clear to North Korea that the United States is prepared to put at risk the one thing that the DPRK holds even more dear than its nuclear weapons—the preservation of its regime—to compel Pyongyang to end its nuclear weapons program. To implement this approach, the United States should aggressively pursue the financial lifeblood of the Kim regime, starve it of foreign currency, cut Pyongyang off from the international banking and trading systems, greatly intensify sanctions, interdict its illicit commerce, and use covert means to exploit the regime's vulnerabilities. The military dimension of U.S. policy will be equally important.

This approach is risky and will complicate relations with China, which sees Pyongyang as an asset in its rivalry with the United States. Importantly, however, America's South Korean ally appears willing to assume more risk to end the North's threat. However, political developments in South Korea (Republic of Korea; ROK) will bear careful watching and there is some potential for a political shift in Seoul that could find the United States at odds with a new, center-left government. The Trump administration should carefully listen to South Korean concerns and not take the South for granted. With a rising North Korean threat, America will need allies. Building strong ties with Seoul will be critical to ensuring that Washington and Seoul stay on the same page and pursue an effective policy against Pyongyang.

THE THREAT

A nuclear-armed North Korea will present the Trump administration with one of its most urgent foreign policy and security challenges. President Trump will face a more dangerous North Korea than did any of his predecessors. He will also inherit a legacy of U.S. policy failure in dealing with Pyongyang's nuclear ambitions.

Four U.S. administrations have tried and failed to stop North Korea's pursuit of nuclear weapons. Pyongyang has been offered incentives, presidential assurances, and security guarantees on the one hand, and Washington has also tried sanctions, threats, and isolation on the other. Nothing has worked more than temporarily. As a result, America now faces the nightmare of a nuclear-armed North Korea that is threatening to use those weapons.

North Korea can probably already target South Korea, Japan, and U.S. bases in those countries with nuclear-tipped ballistic missiles. And Pyongyang will likely be able to strike more distant targets, including U.S. bases in Guam and Hawaii, and eventually the continental United States itself, within two to three years. Meanwhile, North Korea is also developing solid-fuel ballistic missiles that would enable it to disperse and hide those missiles and give the regime a survivable second-strike capability.

WHAT DOES PYONGYANG WANT?

What is Pyongyang's goal in building nuclear weapons? For years, some argued that Pyongyang's nuclear weapons were "bargaining chips" to be "traded" for aid, concessions, and inducements, including diplomatic normalization and security guarantees. But over the years, U.S. diplomats negotiating with North Korea came to realize that incentives were of little value. They discovered that Pyongyang was *not* building nuclear weapons just to trade them away.

Today, we know that nuclear weapons fulfill two core requirements for the regime. First, nuclear weapons ensure the regime's survival. Pyongyang is convinced that the United States will not attack a country that has nuclear weapons and is prepared to use them. But a second reason for North Korea's nuclear weapons and missiles now seems clear: DPRK representatives say privately that, thanks to their nuclear weapons, they have the United States "deterred." They assert that the United States must now live with a nuclear-armed North Korea and accept its demand to negotiate a peace treaty to replace the Korean War armistice agreement and conduct U.S.-DPRK "arms control talks." The goal of these talks, they declare, would be to remove the U.S. "threat," which they define as the U.S.-ROK alliance, American troops in South Korea, and the U.S. "nuclear umbrella."

Pyongyang appears to believe that its nuclear weapons have fundamentally changed the dynamics of U.S.–North Korea relations. Pyongyang thinks it can now compel Washington to end the U.S.-ROK alliance and remove the U.S. extended deterrent, allowing the North to achieve its ultimate goal: the reunification of the peninsula on its terms. And by threatening to use nuclear weapons, Pyongyang's message to the United States is: "We are willing to risk nuclear war to achieve our goals, are you?"

Pyongyang's belief that it has changed the balance of forces on the Korean Peninsula is troubling. So, too, is its desire to leave the United States with no alternative but to deal with a nuclear-armed North Korea. That is why it has declared the goal of denuclearization dead, and why the North says it will continue to expand its nuclear arsenal. By making its intentions explicit, Pyongyang hopes to force the United States to choose between accepting a nuclear-armed North or risking war to prevent it.

THE CHINA FACTOR

Many believe that Beijing is the key to solving the North Korea nuclear challenge, but China is increasingly part of the problem. We have probably reached the limits of Beijing's willingness to do more to pressure the DPRK. Chinese cooperation in implementing international sanctions has been grudging and filled with loopholes, and efforts to approve a tough UN Security Council resolution after Pyongyang's fifth nuclear test were fraught with difficulties.

China's position on North Korea is increasingly driven by broad, geopolitical factors, especially Beijing's growing strategic rivalry with the United States. In this context, China's leaders do not necessarily see North Korea as a liability. For that matter, China's leaders continue to believe it is better to keep a troublesome North Korean ally afloat than to risk the chaos that might result if the regime collapses.

Accordingly, the United States should be modest in its expectations of China when it comes to pressuring Pyongyang. Washington should also avoid characterizing North Korea as "China's problem" to solve. Pyongyang's nuclear weapons are aimed at U.S. bases and U.S. allies, and soon will target the U.S. homeland. For that reason alone, subcontracting America's security to a Beijing that is inclined to sympathize with Pyongyang would be a grave mistake. Instead, when Beijing repeats the familiar mantra that it has "little influence" over North Korea, U.S. policymakers should respond that China's inability (or unwillingness) to act makes it necessary for the United States and its allies to do so as a matter of self-defense.

The new administration should also recognize that steps it takes to intensify sanctions on Pyongyang, including targeting Chinese companies that are violating sanctions, could complicate U.S.-China relations. But these concerns cannot be allowed to prevent the United States from defending its interests.

U.S. POLICY OPTIONS: PLUSES AND MINUSES

So what is to be done? The list of policy options the Trump administration will consider is an unsatisfying one. It includes choices that are deficient, defunct, dangerous, defeatist, and even delusional. Here are several possible options.

"Staying the Course-Plus"
First, the new administration could pursue a version of recent policy and gradually increase sanctions on North Korea and hope the cumulative effect of sanctions over time will convince Pyongyang to resume denuclearization talks. However, this approach has not worked, and is not likely to work in an acceptable timeframe, as Pyongyang's nuclear and missile threats become increasingly urgent in the coming months. And with North Korea having rejected denuclearization dialogue and made clear its determination to rapidly expand its nuclear arsenal, gradualism is unlikely to work.

Military Action
The United States and South Korea could take military action against North Korea, destroying its known nuclear, missile, and military infrastructure, including nuclear production and storage facilities. Such an attack would leave the DPRK incapable of mounting a significant conventional counterattack and render its army largely ineffective as a fighting force. But North Korea could still inflict major damage on South Korea, and even a broadly successful air campaign would not guarantee that North Korea could not use its nuclear or other weapons of mass destruction against South Korea, Japan, and U.S. bases. Military action against North Korea is a dangerous option that could undermine regional stability, risk a conflict with China, create peninsula-wide chaos, and cause major damage to our South Korean ally.

Living with a Nuclear North Korea
Some argue that the United States should accept the inevitability of a permanently nuclear-armed DPRK. In this view, the United States could opt to live with a nuclear North Korea and rely on containment and deterrence to defend itself and its allies and prevent nuclear proliferation.

Doing so would reverse decades of U.S. policy. It would damage, perhaps fatally, the international nuclear nonproliferation regime and emasculate the Nuclear Nonproliferation Treaty (NPT). It would shake the confidence of America's South Korean and Japanese allies, who refuse to accept Pyongyang's nuclear status. Calls would escalate in both Seoul and Tokyo to develop nuclear weapons. This approach would allow Pyongyang to continue to enhance its nuclear and missile arsenals to threaten U.S. allies. The North's temptation to engage in proliferation would be strong, especially since the fabric of the NPT had been damaged and American resolve was in question. Accepting the North as a de facto nuclear weapons state would make things worse, not better.

A New Goal for Dialogue?

What about accepting Pyongyang's proposal to discuss replacement of the Korean War Armistice Agreement with a peace treaty, instead of or in advance of a denuclearization discussion? A peace treaty would defuse tensions, it is said, and would convey U.S. seriousness about dealing with Pyongyang's concerns and remove what Pyongyang claims is the "root cause" of its development of nuclear weapons.

Such thinking is delusional. Accepting North Korea's proposal would damage ties with the ROK, which is not prepared to negotiate a peace treaty with a nuclear-armed DPRK. And Seoul surely would not accept a peace treaty discussion in which it is not a central player. Moreover, entering a peace treaty discussion with a nuclear North Korea and foregoing denuclearization discussions would buy into the North Korean game plan mentioned earlier. North Korea wants a peace treaty that leads to the end of the U.S.-ROK alliance. The Trump administration cannot accept this.

A "Freeze"

For some, "freezing" or "capping" the North Korean nuclear program and trying to eliminate it over time through dialogue should be the goal.

It is important to recall that a freeze leading to denuclearization was the central premise of both the October 1994 Agreed Framework and the September 2005 six-party agreement. Both efforts failed. Importantly, a credible freeze or cap is only as good as our ability to verify it, and North Korea has made clear it will not accept international verification. U.S. inability to verify a freeze would leave North Korea's uranium enrichment facilities in operation. Pyongyang would also be free to improve its warheads, manufacture larger warheads, and make other refinements to its nuclear weapons during a so-called freeze. A freeze that does not halt the testing and deployment of ballistic missiles also would allow Pyongyang to continue to improve its delivery systems.

If the goal of a freeze is to prevent the North from making additional nuclear weapons, it will not work. It would leave the United States and its allies dangerously vulnerable. Unless a *temporary* freeze on nuclear testing and plutonium production is part of a *firm* agreement that leads quickly to complete and verifiable denuclearization, it runs the risk of creating the illusion of security and progress where none exists.

"Nukes for Everybody"

Finally, some have suggested that the solution is to allow Japan and South Korea to develop their own nuclear weapons. This proposal is ill advised and dangerous and would lead to the further deterioration of the NPT and provide justification for Pyongyang to keep its nuclear weapons. When a dangerous resident is threatening to blow up the neighborhood, responding to the threat by giving everyone in the neighborhood a can of gasoline and matches is unlikely to be an effective approach.

TIME FOR A DIFFERENT APPROACH

The Trump administration needs a new approach. And the rapidly rising danger from Pyongyang requires the United States to adopt a strategy that reflects the growing urgency of the threat. The United States must apply immediate and unprecedented pressure on the North Korean regime to compel it to change course.

Going forward, U.S. policy should be built on a much stronger foundation than exists today, one that includes the following strategies:

- Deploying improved U.S. and allied military capabilities on and around the Korean Peninsula;

- Enhancing extended deterrence and measures to physically demonstrate U.S. determination to fulfill its commitments; and

- Increasing the scope and frequency of military exercises, to include participation by other members of the UN command, such as the United Kingdom and Australia.

North Korea must be convinced that it will never be accepted as a nuclear state and that the United States is prepared to respond with steps designed to deter and contain any of the North's nuclear activities, and that the United States will raise the cost to Pyongyang of its pursuit of nuclear weapons to an unacceptable level. U.S. policy should make clear that Washington's preference is for the resumption of meaningful dialogue with Pyongyang, and that the United States stands by past agreements to eventually normalize relations with a *nonnuclear* DPRK. The United States should assure Pyongyang that it is prepared to engage at the highest levels with the DPRK to address the full range of its concerns, *if and only if* Pyongyang is prepared to reopen a serious denuclearization dialogue.

To do this, the United States should be prepared to hold at risk the one thing that the DPRK holds more dearly than its nuclear weapons—the preservation of its regime—in order to convince Pyongyang to end its pursuit of nuclear weapons. North Korean officials say their goal is the preservation of their regime, and they believe nuclear weapons will help them achieve this goal. The United States must convince Pyongyang otherwise. U.S. policy should emphasize a central new message to Pyongyang: If regime survival is your goal, nuclear weapons will prevent you from reaching this goal.

THE TOOLKIT

The tools to convince North Korea to take a different path include greatly strengthened economic, trade, financial, and other measures designed to starve the Pyongyang regime of hard currency and disrupt its companies' ability to do business in violation of UN and other sanctions.

Sanctions on North Korea should be intensified to the level once applied on Iran. This should *not* be done in an incremental way, but as quickly as possible to achieve maximum effect. The United States and like-minded countries should expel North Korea from the international banking system, including denying Pyongyang access to the global financial transaction clearing system. Secondary sanctions should be applied on third-country entities, including Chinese firms, that do business with suspect North Korean entities. Existing authorities under UN Security Council resolutions and relevant unilateral sanctions should be used to pressure and, if possible, shut down firms, including travel and tourism companies, currently doing business in North Korea.

The international community should intensify inspection and interdiction of suspect North Korean vessels and aircraft, and third-country vessels and aircraft trading with the DPRK. The United States also should consider imposing a naval quarantine to prevent North Korea from violating existing UN Security Council sanctions or trading in illicit materials.

Overseas North Korean assets should be frozen or seized if they are linked to illicit activities or violation of UN Security Council sanctions.

Surveillance of overseas DPRK trading offices should be increased with an eye toward shutting these offices down in cases where they violate sanctions. The United States should encourage the international community to stop trading with North Korea and be prepared to exclude from the U.S. market firms that do business with North Korea.

Other, more technical efforts can be made against North Korea's domestic and foreign vulnerabilities. Using new U.S. legislation that calls for an increase in information operations against the DPRK, the United States and its partners should explore vulnerabilities in the DPRK's cellphone system to maximize the flow of information into the country. Efforts also should be made to encourage overseas representatives of the DPRK to defect and to cooperate with international law enforcement to stop illicit trade and other activities. Covert activities designed to exploit vulnerabilities in the DPRK's communications, banking, and financial systems should be considered—but the less said publicly about these measures, the better.

A WORD ABOUT RISK AND UNCERTAINTY

The above policy recommendations carry some risk, but the risk of allowing North Korea to increase its nuclear threat is much greater. The Trump administration must be prepared to act from the outset with a sense of urgency, determination, and intensity, especially since Pyongyang may challenge it early on.

No country knows the risks associated with the above approach better than South Korea. Importantly, Seoul's consistent message to Washington in recent months has been one of firm determination and a clear willingness to accept the risks. But South Korea's recent political crisis has created uncertainty about its ability to stay the course, and we cannot rule out the possibility that a successor, center-left South Korean government might opt for a different approach to deal with Pyongyang. This bears careful watching.

The new U.S. administration must carefully consider South Korea's concerns, sensitivities, and politics. As the Trump administration works with Seoul to coordinate next steps against North Korea, it must avoid alienating our important ally or taking it for granted. The administration should also avoid fueling South Korean fears that Washington might abandon its ally. The words of reassurance President-elect Trump used in his postelection call with South Korea's President Park were important—and absolutely necessary.

In the current atmosphere of continuing uncertainty about how the United States views alliances, providing reassurance to America's best friends is essential. As the United States faces the rising danger of a nuclear-armed North Korea, it will need partners. The new administration must prioritize building the closest possible ties of trust and confidence with its allies, particularly South Korea, which has always stood shoulder-to-shoulder with the United States. Therein lies the best hope for success in dealing with North Korea.

32

President Trump's Options for Israeli-Palestinian Deal Making

MARTIN INDYK

SUMMARY: The Israeli-Palestinian conflict has defied the peace-making efforts of successive U.S. presidential administrations. As the incoming Trump administration considers how it will attempt to resolve the conflict, this chapter presents three possible approaches to negotiations—a provocative, high-risk "top-down" approach that would focus on the contested status of Jerusalem; a more measured "bottom-up" approach that would work with regional players to change the situation on the ground; and a summit-driven "outside-in" approach that would establish internationally supported terms of reference for negotiating a two-state solution. All three options are likely to have critical political consequences for the Trump administration, but if there is a desire to break the stalemate of distrust in the Middle East, their potential merits should be considered.

President-elect Trump has repeatedly declared his desire to make peace between Israelis and Palestinians "for humanity's sake," viewing it as the "ultimate deal," and suggesting that he would appoint his son-in-law, Jared Kushner, as his special envoy for this purpose. He would not be the first American president to hear the siren song of the Nobel Peace Prize committee, but he would be the first real estate developer to try to reach for the "brass ring," and his experience with making land deals as well as his unconventional, disruptive approach to diplomacy might just generate new possibilities when all other efforts have failed. However, President Trump would be taking on the task at a uniquely difficult moment when neither side trusts in the peaceful intentions of the other or believes in the possibility of a peace deal based on the establishment of a viable Palestinian state living alongside the Jewish state of Israel in peace and security.

This "two-state solution" has been thwarted by two abiding realities that would have to be fundamentally altered for its chances to be revived. The first is the power of the Israeli settler movement and its supporters in Israeli prime minister Benjamin Netanyahu's right-wing coalition government. They regard all West Bank territory as part of the Land of Israel and firmly reject the two-state solution. Consequently, they are pursuing apace an effort to annex the 60 percent of the West Bank that remains under complete Israeli control (known as "Area C" in the Oslo Accords that govern Israel's relations with the Palestinian Authority) through expanding settlements there, attempting to legalize some 50 outposts that are illegal under Israeli law, and preventing any Palestinian development of the land.

The second reality is a politically and physically divided Palestinian polity in the West Bank and Gaza Strip between the Hamas and Fatah political parties, in which Hamas remains dedicated to the destruction of Israel and is consolidating its grip on Gaza while building its influence in the West Bank. Meanwhile, Fatah is going through a succession process that has left its leadership preoccupied and, for the time being, unable to engage in any kind of peace initiative.

In other words, there are two powerful forces—the Israeli settler movement and the Hamas Islamist movement—that are driving toward one-state solutions of their own design. However momentarily attractive these alternatives may look to people on either side of the conflict, they cannot produce a peaceful solution brought about by a negotiated deal between the two sides. Indeed, such a negotiated peace deal is anathema to both of them. Little wonder they have done all they can—the one through settlement activity, the other through violence and terrorism—to thwart the negotiations that have taken place. Their solutions do not solve the conflict between the two peoples that inhabit the same land. On the contrary, they are bound to perpetuate it.

Nevertheless, these realities constrain both Prime Minister Netanyahu and Palestinian president Mahmoud Abbas (Abu Mazen) from engaging in meaningful peace negotiations. Netanyahu's right-wing coalition would collapse if he were to pursue territorial concessions in the West Bank. The alternative of forming a more flexible centrist coalition with the Labor Party would leave him dependent on parties to his left while his rivals to his right robbed him of the support of his natural constituency. Meanwhile, Abbas's electoral mandate expired some six years ago, and he no longer feels he has the legitimacy to make compromises over what his people believe are their inalienable rights. If he attempted to do so, he would be denounced as a traitor by his rivals in Hamas and Fatah alike.

This situation generates an acute policy dilemma: current circumstances do not permit the achievement of a negotiated resolution of the Israeli-Palestinian conflict, and yet failure to pursue that resolution now will make it even less possible to achieve it in the future. In attempting to address this dilemma, President-elect Trump and his would-be special envoy would do well to heed the lesson of the last attempt by Secretary of State John Kerry (in which I served as his special envoy to the negotiations): American willpower alone, no matter how artful, cannot substitute for the will and ability of the parties themselves to make the politically costly and emotionally fraught compromises necessary to achieve the deal. And yet, another failed effort will not only make matters worse, potentially sparking a new round of conflict, but also tarnish the credibility of the new president, making him look like a loser.

If President-elect Trump is nevertheless intent on trying his hand at the "mother of all deals" despite all these difficulties, he might do well to choose from three options:

"JERUSALEM FIRST"

Given the President-elect's penchant for throwing away the established rule book, he could adopt a completely novel, high-risk approach designed to inject a new and very different dynamic. One of the basic rules of Israeli-Palestinian negotiations is that the status of Jerusalem is an issue that should be left until all the other issues are resolved. Negotiators have learned from bitter experience that the room for compromise there is more limited than on any other issue. The 2000 Camp David negotiations collapsed over Jerusalem, sparking the second intifada that resulted in the deaths of thousands of Palestinians and Israelis.

The reasons for the intractability of the Jerusalem issue are quite clear: neither side accepts the legitimacy of the other's claims. Arab east Jeru-

salem was annexed to Israel in 1967, and since then every Israeli government has claimed undivided Jerusalem as "the eternal capital of Israel."
Jewish suburbs have been built throughout east Jerusalem, cutting the city
off physically from the West Bank, leaving only one area (known as E1)
that can still connect the two territories. Conversely, Palestinians claim all
the area of east Jerusalem that Israel occupied in 1967, including the Old
City, as the capital for their state and view the Jewish suburbs built there
as illegal. Both sides also demand sovereignty over the area in the Old City
known as the Temple Mount to Jews and the Haram a-Sharif to Arabs and
Muslims. That area contains the Al-Aqsa mosque, the third holiest site in
Islam, and the Western Wall and the ruins of the Second Temple that lie
behind it, the holiest site in Judaism. The fact that Islam and Judaism both
lay religious claim to the same holy area makes touching this issue in negotiations particularly sensitive and potentially explosive.

Rational solutions to all these competing and overlapping claims have
been developed. For example, the undivided city could become the shared
capital of the two states. Jewish suburbs would be under Israeli sovereignty,
Arab suburbs would be under Palestinian sovereignty, and the Palestinian
state would be compensated with equivalent land swaps for the land in east
Jerusalem on which the Jewish suburbs were built. The area bounded by
the walls of the Old City, which contains the sites holiest to the three great
religions (including the Church of the Holy Sepulchre), would be declared
a special zone where neither side would exercise its claims to sovereignty
and a special regime would instead be established to administer the area,
ensure freedom of access to all the holy sites, and maintain the religious
status quo in which the three religious authorities continue to administer
their respective holy sites. However, such rational compromises have not
proven remotely acceptable to either side.[1]

President Trump could decide to ignore all these obstacles and instead
adopt a strategy of "Jerusalem first." He could begin by announcing that
he had decided to move the U.S. embassy to Jerusalem, as he promised to
do during the election campaign. This would likely spark an explosion of
anger in the Palestinian, Arab, and Muslim worlds and generate a rallying
cry for Islamic extremists everywhere. American embassies and American
citizens in Muslim countries would likely be targeted by violent demon-
strators. Confrontations between Palestinians and Israelis would likely
erupt in the West Bank, and the Palestinian security forces would likely
stand aside, unable or unwilling to continue cooperating with their Israeli

counterparts to tamp down the violence. Hamas might resume rocket attacks from Gaza, but because of fear of an Israeli response it would more likely seek to stoke the fires of violent resistance in the West Bank and Jerusalem. Arab and Muslim states would likely demand that Trump rescind the decision.

Alternatively, in parallel with moving the U.S. embassy in Israel to Jerusalem, the president could also announce that he has decided to establish a U.S. embassy to the state of Palestine in east Jerusalem, while opposing any division of the city. This decision would likely provoke an equally vociferous but less violent howl of protest from Israel and its friends in Congress and the organized Jewish community, since it would not only acknowledge Palestinian claims in east Jerusalem but also grant recognition to the Palestinian state, prefiguring Jerusalem as the shared capital of the two states.

Having provoked the crisis, President Trump could then seek to end it by declaring that he was willing to suspend U.S. recognition of Jerusalem as Israel's capital (and as Palestine's capital, in the alternative approach) until both sides resolved its status. He would then need to summon Israeli and Palestinian leaders to Washington to begin direct negotiations on the issue of Jerusalem. President Abdel Fattah al-Sisi of Egypt and King Abdullah of Jordan and the other members of the Quartet (the European Union, Russia, and the United Nations) would need to be invited to join President Trump in overseeing the negotiations to lend weight and legitimacy to the effort. And a short timetable, perhaps three months, would need to be established to conclude the negotiations, during which time there would need to be a construction freeze in east Jerusalem.

To ensure that both sides negotiated in good faith, President Trump could declare that if they fail to turn up or fail to reach agreement, the Quartet, Egypt, and Jordan would resort to a UN Security Council resolution setting out the parameters of the rational solution on Jerusalem, in effect threatening to impose it on the two sides. Israel would be required to accept a Palestinian capital in Arab east Jerusalem in return for Arab, Muslim, and international recognition of Israel's capital in an undivided Jerusalem. The United States could then go ahead and locate two embassies in Jerusalem, one on the west side for Israel and the other on the east side for Palestine. This could then open the way to negotiation of the other final status issues.

It is important to underscore that this is a high-risk, provocative option in which American lives and interests around the world could well be at stake, not to speak of Israeli and Palestinian lives. Once the fire is lit, it may not be possible to extinguish it by a diplomatic initiative. But if President Trump is determined to go ahead with his promise to move the U.S. embassy to Jerusalem, then wedding it to a preplanned diplomatic effort to resolve the conflict is more advisable than just battening down the hatches and hoping that the storm of adverse reaction will pass.

BOTTOM UP

President Trump could instead choose a more conventional effort that attempts to use time to shape a more favorable negotiating environment, laying the groundwork for a negotiated solution later in his presidency. In his first two years, he would instead focus on arresting the negative dynamics on the ground in the West Bank and work with Egypt and Jordan to promote a united Palestinian leadership with a mandate to negotiate peace with Israel.

Under this option, he would need to insist at the outset that Israel stop all construction east of the security barrier that it has built that runs more or less parallel to the 1967 lines inside the West Bank and incorporates the major Israeli settlement blocs as well as east Jerusalem. The right-wing Israeli defense minister, Avigdor Lieberman, has already offered a similar deal to President-elect Trump. Construction in the blocs west of the barrier could continue without American objection. Construction in east Jerusalem could also continue but on a 1:1 basis for building in Arab as well as Jewish suburbs. There could be no construction in E1 or other sensitive areas such as Givat Hamatos, which would block east Jerusalem's connection with the West Bank in the south. Israel also would have to agree to handing over significant territory in Area C, contiguous to the Palestinian-controlled Areas A and B, to allow for Palestinian construction and development.[2] If the Netanyahu government prefers to continue settlement construction in Area C beyond the barrier, President Trump should make clear that he is willing to have the United States abstain on a settlements resolution in the UN Security Council that would declare settlement activity illegal. Prime Minister Netanyahu cannot say so, but he needs this threat to constrain the settlers in his governing coalition. Trump's insistence on this approach might precipitate a change in Prime Minister Netanyahu's coalition, since it would be unacceptable to Naftali

Bennett's Jewish Home Party, but it has been one of the preconditions for Isaac ("Buji") Herzog to bring the Labor Party into the coalition. With Jewish Home out and Labor in, Netanyahu would be more capable of entering into meaningful negotiations.

Meanwhile, President Trump would need to work with President Sisi and King Abdullah on generating a change in Palestinian leadership and reconciling Hamas and Fatah on grounds that would enable a unified leadership to enter peace negotiations with Israel. In return, the building of state institutions and the development of the Palestinian economy in the West Bank and Gaza initiated by former prime minister Salam Fayyad should be boosted by a new injection of funds from the United States, the Arab states, and the international community.

As these processes on both sides began to take hold, President Trump's special envoy could begin to talk to both sides about terms of reference for resuming final status negotiations in the last two years of the president's term. If the Palestinians refused to enter negotiations based on these Israeli constraints on settlement construction, or demanded additional preconditions such as prisoner releases, President Trump could make clear that he would no longer be willing to constrain Israeli settlement activity anywhere.

OUTSIDE IN

If President Trump judges the bottom-up option to be too conventional, slow, and "in the weeds" for a nonconventional leader, he might consider taking up an "outside in" approach, which would involve Trump convening the leaders of the Quartet (the United States, Russia, the EU, and the UN) and the Arab Quartet (Egypt, Jordan, Saudi Arabia, and the United Arab Emirates) in a summit meeting to announce a set of agreed principles that would serve as the terms of reference for direct Israeli-Palestinian negotiations to achieve a two-state solution. The purpose of convening the summit would be to draw on the collective will of the international community to jumpstart direct negotiations based on these agreed principles.

The principles would need to be based on the final status negotiations that Secretary Kerry conducted, which reflect the requirements of both sides that were articulated in those negotiations. They would need to look something like this:

- The negotiations should lead to an agreement that would end the conflict, end all claims, and establish two states living side by side in peace and security.

- The border between the two states should be based on the 1967 lines with mutually agreed swaps.

- The security arrangements should ensure that Israel can defend itself against any threat, end the occupation that began in 1967, and enable the Palestinians to live securely in an independent, demilitarized state.

- Jerusalem should serve as the shared capital for the two states, with special arrangements to maintain the status quo in the religious sites.

- There should be a just and agreed solution to the Palestinian refugee problem based on UN General Assembly resolution 181 that provided for the establishment of independent Arab and Jewish states in Palestine with equal rights for all their citizens.

Trump would need to be willing to use the goodwill he would gain with these states because of his willingness to adopt a harder line on Iran and political Islam, and a softer line on Egypt, to convince them to join him at this summit.

The Israelis and Palestinians would be invited to attend, but he should not accept their refusal as reason not to convene the summit. Nor should he allow himself to be dragged down into the weeds by agreeing to pre-negotiate the principles with the two sides. That is a well-practiced technique that both sides have deployed repeatedly in the past to bog down a new American president and prevent him from making any progress.

Netanyahu might be attracted by the opportunity to engage with the Gulf states at such a summit, but he will likely be constrained by the right-wing parties in his coalition. The Arab states would have to press the Palestinians to attend. If one side agreed to attend, the other side would come under immense pressure to do so as well. But if only one side were willing to attend, the summit should go ahead anyway, highlighting the recalcitrance of the other side. President Trump might also indicate that if one or both sides were unwilling to attend or begin negotiations based on these terms of reference, then the United States might have to vote for a UN Security Council resolution that incorporated these principles and that called on the two sides to negotiate based on those principles.

NO PAIN, NO GAIN

Before President Trump decides to fulfil his desire to make the ultimate deal, it is important that he also be willing to bear the political consequences of doing so. Neither Israelis nor Palestinians at this moment believe that peace is either possible or desirable because the costs seem too high and the benefits too small. For both leaders, the status quo is quite sustainable, even as outside parties fret that the two-state solution is being buried in the process. Moreover, given the nature of his coalition, the maximum that Netanyahu can concede falls far short of the minimum that Mahmoud Abbas will insist upon, given the weakness of his position. There simply may be no zone of possible agreement. Therefore, the president should not assume that this will be an easy lift, his negotiating skills notwithstanding.

Moreover, Israel has a way of extracting a high, upfront political cost via its supporters in Congress if the president makes any effort to apply pressure. Likewise, Palestinian weakness makes it particularly difficult to move them since, like a business venture that is close to bankruptcy, they can always threaten collapse if they are forced to compromise. Meanwhile, the Arab states are all preoccupied with other more serious threats to their security and stability. They will be reluctant to risk Palestinian ire or, for Egypt and Jordan, the unhappiness of their Israeli security partner, to assist the president unless they understand that a final settlement is a high priority for him personally. Even so, none of them will be convinced solely by his confidence that he can do the deal. He will need to embed his effort in a broader strategy for peace and security in the Middle East that is seen to serve their wider interests.

President Trump will therefore have to be prepared to overcome all the local resistance that is now baked into the situation. He will also need to resist the advice of his experts, some of whom will be quick to tell him that this is not a good place to risk his prestige and dissipate his energy, while others will argue that he should just leave Israel to deal with the Palestinians as it prefers. The president does have one thing going for him, however, should he nevertheless decide to ignore the naysayers and try to seize the brass ring: the support of the international community. Except for outliers like Iran and North Korea, there is an international consensus behind the idea of an American-led effort to resolve the Israeli-Palestinian conflict. Despite all the friction with the Obama administration, Russia has been fully supportive of Secretary Kerry's efforts, so President Trump can easily find common ground with President Vladimir Putin. Similarly, he will find a willing partner in the EU, which believes that the failure to solve the Palestinian problem exacerbates the other Middle Eastern conflicts that threaten stability in Europe. While the Arab states will be more reluctant to take risks, President Sisi and King Abdullah both strongly believe in the importance of a resolution of the Israeli-Palestinian conflict for their own well-being. The Gulf Arabs are less persuadable, but will be attracted by the ability to engage openly with Israel if progress is made in this arena, and that will be an attraction to Israel, too. These converging interests will also help cement the Arab-Israeli cooperation that President Trump will need if he is to get them to share together the burden of restoring stability in the Middle East.

Ironically, then, if President Trump wants to overcome the reluctance of the Israelis and Palestinians to do the ultimate deal, he will need to draw on the support of the international community to achieve it, including the desire of key players, like Putin and Sisi, to work with him. Without their support, he will not have the leverage to move the two sides forward. But if he combines that support with the halo effect of his upset victory, he might just succeed where Clinton, Bush, and Obama have all failed. Just as he dared to be president, he will need to be willing to dare to be the ultimate dealmaker.

Notes

1. For example, in the Kerry negotiations, the most that Netanyahu was willing to concede was that the Palestinians "aspired" to have their capital in Jerusalem, while Abbas insisted on Palestinian sovereignty over all Arab east Jerusalem.

2. On the last night of the Kerry negotiations, in April 2014, the Israeli negotiators offered to hand over "tens of thousands of dunams" (some 5,000 acres) of Area C to the Palestinian Authority for it to develop without Israeli permits, in return for Palestinian acquiescence in Israeli construction in east Jerusalem and the settlement blocs.

33

Iraq and a Policy Proposal for the Next Administration

KENNETH M. POLLACK

SUMMARY: Although concerns about ISIS have overshadowed the depth of the ongoing civil war in Iraq, the incoming administration will need to reorient its policy approach to focus on both the causes and the effects of the conflict in order to address it. In particular, the United States will need to reach out to all of Iraq's disparate communities to develop new power-sharing agreements and strengthen Iraq's central government to provide a firmer foundation for security, democracy, and rule of law even as it moves toward a more decentralized, federal structure.

During the 2016 presidential campaign, Donald Trump excoriated President Obama for prematurely disengaging from Iraq and so plunging it back into civil war. President Trump will now have the ability, and the responsibility, to avoid repeating Obama's mistake. However, doing so is going to require treating Iraq as more than just a host for ISIS—let alone a gas station to be robbed—and instead enact policies that will help Iraq to slowly heal the wounds that allowed ISIS to spawn there. That isn't as hard as it sounds, but it will require the new administration and its principal officials to see Iraq in a very different light.

What needs to be understood is that Iraq is caught in a quintessential ethno-sectarian civil war. It is not the case that Iraq is in civil war because ISIS is there; it is instead the case that ISIS is there because Iraq is in civil war, and eliminating the former will mean confronting the latter. Unfortunately, however, American policy toward Iraq has been badly misguided because it has attempted to address one of the symptoms of the civil war—the rise of ISIS—without addressing the dynamics of the civil war itself.

CIVIL WARS AND THE LESSONS OF HISTORY

The modern world has a great deal of experience with civil wars, and one of the stark lessons of this history is that civil wars do not lend themselves to half-measures. While it is entirely untrue that external actors cannot end a civil war, as is often claimed, such wars cannot be ended easily. History demonstrates that half-hearted interventions do not quell a civil war: they exacerbate it.

There is essentially only one approach that a well-meaning external actor can take to end someone else's civil war. Very crudely, the approach requires three steps: (1) changing the military dynamics such that none of the warring parties believes that it can win a military victory, or that it will be slaughtered by one of its rivals if it lays down its arms; (2) forging a power-sharing agreement by which political authority and economic benefits are divided more or less in keeping with demographic realities; and (3) establishing at least one internal or external institution that is capable of ensuring that the first two conditions endure until trust among the communities and strong internal institutions can be rebuilt. There are multiple ways to handle each of these tasks, but any intervening nation that does not pursue this course of action, that does not bring enough resources, or that is not willing to sustain its commitment long enough to succeed will only make the situation worse.

Consequently, the minimalist approach to Iraq that the United States employed under the Obama administration is highly unlikely to secure American interests there over the long term. The military progress has been admirable, but without comparable political progress along the lines required to end a civil war and prevent its recurrence the exertions so far are likely to prove ephemeral. For Iraq, destroying ISIS and then leaving the country to the Iraqis to sort out their own political problems will not do it. The Iraqis are capable of addressing their myriad problems, but only with American assistance. Unless the United States wants to fight yet another war in Iraq in the near future, the incoming administration needs to be willing to deepen America's role there.

THE BIG PICTURE OF A NEW IRAQ POLICY

One of the big dangers in Iraq for the new administration is overcoming the false sense of security that ISIS is now effectively defeated and therefore there is nothing more to worry about in Iraq. While the military campaign to evict and eradicate ISIS in Iraq and Syria seems well in train, it cannot be the end of America's involvement. If Washington repeats the same mistake it committed in both 2003 and again in 2011 by ignoring the political requirements to translate a successful military campaign into an enduring foreign policy achievement, none of the gains are likely to prove lasting. Iraq is likely to fall apart all over again, and President Trump will then face the same frustrating choice of paying the costs to stabilize Iraq yet again or running the potentially catastrophic risks of trying to walk away as both of his predecessors did.

Indeed, if the final eviction of ISIS is not handled properly, it could simply create the circumstances for more widespread conflict. Right now, fear and hatred of ISIS is perhaps the only thing that all Iraqis have in common. The danger is that if it is removed without establishing a process of national reconciliation—or better still, an actual accord—that gives Iraqis faith that their polity remains viable, the civil war will reignite and will shift from a fight of all against ISIS to a fight of all against all.

Iraq's first great problem now is that its communities have once again lost their trust in one another. Trust is always the first casualty of civil war, and Iraq had only started to rebuild it in 2007–9 before the American withdrawal allowed Prime Minister Nouri al-Maliki to pursue a sectarian agenda and strip Sunni trust of the Shi'a all over again. After the fall of Mosul, rebuilding that trust must be a top priority. In part for that reason, Iraq will almost certainly need to transition eventually to a combination of federalism and either confederation with the Kurds or independence for an Iraqi Kurdish state.

With regard to the latter, the Kurds constitute a separate nation, and they have made clear for the past century that they do not want to be a part of Arab Iraq. Their forced inclusion in the Iraqi state has resulted in nothing but conflict and misery for *both* the Kurds and the Arabs. Iraq and the Kurds would both be better off with an amicable divorce, but ensuring its amicability will take time, goodwill, and constructive diplomacy that seem in short supply right now. The United States has important interests in seeing this separation happen peacefully, but little else. The ways in which the Kurds and Arabs will choose to handle territorial issues (including the status of Mosul and Kirkuk), the distribution of oilfields, and the return of displaced persons are not issues on which the United States needs to take a position, but it will be critical that Washington serve as honest broker in helping the parties find solutions that both can accept. It may also be necessary for the United States to help each side make painful concessions, in part by providing bilateral or multilateral aid as compensation. Allowing the Kurds to opt out of Iraq would also increase the demographic and therefore electoral weight of Iraq's Shi'a Arab community, which will make it all the more important for the United States to help Arab Iraq devise a more stable, equitable, and self-regulating political system of its own.

For this reason, and because the opposite approach had failed miserably by 2014, paving the way for ISIS, Arab Iraq will have to develop a federal structure (as envisioned in the current Iraqi constitution) that delegates greater authority and autonomy to its various ethnic, sectarian, and geographic components. The traumatic experiences of three-and-a-half decades of Saddam Hussein's tyranny, two bouts of civil war, and Maliki's brutal attempt to consolidate power in between, have made it inconceivable that Iraq's communities will accept a return to an all-powerful, highly centralized Iraqi state.

However, in fittingly ironic fashion, the goal of a more decentralized, federal political system now requires a dedicated effort to *strengthen* Iraq's central government. The problem is best understood this way: Decentralization can take two forms, empowerment or entropy. Obviously, the former is a positive form that can produce a functional state; the latter a disaster likely to produce war and misery. Decentralization via empowerment requires a reasonably strong and functional central government that grants specific authorities and the power to execute those tasks to subordinate and/or peripheral entities. Decentralization via entropy, in contrast, occurs when the central government lacks the strength to control its constituent parts—let alone to empower them—and so subordinates, peripheral entities, and actors outside the system altogether simply grab authority and resources and do with them whatever they like. Not only does such anarchy invariably dissolve into chaos and conflict, but the actors arrogating power to themselves also are rarely as strong as they would be if their power was delegated by an effective central government. One example of the distinction is the United States created by the Articles of Confederation compared to the United States created by the U.S. Constitution.

Under the former, the central government was too weak and so the federal structure did not work, even though the states were far more powerful than they were under the Constitution. The result was anarchy, chaos, and internal conflict. The Constitution provided for a stronger central government, which paradoxically made a stable federal system—with still strong states—both possible and practical.

Unfortunately, what is happening in Iraq today is largely decentralization by entropy, not empowerment, and this is the second, related factor that is likely to produce renewed conflict in the future. It is this entropic pull that is causing the fragmentation that is now the leitmotif of Iraqi politics. The Sunnis have long suffered from a badly atomized leadership, but even that has worsened in recent years, exacerbated by Maliki's brilliance in targeting any moderate, capable, and charismatic Sunni leader who might have unified that community. But now the Kurds, whose leadership once consisted of Mas'ud Barzani (head of the Kurdistan Democratic Party [KDP]) and Jalal Talabani (head of the rival Patriotic Union of Kurdistan [PUK] party) and no one else, are now increasingly beset by divisions. The long-dormant KDP-PUK split has been reopened, to be joined by a split between the KDP and the opposition Gorran ("Change") movement, and splits within each of these parties as well. Even the Shi'a leadership is fracturing. Iraqis often like to argue that the Marja'iye (the Shi'a religious establishment centered in Najaf) provides the Shi'a with a unified voice, but if that were ever true, it is proving less and less so. Now, dozens of Shi'a figures can claim leadership over important constituencies, including dozens of new militias, many of which operate outside the control of the central government. This centrifugal trajectory simultaneously paralyzes the Iraqi political system and pushes the country toward chaos and renewed conflict.

SPECIFIC STEPS FOR POST-ISIS IRAQ

In this context, a new American policy that would have a reasonable prospect of helping Iraq to avoid slipping back into civil war once ISIS is defeated will require the United States to pursue a number of interwoven courses of action.

Forge a New National Reconciliation Agreement

There is simply no way around this foundational requirement. Iraqis need a new power-sharing agreement that will allow all of the rival communities, but particularly the Sunni and Shi'a Arabs, to begin cooperating again. Without this, the military successes against ISIS will evaporate. In recent months, both the United States and the government of Iraq have trumpeted local reconciliation efforts as a bottom-up substitute for a top-down process of national reconciliation. While such grass-roots efforts can be very useful, historically they are no substitute for high-level reconciliation. Without the latter, local efforts are typically undone by rivalries among senior leaders and the result, once again, is renewed civil war. Yet the United States has made far too little effort to bring Iraq's senior leadership together, hiding behind Baghdad's desire to handle this matter itself and the self-fulfilling prophecy that Iraq's leaders are too fragmented. The current Iraqi-led "process" has so far achieved nothing. On the other hand, it is worth noting that in 2007–8, Ambassador Ryan Crocker faced a similar problem of fragmented leadership, yet he and his team brokered exactly the kind of informal but effective national reconciliation that Iraq desperately needs once again.

Push Baghdad and Erbil Toward Short- and Long-Term Solutions

As noted above, it would be better for both Arab Iraqis and Iraqi Kurds if Iraqi Kurdistan were a separate country. Unfortunately, getting to that point without large-scale violence will be very difficult. There are borders to be negotiated, populations to be consulted, and foreign powers to be placated (or stonewalled). Moreover, in the near term, Kurdish political, economic, and security needs may require a closer relationship with Baghdad rather than a more distant one. The Obama administration has put considerable effort toward handling these immediate problems and has helped achieve a certain amount of success. However, without the framework of a long-term plan that creates the circumstances for peaceful Kurdish secession (along the lines of the Czechoslovak model), these near-term gains will erode and eventually collapse as they have so regularly in the past.

Help Baghdad Regain the Basic Capacities of Governance

Even the most extreme advocates of federalism in Iraq recognize that the central government will have to retain certain powers and prerogatives because they are responsibilities that only the central government can realistically discharge. This starts with the role of defending Iraq from external attack and helping its governorates and regions defend themselves against major internal security threats. It means helping Baghdad regain its Weberian monopoly on the use of violence, including demobilizing the Hashd ash-Shaabi (the militias created in 2014 after the fall of Mosul) and/or integrating them into the formal Iraqi security forces. Only after such a reform program will the central government be able to delegate part of its security authority to the internal security forces of its governorates and regions. Strengthening the central government would also give Baghdad the ability to conduct basic functions like gathering revenue and spending it on nationwide services such as power generation and distribution, infrastructure improvements, and economic development—functions that everyone accepts Baghdad will have to retain. That, in turn, requires both wider political reform to ensure a more functional central government overall and more specific reforms to address Iraq's paralyzed legislature, its corrupt executive branch, and its politicized judiciary.

Strengthen the Abadi Government
The United States can provide Iraq with guidance and some resources to enact the kinds of reforms enumerated above, but most of that work can only be undertaken by the Iraqi government itself. This places a premium on helping the Iraqi government as best we can and far more than we have over the past eight years, which also raises the question of whether the United States should support the current Iraqi government or push for a different one. Although Haider al-Abadi has made mistakes as prime minister, he is still the best we are likely to get. Of greatest importance, he has a number of highly desirable qualities: He is politically courageous, he is not corrupt (as best anyone can tell), he has a clear and correct sense of what Iraq needs to do to escape the civil war trap, and he has shown a willingness and an ability to learn from his mistakes. We could have done a lot worse than Haider al-Abadi. Moreover, replacing him would be more likely to bring to power a worse leader than a better one. Consequently, Washington's best bet will be to double down on Abadi in the expectation that greater American backing and partnership will enable him to pursue the national reconciliation and political reform that Iraq so desperately needs and that he has repeatedly called for. But that means keeping American skin in the game.

Develop a Robust, Long-Term Aid Program for Iraq

The Obama administration has proven that its early refusal to invest resources in Iraq—and its perverse claim that doing so was senseless because the United States had no influence there—was wrong. Since 2014, the United States has invested considerable resources in Iraq, including 5,000 ground troops, large-scale weapons deliveries, a major air campaign, and significant financial assistance, and as a direct result now has considerably more influence than at any time since 2011. After the fall of Mosul, the United States should maintain this commitment of resources to Iraq. Ideally, the United States would decrease some aspects of its support, like airstrikes and other fire support, and increase other elements to focus more on the political and economic tasks that need to be accomplished after the defeat of ISIS, which arguably are more challenging than the military task of liberating Iraq.

Retain and Rebuild the American Military Presence

Ideally, the United States would keep about five to ten thousand ground troops in Iraq. In terms of missions, these personnel are needed to thoroughly rebuild the Iraqi Security Forces—as the United States finally did in 2007–9—with large numbers of U.S. personnel training, advising, partnering with, and accompanying Iraqi forces down to company level or lower. As part of this, it would be helpful to have American combat battalions, or even brigades, regularly rotate into Iraq to exercise with Iraqi forces. The United States should retain a large special operations counterterrorism force to help Baghdad with the inevitable residual terrorist problem that will persist for some time, even under the best of circumstances, after the fall of Mosul. Further troops would be necessary for force protection, medical support, transportation, communications, and other administrative and security tasks. In addition to carrying out these key missions, the initial size of the force will also be important from a psychological perspective. The Iraqis need to believe that the United States is not abandoning them again, and that the American military presence left behind after the defeat of ISIS is large enough to prevent the country from coming apart at the seams or its government from using force against any of its constituent communities. While even a ten-thousand-man force would have only a very limited prospect of playing that role in practice, history has demonstrated that in postconflict scenarios, the symbolic role is of far greater significance than actual military capability as long as the peacekeeping force is believed to have some degree of capacity and a willingness to employ it.

Establish a Sustained Economic Aid Program

Low oil prices have created dire financial problems for Baghdad, and even more so for Erbil. A World Bank loan of $5.4 billion over three years will help, but it is far from making up Iraq's shortfall. Additional outside aid can also have an outsized effect in Iraq because Baghdad is so inefficient, corrupt, and bottlenecked that foreign assistance provided directly to those who will spend it comes faster and is of greater utility than trying to squeeze dinars through the Iraqi political process. Moreover, as with a five- to ten-thousand-man military commitment, an economic aid program of (ideally) $1 billion to $2 billion per year for five years would reinforce the impression that the United States is renewing its long-term commitment to Iraq's stability and development. That symbolism is worth far more than the practical impact of the dollars spent. Moreover, if that money is spent wisely, it can be used to further empower Prime Minister Abadi and other Iraqi leaders looking to move past sectarian differences and break the deadlocks suffocating the Iraqi political system. In this sense, and again coupled with a slightly enlarged long-term American military presence, such an aid program would go a long way to preserving (and perhaps expanding) the hard-won American influence in Iraq to help guide the country down the right path in the years ahead.

34

Deconstructing Syria

A Confederal Approach

MICHAEL E. O'HANLON

SUMMARY: U.S. policy toward Syria since the Arab spring uprisings of 2011 has tragically failed. Despite the ebb and flow of battle, as well as occasional temporary and partial cease-fire arrangements, there is no likely end in sight to the war, even with the recent changes in Aleppo. As a result, the Syrian people will continue to suffer enormously. Refugee flows will likely remain intense, the stability of other key regional states will remain at risk, and the possibility of extremist elements using Syria as a safe haven as well as a rallying cry for their cause will remain (even if ISIS itself continues to lose ground within Syria). A new approach is needed, based on the notions of possibly expanding military means we bring to bear to the problem and making the political vision for a future Syria more realistic as well as more commensurate with battlefield realities, and, to some extent, Russian interests too.

The Islamic State in Iraq and Syria (ISIS, also known as ISIL or Daesh), a major element of the opposition to the Bashar al-Assad regime, may not amount to an imminent threat to American security. But ISIS's rise does place at much greater risk the security of Iraq, the future of Syria itself, and the stability of Lebanon and Jordan.[1] It could jeopardize the safety of American citizens as well, given the possibility of more attacks by "lone wolves" inspired in their western home by ISIS propaganda, or by westerners returning from the Syrian jihad to carry out attacks at home. Istanbul, Ankara, Paris, Brussels, San Bernardino, and Orlando may not be the last of such tragedies in western nations—and the interest of extremists in gaining access to weapons of mass destruction should give pause to anyone inclined to trivialize the strategic implications of attacks against the homeland. The refugee flows into Europe in 2015 highlight the human costs of a war that has killed several hundred thousand and displaced more than 10 million. The potency of the al-Nusra organization, al Qaeda's loyal affiliate, within the Syrian opposition raises additional concern, even if that organization is now renamed and rebranded as the Front for Conquest with a supposed independence from al Qaeda.

This chapter makes a case for a new approach that I call "deconstructing Syria" that attempts to bring ends and means more realistically into balance. It aims for a Bosnia-like confederal model within the current borders of the Syrian nation, but with devolution of most powers to regions or states. Ultimately, this arrangement would be negotiated and formalized and upheld by international peacekeepers, but in the short term the United States and partners would seek to help local allies expand de facto safe havens and bring governance to them. It would not declare safe havens formally in the beginning, but could offer warnings to Assad not to bomb certain areas and neighborhoods lest his air force face reprisal action later. Over time, ISIS and related groups would have to be defeated. Assad or his close associates could be tolerated within a sector consisting mostly of Alawites and Christians. (Perhaps Assad could even nominally remain president for a time, if truly necessary, as long as he did not deploy security forces in those parts of Sunni-dominant Syria granted autonomy.)

The idea here builds on a paper I wrote in 2015, before the Russian intervention in the war, that made a similar case. The argument has only strengthened since Russia's intervention. Decisive defeat of President Assad now looms as an even more improbable prospect; decisive victory by Assad also remains improbable, and highly undesirable, even as his regime's forces consolidate control in Aleppo. ISIS is weaker, but far from defeated, and even if Raqqa were soon to be liberated, the likelihood of an ongoing civil war could provide the raw materials for the rise of a similar group in the future. My approach seeks to end the Hobson's choice currently confronting American policymakers, whereby they can neither attempt to unseat President Assad in any concerted way (because doing so would clear the path for ISIS and other extremists, and because he is now propped up by Russia), nor tolerate him as a future leader of the whole country (because of the abominations he has committed, and because any such policy would bring the United States into direct disagreement with many of its regional allies).

The new approach would seek to break the problem down in a number of localized components of the country, pursuing regional stopgap solutions while envisioning ultimately a more confederal Syria made up at least in part of autonomous zones or states. It also proposes a path to an intensified train and equip program, married with more assertive use of American airpower, and ultimately the reinforcement of emergent safe zones. When appropriate, the safe zones would also be used to accelerate recruiting and training of additional opposition fighters who could live in, and help protect, their communities while going through basic training. These zones would, in addition, be locations where humanitarian relief could be provided to needy populations and local governance structures developed.

DECONSTRUCTING SYRIA—TOWARD A REGIONAL, INK-SPOT STRATEGY

A realistic comprehensive plan for Syria seems elusive at this stage, without even factoring in self-imposed U.S. political constraints. American allies are, even in aggregate, not the strongest players on the battlefield. Other key players include Assad's own army, pro-regime paramilitaries, ISIS, al-Nusra/Front for Conquest, Russia, and even Hezbollah. And some of these so-called allies may not be so moderate, or dependable. The ability of the Kurds to liberate any territory further south is unclear, and Turkey's willingness to go along with any escalation of the Kurdish role also is dubious.[2]

The central peace process attempted in 2015–16 is in tatters. Moderate groups are not currently strong enough to achieve any significant governing role through any plausible negotiation outcome (see table 34.1).[3] Any willingness by Assad to defect as part of an integrated plan to produce a new power-sharing government is not in the cards, after the Russian intervention of late 2015 and the generally favorable battlefield trends for Assad's forces since that time.

Counterintuitively, the only credible path forward may be a plan that in effect deconstructs Syria, at least in part for some amount of time. A comprehensive, national-level solution is too hard even to specify at this stage, much less achieve. Instead, the international community should work hard, and devote substantial resources, to create pockets of more viable

TABLE 34.1   ESTIMATED PERSONNEL STRENGTH OF KEY
COMBATANTS IN SYRIAN CIVIL WAR, AS OF AUGUST 2016

Syrian Government Armed Forces	130,000
Syrian Government Paramilitaries	150,000
Hezbollah	4,000 to 8,000
Russia	4,000
Iran/IRGC	2,000
ISIS	10,000 to 30,000
Al-Nusra (now Jabhat Fatah al-Sham or Front for Conquest of the Levant)	5,000 to 10,000
Ansar al-Sham, other hardline/Islamist groups	20,000 to 50,000
Moderate groups in Free Syrian Army/ Syrian Democratic Forces	20,000 to 50,000
YPG (Kurdish Fighters)	30,000 to 65,000
U.S. forces on ground in Syria	300 to 500
Other coalition forces on ground	500 to 2,000
U.S. airpower in region engaged in Syria	2,500 to 10,000

Sources: International Institute for Strategic Studies, *The Military Balance 2016* (Oxfordshire, England: Routledge, 2016), pp. 353–55; Jennifer Cafarella and Genevieve Casagrande, "Syrian Armed Opposition Powerbrokers," Middle East Report No. 29 (Washington, D.C.: Institute for the Study of War, March 2016) (www.understandingwar.org/sites/default/files /Syrian%20Armed%20Opposition%20Powerbrokers_0_0.pdf); "Kurdish People's Protection Unit YPG," Globalsecurity.org, 2016 (www.globalsecurity.org/military/world/para/ ypg.htm); Andrew Tilghman, "Size of ISIS Force Declining in Iraq and Syria, According to New Intel," Militarytimes.com, February 4, 2016 (www.militarytimes.com/story/milit ary/2016/02/04/new-intel-shows-isis-force-declining-iraq-syria/79819744); James R. Clapper, "Worldwide Threat Assessment of the U.S. Intelligence Community," Senate Select Committee on Intelligence, February 9, 2016 (www.dni.gov/files/documents/SSCI_Unclas sified_2016_ATA_SFR%20_FINAL.pdf); Jabhat Fatah al-Sham, "Mapping Militant Organizations," Stanford University, August 2016 (http://web.stanford.edu/group/map pingmilitants/cgi-bin/groups/view/493); Lina Sinjab, "Guide to the Syrian Rebels," BBC News, December 13, 2013.

security and governance within Syria over time. With initial footholds in place, the strategy could develop further in a type of "ink-spot" campaign that eventually sought to join the various local initiatives into a broader and more integrated effort. The ink spots would not be formal areas designated as official safe havens by the United States, NATO, or the United Nations. Rather, they would be zones like the current Kurdish regions in the north that the United States helped emerge as sanctuaries of sorts— and also as staging grounds for further development of opposition forces.

This strategy might produce only a partial success, liberating parts of the country and then settling into stalemate. It also might not initially help those pockets of opposition-controlled territory in or near cities like Damascus, Homs, Hama, and Aleppo that are largely encircled by pro-government forces. They might have to await a negotiated deal, based on concepts of confederation and protection of minority rights, to gain significant relief. Such a deal cannot be specified in detail now, and would have to be one that Syrians themselves negotiated. It could include mechanisms for helping people relocate to areas where they might feel safer, if desired. Ideally, however, it would also develop legal and security mechanisms to help them feel safe even in their current homes, while also allowing the displaced to return to wherever they wished.[4]

Meanwhile, in the short term, even a partially successful strategy would have major benefits. It would help the United States and other outside powers protect several million Syrians who would no longer have to fear being overrun by Assad or ISIS, allow them to collectively attack and pressure ISIS from other locations than is possible today, reduce refugee flows, and send a clear message of U.S. engagement to regional partners.

Turkey could be expected to have serious misgivings about the strategy, given that it would envision greater Kurdish autonomy in a future Syria. The United States would have to address these concerns by underscoring to the Kurds that all American support—military material, airpower assistance, and future economic and development aid—would be contingent on Kurds respecting clear limitations on their future autonomy. Independence would be ruled out. Aid flows would depend on Kurds verifiably reining in any extremists who sought to support the PKK movement within Turkey itself. And Kurdish areas in Syria might need to be broken up into two state-like entities, rather than a single truly autonomous zone as in Iraq, to limit the potential for a self-governing single entity to develop aspirations for greater self-rule down the road.

Ideally, vetting of opposition fighters wishing U.S. training, equipment, and battlefield assistance would be relaxed under this approach. They would no longer be required to be untainted by any and all past tactical associations with extremists, and they would no longer be required to swear to fight only ISIS. To avoid American legal issues, the subject could simply not be raised the way it is now. The United States would not have to bless, or encourage, their aspirations for liberating Sunni-majority areas from Assad. But it could stop trying so proactively, and unrealistically, to squelch those ambitions. However, if President Trump opposes this part of the strategy, others parts could still be attempted.

This strategy would also include a new element of air campaign. Washington and allies would declare that any Syrian aircraft seen attacking helpless civilians (especially in the emergent safe areas) or American and allied troops on the ground would be subject to destruction at a subsequent time and place of U.S. choosing. This approach to a no-fly-zone would be easier and safer to conduct than classic no-fly-zone operations, with less risk of accidentally shooting down Russian aircraft in the process.

The ultimate end-game for these safe zones would not have to be determined in advance. The interim goal might be a confederal Syria, with several highly autonomous zones. One of those zones might be principally for Alawites, in the nation's northwest. But none could be for ISIS, al-Nusra, or Assad and his inner circle. Minority rights would have to be protected in all zones. Key central cities—Damascus, Homs, Hama, Aleppo, perhaps Idlib—might even be divided in some cases between two different autonomous zones. Or, as one variant of the strategy, a new city or two could effectively be created in one of the Sunni zones, using external financial assistance (such financing would presumably not be offered by Washington to any area Assad still controlled, except in very limited amounts). Kurdish areas would probably have to be divided into two noncontiguous areas as well, as noted, to assuage Turkish worries that they could otherwise form the embryo of a future attempt at an independent Kurdish state within Syria. Indeed, Turkey could even deploy forces to the zone between the two Kurdish areas in any future peace enforcement operation.

A peace enforcement force would almost surely be needed to solidify any negotiated accord. It could be authorized by the United Nations and run by NATO, perhaps, but with strong participation by Muslim states from the broader region as well as South Asia and Southeast Asia. The American role could be focused on command and control, intelligence, logistics, airpower, and special forces/rapid-reaction capabilities and might number, at that stage, up to a few thousand personnel. That is roughly the number that could be needed to produce the conditions for peace in the shorter term, as well, under the contours of the strategy proposed here.

The confederal Syria that would emerge from this process would have a weak central government with a limited military force; most governance and most security would occur region by region or state by state, at least in Sunni and Kurdish areas. This approach, while not ideal for many elements of the opposition who surely seek more systematic revenge against Assad and his cronies, could nonetheless provide a workable basis for making common cause. It would, in fact, ultimately aim for an end to Assad's rule over the nation as a whole (though not necessarily in Alawite or Christian areas). For these reasons, whether they fully endorsed it or not, America's main regional allies in the effort—Turkey, Jordan, Saudi Arabia, other GCC countries—would likely find it welcome since it would move significantly in the direction they have advocated. Moreover, it would be more credible than previous American strategies, stated or implied, because its means would better match ends. And for those Syrians and others reluctant to give up on the notion of a future highly integrated and cohesive state, the weak confederation could be subject to reconsideration and constitutional revision at some date—say 10 to 20 years into the future—when peace had been robustly reestablished. In the short term, however, it is time to realize that Humpty Dumpty cannot be put back together anytime soon, and insisting on such an outcome will only prolong the conflict.

The basic logic of this ink-spot and regional strategy is not radical. Nor is it original or unique to Syria. In effect, variants of it have guided western powers in Bosnia, as noted, in Afghanistan in the 1980s, in Iraqi Kurdistan, and since 1993 in Somalia. The last case is particularly relevant. Somalia, while a site of tragedy for U.S. forces in 1993 followed by withdrawal and defeat in 1994, has wound up showing some signs of hopefulness. The Puntland and Somaliland in the north are largely self-governing and autonomous. Similar types of zones would be the interim goal for Syria as well.

CONCLUSION

The tragedy of Syria today does not require an invasion by tens of thousands of western ground forces. But nor is it a situation that can be allowed somehow to burn out on its own. Hoping for the latter outcome through some variant of a containment policy has been tried for five years. One need not condemn the logic, or the motives, of those who favored containment at an earlier time to recognize that empirically speaking, it has failed.

A confederal political model for the country's future governance and organization of security forces should provide the vision for Syria and the objective toward which a new strategy seeks to move. That strategy should ideally include expanded military assistance of various types to key resistance elements, a more potent and expansive air campaign, and accelerated help to emergent safe areas in a sort of ink-spot strategy as conditions permit. Over time, the arrangement could be codified by negotiations and backed up by peacekeepers.

Together, these ideas provide the most realistic concepts for making major progress in defeating ISIS and ending the civil war in Syria. It will not be easy or quick to implement such a strategy. But it should bear considerable fruit in the first term of the next president, while limiting U.S. exposure and American risks along the way.

Notes

1. See, for example, Will McCants, "Why ISIS Really Wants to Conquer Baghdad," Brookings blog, November 12, 2014, www.brookings.edu/blogs/markaz/posts /2014/11/12-baghdad-of-al-rashid-mccants.

2. Charles Lister, "A Long Way from Success: Assessing the War on the Islamic State," *Perspectives on Terrorism* 9, no. 4 (2015), www.terrorismanalysts.com/pt/in dex.php/pot/article/view/439/html.

3. Michele Flournoy and Richard Fontaine, "An Intensified Approach to Combatting the Islamic State," Center for a New American Security, Washington, D.C., August 6, 2015, www.cnas.org/combatting-the-Islamic-State.

4. Edward P. Joseph and Michael E. O'Hanlon, "The Case for Soft Partition in Iraq," *Brookings Center for Middle East Policy Analysis Papers,* June 1, 2007, www .brookings.edu/research/the-case-for-soft-partition-in-iraq/.

35

Addressing the Syrian Refugee Crisis

JESSICA BRANDT and ROBERT L. MCKENZIE

SUMMARY: Five years into Syria's civil war, the international community has come to recognize that 5 million Syrian refugees will not be returning home anytime soon. The scale of the refugee crisis poses vast and consequential challenges to Lebanon, Jordan, and Turkey and, by extension, to American interests in the region. As this chapter shows, resolving this conflict will require the incoming presidential administration to renew its commitments to the U.S. refugee resettlement program and to challenge the international community to provide greater support to the frontline states.

President-elect Trump is soon to inherit the Syria conflict, an enormous engine of suffering that has taken the lives of nearly 500,000 people[1] and displaced more than 10 million, nearly half of Syria's prewar population.[2] Today, 13.5 million are in need of humanitarian assistance within Syria, of which more than 6 million are internally displaced. Nearly 5 million more have sought refuge in neighboring countries.[3]

Resolving the conflict will be Mr. Trump's most daunting foreign policy task. Under President Obama, Washington's Syria policy was almost singularly focused on defeating the Islamic State, an approach that allowed the conflict to fester, and thereby contribute to one of the worst humanitarian crises of our time.

As the Trump administration begins to formulate a Syria policy, the nearly 5 million Syrian refugees in neighboring countries—who represent nearly one-quarter of Syria's population before the civil war—should not be overlooked.[4] The sheer scale of the refugee crisis poses unparalleled humanitarian, economic, and political challenges in an already fragile region. Turkey hosts more than 2.8 million refugees from Syria, more than any other country in the world and more than half the refugee population in the region. Lebanon hosts more than 1 million refugees, which amounts to more than one in five people in the country. In Jordan, that number is one in ten at least.

Despite the high-level attention paid to the tremendous scale of need at a series of global conferences this year, substantial resource gaps remain. Those resource gaps have consequences. The United Nations High Commissioner for Refugees (UNHCR) and the World Food Program, both of which are critical to aid delivery in frontline states, face funding shortfalls that have resulted in housing and food insecurity. This lack of institutional support, coupled with deepening poverty and hurdles to legal residency, led hundreds of thousands of refugees to make their way to Europe, often at great personal risk. In their wake, politics on the continent have been reshaped, largely in ways that strain the transatlantic relationship (for example, Brexit and the rise of extreme forms of populism). Because of its potential to drive instability that runs counter to American interests, the United States should increase its already substantial contribution to help fill these resource gaps.

This chapter argues that there are steps the next administration should take to address the Syrian refugee crisis that will improve the lives of those in need while advancing American security interests. It presents three policy recommendations that focus on America's own resettlement program, efforts in the frontline states, and a coordinated international response to the crisis.

CORRECT THE RECORD AND CONTINUE AMERICA'S LONGSTANDING RESETTLEMENT PROGRAM

Since 1975, the United States has taken in more than 3 million refugees from around the world.[5] Working with the U.N. Refugee Agency and its implementing partners, the program resettles the most vulnerable refugees whose specific needs cannot be addressed in the country where they have sought protection. Those include single-parent, female-led families; orphans, unaccompanied minors, and adolescents at risk; women and girls at risk; the disabled and infirm; and survivors of torture.[6]

Since 9/11, the United States has resettled almost 860,000 refugees. Of those, only three individuals have been convicted on terrorism-related charges: all were for plots outside of the United States, and none were successful.[7] Every refugee resettled to the United States must complete a multilayered, dynamic vetting process while overseas, which often takes two or more years to complete. It is the most stringent security procedure for an individual entering the country. The chances of being murdered by a refugee-related terrorist attack in the United States has been 1 in 3.4 billion a year.[8] This is a fact that the incoming administration needs to convey to the American public.

Just as the threat of Syrian refugees has been overstated in public discourse, so too has the number of Syrian refugees being resettled in the United States. This past presidential cycle, candidates routinely and incorrectly suggested that America risked being "flooded by Syrian refugees." Yet since the Syrian uprising began in 2011, the United States has resettled a fraction of the nearly 5 million Syrians in need—only 10,000 to date.[9] The overwhelming majority will not have the opportunity for resettlement in Western countries. Less than 1 percent of the world's 21 million refugees will be resettled. However, the resettlement of even this small number of refugees is important. First, it provides a pathway out of frontline states for those who are particularly vulnerable and cannot safely be accommodated there. Second, resettling refugees has a symbolic importance. It demonstrates solidarity within the transatlantic relationship and makes it clear that the United States supports rights and refuge for all. Third, the United States will not be able to encourage other countries to step up their efforts if it does not shoulder its share of responsibility. For these reasons, the United States should neither pause nor discontinue its refugee resettlement program but instead reaffirm its commitment to it. The next administration should maintain course on America's commitment to resettle 110,000 refugees in fiscal year 2017 (a 30 percent increase from 2016).

FOCUS ON EDUCATION AND LABOR MARKETS IN FRONTLINE STATES

Five years into Syria's civil war, the international community has come to recognize that refugees will not be returning home any time soon. The average length of major protracted refugee situations is 26 years.[10] The resources and infrastructure of Lebanon, Jordan, and Turkey have been strained by the crisis, which was a contributing factor to large-scale, irregular migration to Europe in 2015. Therefore, for political reasons as well as humanitarian ones, advancing the well-being of the displaced *where they are* is imperative. The key to doing so is better access to education and employment.

Increase Access to Education for Refugee Children in Frontline States
President-elect Trump should make Syrian refugee education a top priority. Before the Syria conflict, 94 percent of children in Syria attended primary and lower secondary education. However, access to education for Syrian refugees is limited and uneven in Lebanon, Jordan, and Turkey. Mr. Trump should challenge the international community to work with and support frontline states to set a bold agenda to ensure that every Syrian refugee child has access to primary and secondary education by September 2017. The international community must ensure that these efforts to support refugee children do not overlook or come at the detriment of the needs of children in host communities.

The returns on investing in Syrian refugee education are enormous, far reaching, and long lasting. Schools and classrooms provide an environment for refugee children to learn from and about one another, strengthen interpersonal skills, develop resilience, and build conflict resolution skills. When children are unable to attend school, they have difficulty integrating into their host societies and are likely to be a greater burden on the host country's economy in the future. In the immediate term, Syrian school-aged refugees need psychosocial support because many of them have experienced tremendous suffering. They should be in learning environments where they can develop a sense of peace, belonging, trust, and respect. In the long term, access to high-quality education gives refugees the skills to become valuable and valued contributors to their host communities, as well as to their country of origin when they can return home. By failing to educate refugee children, the international community is not only dashing their hopes and aspirations but also turning a blind eye to potential environments where violent extremism can take hold.

There are several common obstacles to access to education in frontline states, including a lack of funding for public schooling and economic hardship that drives families to send children to work instead of the classroom.

In the case of Turkey, there is also a language barrier. The only way to overcome these obstacles is for the next administration to challenge the international community, host governments, and implementing partners to act.

Encourage and Resource Education Reform in Lebanon   In Lebanon, the education system has struggled to keep up with demand, and nearly 250,000 Syrian children—half of the Syrian school-aged children there—are out of school. The sheer number of Syrian children has required the Education Ministry to introduce two-shift school days in the public education system. The first shift is for Lebanese students and is open for Syrian students if there is space. The second shift, starting between 2:00 and 2:30 p.m., is only for Syrian children. To improve the situation, Lebanon will need to embrace major reforms to strengthen public education and receive donor funding earmarked for this purpose. The responsibility of hosting so many refugees has cost Lebanon over $13 billion, and stretched the government's capacity on virtually every single public good.

Increase Political and Financial Support for Turkish Language Instruction in Turkey   To its credit, Turkey has lifted legal barriers for Syrian refugees to access education. However, language is an obstacle for many Syrian children, who are primarily Arabic speaking, and most instructors do not have the ability to teach Turkish as a second language. They will need special training.

Economic hardship is the primary reason most Syrian school-aged children are out of school, and it is forcing many refugee children into employment to provide for their families. Of the nearly 5 million Syrian refugees, 35 percent are children and 900,000 are out of school.[11] In Jordan, 84 percent of employers employ Syrian refugee children.[12] In Iraq, 77 percent of Syrian children are supporting their families.[13] In Lebanon and Turkey, girls and boys as young as six years of age are working to help make ends meet. Under these conditions, refugee children are extremely vulnerable to multiple forms of exploitation and abuse, and an entire generation is at risk of missing out on an education. Getting Syrian school-aged children into classrooms will require that their parents be allowed to work, making families less dependent on children's labor.

Expand Access to Employment Opportunities in Frontline States

Opening labor markets to refugees is a politically sensitive matter. The United States, together with the international community, has a role to play in encouraging countries to take steps in that direction and supporting them when they do.

Partner with the Private Sector   Washington could employ a range of incentives to encourage companies to make measurable commitments that would expand labor market integration, especially in communities on the frontlines of the crisis. These incentives could include ensuring that refugees have access to financial services, even if they do not have a place of permanent residence; enabling refugees to access seed funding to start new businesses, and where necessary providing them with the technical assistance to do so; and procuring goods and services from businesses that hire refugees.

Increase Financial Support for Jordan's Refugee Response Plan   In response to the Syrian refugee crisis, the government of Jordan recently produced a three-year plan that promotes a resilience-based approach.[14] To the extent that such an approach is sustainable and can offer benefits to host communities as well as refugees, it is an important mechanism for ensuring stability. Although the international community has supported the plan, only $1 billion (37.5 percent) of the $2.7 billion required to fund it for 2016 has yet been raised. As Michael Ignatieff and a team of researchers pointed out in a paper they wrote for Brookings earlier in 2016, the success of the plan depends on the extent to which it is supported.[15]

Jordan has indicated that it could generate 200,000 jobs suitable for Syrian refugees, including 150,000 jobs in a set of five new industrial zones and 50,000 jobs in labor-intensive infrastructure projects. That number could rise with additional support from the international community, in particular for the development zones. Earlier this year, the European Union granted trade concessions that allow goods produced there to be sold on European markets free of taxes and quotas, provided that the manufacturer's workforce is at least 15 percent Syrian. The United States, which has its own trade agreement with Jordan, should encourage other countries to follow suit.

Encourage Turkey to Further Open its Labor Market   Turkey hosts more than 2.8 million refugees from Syria, more than any other country in the world and more than half of the refugee population in the region. In January, Turkey opened up its labor market, passing legislation that allows registered Syrian refugees who have been in the country for at least six months to apply for work permits in the province where they first registered. Under the new law, employers are required to pay permit holders minimum wage. Given the extent to which many Syrians in Turkey work illegally, for low wages, and sometimes under exploitative conditions, the measure is an important one.

However, it is not clear that the new law goes far enough. First, it does not automatically give refugees a path out of the black market; most notably, it requires an employer to give his or her employee a work contract before the employee can apply for a permit. Employers who have benefitted from the exploitation of refugees are unlikely to offer these contracts. Perhaps for that reason, very few permits have yet been issued. Second, the law does not apply to all Syrians. To be eligible, would-be permit holders must have held a Turkish identification card for at least six months. These cards are not always easy for refugees to procure.[16]

Washington can use financial commitments to incentivize Erdoğan's government to expand the pathway to legal work. This approach will be harder to make in the wake of the attempted coup in Turkey in July 2016, which led to a series of crackdowns that have introduced substantial uncertainty in the relationship between Ankara and Washington. However, it is an effort worth making.

COLLABORATE WITH NONGOVERNMENTAL ORGANIZATIONS AND FOSTER COLLABORATION AMONG THEM

Across each of these initiatives, collaboration between government and civil society organizations, as well as among civil society organizations themselves, has the potential to contribute substantially to success. Faith-based organizations and diaspora groups have an important role to play in providing on-the-ground services to those in need. So too do refugee advocates. Washington-based think tanks should work with organizations like the International Rescue Committee and smaller outfits doing refugee-specific work, helping to leverage their impact.

CONCLUSION

Providing assistance to refugees fleeing the violence in Syria will require substantial financial and political investment. But the costs of doing otherwise are much higher. Scaling back America's commitment to those in search of safety would reverberate within the transatlantic alliance, strengthen the forces of nationalism and populism breeding disunity within Europe, deny a needed form of support to fragile states in the Middle East that are already struggling to cope with the crisis, and make the United States a bystander in a catastrophe that cries out for leadership.

For these reasons, the next administration should continue America's long-standing refugee resettlement program while providing additional support to Syrian refugees in frontline states. It is also important that Mr. Trump build and lead a global coalition of countries to advance the needs of Syrian refugees and the communities that host them—only then can the pressure on fragile states in the Middle East and America's allies in Europe be relieved. Both are strained by the weight of the crisis, and both are critical to America's security interests. If the next administration is to take such concerns seriously and make Syrian refugees more than a political slogan, Mr. Trump must challenge the international community to take action. It can only do so if America takes action itself.

Notes

1. Priyanka Boghani, "A Staggering New Death Toll for Syria's War –470,000," *PBS Frontline*, February 11, 2016, www.pbs.org/wgbh/frontline/article/a-staggering-new-death-toll-for-syrias-war-470000/.

2. Mark Bixler and Michael Martinez, "War Forced Half of All Syrians from Home. Here's Where They Went," CNN, April 18, 2016, www.cnn.com/2015/09/11/world/syria-refugee-crisis-when-war-displaces-half-a-country/.

3. "Figures at a Glance," *Global Trends 2015 Statistical Yearbooks*.

4. "Syria Complex Emergency – Fact Sheet #5," U.S. Agency for International Development, September 30, 2016, www.usaid.gov/crisis/syria/fy16/fs05.

5. Ruth Igielnik, "Where Refugees to the U.S. Come From," Pew Research Center, June 17, 2016, www.pewresearch.org/fact-tank/2016/06/17/where-refugees-to-the-u-s-come-from/.

6. "Information on UNHCR Resettlement in the United States," UNHCR, n.d., www.unhcr.org/en-us/information-on-unhcr-resettlement.html.

7. Alex Nowrasteh, "Syrian Refugees Don't Pose a Serious Security Threat," Cato Institute, November 18, 2015, www.cato.org/blog/syrian-refugees-dont-pose-serious-security-threat.

8. Alex Nowrasteh, "The Terrorism Risk of Asylum-Seekers and Refugees: The Minnesota, New York, and New Jersey Terrorist Attacks," Cato Institute, September 20, 2016, www.cato.org/blog/terrorism-risk-asylum-seekers-refugees-minnesota-new-york-new-jersey-terrorist-attacks.

9. *Washington Post* Editorial Board, "America Has Accepted 10,000 Syrian Refugees. That's Still Too Few," *Washington Post*, September 2016.

10. Bureau of Population, Refugees, and Migration, "Protracted Refugee Situations," U.S. Department of State, n.d., www.state.gov/j/prm/policyissues/issues/protracted/.

11. "UNHCR Reports Crisis in Refugee Education," UNHCR, September 15, 2016,

www.unhcr.org/en-us/news/press/2016/9/57d7d6f34/unhcr-reports-crisis-refugee
-education.html.

12. "Economic Impacts of Syrian Refugees: Existing Research Review & Key Takeaways," Policy Brief no. 1 (International Rescue Committee, January 2016), www
.rescue.org/sites/default/files/document/465/ircpolicybriefeconomicimpactsof
syrianrefugees.pdf.

13. "Small Hands, Heavy Burden: How the Syria Conflict is Driving More Children into the Workforce," Save the Children, July 2, 2015, http://childrenofsyria.
info/wp-content/uploads/2015/07/CHILD-LABOUR.pdf.

14. "Executive Summary," *Jordan Response Plan for the Syria Crisis, 2016–2018*, Jordan Ministry of Planning and International Cooperation, n.d., https://static1.
squarespace.com/static/522c2552e4b0d3c39ccd1e00/t/56979abf69492e35d13e
04f3/1452776141003/JRP+2016-18+Executive+Summary.pdf.

15. Michael Ignatieff, Juliette Keeley, Betsy Ribble, and Keith McCammon, "The Refugee and Migration Crisis: Proposals for Action, U.N. Summit 2016," Brookings, September 12, 2016.

16. Patrick Kingsley, "Fewer than 0.1% of Syrians in Turkey in Line for Work Permits," *The Guardian*, April 11, 2016, www.theguardian.com/world/2016/apr/11/
fewer-than-01-of-syrians-in-turkey-in-line-for-work-permits.

36

Dealing with a Simmering
Ukraine-Russia Conflict

FIONA HILL and STEVEN PIFER

SUMMARY: Ukraine and its conflict with Russia will pose a significant foreign policy challenge for the Trump administration. Washington should insist that Kyiv accelerate reform efforts, continue current military aid to Ukraine, maintain pressure on Moscow, keep U.S. policy aligned with Europe, be prepared to enter a negotiating process if a prospect emerges, avoid displacing Germany and France in negotiations, and continue not to recognize Russia's illegal annexation of Crimea.

A major foreign policy challenge that will confront the Trump administration from its start is Ukraine and its conflict with Russia, which has killed nearly 10,000 Ukrainian and Russian combatants and civilians. A settlement of the conflict in Ukraine will likely be a prerequisite for any restoration of normalcy in U.S.-Russian relations.

The February 2015 Minsk II settlement that was to end the fighting in eastern Ukraine's Donbas region has yet to be implemented. There is little sign that Moscow wants a settlement, apparently preferring a "simmering" rather than "frozen" conflict, where it can turn the heat up or down to pressure Kyiv, and prevent the country from allying with the West by associating with the European Union (EU) and, the Kremlin fears, ultimately by joining NATO.

U.S. policy has focused on three fronts: assisting Ukraine; supporting the German/French-led effort to reach a negotiated settlement for the Donbas war; and maintaining pressure on the Kremlin, including by working with the EU to uphold the sanctions regime imposed on Russia after Moscow's March 2014 illegal annexation of Crimea and the subsequent violence in Ukraine's eastern region. Kyiv has no leverage to change Crimea's status and has put the issue on the back burner. The diplomatic focus is on Donbas and the Minsk agreement.

In 2017, sustaining the diplomatic momentum around Minsk II will become especially difficult. In Ukraine, President Petro Poroshenko's popularity is eroding. The country remains dependent on Western loans and assistance, and thus on the (already overstretched) goodwill of Western governments. The ongoing conflict distracts the Ukrainian government from much-needed domestic reforms, including tackling the culture of corruption that permeates Ukraine's politics and economics. In Europe, key constituencies have pushed to end EU sanctions that impede trade and business relations with Russia, although Germany has thus far managed to maintain a unified EU stance.

Europeans—on both the EU and member-state levels—are critical actors in the Ukraine-Russia crisis. Washington has closely coordinated with Brussels and individual member states on policy toward Ukraine over the past several years. The EU supported International Monetary Fund credits for Ukraine and has provided additional financial assistance to Kyiv alongside the United States. EU sanctions on Russia, while not identical to those imposed by the United States, have certainly been tougher than Moscow anticipated. The EU adopted more severe sanctions after separatist forces used a Russian-provided missile to shoot down Malaysian Airlines Flight 17, and in response to Moscow's duplicitous denials of separatist involvement. These denials have continued despite the publication in September 2016 of a detailed report by a Dutch-led investigative team, based on a painstaking two-year review of all available evidence.

The European political cycle will be intense in 2017. The French and German leaders face general elections, as do their counterparts in Italy, the Netherlands, and the Czech Republic. Anti-EU parties have secured seats in European national assemblies and the EU Parliament, propelled by a popular backlash against the wave of refugees and migrants seeking entry. Russian president Vladimir Putin has stalled on Russia's compliance with the Minsk II agreement, waiting to see if these developments will weaken Western resolve and allow Moscow a freer hand in Ukraine.

The Trump administration should stick to the current policy course at the outset, but with an eye to making adjustments as the situation on the ground in Ukraine or as policy in Moscow changes. The U.S. should:

- Insist that Kyiv accelerate reform efforts and, if it does, work with Europe to offer greater assistance;

- Continue current military aid to Ukraine and consider provision of defensive arms, depending on circumstances on the ground;

- Maintain pressure on Moscow to comply with Minsk II, while signaling that Russian implementation of Minsk II would lead to better relations with the West;

- Be ready to enter the negotiating process if and when a real prospect emerges for a solution to the Donbas conflict;

- Avoid displacing Germany and France in the negotiations and make sure that Ukraine is present and represented in any supplemental diplomatic frameworks; and

- Continue the policy of nonrecognition of Crimea's illegal annexation by Russia.

Sequencing the security and political provisions of Minsk II will remain the heaviest lift in the negotiations in 2017. Russia provides leadership, weapons, funding, and, in some cases, regular units of the Russian army to support the separatists. It has shown no sign that it wants the separatists to fulfill their Minsk II obligations. Moscow prefers to use the conflict to destabilize Ukraine. The Ukrainian government argues that it should not be expected to implement political elements of Minsk II until Russia and the separatists implement the security provisions for a cease-fire and withdrawal of heavy weapons from the line of contact. If the security provisions *are* implemented, however, the Ukrainian government does not have sufficient parliamentary support to pass a constitutional amendment devolving governmental authorities to the separatist Donbas entities, in line with Minsk II. In sum, the process has little prospect of success unless there is a major change in Kremlin policy *and* an improvement in Kyiv's political capacity.

In light of the impasse, some in Ukraine and the United States have recommended abandoning the Minsk process. That would be unwise. There is no obvious diplomatic or political instrument to replace it. A precipitous withdrawal from Minsk could leave Ukraine in a one-on-one face-off with Russia. German chancellor Angela Merkel and French president François Hollande could choose not to reengage in a new set of negotiations in a critical domestic election year for them; and the United States would not be able to fill the diplomatic vacuum given the separate demands on Washington to find a deal with Russia on Syria. There is no "grand bargain" to be had with Russia in which the future of Ukraine is traded for other strategic goals in the Middle East. The conflict has to be dealt with on its own terms, in the context of its own complexities.

When Minsk II was concluded in February 2015, the first iteration of a negotiated settlement, Minsk I, had irrevocably frayed. A major debate about the provision of lethal weapons to Ukraine was under way in Washington, with the intent of helping Kyiv to establish a better balance of forces on the Donbas battlefield and deter further separatist/Russian attacks. The Kremlin wanted to head off the prospect of the United States unilaterally arming the Ukrainian military. Putin, therefore, preemptively moved to rupture this debate by switching to the diplomatic track. He negotiated a new Minsk agreement with Germany and France that put considerable emphasis on political concessions from Ukraine in addition to concluding another cease-fire. Moscow's initiative was greatly facilitated by the fact that Germany opposed arming Ukraine for fear of further escalating the conflict with Russia.

Minsk II—and German insistence that the agreement must be fully implemented before there can be sanctions relief for Moscow—is now a major impediment to Russian interests. Western sanctions have contributed to the contraction of the Russian economy over the past two years at a time of low oil prices. They have impinged on the Russian government's and private sector's ability to borrow money on international financial markets and blocked new foreign investment in manufacturing, banking, and services. Although the Russian government has taken measures to adjust, Moscow remains concerned that continued sanctions will lead to a long-term economic stagnation.

Sanctions have not, however, deterred Russia from pursuing its goals in Ukraine. Since the annexation of Crimea, Moscow has made it clear that it considers Ukraine, as well as other former Soviet republics, as part of its sphere of influence. It demands explicit U.S., EU, and NATO acknowledgment that Ukraine and other countries in Eastern Europe and Eurasia are off limits for membership in Western economic, political, and security institutions—unless by some prior agreement, directly negotiated with Moscow. Russia thus wants to prevent Ukraine from implementing the terms of the association agreement and free trade agreement it signed and ratified with the EU in 2014—which precipitated the initial confrontation when Russian forces seized Crimea after the Maidan Revolution. Moscow also seeks to roll back the commitment that NATO made at the 2008 Bucharest Summit to grant Ukraine eventual membership. Keeping Ukraine in a state of perpetual conflict with its international borders under constant question is one way of ensuring that the West keeps Kyiv at arm's length.

Instead of pursuing the implementation of Minsk II, Moscow has focused on different ways to weaken support for the sanctions regime. These efforts have included Russian presidential visits to countries like Italy, Hungary, Greece, and Cyprus that are seen as potentially amenable to lifting sanctions; patching up relations with Turkey (which did not take part in the initial sanctions) and Japan (which was part of the sanctions as a member of the G-7 group, along with Canada); outreach to Western investors whose business has shrunk under sanctions; blatant efforts to sway popular sentiment in Europe against sanctions through Russian-sponsored television, radio, and press outlets and social media; and tactical support for anti-EU parties and their leaders, like the National Front in France, Alternative for Germany (AfD), and the United Kingdom Independence Party (UKIP). Moscow is working hard to shape a narrative among European politicians and populations that lays the blame for the conflict in the Donbas and the failure to implement Minsk II entirely on Kyiv, and to break EU and transatlantic unity on sanctions.

The German chancellor is the most influential European decisionmaker shaping policy toward Ukraine and Russia. Merkel sees Russian aggression against Ukraine as violating the principles of international law that underpin the European security order, including that states should not use military force to seize territory from their neighbors. Senior German officials routinely describe Russia as their number-one foreign policy challenge and publicly decry Moscow's media and public relations campaigns to influence Germany's domestic policy, as well as the Kremlin's outreach to political parties.

The United Kingdom's decision to leave the EU greatly complicates European and U.S. policy coordination. In conformity with the June 2016 "Brexit" referendum, the British government announced in early October that it intended to initiate the Article 50 process to leave the EU by the end of March 2017. The United Kingdom will thus remove itself from the center of EU policy debates, where British diplomacy played a critical role in hardening resolve on dealing with Russia (along with Denmark, Poland, Sweden, and the Baltic states) as well as on a range of other EU foreign and security issues. The United Kingdom alone accounts for 16 percent of EU GDP. It was the major recipient of foreign direct investment into the EU, primarily into the goods and services sector in the City of London—an area of considerable importance for Russia. Without the United Kingdom, the EU will have less economic clout with Moscow.

The impact of the Brexit negotiations, along with other internal EU matters such as the migration crisis and the ongoing vulnerability of the eurozone (whose weakest point now appears to be the Italian banking system), will dominate EU summit meetings. European leaders will have less time for serious discussion of EU foreign policy issues like Russia and Ukraine, as well as less time (and perhaps less incentive) to engage and coordinate with the United States.

European trade with Russia was roughly 10 times the size of trade between Russia and the United States. Sanctions, including the counter-sanctions that Moscow imposed on European countries in retribution, have had a greater impact on individual European economies like France, Germany, Greece, Hungary, and Italy than on the United States. While Hollande has worked closely with Merkel in steering the Minsk negotia-tion process, other French politicians have called for ending EU sanctions, which Brussels currently reviews and renews on a semiannual basis. In both the French and German elections, Hollande and Merkel face op-ponents who almost certainly would seek to adopt softer policies toward Russia and reduce support for Ukraine.

If Russian efforts succeed, and sanctions are lifted without any signifi-cant progress having been made in implementing the Minsk II security provisions, Western credibility will be undermined. The Kremlin will feel emboldened to act in a similar fashion elsewhere in the post-Soviet space. Even without further military interventions, there are a range of other troubling actions Russia could undertake: increased violations of Euro-pean air and sea space; state-sponsored hacking of European politicians, political parties, and Kremlin critics during the 2017 election cycle; cy-berattacks against institutions and critical infrastructure; and the encour-agement of political violence by fringe groups in vulnerable states with disaffected minority groups, like the Baltic states. It will thus be important for the new U.S. administration to maintain parallel support for sanctions and the Minsk II process, in coordination with the EU, to make clear that Russian actions do have a cost. Additionally, the administration should push back against the Moscow narrative that Kyiv is solely at fault for Minsk's failed implementation.

Nonetheless, Washington should recognize that Kyiv needs to do more on reform to sustain Western support. Ukraine cannot afford the perception that the post-Maidan government, like its predecessors since the 2004 Orange Revolution, lacks the will and ability to genuinely transform. The Trump administration should press the Ukrainian government to accelerate anticorruption efforts. Kyiv's slowness to tackle this problem is sapping public confidence at home and abroad. This will entail making U.S. and EU assistance conditional on Ukrainian actions, and will require coordinated blunt talk from Washington and Brussels to push the Kyiv leadership to move forward on measures it has so far resisted. If Kyiv moves more quickly, the United States and the EU should consider additional financial and technical assistance.

In parallel, the United States should continue to provide Ukraine with military assistance. Current policy limits U.S. support for Ukraine to nonlethal assistance, including training for the Ukrainian armed forces. Any changes in this policy should be closely coordinated with Germany and other EU partners, given their previous strong opposition to providing lethal weaponry. Depending on the circumstances in Donbas and feedback from Berlin, Washington might wish to consider the provision of some defensive arms, such as man-portable antiarmor weapons.

The United States should also work within NATO to ensure full implementation of the decisions taken at the 2016 Warsaw Summit to enhance the alliance's military capabilities, particularly in the Baltic region. Assuring NATO's eastern allies will be an important element in boosting the confidence of European states to push back against Russian efforts to intimidate governments and populations through massive military exercises and nuclear saber-rattling. While it is not impossible that the conflict in Donbas might escalate or expand in 2017, the combination of U.S. and EU sanctions, NATO deployments to Poland and the Baltic states, and NATO's continued engagement with Ukraine has made it clear to the Kremlin that the costs of such a course could be prohibitive. In addition to continuing these policies, the United States and EU will also have to invest in Europe's political, economic, and societal resilience. Russia's interference in West-ern political and societal dynamics is far less attributable, much cheaper and easier for Moscow to carry out, and possibly much more damaging to U.S. and EU interests than all the military maneuvers.

It will be critical to keep Europe closely aligned with U.S. policy in 2017. Regular high-level consultations with Berlin and other EU member states will be necessary to sustain trans-Atlantic coordination. The United States has not directly participated in the Normandy format negotiations (among France, Germany, Ukraine, and Russia) that support the Minsk II process. However, if a prospect emerges for finding a settlement to the Donbas conflict that builds on this process, and direct U.S. participation would prove helpful, Washington should seek to enter the negotiations. In doing so, the United States should take care not to be seen to displace Ger-many or France in any way, or fall into a bilateral or multilateral negotia-tion format with Russia that is conducted over the heads of the Ukrainians or the (other) Europeans.

Finally, it is entirely possible that Russian policy regarding Ukraine and Donbas could evolve. U.S. policy should be prepared to evolve with it. Donbas is a sprawling territory with an impoverished population, de-stroyed infrastructure, and, by now, a deeply damaged economic base that will take years, if not decades, to restore. The Kremlin has shown zero interest in annexing the occupied region, which would entail costs far in excess of annexing Crimea. This suggests that, at some juncture, Moscow will be open to an accommodation with Kyiv.

The situation with Crimea is different. Russia has absorbed Crimea into its existing federal structures, annulled its autonomous status, and included the peninsula in its September parliamentary elections. It is hard to see how Kyiv can restore Ukrainian sovereignty there. The West cannot and should not accept Moscow's use of force to redraw borders. The United States and the EU should maintain a coordinated policy of not recogniz-ing Crimea's illegal incorporation into Russia until such time as Crimea is returned to Ukraine, or until Kyiv voluntarily accepts the peninsula's changed status. This is a similar proposition to the U.S. and European nonrecognition of the status of the three Baltic states after Moscow forc-ibly incorporated them in the Soviet Union at the end of World War II, and the nonrecognition of occupied East Berlin in the same time frame. Like the policy of Baltic nonrecognition, this approach to Ukraine will require patience and persistence, until circumstances change, in order to succeed.

37

Nuclear Arms Control Choices and U.S.-Russia Relations

STEVEN PIFER

SUMMARY: One issue for the Trump administration will be arms control. It has long figured on the agenda between Washington and Moscow, in times of both good and difficult relations. In the past few years, however, Moscow has refused to engage on further nuclear arms reductions, raising instead related issues such as missile defense, advanced conventional strike weapons, and third-country nuclear forces. Prospects for bilateral progress in the near term appear bleak.

Arms control can make a significant contribution to U.S. security and is more important when relations are adversarial than when they are working. The Trump administration should prepare a position in case Moscow decides to reengage. It should seek a negotiation on further nuclear arms reductions that would include all U.S. and Russian nuclear weapons while also indicating that it is prepared to address the related issues raised by the Russians. Doing so could revive the arms control dialogue and perhaps produce agreements that would strengthen U.S. and allied security.

ARMS CONTROL AND RUSSIA

Russia is the one country that could physically destroy America. Successive administrations since the 1960s have sought to limit and reduce the number of Soviet and Russian nuclear weapons that could threaten the United States. Enhancing strategic stability—minimizing the incentives a side might have to use nuclear weapons first in a crisis—has served as a prime motivator for U.S negotiating efforts. Other reasons include increasing transparency and predictability, reducing the costs of U.S. nuclear forces, and bolstering America's nonproliferation credentials.

Negotiations between Washington and Moscow have produced a string of agreements. These agreements and the two countries' unilateral measures have dramatically reduced the number of their nuclear weapons. When the 2010 New Strategic Arms Reduction Treaty (New START) is fully implemented in February 2018, the United States and Russia will each be limited to no more than 1,550 deployed strategic warheads on no more than 700 deployed strategic ballistic missiles and bombers. The total U.S. nuclear stockpile—including nondeployed (reserve) strategic warheads and nonstrategic nuclear weapons—numbers some 4,500 weapons. Russia is believed to have a stockpile of roughly equivalent size.

Over the past few years, a clear difference has emerged between the U.S. and Russian approaches, contributing to the current standstill in the arms control dialogue. The Obama administration sought further cuts in U.S. and Russian nuclear weapons, but Moscow focused on questions such as missile defense, advanced conventional strike systems, and third-country nuclear forces. Meanwhile, the overall political relationship between Washington and Moscow has tumbled to a nadir. Ukraine and Syria remain points of contention. Problems have arisen with existing arms control arrangements. The U.S. government in 2014 announced that Russia had violated the 1987 Intermediate-range Nuclear Forces (INF) Treaty by testing a ground-launched cruise missile of intermediate range. (U.S. allies in Europe and Asia want to see the treaty preserved.)

The more belligerent approach that Russia has adopted toward the United States and West comes against the backdrop of a major Russian military modernization effort, including modernization of its strategic nuclear forces, though much of that aims to replace older systems that are aging out. Putin and other Russian officials have engaged in nuclear saber-rattling of a kind not seen since the Cold War. The Kremlin seems to prefer an adversarial relationship, driven in part by domestic political factors and a sense of grievance against the United States and West.

Although U.S. and Russian interests clash on a number of issues, they converge on other questions, where Washington and Moscow have cooperated. These include the efforts to curb Iran's nuclear arms program and eliminate Syria's chemical weapons. The bilateral relationship for the foreseeable future will likely consist of confrontation on some questions mixed with issues where the two cooperate, though the balance has shifted in the direction of greater confrontation. It is not clear how quickly this might be changed.

If anything, the downturn in U.S.-Russia relations makes agreements such as New START count more. Having a cap on the other's strategic nuclear capabilities and transparency measures that provides enhanced predictability regarding the other's nuclear forces is more valuable in times of tension than when the bilateral relationship is working well.

There are currently few grounds for optimism about near-term arms control prospects, but one should not completely write them off. Russian officials reportedly said they might be prepared to reengage on nuclear arms control once New START is fully implemented in February 2018. The tone and substance of the arms control dialogue between Washington and Moscow have changed dramatically in the past—often in connection with a change of leadership in one of the capitals.

While President Trump should not expect such a positive reversal, he should not exclude it. If the Russians indicate a readiness to reengage, Washington will need a position on reducing nuclear forces and related questions. Without appearing too eager, the Trump administration should look for an opportunity to signal to Moscow that it is open to a resumed dialogue on nuclear arms control and is prepared to discuss related questions raised by the Russians. A security deal may be doable.

Even if the Kremlin is not prepared to reengage, there may still be value in a forward-looking position on arms control. It can be important for sustaining allied support, including for the modernization of U.S. nuclear forces. Moreover, the UN General Assembly has mandated a negotiation aimed at concluding a ban on nuclear weapons—which most, if not all, nuclear-armed states will boycott. That negotiation will invariably result in more international pressure on the United States than others. Having an arms control position calling for further U.S. and Russian nuclear reductions would put Washington in a better position to withstand such pressure.

NUCLEAR WEAPONS, RELATED ISSUES, AND OPTIONS

Strategic modernization. The Trump administration will inherit the modernization program of record that the Obama administration deemed necessary to meet its strategic force requirements, entailing a new ballistic missile submarine, a new intercontinental ballistic missile (ICBM), a new bomber, and a new nuclear-armed air-launched cruise missile. The new administration will want to review this program, including whether it is affordable. Many believe that it is not, or that it can be funded only by taking resources from critical conventional military capabilities.

New START allows the United States and Russia each to maintain up to 1,550 deployed strategic warheads on no more than 700 deployed strategic ballistic missiles and bombers. The Pentagon has planned a force of 700 deployed ICBMs, submarine-launched ballistic missiles (SLBMs), and nuclear-capable bombers. The Trump administration's review could ask: Does the United States need to maintain a triad of ICBMs, SLBMs, and bombers? Should the numbers planned by the Obama administration be adjusted? Should the Pentagon proceed with the new nuclear-armed air-launched cruise missile?

Further nuclear reductions. As for dealing with Russia, the administration will have to decide whether and when it might seek to extend the New START Treaty, which expires by its terms in 2021 but can be extended for up to five years. Should Moscow be prepared for negotiations going beyond New START, the administration will have to decide whether to seek to reduce limits on deployed strategic warheads and deployed strategic delivery vehicles and, if so, by how much. It will need to weigh other questions related to New START, such as whether it would want to change the counting rules for bomber weapons, which attribute each deployed bomber with only one deployed strategic warhead, even though they can carry many more.

The Trump administration should consider how to deal with reserve strategic nuclear warheads and nonstrategic nuclear weapons, which the Obama administration sought to bring into a negotiation of a follow-on treaty to New START. These weapons are unconstrained. Their relative importance in the nuclear balance grows as the number of deployed strategic warheads is reduced. Would a negotiation be possible for an aggregate limit that would cover all U.S. and Russian nuclear weapons as opposed to just deployed strategic arms?

Missile defense. Missile defense has been a difficult issue on the U.S.-Russian agenda. Moscow seeks to limit U.S. capabilities in this area. Are there options regarding missile defenses, particularly missile defenses in Europe, which Washington could exercise that might interest Moscow and could Washington secure Russian agreement to further nuclear arms reductions?

Advanced conventional strike weapons. The Russians have raised advanced conventional strike systems as potentially affecting the strategic nuclear balance, given the increasing accuracy of conventional weapons. The main issue appears to be long-range hypersonic glide vehicles, which both sides are developing though neither has yet deployed. These would not be limited by New START. The Obama administration regarded these as a "niche" capability and planned to build only a small number. Would it be possible to constrain such weapons in a way that would remove them as a problem issue on the agenda? A separate question is whether and how to deal with conventionally armed cruise missiles.

Third-country nuclear forces. Arms control cannot forever remain a U.S.-Russian enterprise, but expanding the process to bring in third countries is complicated, in part owing to the disparity in numbers between the United States and Russia on the one hand (about 4,500 nuclear weapons each), and all other nuclear weapons states on the other (no more than 300 weapons each). One might first look at bringing in the United Kingdom, France, and China, perhaps by having them adopt unilateral commitments and/or transparency measures.

RECOMMENDATIONS

Nuclear posture review. The Trump administration should carry out a nuclear posture review early in its term to examine the requirements for U.S. nuclear forces and policy and whether current and planned nuclear forces meet those requirements. Special attention should go to Russia, given the size and variety of its nuclear forces, the more belligerent stance it has adopted toward the West, and Moscow's loose talk about nuclear use.

The nuclear posture review should examine the U.S. force structure and planned modernization program and ask if that is the right structure and whether it is affordable. Ideally, requirements, policy, and strategy, rather than budgets, dictate force structure. It would be unwise, however, not to factor the budget situation into the decision process.

The nuclear posture review should reaffirm that the triad of ICBMs, SLBMs, and bombers will be maintained. It should, however, suspend the Long-Range Standoff (LRSO) weapon program and take a hard look at whether a new nuclear-armed air-launched cruise missile is needed. A nuclear-armed air-launched cruise missile made sense when the B-52 could no longer penetrate Soviet air defenses, but the new B-21 will have advanced stealth and electronic warfare capabilities.

While maintaining the triad, the nuclear posture review should consider whether it is necessary to keep the current planned force structure of 700 deployed strategic delivery vehicles. A force structure of 500 deployed ICBMs, SLBMs and bombers could carry close to New START's permitted 1,550 deployed strategic warheads while producing significant cost savings. Such a force could also readily accommodate a smaller number of deployed strategic warheads, were there to be a new arms reduction agreement or a decision to make a unilateral reduction.

Nuclear policy. The nuclear posture review should consider ways in which to give the president more time to make a decision regarding use of nuclear weapons—hours, even days. The Trump administration may want to consider whether it wants to maintain the ability to launch ICBMs under attack (which would require a presidential decision in a matter of minutes). An easing of the requirement for prompt launch would have implications for the U.S. force structure, as well as send important signals regarding U.S. strategy and intentions.

If the Trump administration decided to adopt some or all of the above recommendations, it would need to decide when and how to roll them out. A major consideration would be the state of the U.S.-Russia relationship. The administration would not want to adopt and announce policies that seemed to ignore or reward egregious Russian behavior. At the same time, it would not want to wait and lock itself into an unaffordable modernization program. This will be a tough dilemma.

Parity with Russia matters less today in strategic terms. In 2012, the Pentagon stated that even if Russia built up nuclear forces that exceeded New START's limits, strategic stability would be maintained due to the secure U.S. second-strike capability, based primarily on SLBMs on submarines at sea. Still, parity can matter politically. Allies may become concerned if the numbers gap between the United States and Russia appears too large, even if the gap may not have much strategic meaning. Also, negotiating with Russia may become more difficult if the United States has significantly lower numbers. Although the United States should not foreclose unilateral decisions regarding its strategic forces, it would be wise first to seek to engage Russia in a negotiation aimed at mutual reductions. The administration should in any case suspend the LRSO program.

When exploring Moscow's readiness to reinvigorate the arms control dialogue, the administration should indicate that, in the context of an agreement that further reduced U.S. and Russian nuclear weapons, it would be prepared to consider measures in the areas of missile defense, advanced conventional strike weapons, and third-country nuclear forces that would address stated Russian concerns. It should make clear the need to resolve concerns regarding compliance with the INF Treaty.

Further nuclear arms reductions. The Trump administration should seek a negotiation that covers all U.S. and Russian nuclear weapons—strategic and nonstrategic, deployed and non-deployed. The U.S. position should aim to limit each country to no more than 2,200 total nuclear weapons, with a sublimit of 1,000 deployed strategic warheads, the weapons of greatest concern. The position should seek to limit each side to no more than 500 deployed strategic delivery vehicles. Within such a limit, the United States could deploy a modern, secure, and effective strategic triad.

Missile defense. The administration should reiterate the 2013 U.S. proposal for a U.S.-Russian executive agreement on missile defense transparency, under which the sides would annually exchange data on their current numbers of interceptors, radars, and other key missile defense elements, as well as projected numbers for each of the subsequent 10 years. That would allow the sides to judge whether the other's prospective missile defenses posed a real threat to its strategic forces. In addition, U.S. officials should consult with NATO on indicating that Washington would be prepared to consider steps to cap the number of SM-3 missile defense interceptor missiles in Europe, perhaps forgoing emplacement of SM-3 interceptors in Poland, depending on how far Moscow was prepared to go in negotiating nuclear reductions.

Advanced conventional strike weapons. If the administration decides that it wants to field long-range conventionally armed hypersonic glide vehicles, it should offer to negotiate with Moscow a separate agreement limiting each side to no more than 20 or 30 such systems. There is a limited requirement for such systems, which will be expensive compared to other means to conduct conventional attacks. Conventionally armed air-launched and sea-launched cruise missiles do not readily lend themselves to limitation, given their importance for force projection in both militaries, but it would be worthwhile to offer a dialogue on cruise missile capabilities and their impact on the U.S.-Russian strategic balance.

Third-country nuclear forces. The Trump administration could inform Moscow that, in the context of a negotiation of a new nuclear arms reduction agreement along the lines described above, Washington would be prepared to work with Russia to elicit from the United Kingdom, France, and China politically binding unilateral commitments not to increase the total number of their nuclear weapons as long as the United States and Russia were reducing theirs. That could begin to set the stage for later, more meaningful limits on third-country nuclear forces.

These ideas might make it possible to bridge the gap that has emerged between the United States and Russia on arms control and related issues. Even if the Russian government was not prepared to engage—at least not immediately—a stated U.S. readiness to negotiate a 50 percent cut in total U.S. and Russian nuclear weapons could serve as a powerful sign of American commitment to reduce the nuclear danger and would secure the international high ground.

A negotiated outcome along the above lines would advance U.S. security interests in several ways. It would reduce the number of nuclear warheads capable of striking the American homeland, U.S. allies, or U.S. forces; enhance strategic stability; and increase transparency and predictability, particularly regarding missile defenses and nonstrategic and reserve strategic nuclear arms. It would also lower the cost of nuclear modernization, freeing up resources for conventional forces, such as additional warships. It would bolster U.S. nonproliferation credentials and begin the process of bringing third countries into the nuclear arms control process. It might also contribute to an overall improvement of the broader U.S.-Russian relationship, as arms control has done in the past.

This outcome should offer similar benefits to Russia. The big question will be whether Moscow sees things the same way. If so, there may be prospects for nuclear arms control. If, however, the Kremlin sees things differently and does not regard arms control as meeting its security goals, the Trump administration will face more difficult choices. In such a situation, it would be harder to adopt some of the changes described above on a unilateral basis. Nevertheless, the administration should not exclude the possibility of doing so, depending on its calculation of what is needed to support its deterrence, assurance, and stability requirements.

38

Forging an Enduring Partnership with Afghanistan

VANDA FELBAB-BROWN, BRUCE RIEDEL, JOHN R. ALLEN,
MICHAEL E. O'HANLON, RYAN CROCKER, JAMES B. CUNNINGHAM,
ROBERT FINN, ZALMAY KHALILZAD, RONALD E. NEUMANN, DAVID BARNO,
JOHN F. CAMPBELL, STANLEY McCHRYSTAL, DAVID H. PETRAEUS,
JAMES DOBBINS, MARC GROSSMAN, SETH JONES, CLARE LOCKHART,
DAVID SEDNEY, and EARL ANTHONY (TONY) WAYNE

SUMMARY: Since the attacks of September 11, the United States has engaged in and with Afghanistan in pursuit of common strategic interests. Our cooperation with the Afghan government and Afghan people remains a key front in a generational conflict against violent extremists across the greater Middle East. Although the extensive turmoil there leads some to believe that the United States is incapable of playing a constructive role in stabilizing and transforming the region's politics and security situation, we cannot escape this conflict. To succeed, we need, above all, allies in the region with whom we can partner militarily and politically. Our strategies and policies going forward should include ensuring the success of this American-Afghan partnership.

This chapter is excerpted from a longer essay, published by the same group in September 2016 at www.nationalinterest.org, that can also be found in full at www .brookings.edu/research/forging-an-enduring-partnership-with-afghanistan.

The Obama years have encompassed an intense, challenging period in Afghanistan policy. The U.S. role in the war in that country, dating back to 2001, has cost more than 2,300 American lives and $800 billion in American resources, most over the last eight years. We mourn the dead and wounded and grieve for their families, and profoundly cherish their service to the nation. The mission has demanded enormous military, diplomatic and economic attention and investment. The numerous complexities were made more challenging by difficult relations with former Afghan leader President Hamid Karzai during his latter years in office, from an unsettled Afghan political environment more generally, from the legacy of disintegration of an Afghan state that had historically never been strong, and from the dual role of Pakistan—part friend, part strategic challenge in the conflict.

President Obama has attempted to use the prospect of possible American/NATO withdrawal from the country to induce Afghan reforms and an Afghan sense of self-reliance. But ultimately, while progress has been achieved, he concluded that he cannot end the U.S. role in Afghanistan and that he would have to hand off an ongoing mission to his successor. Fortunately, that U.S. role today is much more modest than before—less than 10 percent of earlier American troop levels, less than 20 percent of earlier financial costs, and less than 5 percent of earlier U.S. casualty rates, as of this writing late in 2016.

The next American president will have an opportunity to settle Afghan policy onto a more durable, more effective, and less demanding course. In our view, the watchword for this new approach should be one of an enduring partnership, based on mutual commitment. We should plan for a long-term American—and coalition—role in the country that avoids the recent pattern of nearly annual reassessments of whether the United States should stay, militarily and as a major donor. We should also avoid publicly announced withdrawal timelines. Instead, we should take a quieter and more patient approach, consistent with the commitments the international community made at Bonn in 2011 to help make the entire 2015-2024 period the "decade of transformation" in Afghanistan. The U.S.-Afghan partnership should be recognized as generational in duration, given the nature of the threat and the likely longevity of its future manifestations. Less attention should be placed on troop numbers, and troop caps, as the barometer of whether an exit strategy is being successfully implemented. Rather, the emphasis should be on securing Afghanistan as a crucial pillar of America's global anti-terror campaign and as a needed contributor to stability in the region.

The U.S. and broader international commitment should not, however, be unconditional. Indeed, the notion of conditional engagement was agreed between donors and the Afghan government in the Tokyo Mutual Accountability Framework of 2012 and remains valid today. If the enormous investment that the world has made in Afghanistan since 2001 is to be worthy of continuation, Afghans must do their part to improve governance and economic well-being, and thereby build public support for the government. The very enormity of that U.S. investment to date, and the value of Afghanistan in the broader struggle against jihadi extremism, argue strongly for trying to sustain—and build on—the progress we have collectively achieved so far. And while there is no easy answer about how to improve U.S. relations with Pakistan, we expect that clear articulation of an enduring American commitment to Afghanistan and the region can only help in gradually reducing the distrust and rivalry that often predominate in the relationships in Central and South Asia today.

THE PATH AHEAD

It is not our purpose here to recommend a detailed way forward for the United States in 2017 and beyond. President Trump and his advisers will have to carry out that task, after first wrestling with the big strategic questions we discuss above and taking stock of actual conditions as they present themselves in the region next year. We would only wish to identify several of the lines of analysis and inquiry that any such review should squarely address:

Is a U.S. troop presence of some 8,500 Americans, as now planned, adequate? What strategy should guide their deployment? What force mix is most appropriate? We would counsel less attention to numbers, and less public emphasis on the size of the American troop presence as the central metric in evaluating the success or failure of U.S. policy in Afghanistan. The stability of Afghanistan and our ability to keep pressure on extremists in the region matter more than continual progress towards a smaller international military presence. But that said, it is worth noting that three years ago, U.S. commanders developed an option requiring 5,000 more foreign troops, and more intelligence capabilities, than are now envisioned. That larger posture, in conjunction with other NATO forces, would have provided the ability to work with each of Afghanistan's six major Army corps throughout the country, while also providing counterterrorism and intelligence and training capabilities. Some of the deterioration in the Afghan security environment in recent times can be directly traced to the absence of these U.S./NATO capabilities—though Afghan leaders themselves must accept their fair share of the blame.

Is U.S./NATO airpower being used intensively enough? President Obama gave authorities to commanders to target ISIL in 2016. He subsequently gave authorities to expand certain operations against the Taliban as well. But since the Afghan air force is not likely to be fully built for some years, there is a case for further reassessment. It will be important to ask if the relaxation of rules of engagement that President Obama provided to American/NATO forces in Afghanistan in 2016 should go further, allowing even more substantial use of their airpower against the Taliban.

How should Washington try to engage Afghan politics? Political and diplomatic efforts in Afghanistan today are focused on managing immediate crises, of which there is never any shortage. It would be highly desirable to change this dynamic. Indeed, given the daunting challenges, the United States can be flexible about how the future government is structured, and about when already overdue parliamentary and district council elections will be held, as long as such decisions reflect general agreement among Afghan political leaders including President Ghani and Chief Executive Abdullah. Political processes in general should comport with the Afghan constitution and with the goal of achieving as much reasonable political consensus as possible. (In this context, it is worth noting that the Afghan constitution allows only two terms per person over a lifetime.) The United States should help Afghans remain politically united and improve governance, while remaining alert that some there would likely seek to manipulate us for their own purposes. For the longer term, we should engage constructive groups across Afghan society and encourage them to find ways to press for deeper political reforms.

Can development assistance be better focused? Ongoing U.S. development assistance levels of about $1 billion a year (in addition to the $4 billion annually that the United States is still providing to support Afghan security forces) are complemented by comparable aggregate donations from other governments, multilateral development banks, the United Nations, and select NGOs. It is very important to continue the long, hard task of improving accountability and efficiency in dispersing assistance and reducing corruption, while improving the delivery of government services. That means, in part, channeling more funds through the national government while carefully monitoring their use, so as to improve public finance. Ideas like strengthening the role of the U.N. Special Representative to coordinate the aid flows in partnership with the Afghan government are worth examining. And predatory corruption in particular needs to be targeted—blatant theft of large sums of funds from the public purse.

How should the United States adjust its Pakistan policy? Washington and Islamabad have common interests in many areas. Moreover, it is critical that this nuclear-armed country of 200 million remain stable. We wish to see a Pakistan that is at peace with its neighbors, peaceful internally, and economically thriving. Sustaining operations in Afghanistan without Pakistani ground lines of communication, while possible, would be very difficult and costly. These considerations argue strongly for cooperation.

However, it is clear that the course of action we have pursued since the early 2000s has not produced the needed changes in Pakistan's policies in Afghanistan. Pakistan tolerates and in some cases supports the forces that target and kill U.S. military and civilian personnel, other foreigners, and many Afghans. The Taliban have safe havens within parts of Pakistan and access there to funds and equipment. The United States needs to oppose Pakistan's role in these dynamics at every turn. In its dealings with Islamabad, Washington should prioritize these issues even more than on requesting Pakistan's help with peace talks between the Afghan government and the Taliban.

Some believe that Pakistanis tolerate the Taliban out of conviction that America will again desert them—just as it did in 1989. But the United States has already stayed in Afghanistan 15 years this time, with no plans to leave. Under our proposal it would envision staying in the region a good deal longer. This is desirable, and it should help allay Pakistani fears that it will again face an Afghanistan in chaos or an Afghanistan dominated by its rival, India. Our purpose should be to change Pakistan's calculus over time, while recognizing that whatever policies we adopt, Islamabad will likely not change its Afghanistan policy quickly (even if civilian leaders in Pakistan decide they favor that outcome).

This serious situation calls for a fundamental review of available options by the next U.S. administration. Without advocating these as a group, we would suggest serious consideration of some or all of the below (though some of us are more wary of the last two options):

- The United States could take further steps to pressure Taliban sanctuaries within Pakistan (with or without the support of Islamabad). The May 2016 killing of Mullah Mansour, the head of the Afghan Taliban, while he was traveling through southwestern Pakistan indicates the kind of direct action against the Taliban and Haqqani Network that could make an important difference.

- The Obama administration and Congress have already reduced Coalition Support Funds to Pakistan in recent years, and curtailed the use of Foreign Military Financing as well. But even today's reduced amounts of U.S. assistance could be cut further. If Pakistan's role in Afghanistan does not improve, in fact, the U.S. Congress will likely see to that, whatever President Trump may wish.

- Targeted economic sanctions could be selectively applied against certain specific organizations and individuals; Washington could encourage other countries to consider similar steps.

- Pakistan could even be designated as a state sponsor of terrorism, a finding that would not only be embarrassing to the country but also harmful to its economic prospects, given the likely influence on potential investors.

In more positive terms, Washington might also sketch out a vision of an improved relationship with Pakistan if Islamabad would show more forthright and consistent support for the goals of NATO in Afghanistan. This outcome would be highly desirable for broader American interests, given Pakistan's central role in the stability of the entire region—and its ability to upend that stability. Washington should underscore that it could only be realized after Pakistan had verifiably acted to end its policies of sanctuary and support for the insurgents.

CONCLUSION

The situation in Afghanistan today is difficult. But it may not be measurably worse than one might have projected back in 2012 or 2013, when the Taliban resistance had already proven itself resilient in the wake of a NATO troop surge, and when elections loomed in Afghanistan as President Karzai's second term in office neared its end. Compared with that benchmark, and in light of the fact that NATO withdrew 125,000 of the world's best soldiers over the last five years and then circumscribed the role of U.S./NATO airpower, some deterioration was to be expected. The situation also remains considerably improved, in terms of the economy and human rights and human welfare, from what it was before—not only in the 1980s and 1990s but even in the early years after the overthrow of the Taliban. Since then, life expectancy has increased at least 10 years, child mortality has been cut at least in half, several million more children including millions of girls are in school, GDP per capita has more than doubled, a ring road has been completed (even if security conditions along it are not consistently as good as they should be), and many millions of Afghans have unprecedented access to cellphones, Internet, and media. And the United States has a coalition of international partners willing to stay the course with it.

While dangers are always present, new possibilities lie ahead. Determined collaboration between the White House and Congress as well as Afghan leaders can break the cycle of yearly approaches to the brink of the policymaking cliff. That can in turn help create a longer time horizon for security, political, and economic reforms that will surely take an additional decade or more even to reach a modest degree of success. In light of the continued extremist threat in Central and South Asia, and thus the importance of Afghanistan to western security, this is a burden that we can afford to bear—and one to which we should mutually commit in partnership with the Afghan people and government.

Contributors

SCOTT ANDES, Senior Policy Analyst and Associate Fellow, Centennial Scholar Initiative, Anne T. and Robert M. Bass Initiative on Innovation and Placemaking at Brookings

BEN S. BERNANKE, Distinguished Fellow in Residence with Economic Studies at Brookings.

JESSICA BRANDT, Associate Fellow and Special Assistant to the President, Brookings

RICHARD BUSH, Michael H. Armacost Chair, Chen-Fu and Cecilia Yen Koo Chair in Taiwan Studies, Director, Center for East Asia Policy Studies, Senior Fellow, John L. Thornton China Center, Foreign Policy at Brookings

DAVID DOLLAR, Senior Fellow, John L. Thornton China Center, Foreign Policy, and Global Economy and Development at Brookings

DOUGLAS W. ELMENDORF, Dean, Harvard Kennedy School of Government, and former Senior Fellow and Director of the Hamilton Project at Brookings

VANDA FELBAB-BROWN, Senior Fellow, Center for 21st Century Security and Intelligence, Foreign Policy at Brookings

WILLIAM G. GALE, Senior Fellow, Economic Studies, Director, Retirement Security Project, Co-Director, Urban-Brookings Tax Policy Center

WILLIAM A. GALSTON, Ezra K. Zilkha Chair and Senior Fellow, Governance Studies at Brookings

CAROL GRAHAM, Leo Pasvolsky Senior Fellow, CERES Economic and Social Policy in Latin America Initiative, Global Economy and Development at Brookings

RON HASKINS, Senior Fellow, Economic Studies, and Co-Director, Center on Children and Families at Brookings

SUSAN HENNESSEY, Fellow, Governance Studies at Brookings

FIONA HILL, Director, Center on the United States and Europe, Stephen and Barbara Friedman Senior Fellow, Foreign Policy at Brookings

NATE HULTMAN, Nonresident Senior Fellow in the Global Economy and Development program at Brookings, and Director, Center for Global Sustainability and Associate Professor at the University of Maryland's School of Public Policy.

MARTIN INDYK, Executive Vice President of Brookings Institution, and Special Envoy for the Israeli-Palestinian Negotiations, 2013–14

GEORGE INGRAM, Senior Fellow, Global Economy and Development at Brookings

BRUCE JONES, Vice President and Director, Foreign Policy, Project on International Order and Strategy, Foreign Policy at Brookings

ROBERT KAGAN, Senior Fellow, Project on International Order and Strategy, Foreign Policy at Brookings

ELAINE C. KAMARCK, Senior Fellow, and Director of the Center for Effective Public Management, Governance Studies at Brookings

JOSEPH KANE, Senior Research Analyst and Associate Fellow, Metropolitan Policy Program at Brookings

BRUCE KATZ, Centennial Scholar, Centennial Scholar Initiative at Brookings

AARON KRUPKIN, Senior Research Analyst, Urban-Brookings Tax Policy Center

DAYNA BOWEN MATTHEW, Visiting Fellow, Center for Health Policy, and University of Colorado School of Law, the Colorado School of Public Health, and the Center for Bioethics and Humanities at the University of Colorado Health Sciences Center

ROBERT L. McKENZIE, Visiting Fellow, Center for Middle East Policy, U.S. Relations with the Islamic World, Foreign Policy at Brookings

MICHAEL E. O'HANLON, Senior Fellow, Sydney Stein Jr. Chair, and Director of Research, and Co-Director, Center for 21st Century Security and Intelligence, Foreign Policy at Brookings

PETER OLSON, Research Analyst, The Hutchins Center on Fiscal and Monetary Policy, Economics Studies at Brookings

DAVID H. PETRAEUS, Partner, KKR, and Chairman, KKR Global Institute, and former Director of the CIA, former Commander of Coalition Forces in Iraq and Afghanistan, and former Commander of U.S. Central Command

STEVEN PIFER, Director of the Brookings Arms Control and Non-Proliferation Initiative and Senior Fellow in the Center for 21st Century Security and Intelligence and the Center on the United States and Europe, in Foreign Policy at Brookings

SERGIO PINTO, Doctoral Student, University of Maryland

KENNETH M. POLLACK, Senior Fellow, Center for Middle East Policy, Foreign Policy at Brookings

ROBERT J. PUENTES, President and CEO, Eno Center for Transportation, Affiliated Professor, Georgetown University Public Policy Institute, and Nonresident Senior Fellow, Metropolitan Policy Program at Brookings

RICHARD V. REEVES, Senior Fellow and Co-Director, Center on Children and Families, Economic Studies at Brookings

ROBERT D. REISCHAUER, Distinguished Institute Fellow and President Emeritus, Urban Institute

EVANS J. R. REVERE, Senior Director with the Albright Stonebridge Groupon, and Nonresident Senior Fellow, Center for East Asia Policy Studies, Foreign Policy at Brookings

ALICE M. RIVLIN, Senior Fellow, Center for Health Policy, Economic Studies at Brookings

EDWARD RODRIGUE, Senior Research Assistant, Economic Studies at Brookings

ISABEL SAWHILL, Senior Fellow, Economic Studies at Brookings

MIREYA SOLÍS, Senior Fellow, Center for East Asia Policy Studies, Philip Knight Chair in Japan Studies, Foreign Policy at Brookings

REBECCA WINTHROP, Director, Center for Universal Education, and Senior Fellow, Global Economy and Development at Brookings

ADIE TOMER, Fellow, Metropolitan Policy Program at Brookings

DAVID G. VICTOR, Nonresident Senior Fellow and Co-Chair, Energy Security and Climate Initiative, Foreign Policy at Brookings, and Professor of International Relations at the University of California–San Diego

DAVID WESSEL, Director, The Hutchins Center on Fiscal and Monetary Policy, and Senior Fellow, Economic Studies at Brookings

DARRELL M. WEST, Vice President and Director, Governance Studies, Founding Director, Center for Technology Innovation at Brookings

BENJAMIN WITTES, Senior Fellow, Governance Studies at Brookings.

NOTE: Affiliations for contributors to the chapter on Afghanistan—Vanda Felbab-Brown, Bruce Riedel, John R. Allen, Michael E. O'Hanlon, Ryan Crocker, James B. Cunningham, Robert Finn, Zalmay Khalilzad, Ronald E. Neumann, David Barno, John F. Campbell, Stanley McChrystal, David H. Petraeus, James Dobbins, Marc Grossman, Seth Jones, Clare Lockhart, David Sedney, and Earl Anthony (Tony) Wayne—may be found where the full writing has been posted on the Brookings website: www.brookings.edu/research/forging-an-enduring-partnership-with-afghanistan

Index